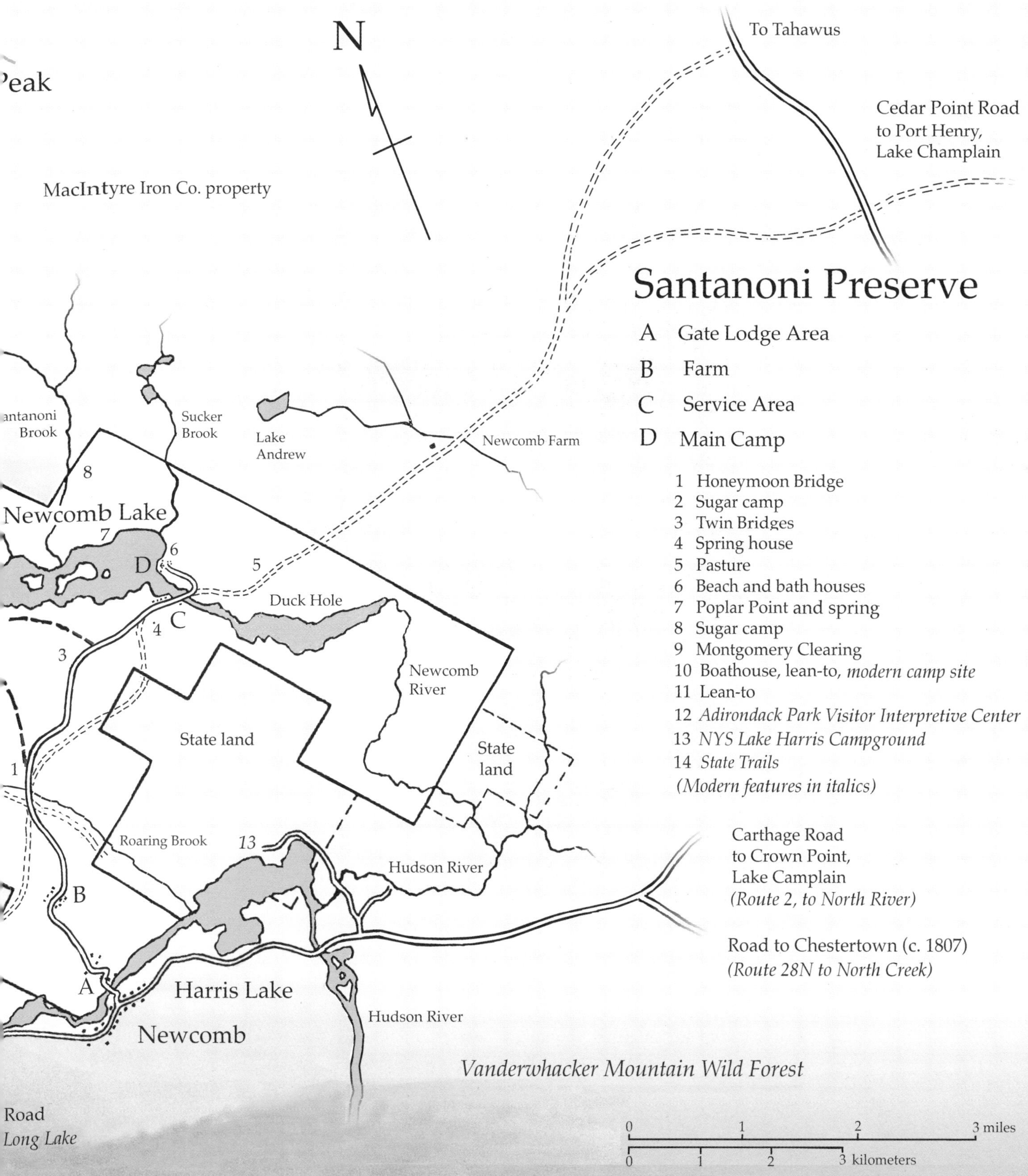

Peak

N

MacIntyre Iron Co. property

To Tahawus

Cedar Point Road
to Port Henry,
Lake Champlain

# Santanoni Preserve

A Gate Lodge Area
B Farm
C Service Area
D Main Camp

1 Honeymoon Bridge
2 Sugar camp
3 Twin Bridges
4 Spring house
5 Pasture
6 Beach and bath houses
7 Poplar Point and spring
8 Sugar camp
9 Montgomery Clearing
10 Boathouse, lean-to, *modern camp site*
11 Lean-to
12 *Adirondack Park Visitor Interpretive Center*
13 *NYS Lake Harris Campground*
14 *State Trails*
*(Modern features in italics)*

antanoni Brook

Sucker Brook

Lake Andrew

Newcomb Farm

8

Newcomb Lake

7

D

6

5

Duck Hole

C

4

3

Newcomb River

State land

State land

1

Roaring Brook

13

Hudson River

B

Carthage Road
to Crown Point,
Lake Camplain
*(Route 2, to North River)*

Road to Chestertown (c. 1807)
*(Route 28N to North Creek)*

A

Harris Lake

Newcomb

Hudson River

*Vanderwhacker Mountain Wild Forest*

Road
*Long Lake*

0 1 2 3 miles
0 1 2 3 kilometers

Island in Newcomb Lake

Pruyn bookplate, enlarged, showing Moose Mountain and islands in lake,
by Herbert Myron Lawrence of Albany

*Santanoni*

Santanoni Peak

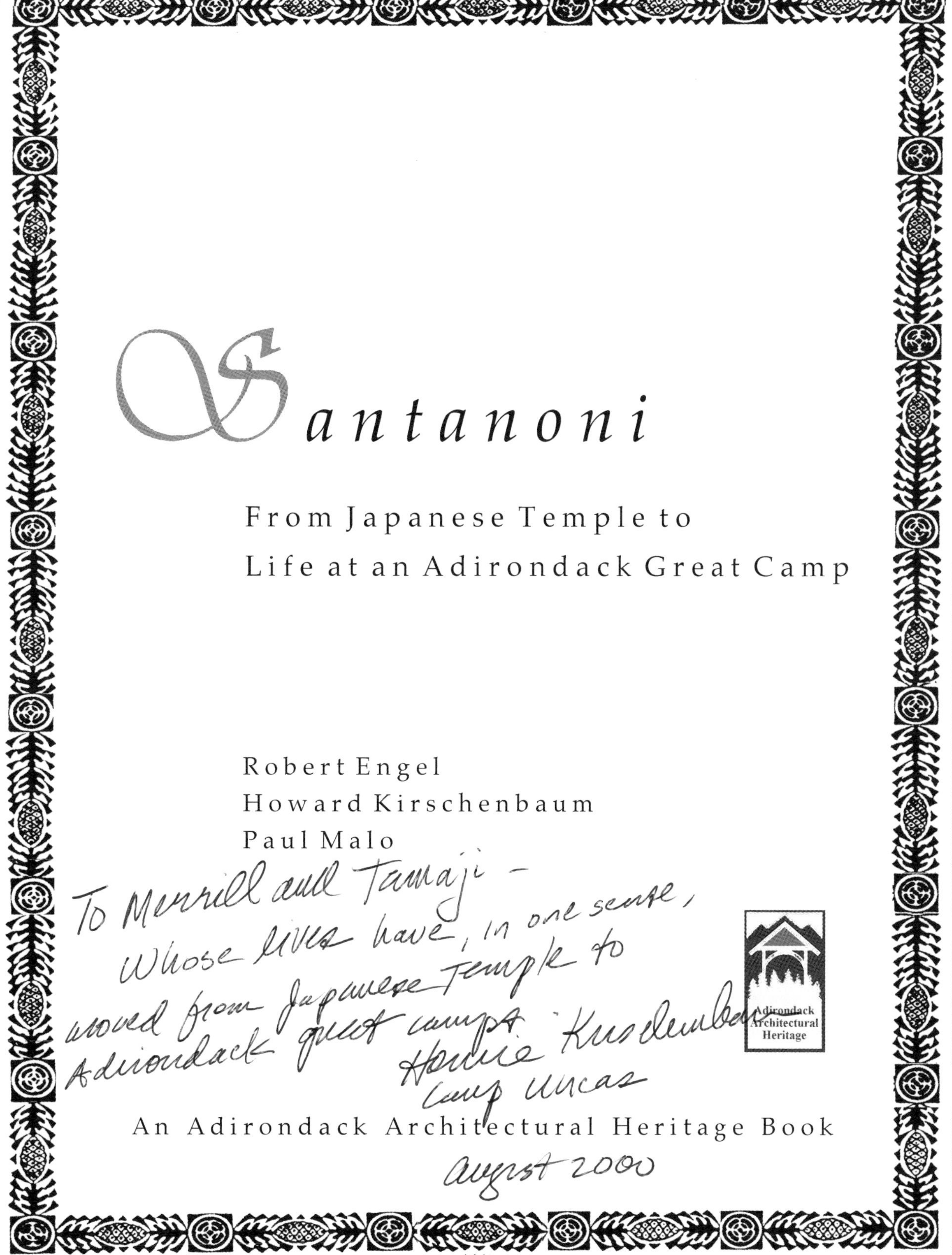

# Santanoni

## From Japanese Temple to Life at an Adirondack Great Camp

Robert Engel
Howard Kirschenbaum
Paul Malo

To Merrill and Tamaji –
Whose lives have, in one sense,
moved from Japanese Temple to
Adirondack great camps.
Howie Kirschenbaum
Camp Uncas
August 2000

Adirondack Architectural Heritage

An Adirondack Architectural Heritage Book

1790 Main Street, Suite 312
Keeseville, New York 12944
(518) 834-9328 Aarch1@aol.com



00 01 02 03 04 05 6 5 4 3 2 1

This book is published with a grant from Furthermore…,
The publication program of the J. M. Kaplan Fund

Includes Bibliographic References and Index

ISBN 0-9670388-1-2
Library of Congress Catalogue Card Number: 00-130126

PRINTED IN CANADA

# Contents

Santanoni Peak from Newcomb Lake, with Wintergreen Island

# Preface

SANTANONI PRESERVE is a central component of the Adirondack Forest Preserve, a National Historic Landmark.[1] Robert Clarence Pruyn and Anna Williams Pruyn of Albany developed Santanoni as their private wilderness estate. The Pruyns were an old New York family of Dutch descent (the family name is pronounced "Prine"). Like virtually all of the nineteenth century "Great Camps" of the Adirondacks, the Santanoni Preserve, situated on an upper branch of the Hudson River, was related culturally to the lower Hudson Valley that links Albany, the state capital, and New York City.[2] Networks of gentry extended throughout New York State. "Yorkers," as these elite landowners were known, tended to be aristocratic and anglophile. The roots of Santanoni accordingly are English and Dutch, but its greater distinction, as an idea as well as a work of architecture, derives more directly from a place far more remote—Japan.

[1] Although the National Historic Landmark is designated as "The Adirondack Forest Preserve" (NR 66000891), the New York State Forest Preserve incorporates state-owned land both in the Adirondack and in the Catskill Mountains.

[2] The term "Great Camps" became common in the 1980s, largely due to publication of Harvey Kaiser's *Great Camps of the Adirondacks* (Boston: Godine, 1982), but was introduced more than a decade earlier, as will be mentioned in Chapter 2.

THE PRUYNS enjoyed their isolated country house and game preserve for sixty years. The prominent Melvin family of Central New York owned the estate for two more decades. Except for its owners, their family and friends, and the workers who were employed on the Preserve, few people visited or even knew of the vast estate, until a personal tragedy there in 1971 catapulted Santanoni into the public's awareness. The Nature Conservancy acquired the property the following year and transferred it to the State of New York. Because of its remote location and difficult access, however, little was known about the collection of thirty or more buildings spread out over a distance of some five miles amid nearly thirteen thousand acres.

The term "Great Camp" had not yet entered popular parlance to describe the grand, rustic estates of the Adirondacks. State officials recognized that the Santanoni buildings had "historical interest as an example of an early Adirondack lodge of the type built by the wealthy summer residents who sought refuge in the wilds of the North Country."[3] Nevertheless, because of conflicting legal interpretations as to whether the state could maintain these buildings in the "forever wild" Forest Preserve, state policy was divided about Camp Santanoni, and some wilderness advocates urged its removal.

The late Paul Schaefer, fondly remembered as an advocate of Adirondack conservation, was among the first to appreciate the design distinction and fine craftsmanship of Santanoni's "great log villa," as he called it; but no one fully understood the historical genesis of Santanoni or adequately appreciated its architectural significance. Without a

[3] Division of Lands and Forests, Department of Environmental Conservation, "Management and Use Plan: Santanoni Preserve," October 22, 1971, 13.

compelling case for retaining and maintaining obscure buildings deep within the Forest Preserve, the state remained ambivalent. While some structures were razed, all the major buildings on the Santanoni Preserve stood empty and deteriorating for twenty years.

This book has evolved with the recent history of Santanoni. Paul Schaefer alerted Paul Malo, then President of the Preservation League of New York State, about Santanoni's precarious status. Malo shared his concern with Howard Kirschenbaum, then co-director of nearby Sagamore Institute, who began leading regular tours of Santanoni's abandoned buildings in the 1980s to call attention to their plight. He, Paul Malo and others collected bits and pieces of information about the Pruyns and Santanoni, both to enrich the tours and bolster the argument for preservation. In 1990 they helped form the regional preservation organization, Adirondack Architectural Heritage (AARCH), which initiated a campaign to preserve and interpret Santanoni as a public resource of the State of New York.

Still relatively little was known about the history of the property when Robert Engel, a history student in the Cooperstown Graduate Program, who had deep family roots in the region, became Adirondack Architectural Heritage's first summer interpreter at Camp Santanoni. He gained insight by living with the place intimately, hearing and recording recollections of Newcomb natives and others who had known the camp in its heyday. Engel went on to write his master's thesis on the history of Santanoni, which became the nucleus of this book.[4]

As Engel was conducting his research, two important sources of information emerged. Kirschenbaum received a letter from a woman who had read a newspaper article about AARCH's efforts on behalf of Santanoni. "My grandfather, Robert C. Pruyn, built Santanoni Preserve. My best memories of childhood are of times spent there."[5] The author, Susan Pruyn King, explained that she possessed the family photograph albums dating from the nineteenth century and that she had long been an advocate of Santanoni's preservation. A dozen or so scrap books, guest books, and related materials contained many hundreds of photographs, letters and assorted documents dating from 1892, the year of construction, through the 1930s, after Robert C. Pruyn had died. These materials provided a rich portrait of the physical development of the property and of camp life at Santanoni during the Pruyn tenure.

Susan Pruyn King and her husband Thomas King became strong supporters of the effort to save the buildings at Santanoni. They, in turn, introduced other Pruyn descendants, especially Beatrice ("Sis") Pruyn Thibault (1916–1994) and Cynthia Pruyn Green (1920–1999) who, along with Susan, have shared vivid memories and additional photographs that make this work come alive.

The next boon was John Winthrop Aldrich. Now Deputy Commissioner for Historic Preservation at the New York State Office of Parks, Recreation and Historic Preservation, Aldrich served as Assistant to the Commissioner of the Department of Environmental Conservation (DEC) when he became intrigued with Santanoni. DEC was responsible for Camp Santanoni, and Aldrich not only became an in-house advocate for its preservation, but also undertook extensive research about the Pruyns and the Santanoni Preserve. He compiled a voluminous collection of materials including his 190-page "Source Book," an important foundation for this book.

The researchers shared information with one another and increasingly with wider circles by leading tours, delivering lectures, and writing articles to help strengthen the growing case for Santanoni's preservation. Their work was further enhanced when AARCH commissioned Wesley Haynes, a historic preservation consult-

4 Robert Engel, "A History of Camp Santanoni, The Adirondack Retreat of Robert Pruyn," unpublished master's thesis, State University of New York College at Oneonta, Cooperstown Graduate Program, 1996.

5 Susan Pruyn King, letter "To Whom It May Concern," April 16, 1991.

ant and building conservator, to undertake a series of reports on some of the historic structures at Camp Santanoni. His report on the Santanoni Farm Complex, in particular, added greatly to our understanding of Santanoni's history and significance, and was an invaluable resource in writing this book. His report on the Gate Lodge complex provided additional information and insights.[6]

When completed, Robert Engel's academic thesis focused on the Pruyns at Santanoni, 1892–1951. Howard Kirschenbaum expanded content throughout, adding a fuller narrative of history after state acquisition. He also viewed Camp Santanoni in relation to development of the Great Camps of the Adirondacks and placed the Santanoni Preserve in context of the region's conservation movement, which is of national significance. Paul Malo assessed Santanoni's architectural value, extended interpretation of its cultural context, and contributed additional material throughout.

The research of three authors and two major contributors over many years has produced a large archive. This book, to be manageable, necessarily has become an abridgment of a larger, more fully footnoted version, which is available for reference on computer disk.[7]

Within less than a decade, Santanoni has gone from being one of the least understood Great Camps to one of the most extensively documented historic sites in the Adirondacks. The concern about saving Santanoni motivated substantial historical research; reciprocally, the on-going research contributed to an appreciation of Santanoni's significance that aided its preservation. No doubt this process will continue in the coming years. We hope this work will play a small part in that process.

[6] Wesley Haynes, "Farm Complex, Santanoni Preserve, Newcomb, NY: Historic Structures Report" (prepared for Adirondack Architectural Heritage, July 1996). Wesley Haynes, "Gate Lodge Complex, Santanoni Preserve, Newcomb, NY: Historic Structures Report" (prepared for Adirondack Architectural Heritage, May 1998).

[7] The disk is available from Adirondack Architectural Heritage, which maintains a Santanoni archive.

DEDICATION of this work caused a quandary; the three authors had a surfeit of candidates. In his thesis, Robert Engel had honored three granddaughters of Robert and Anna Pruyn: Beatrice Pruyn Thibault, Cynthia Pruyn Green, and Susan Pruyn King, who shared many mementos and personal memories. Howard Kirschenbaum felt indebted to George Canon, Supervisor of the Town of Newcomb and influential voice for the Adirondack constituency. Without George's enthusiastic advocacy and unflagging support, Santanoni would not have been saved and this book would not have been written. Paul Malo thought we ought to acknowledge the critical role played by the late Harold Hochschild, whose generous gift saved Santanoni for the People of the State of New York. The authors dedicate their work to these friends of Santanoni, and thank all the others whose contribution has preserved Santanoni and made this book possible.

First of all, we thank J. Winthrop Aldrich, whose major research has been mentioned, and likewise Wesley Haynes, whose professional studies are indispensable to interpreting and preserving Santanoni.

The friendly people of the town of Newcomb have supported Camp Santanoni's preservation and been helpful in many ways, especially Ken Helms and Tom Dillon, who operate the horse-drawn wagons to Santanoni, and Andy Blanchette, DEC operations staff member based at Santanoni. The citizens of Newcomb have shared much valuable information about Santanoni's history and have been most helpful to Adirondack Architectural Heritage and its summer interns. The names of others who have helped us are too many to list here, but we hope to mention many in the text.

A special contribution was made by Dr. Langdon G. Wright, Associate Professor, Cooperstown Graduate Program, who guided Robert Engel's thesis on Camp Santanoni.

Jim Meehan, photograph registrar, and Jerry Pepper, librarian at the Adirondack Museum, were helpful in providing access to the Pruyn photograph and document collection.

Chuck Vandrei, Historic Preservation Officer of the Department of Environmental Conservation, and a staunch and effective supporter of Santanoni, facilitated access to DEC's Santanoni archives.

Taya Dixon, an AARCH Intern at Santanoni, completed her master's thesis on Edward Burnett.[8] Mrs. E. Burnett Vaughan, daughter, and John Vaughan, grandson, provided further information about Edward Burnett. Both sources enrich the discussion of the Santanoni Farm.

Valerie Stevens, a Trust Officer at Key Trust Co., successor to R.C. Pruyn's bank, provided access to important records.

Merle Melvin, Jr. generously shared his memories of the Melvin years at Santanoni.

We are grateful as well to Donald and Beverly Williams, Warder Cadbury, John Deming, David Gibson, Tom Bissell, Robert Birrell, Ray Masters and Richard Holden Waite for their help in obtaining additional information on Santanoni history. We also thank the many contributors of photographs who will be mentioned in the section on illustrations.

Richard Longstreth, Ted Comstock, Jr., J. Winthrop Aldrich, Mary Hotaling, Wesley Haynes, and Susan Pruyn King read preliminary drafts of the manuscript, offering many helpful suggestions. After their careful reading and thorough feedback, any remaining errors or misinterpretations are surely our responsibility, not theirs. We are also indebted to Carl Engelhart and Peg Mauer for their careful proofreading and suggestions, and to Laurie Winship, who prepared the index.

The Preservation League of New York State, which has long been interested in saving Adirondack landmarks, including Camp Santanoni, has been especially helpful by assisting in the preparation of historic structures reports.

Special gratitude is due our publisher, Adirondack Architectural Heritage. Steven Engelhart, Executive Director, has participated throughout the Santanoni campaign and has made innumerable contributions to the writing and publishing of this book. Founding board member Carl Stearns has been a long-time participant in the Santanoni preservation campaign. Mary Hotaling, newsletter editor and Adirondack historian, has been helpful, as has William Johnston, current board president. We thank board members for their confidence in this project.

Joan K. Davidson has been an important supporter of this project. The J. M. Kaplan Fund and Open Space Institute assisted preparation of historic structures reports, while the publication program of the J. M. Kaplan Fund, "Furthermore...," provided a generous grant to enable the publication of this book. We also thank Finch, Pruyn & Company of Glens Falls, New York for donating a portion of the paper cost.

Finally, we owe genuine gratitude to our spouses, Judy Watson, Mary Rapp, and Judith Wellman, for their forbearance over these many years.

Still another and even longer list of individuals and organizations would have to follow here, were we to thank all those who have worked so hard over the years for Santanoni's preservation. We hope that this book may confirm their confidence in the value of this historic and architecturally important place. Perhaps for all who visit Santanoni it may likewise confirm their intuitive recognition that environmental conservation and historic preservation go hand in hand.

8 Taya Dixon, "Edward Burnett: An Agricultural Designer of Gentlemen's Estates," unpublished master's thesis, University of Pennsylvania, 1998.

Santanoni Peak, Newcomb Lake and islands, from Baldwin Mountain, 1905

# Arrival

Newcomb, May 15: The refreshing showers of last Saturday have started everything fresh and green. It was very warm the first of the week and forest fires were raging considerably.

*The Essex County Republican, May 18, 1893*

Rumors of the proposed party had floated around town through the late winter," wrote Robert Pruyn's young cousin Huybertie, "and as we heard a great deal of the Santanoni Preserve, we were crazy to be invited.[1]

"When the coveted invitations arrived, all was excitement, but Mother was much worried over the bears and other wild animals—the Adirondacks were indeed a wilderness to that generation— and she was doubtful about letting me go, which almost disrupted the family. I told Cousin Robert about her fears and he caustically remarked that there was less danger for me than going to Guy Baker's party at Balston Spa for New Year's."

[1] Huybertie Pruyn Hamlin, "The Four Spring Parties to Santanoni" (typescript, Albany Institute of History and Art, n.d.), 7. "Bertie" Pruyn Hamlin is quoted throughout this segment unless noted otherwise. Details of the inaugural house party generally were provided by this delightful memoir.

It is doubtful that Huybertie's mother was reassured; nevertheless she allowed her daughter to attend the inaugural house party at Camp Santanoni. In fact "Bertie" became a Santanoni regular, the young life of the party, whose chronicles of camp life enrich the history of Santanoni Preserve.

On May 21, 1893 the Pruyns and their thirteen guests gathered at Albany's Delaware and Hudson station for the 4 p.m. train to Saratoga. There they changed trains for North Creek where they spent the night at a "primitive hotel." Bertie soon had a chance to demonstrate her capacity to deal with the creatures she might encounter in the Adirondack wilds. Verplanck Colvin was a guest at the same hotel. The eminent Adirondack explorer, surveyor, and wilderness advocate had by now begun a period of declining mental health. Apparently he took a fancy to young Bertie and followed her about the hotel; hence she dubbed him "the Panther." "That idiotic old Panther" regaled her with unwanted Adirondack tales and advice on surviving in the wilderness to the point where she climbed out of a window in order to avoid encountering him. "He had hardly vanished before there was a wild outburst about my wild beau."

The next morning, shortly after eight, the party left for Newcomb, a thirty-five mile ride farther north to the heart of the Adirondacks. Leading the procession, "Cousin Robert drove Cousin Anna himself in a light yellow, one-seated buggy and pair," Bertie tells us. The rest of the group followed in open "cut-unders," each lurching behind a pair of horses, three guests plus driver to a wagon. In one wagon rode eighteen-year-old Edward ("Ned") and fifteen-year old Ruth Pruyn, the older of Robert and Anna's four children. Robert and Frederic Pruyn, thirteen and eleven, respectively, may still have been at school or deemed too young to participate on this occasion.

Capped and gloved, the passengers were prepared to enjoy the lovely spring morning with newly emerging tree buds covering the hillsides, still bright yellow-green. This often proved difficult as they soon were jouncing over dry, rutted roads that were "beyond description." The wagons "plunged from one hole to another," averaging four miles to the hour, a fast walking pace. At one point they entered an area where a serious forest fire was raging, so the horses were made to run through as fast as possible while the driver had the passengers crouch in the bottom of the wagons to avoid inhaling the smoke.[2] Merely *getting to camp* was proving to be an adventure.

They recuperated at the roadside inn, Aiden Lair, where the party enjoyed a pleasant luncheon. "The table was spread outside by the brook from which the trout that we ate with so much relish, had been caught." Continuing the journey, the wagons finally reached the preserve around six, the passengers dusty, tired, and "bounced and trounced to jelly."

Emerging from the forest into a clearing, the Pruyns and their guests got their first glimpse of the new, almost completed camp, a massive and rambling structure with many windows and stone chimneys. Like no other large country house they had ever seen, it was built of logs. Peeled of bark, the logs were smooth and shiny, coated with bright varnish. In every window were many tiny panes of glass, sparkling clean, set in a lattice of thin dividers, painted red. Camp Santanoni was a dazzling sight in the spring sunshine.

Robert Pruyn drove through the porte cochère where he reined in the horses, stopping the buggy under the roof, the others following a short distance behind. In the shade of the verandah several people waved and smiled, then hurried to help the passengers disembark.[3] While one of the men held the horses, the master of Santanoni Preserve stepped down, a small man, dignified and buttoned-up, a handkerchief in his breast pocket. His neatly trimmed beard nearly concealed a high, starched collar. Although he must have had many feelings at this moment, beholding his grand achievement and sharing it with his family and closest friends, it was not his custom to show emotion; rather it was his decided manner to maintain composure. That would be demeanor proper for Albany's leading banker and the responsible governor of the household. Male attendants tipped their caps as Mr. Pruyn stepped down; a smile from the proprietor was sufficient recognition in return.

The men extended their hands to help his wife step down. Anna Pruyn, impeded by a large hat with long feathers, hesitated. She handed her furled parasol to one of the waiting men, so that she could gather up her large skirts and ruffled cape before extending a gloved hand, smiling to the waiting staff, and joining her husband on the porch.

[2] The summer of 1893 was marked by major forest fires, largely caused by poor logging practices of the time.

[3] This scene has been imagined.

The understated covered entry to Santanoni's main camp, embedded in the woods.

As Robert and Anna's buggy was led away, the other wagons pulled in to the porte cochère. Young Ruth Pruyn jumped down independently, careless of her long skirt and straw hat. One of the aproned women hugged the teenage girl, as Bertie also jumped from her wagon and ran about, giddy with excitement. Trying bravely not to acknowledge that they were disheveled, other elaborately dressed travelers disembarked, stretched their tired muscles, and looked about them. Not all were as insouciant as Ruth and Bertie. Among those stepping onto the wide verandah were James Fenimore Cooper III of the old Cooperstown family and his wife Mary Barrows, together with Howard Van Rensselaer of the Dutch patroon family, Henry M. Sage of the Albany philanthropist family, and members of other prominent families, including those of several Albany industrialists.[4]

Robert and Anna Pruyn, both now hatless, greeted their guests on the "piazza," he wearing a tweed Norfolk jacket, she a balloon-sleeved dress with high collar—her parasol exchanged for a familiar cane.[5] Host and hostess were framed within a wide aperture between log buildings, two of many separate structures under one great roof. Behind the Pruyns, beyond a screen of trees, appeared the first view of the lake, shimmering in the early evening sun. Robert and Anna escorted their guests from this wide portal along the extended verandah promenade that led, with several turns, to the center of the complex, where overhead a lofty gable of logs reflected the triangle of a distant mountain. From here they could look out on what one writer called the "fairest waters of this lake-bespangled and leafy solitude," a "sequestered loch, . . . crescent-shaped, island-adorned, and mountain-locked,

---

4 Cooper was grandson of the novelist. Others who signed the Guest Book at the initial house party on May 23, 1893 were: Edward Bowditch, Lucy R. Bowditch, Frederick W. Kelley, Charles Dickinson Meneely, Elizabeth Shaw Oliver, Huybertie Lansing Pruyn, Cornelia Kane Rathbone, Henry M. Sage, Mabel Bookerton Sard, and Grange Sard.

5 Granddaughters remembered that Anna, as result of a horseback riding accident, walked with a cane.

Moose, Baldwin, Santanoni, and other peaks rising grandly near the shores."[6]

Only gradually did the visitor begin to realize the extent of the house, which extended 264 feet along the lake.[7] The great log villa was not intended to be imposing; to the contrary, it was built purposefully where few people could see it and was arranged so that it could not be seen all at once. Similarly, the Pruyns' style of entertaining was understated, not at all ostentatious. They met their guests personally as they disembarked. Only later would visitors become aware that there was a butler, lurking with other staff unseen. Maids wore plain white dresses with aprons, rather than fancy uniforms, to wait on guests. The help remained in the background, out of sight as much as possible. The intent was to create an illusion of simplicity, of effortless ease.

Although a wilderness retreat, the main compound at Santanoni Preserve was no mere hunting camp or family summer cottage. It was a "country house," as known in England. Designed for entertainment of large house parties, the main lodge could accommodate twenty family members and guests.[8]

Guests were impressed not so much with grandeur, but with the unexpected discovery of untamed wilderness that was not hostile, of life in the wild that was not arduous but, to the contrary, was idyllic. "I can never forget the first impression of it," recalled Bertie, "and how we rushed about admiring and wondering at everything. . . . When we discovered real bath tubs and then a piano, we were lost in amazement. How had they even been brought in over such roads! I believe as a matter of fact they came in on sledges over the snow."

Visitors viewed the Pruyn country house, still being completed in May of 1893, as a wonder. Despite its rustic understatement, the log villa was impressive, "the largest and finest [residence] in the entire forest," as judged by the New York State Forest Commission that year.[9]

The Pruyns were a young family to be moving into a large country house on a vast estate. Robert was forty-six and Anna forty years old when they and their four children spent their first season at Santanoni Preserve. Their guests found life at Santanoni Preserve relatively carefree and comfortable, but not very casual. Groups of people, some distinguished and many unfamiliar with one another, often shared elite country houses of the period. Visitors were expected to conform to a structured agenda and behave according to conventional manners, which served all by prescribing mutually agreeable conduct.

The teenage Pruyn children addressed their mother as "Madam."[10] "Grandfather was a very meticulous man about his dress and behavior," recalled granddaughter Beatrice ("Sis") Pruyn Thibault. "He had a special knife in his pocket which he used to open his mail, just so."[11] "Just so" was how things were at Santanoni Preserve. Gentlemen wore pressed trousers or, if sporty, knickers, commonly worn with jackets and ties. A guest referred to the host as "the wearer of the starched shirt collar."[12] Ladies generally wore floor-length dresses or skirts, but if they chose to be sporty, might don culottes or bloomers, worn with calf-high buttoned gaiters. Even a visiting boy would wear jacket and tie when inspecting the estate farm.[13] "The full dress

[6] E. R. Wallace, *Descriptive Guide to the Adirondacks (Land of a Thousand Lakes)* (Syracuse: 1895), 377-380.

[7] Most accounts give this dimension but, according to one, the "combined frontage" is "275 feet." Alice M. Kellogg, "Luxurious Adirondack Camps," *New Broadway Magazine* (August 1908): xxi.

[8] New York State Forest Commission, *Annual Report of the New York State Forest Commission for the Year 1893*. 1: 178. The report said twenty "guests," but the number more likely referred to number of persons, including family. In practice, the Pruyns' house parties did not exceed fifteen guests, according to the guest books.

[9] NYS Forest Commission, *Annual Report*.

[10] Cynthia Pruyn Green, letter to J. Winthrop Aldrich, cc. to Robert Engel, August 1992.

[11] Beatrice Pruyn Thibault, interview recorded by Robert Engel, Santanoni Preserve, July 29, 1992.

[12] Santanoni memorabilia, Adirondack Museum.

[13] The illustration of Robert Pruyn and guests at the farm appears subsequently; many other photographs of this sort may be found in the Santanoni albums.

House-warmers seek May sunshine on verandah, not yet enclosed by railing. Life-of-the-party Bertie is second from right.

parties that I saw showed how the rich of that era enjoyed themselves," a local veterinarian recalled. "Everything was on a scale of luxury."[14] As F. Scott Fitzgerald observed, "the rich are different." If less wealthy than many families with grand Adirondack camps, the Pruyns and their company nevertheless lived differently from mainstream Americans.

On the other hand, like families of all social classes, the Pruyns loved to have a good time. With thirteen thousand acres in their own back yard, the Pruyn brothers and sister had ample room for escape from the protocol of the main house. Bertie's reminiscences are filled with numerous practical jokes the guests played on one another, to the tolerant amusement of their hosts. In a single night, the men put a porcupine in the young women's bedroom, the women retaliated by disassembling and hiding the men's fishing rods and sinking one of their boats in the lake, and the men noisily woke up the girls the next morning to show them how they'd already found and assembled the rods and were going fishing in the resurrected boat. "It was sad but true," wrote Bertie, "we were outclassed by the men. They had beaten us at last."

Fishing was the family's most popular pastime—indeed, a passion. A large lake of their own was steps from the main lodge, while fly fishing often entailed hiking to distant ponds and streams. The estate provided four named mountains and many smaller peaks for climbing. Following a full day outdoors, family and guests dressed for dinner. After a large and leisurely meal, even active youngsters required little entertainment. Yet entertain themselves they did—making music, singing around the piano, playing charades, composing humorous poems and songs, and staging costume dances. Then out early the next morning to fish another pond or stream.

[14] Edward Johnson, letter to Ethel Bissell, October 29, 1982.

The Pruyn family had been attracted to the place "for the rare hunting and fishing which it affords." According to an account of 1893, "the forest which covers the entire preserve and comes to the very doors of the camp, contains the usual kinds of Adirondack game: deer, rabbits, partridges, etc. There are also mink, otter, foxes, and an endless variety of feather and fur. The lakes and streams contain both speckled and lake trout, and land-locked salmon have recently been added." Santanoni Preserve incorporated Newcomb Lake, "one of the most beautiful . . . in the Adirondacks, . . . a large body of water, embellished with well forested islands, and surrounded by picturesque mountain scenery," as well as three ponds and a section of a larger lake, providing a total of 881 acres of water.[15]

The contrast between this wilderness environment and a cultivated lifestyle may seem odd, even highly artificial to us today. Santanoni Preserve, seen through our eyes, would appear to be liberating, providing the freedom of the wilderness; the regimen of the Pruyns, however, may seem stifling. In part, formality was a convention of the time, especially in this class. It would not have seemed so unusual to family and guests. The mannered regime, accepted gracefully by Anna Pruyn and others devoted to the outdoors, was especially consistent with the disciplined ambiance favored by the master of Santanoni Preserve, a courtly gentleman, Robert Clarence Pruyn.

"There is independence, delight and peace in the isolation," wrote Robert Pruyn about Santanoni.[16] Ever fastidious, he would have chosen those three terms carefully. First, Santanoni Preserve provided *independence*. It was not a weekend cottage. It was to be a self-sufficient domain, incorporating a farm and staff to provide needs and comfort. The challenge was not merely to survive isolated in the wilderness, but to prevail there, in control and with style. By *delight*, Robert Pruyn meant not merely pleasure from sports and entertainment, but also an aesthetic or spiritual enhancement of life. Closely related to delight, *peace* suggests contentment. One finds serenity at Santanoni Preserve. Its isolation in the wilderness suggests a Shangri-La quality of other-worldliness, Zen-like in integrating primitive simplicity and urbane sophistication. Isolated and insulated from the larger world, one focuses there on the reality of nature, to experience *mono no aware*, as the Japanese say, "the poignancy of things."[17]

The Pruyns were akin to Japanese aristocrats, barricaded within idyllic villas where "stylized poems were composed and enjoyed and where the composers amused themselves with their abstract, formalized thoughts."[18] Poems written at Santanoni were compiled in two volumes.[19] Visual artists like Ned Pruyn painted in the studio and outdoors.

The Pruyns enjoyed a life of measured cadence, of reserve and understatement. It was a life of style—patrician style.

[15] Quotations in this paragraph are from the NYS Forest Commission, *Annual Report;* other information from "Santanoni Preserve/Adirondack Mountains," typescript, c. 1925, New York State Department of Environmental Conservation.

[16] "Santanoni Preserve/Adirondack Mountains."

[17] Yasuhiro Ishimoto, "Tradition and Creation in Japanese Architecture," in Yasuhiro Ishimoto, ed., *Katsura: Tradition and Creation in Japanese Architecture* (New Haven: Yale, 1960), 22.

[18] Ishimoto, 22.

[19] "Bits of Fact and Fiction by All" and "Santanoni Scrapbook" both contain poems and other writings by family and guests.

Albany's Pearl Street from State Street, a Pruyn house in distance

#  1. The Pruyns 

> It became usual . . . for Dutch towns to be dominated by a closely intermarried group of the wealthiest commercial families, who have been called *patricians* by broad analogy with the ruling class of ancient Rome.
>
> *Alice P. Kenny*

Franz Janse Pruyn came from Holland about 1630 to settle at Fort Orange, later to become Albany, New York, the fourth oldest permanent settlement in North America.[1] By the early eighteenth century, Albany had become "in general the counterpart and competitor of Montreal."[2] "Albany rather than New York City served as the *de facto* capital. . . . "[3]

Albany was an old Dutch city, in which the Pruyns were an eminent old Dutch family. An early Albany resident recalled the eighteenth-century city as "indeed Dutch, in all its moods and tenses; thoroughly and inveterately Dutch. The buildings were Dutch—Dutch in style, in position, attitude and aspect. The people were Dutch, the horses were Dutch, and even the dogs were Dutch."[4] Other writers noted that Albany could "best be described as a city-state. Its frontier location, its almost totally Dutch character, and its fur-centered economy all conspired to emphasize a separate, special, and unique position."[5]

Like most elite gentry of the lower Hudson River valley, patrician Dutch families had not acquired the Yankee sense of democratic participation by individuals, but regarded civic leadership as the obligation of important families.[6]

---

1 "Register of Pedigree," unpublished manuscript. Family tradition recalls an arrival date of 1629, while by another account, the Pruyns were "a pioneer Dutch family whose residence in Albany dated back to 1665." Susan Pruyn King and "Portraits of Presidents of National Commercial Bank and Trust Company" (Albany: National Commercial Bank and Trust Company, 1970), 5. "Albany is one of the oldest of the permanent settlements made in America. . . . Only St. Augustine, Santa Fé, and Quebec antedate it." Frank Oppel, compiler. *New York: Tales of the Empire State* (Secaucus, NJ: Castle, 1988), 224.

2 D. W. Meinig, *The Shaping of America: A Geographical Perspective on 500 Years of History*, v. I (New Haven, Yale University Press, 1986), 126.

3 Meinig, 128.

4 Gorham A. Worth, quoted by William Kennedy, *O Albany: An Urban Tapestry* (New York: Viking, 1983), 79.

5 Patricia Bonomi, *A Factious People: Politics and Society in Colonial New York* (New York: Columbia University Press, 1971), 40.

6 Alice P. Kenny, *The Gansevoorts of Albany: Dutch Patricians in the Upper Hudson Valley* (Syracuse, N.Y.: Syracuse University Press, 1969), xv.

Robert was of the eighth generation descended from Franz Pruyn. In the late eighteenth century, some of the Pruyn family resided on North Pearl Street in "a stately Dutch house, with terraced gable fronting the street."[7] Robert C. Pruyn's grandfather built a landmark house outside the city.[8]

Some of the family became leaders in the lumber and paper industries of New York State, a position that Finch, Pruyn & Company still holds today. Other Pruyns became members of the State legislature and United States Congress. An Albany tradition toward the end of the nineteenth century was a Pruyn New Year's Eve party, generally attended by the Governor. This took place at the home of John Van Schaick Lansing Pruyn, who was preeminent among the Pruyns in that generation.[9] John V. L. Pruyn was a noted lawyer who had aided Erastus Corning in consolidating the New York Central Railroad.[10] John V. L. Pruyn also served as congressman and Chancellor of the State Board of Regents.[11] Pruyns entertained old Hudson Valley families, such as the Roosevelts, both Theodore's and Franklin's families—as well as New York City elite, such as the J. P. Morgans.[12] "The Pruyns were everywhere," observed the Albany historian, William Kennedy, noting "the pervasiveness of their influence, politically, culturally, and socially."[13]

Although some of the Pruyns became successful businessmen and prominent civic leaders, they participated in a society dominated not by the urban elite, but by powerful rural patroons—hereditary lords of large manors of the Hudson and Mohawk River valleys. None of the many branches of the Pruyn family attained the status of the patroons, foremost among whom were the Van Rensselaers of Rensselaerwyck, a 700,000-acre estate that included virtually all of present day Albany County, much of what is now Rensselaer County, and some of Columbia County,[14] or the Schuylers, whose estate encompassed Saratoga Springs and extended to the Adirondacks.

Patrician families of Albany and upstate New York were intertwined by many links. Robert C. Pruyn's father, Robert Hewson Pruyn, married Jane Anne Lansing, "Jennie," whose old Dutch family was connected to other branches of the Pruyn family.[15] Robert Clarence Pruyn, born October 23, 1847, was the first of Robert and Jennie's three sons. A sister died in infancy.

Robert C. Pruyn (like his favorite cousin) was called "Bertie." When a schoolboy attending Albany Academy and Wrightson's preparatory school, Bertie's father, Robert Hewson Pruyn, was becoming accomplished as an Albany lawyer and prominent as a Whig politician, serving twice as Speaker of the New York State Assembly.[16] He was less successful, however, in running the family business, the Albany Iron and Saw Works, which was more important to his income. By the early 1860s he was in serious debt, "hit hard by the effects of [the Civil] war."[17]

William Seward, a longtime friend through Whig and Republican circles and President Lincoln's Secretary of State, offered Pruyn the position of American Minister Plenipotentiary

7 Robert C. Pruyn biography, *National Cyclopaedia of American Biography*. "Albany Fifty Years Ago." *Harper's New Monthly Magazine*, 1857, quoted by Oppel, 66, Illus. IV, 67.

8 The Casparus F. Pruyn House at 207 Old Niskayuna Road, Colonie, N.Y., is listed on the National Register of Historic Places. Casparus married Anne Hewson. Edwin B. Lee, "Robert H. Pruyn in Japan, 1862-1865." *New York History*, April 1985, 124.

9 Huybertie Pruyn Hamlin, *An Albany Girlhood*, edited by Alice P. Kenny (Albany, N.Y.: Washington Square Press, 1990).

10 Allison P. Bennett, *The People's Choice: A History of Albany County in Art and Architecture* (Albany: Albany County Historical Association, 1984), 92.

11 *Who Was Who in America, 1607-1896.*

12 Kennedy, 110.

13 Kennedy, 12.

14 Bennett, 2.

15 Robert Hewson Pruyn (1815-1882) married Jane Anne Lansing in the 1840s. "Jennie" was daughter of Gerrit Yates Lansing and Helen Ten Eyck Lansing. Edwin Lee, 124.

16 Payson J. Treat, *Japan and the United States, 1853-1921* (Boston: Houghton Mifflin, 1921), 52.

17 Edwin Lee, 124. He mentions Pruyn's financial plight when forty-seven years old, which would have been in 1862; preparations for the Civil War had begun during the winter of 1860-61, a year before the Pruyns left for Japan.

to Japan, arguing that it would allow him to recover financially. The first and outgoing Minister, Townsend Harris, had increased his $7,500 annual salary considerably through careful currency exchange in this position.[18] So it was not solely out of a sense of *noblesse oblige* that Pruyn accepted the honor of what was the newest, and probably the most alien, most dangerous, and nearly the most distant post in the American foreign service.[19] Rather, he intended to advance his own branch of the family, to pay his debts and to establish the family fortune.

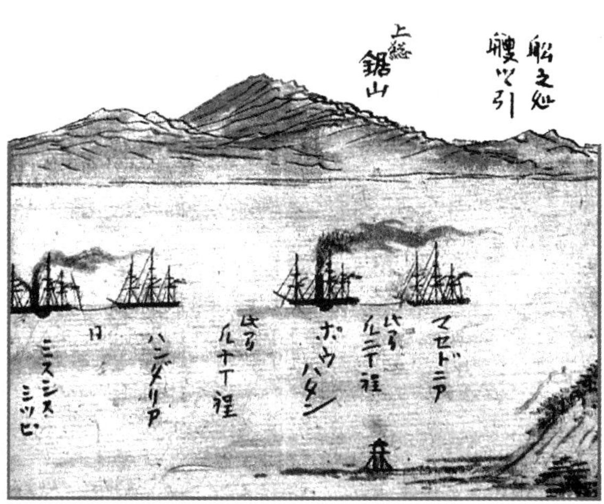

American ships arrive at Japan, 1854

## Father and Son in Japan

The family paid a high price. The ministerial assignment resulted in a long separation, with Jennie Pruyn remaining in Albany. The appointment moreover resulted in loss of a son. Robert H. Pruyn left for Japan with fourteen-year-old Bertie and his younger brother, Edward. The youngest brother, Charles, stayed at home in Albany with their mother. Although Edward was not well when they left, his parents thought that Japan's milder climate might improve his consumptive condition. Edward did not survive the voyage.[20]

Despite its tragic beginning, life in Japan would be exhilarating for father and son. The retiring Minister, Townsend Harris, welcomed the Pruyns when they disembarked in April 1862. Harris escorted them to the nearby capital city of Edo (or "Yedo," later to be called Tokyo).[21]

There were no Western-style hotels in the capital city.[22] Inns had neither chairs nor even beds. A contemporary visitor to Japan vividly described the Pruyns' living situation. "The residence of the American Minister is in the western suburbs of Yedo, [a] mile and a half from the Custom House landing, . . . through streets of shops crowded with buyers and sellers, hucksters, venders of small wares, then by the walled enclosures of some *daimos* [noblemen's villas], and again through a quiet street of humble houses, clean chalets where little yards were separated by green hedges and adorned with shrubbery. Again we descended into a little valley through which flowed a small stream and no building had been permitted to stand on its banks for a large breadth either side so that the city stream retained its country life and meandering gracefully between green banks skirted with clumps of trees."[23]

Amid a neighborhood of modest cottages, some hardly more than shacks, towered a massive red tile roof, brilliant in the sun in contrast to a backdrop of dark foliage. This was Zempukuji, the old temple that was to be their home.

18 Edwin Lee, 124.

19 Susan Pruyn King retains the original proclamation of appointment, signed by President Lincoln.

20 Edwin Lee, 123-4; R. H. Pruyn, letter to J. L. Pruyn, April 1862, Pruyn Papers. Not only was the mission dangerous, but Jennie Pruyn suffered from acute seasickness.

21 Francis Hall in his journal noted the "arrival of Minister Pruyn" on Friday, April 25, 1862. The Pruyns referred to Edo as "Yedo." F. G. Notehelfer, ed., *Japan Through American Eyes: The Journal of Francis Hall, Kanagawa and Yokohama, 1859-1866* (Princeton: Princeton University Press, 1992), 423.

22 The first Western-style hotel in Tokyo opened in 1867. Bernard Rudofsky, *The Kimono Mind* (New York: Doubleday, 1965), 124.

23 Francis Hall in Notehelfer, 258.

Zempukuji Temple, the Pruyns' home away from home in Japan

The Pruyns lived in "the dwelling apartments of the priesthood attached to the large temple."[24] "The temple was in "a beautiful garden at the foot of a hill in Azubu."[25] "[The] interpreter (Mr. Heusken) occupies a small house within the same compound. A large number of officials are posted within the same grounds as a guard. The Minister's residence is pleasant, the back court is shut in by a high hill covered with fine old trees. Here is a fish pond with some remarkably large gold fish or carp."[26]

"By Albany standards, Pruyn's surroundings were thoroughly exotic, and [the minister's] early letters depicted 'Buddhist and Sintou' temples. . . ." No doubt Bertie shared his father's interest and admiration, likewise regarding Japan as "the most lovely country the eye ever rested on."[27]

Robert H. Pruyn inherited an extraordinary situation. Only eight years before their arrival, America's Commodore Perry had opened a virtually unknown Japan to diplomacy and trade. The Japanese, little informed about the West, were wary of foreigners, but their leaders generally were aware of practical realities, like gunboats in the harbors. As first consul, Townsend Harris had succeeded in establishing diplomatic and trade relations, but the Pruyns found a nation tensely divided. Powerful feudal lords had largely usurped the unifying authority of the Emperor. Western nations had recognized, to their advantage, the lords' leader, the Shogun, as the real power in Japan. This faction in return supported open

---

[24] Notehelfer, 258. Francis Hall spelled the name "Iempoogi," apparently phonetically as he heard it, 260. "By a strange turn of fate, it was American bombs which burned down Zempukuji in 1945, but ... the *ginko* tree which marks the site where the American flag fluttered for the first time over the capital" survived. Photograph by the contemporary Yokohama photographer, Felix Beato (Notehelfer, 259).

[25] Noël Nouët, *The Shogun's City: A History of Tokyo* (Sandgate, England: Norbury, 1990), 184.

[26] Notehelfer, 258

[27] Robert H. Pruyn, letter to Jane Anne Lansing Pruyn, May 23, July 7, Nov. 8, 1862, Pruyn Papers, box 3, quoted by Edwin Lee, 126.

ports and the emerging merchant class. A growing anti-Western faction feared colonization and despised all foreigners; recently an American and other foreigners had been brutally murdered. Shortly after the Pruyns arrived, several Englishmen had been murdered and others wounded.[28] Japanese who opposed the rule of the nobles and their leader, the Shogun, rallied around the Emperor, a symbol of traditional Japanese culture. The Shogun's government was on the verge of collapse as factions maneuvered to gain control. Violence was a constant threat as fanatic xenophobes routinely attacked foreigners in the port cities.

Consequently, the British, French and Dutch consuls fled to the safer Yokohama, some fifteen miles distant, leaving Minister Pruyn the only western diplomat to remain in Edo. The Pruyns depended on soldiers loyal to the Shogun for their security, which might vanish with a shift of political positions.[29] Pruyn, with infrequent naval support, was forced to make ministerial decisions on the spot, unable to consult his State Department.

In Japan, Robert H. Pruyn was called "General Pruyn" by others in the expatriate community more often than "minister," although he had little or no military experience.[30] Teenage Bertie Pruyn was honored by the title *attaché*.[31] Both father and son wrote home virtually daily.[32] Bertie's youthful letters to his mother show little awareness of his father's diplomacy. His enthusiasm may seem naively righteous and privileged a century and a half later: "I want to see Japan again when the whole country is open to foreigners. I want to attend church in the Edo cathedral, to eat dinner with the Mikado [Emperor] and to take rides with Satsuma, and to see Mr. Brown preaching on top of Fugi-yama."[33] Despite tense conditions, Bertie would not remain confined. He wrote to his mother: "I have gotten in the habit of taking a bath every afternoon..., not in the house, but in the sea."[34] Bertie also took his fishing rod and tackle to Japan.[35] We ought not envision solitary swims in the surf or lonely fly casting in mountain streams; on canters around the American legation quarters, horseman Bertie was accompanied by an escort of fifty-two armed Japanese guards.[36]

Letters home reveal keen interest in Japan and sensitive perception of its culture, even though foreigners were allowed to travel only twenty-five miles from the few cities where they were permitted to reside. Within this orbit, the Pruyns saw prominent landmarks, but they did not have to travel far to see historic Japanese architecture; the American legation, like those of other nations, was quartered in an old temple structure. Japanese temples had often become noble residences when supplanted by newer buildings. Conversely, sometimes villas of nobles became temples. The Japanese government installed all Western legations in temples. "The heads of foreign missions tried to obtain quarters that were more comfortable than the temples and succeeded in having residences built. . . . The buildings were already well underway in February 1862 when they were burnt down by anti-foreign fanatics."[37]

After the killing of westerners and the burning of the British legation by arsonists, Pruyn contemplated returning to the United States. By 1863 he had profited sufficiently to wipe out his personal debts. The situation

[28] Treat, 46, 47, 54.

[29] Treat, 197-387.

[30] Although Pruyn was in Japan during the Civil War, granddaughter Susan Pruyn King retains a photograph of him in uniform, perhaps because Robert H. Pruyn served as Judge Adjutant General in the New York State Militia and as Adjutant General of the State. *Who Was Who in America, 1607-1896*. Americans did not yet use the title "ambassador".

[31] Bertie did not serve as his father's business secretary; the minister had another business secretary. Notehelfer, 479.

[32] Edwin Lee, 125.

[33] R. C. Pruyn, letter to J. A. L. Pruyn, July 23, 1863, Pruyn Papers, box 11, folder 2. The Prince of Satsuma was one of the great lords of Japan. The Prince was about Bertie's age. Notehelfer 308, 644. Reverend Samuel Robbins Brown (1810-1880), a minister of the Dutch Reformed Church, had been a missionary in China before coming to Japan. Notehelfer, 12, 622. Edwin Lee also mentions Brown, 137.

[34] R. C. Pruyn, letter to Jane Ann Lansing Pruyn, Pruyn Papers, box 11, folder 2.

[35] Inventory of personal articles. Pruyn Papers, undated.

[36] Edwin Lee, 198.

[37] Nouët, 179, 184, 187.

moreover had become perilous. A few months after destruction of the British legation, "the residence of Gen. Pruyn . . . who had courageously remained at his post, was burned over his head, involving the loss of his personal property, though the archives were saved in an injured condition."

> This occurred on a dark, stormy night after a day of pouring rain—the house being surrounded by the usual guard of five-hundred men, and the fire had originated in an unused and detached apartment—thus the suspicion of incendiarism was too palpable. The American Minister, however, still maintained his ground and living with his son and Secretary in the small single apartment of an outbuilding, refused to leave Yedo until the immediate preparation of another residence was promised. On the 30th, after many delays and prevarications, the new residence was promised, and Gen. Pruyn prepared to leave Yedo temporarily, or until the promised house was in readiness.
>
> On the afternoon of the day following, he was waited upon by two Governors of Foreign Affairs, who urged his instant departure to Yokohama. A conspiracy, they said had been discovered, in which a body of 500 *ronins* [Samurai warriors] were engaged, that night to attack and overpower his guard and take his life. The Governors were urgent, fairly compelling the Minister from his house, and placing him on board of a Japanese steamer in the harbor, which, the night following, took him to Yokohama. So Yedo was at last cleared of its last obnoxious foreign inhabitant.[38]

The Japanese adventure bonded father and son. In a letter to his mother, however, Bertie worried that he might be delaying his education too long by staying in Japan, adding: "I want to go home... and be something."[39] After the burning of the legation, Bertie's father determined that one of them, at least, should go home. Reluctantly, father bid son off.[40] They would not see one another for almost two years.

About the time that Bertie sailed, Robert H. Pruyn, convinced that his intervention had averted a war between Japan and the treaty nations of western Europe, wrote to his wife: "I cannot, when I look at the difficulties which have all the time surrounded me, see how it is possible for one so entirely inexperienced to succeed so well."[41]

The American Consul and his legation meet the Japanese Shogun and his court at Yedo (Tokyo)[42]

Pruyn's assessment of his job-well-done has been sustained by history.[43] However, if his diplomacy and courage were admired at the time, his mercenary interest was less highly regarded:

---

38 Francis Hall in Notehelfer 483.

39 R.C. Pruyn Papers, Albany Institute of History and Art.

40 Francis Hall noted in his Journal, on Tuesday, December 1, 1863, "Robt. Pruyn leaves us for home via Europe in the Granada tomorrow." Notehelfer, 516.

41 R. H. Pruyn, letter to J. A. L. Pruyn, April 26, 1864, Pruyn Papers, Box 3.

42 The detail from a contemporary Japanese print depicts predecessor Townsend Harris and Shogun Iesada.

43 "Mr. Pruyn played an important part in securing American rights in the East." *National Cyclopaedia*, 131. Edwin Lee concurs in his estimate of Pruyn's accomplishment, 137-8. A summary of Robert H. Pruyn's achievements in Japan appears in his capsule biography, *Who Was Who in America, 1607-1896.*

> The documents are all authentic . . . and show an amount of official rapacity that is lamentable to behold. . . . The American Minister is down for over $70,000 worth of exchange for a single year, some of which is put down by the Japanese 'as compensation for leaving Yedo'!! . . .
>
> To know what profit this represents, it is only to be added that those receiving exchange for each $100 get 311 ichibus [280 net after commission]. These ichibus they have sold in the markets again in the past year at 240 ichibus per $100 on an average![44]

This entailed a profit of more than sixteen percent, or more than $11,000 for Pruyn that year, an amount that may not seem substantial today, until one recalls that a Massachusetts shoemaker earned about $300 for the same year.[45] In late twentieth-century dollars, the income from the currency-exchange sideline would be about $148,000 for the year.[46]

> The American Minister seems to have the sharpest dodge, for instead of allowing the Japanese to take 4 percent discount of his money he exchanges for his full monthly sum of $3000 and pays them the $120 additional, thus securing the exchange for $120 more than he would if the discount was deducted. . . . What a revelation is this of foreign rapacity in high quarters. . . . Of its entire truthfulness there is no doubt. I myself am knowing personally to the US Minister's monthly receipt of $3000 exchange, at a single time last year as a 'special' favor. . . . It is within bounds to say that the US Minister's place was thus made worth for a single year with salary and exchange privileges alone $25,000.[47]

In late-twentieth-century dollars, Pruyn's income for the year might have been $335,000. "These affairs will one day be exposed to public excoriation."[48]

Considering today's executive salaries, the amount hardly seems to warrant outrage. Nevertheless, one begins to sense why, despite the unpleasantness and even mortal danger of his job, Robert H. Pruyn was in no hurry to depart. He had, moreover, another iron in the fire. He obtained and invested a half-million-dollar deposit, intended by the Shogun's government to purchase American-built ships. The ships never were built. Pruyn refunded the capital, an amount equivalent to about 6.7 million late-twentieth-century dollars, but Pruyn and his agents retained the considerable interest on the investment, which might have earned an additional amount equal to his other income—the total equivalent today to $670,000 a year.[49] In our terms, the revenue was more like a million dollars a year.[50]

The mission to Japan, as Pruyn had hoped, was lucrative. Robert H. Pruyn returned a wealthy man. Representing the United States successfully during the opening of Japan to western trade may have been worth his compensation. Historians have concluded that Robert H. Pruyn's recommendations to his government "showed wise understanding of the real situation." On occasion, even the British government relied more on Pruyn's judgment than on that of its senior envoy. Even the Japanese government heeded his warnings and counsel.[51] ". . . With the Shogun's representative Mr. Pruyn seems always to have been on friendly terms. He appreciated the heavy difficulties under which they labored, and he constantly counseled moderation on the part of his colleagues. . . . It is of interest to note that Mr. Pruyn introduced the

---

44 Notehelfer, 552.

45 Alan Dawley, *Class and Community: The Industrial Revolution in Lynn* (Cambridge: Harvard, 1976), 156-7.

46 Composite Consumer Price Index, 1862-1991, Table A2. John J. McCusker. *How Much Is That in Real Money? A Historical Price Index for Use as a Deflator of Money Values in the Economy of the United States* (Worcester: American Antiquarian Society, 1992), 328, 332.

47 Pruyn accepted the position with the understanding that his salary of $7500 "might be doubled or tripled through a unique exchange rate." He did even better, more than tripling it. Edwin Lee, 124, from letter of Robert H. Pruyn to "Wife, Sister, Brother," May 26, 1862. Pruyn Papers, Box 3.

48 Notehelfer, 552-3.

49 Pruyn's brother-in-law, Charles Lansing, and his Republican political patron, Thurlow Weed (his American agents) shared in the proceeds of the investment. Edwin Lee, 137.

50 Because of the Civil War, there was an income tax from 1862 to 1872. Probably Pruyn would have been in a bracket to owe ten percent.

51 Treat, 60, 65, 64.

principle of arbitration to the Japanese. . . . He had been sympathetic in his endeavor to understand the troubled state of Japanese politics, and he had advocated moderate measures no matter how serious the provocation might seem to be."[52]

The Japan adventure was successful diplomatically; it was for Pruyn financially rewarding, and it was culturally enriching, especially for young Bertie on whom the experience made a profound impression.

## Home Again

Bertie was sixteen years old when his father sent him home from Japan by way of Europe.[53] Back in the United States, the Civil War would continue for another year and a half, which may have motivated a European sojourn. In addition to traveling in Europe, Bertie would have caught up with some schoolwork missed while in Japan. Almost two years after leaving Japan, he entered his father's alma mater, Rutgers College.[54] Many families of Dutch descent favored Rutgers, founded at New Brunswick, New Jersey in the eighteenth century by Dutch settlers and identified with the Dutch Reformed Church. Bertie's father was a trustee and benefactor of Rutgers University.

Family tradition recalls Bertie's bringing back to America a young man who became the first Japanese student at an American university.[55] Indeed, in 1866 the first Japanese students did arrive at Rutgers while Bertie was there.[56] Another classmate of Bertie's was future Orientalist William Elliot Griffis. Evidence of the profound influence Japan had had on young R. C. Pruyn was the dedication of one of Griffis' books, *Japanese Fairy Tales*, written some forty years after he and Bertie graduated. In his lengthy "Foreword of Dedication to Robert Clarence Pruyn" Griffis recalled the conversation, "when in our Alma Mater, 'on the banks of the old Raritan,' in 1865, you first told me about the soul of Japan and of her fairy and folklore, and when in 1866, the first two sons of Dai Nippon came to America to be our fellow-students in Rutgers College."[57]

Robert Hewson Pruyn

Another clasmate of R. C. Pruyn was future architect Robert H. Robertson, who, a quarter century later, would play a central role in the development of Santanoni.

52 Treat, 70.

53 Edwin Lee, 130.

54 If Bertie spent the conventional four years pursuing his Baccalaureate degree, which he earned in 1869, he would have gone to Rutgers in 1865, a year and eight months after leaving Japan.

55 J. Winthrop Aldrich to Paul Malo.

56 "The first who came made the journey unapproved and at risk of their life; and they bore assumed names." Two young Japanese men arrived on a boat at New York City using names Ise and Numagawa. The ship's captain escorted them to the office of the Board of Foreign Missions of the Dutch Reformed Church, who arranged their placement at Rutgers. They did not remain long, and both died soon after return to Japan. Many Japanese students followed in the 1870s. William H. S. Demarest, *A History of Rutgers College, 1766-1924* (New Brunswick, N.J.: Rutgers, 1924), 440-41.

57 Later in this full-page dedication, Griffis added, ". . . please accept this offering of stories, new and old, and walk with me through the jeweled gates you first opened to your fellow-student. With your name and that of your honored father–the envoy of President Lincoln in the land opened to the world's brotherhood by Commodore M.C. Perry and Townsend Harris—the modern progress of Japan will ever be honorably associated." William Elliot Griffis, *Japanese Fairy Tales* (New York: T.Y. Crowell Co., 1908), "A Forward of Dedication," n.p.

About the time that his son was preparing to enter Rutgers, Robert H. Pruyn left Japan, after serving three full years as minister.[58] The Civil War ended as he traveled home, via Europe, arriving in New York about six months after leaving Japan.[59]

On his return in 1865, the senior Pruyn assumed direction again of the Albany Saw Works. He also ran for lieutenant governor, apparently attempting to use his success as diplomat to resume his political career. He was not elected and "ill health obliged him to retire from public life."[60] However, he served as chairman of the State Constitutional Commission, and "some of the most far-reaching reforms . . . were due to his efforts."[61] Soon, probably because of his improved financial status as well as enhanced prestige, Robert H. Pruyn launched a banking career. In 1874, he became vice-president of National Commercial Bank in Albany and the next year became president of the bank, a position he would hold for six years.[62]

Son Robert earned his B.A. degree in 1869 and an M.A. degree, also from Rutgers, in 1872. R. C. Pruyn's first regular employment was as an aide to the Governor in Albany.[63]

In his first year out of college, when twenty-six years old, Robert married Anna Martha Williams, who was descended from early English settlers of Connecticut.[64] Anna, one of five siblings, was daughter of Chauncey Pratt Williams and Martha Andrews Williams.[65] Anna's father was also a prominent Albany banker.[66] Robert and Anna's four children—Edward, Ruth, Robert and Frederic—were born between 1874 and 1881.

Newly married and responsible for a growing family, Robert required additional income, as did his brother, Charles Lansing Pruyn, five years younger.[67] Their father turned over the Albany Saw Works to the brothers, then acquired another business for them, the Albany Embossing Co., which produced checkers, blocks, dominoes and various other games. The brothers were personally close for their entire lives; they managed their joint business enterprises with little friction. Not surprisingly, both brothers eventually entered banking.[68]

Robert C. Pruyn became a director of Robert H. Pruyn's National Commercial Bank in 1881. When his father died the following year, young Robert was elected vice-president.[69] His principal career as banker had been launched.

When Robert H. Pruyn's successor after only three years as bank president went to Washington, Robert C. Pruyn filled the vacancy.[70] Robert became president of a major

[58] "When Mr. Pruyn, the second American Minister, left Yedo in 1865 on a well-earned leave of absence, he fully expected to return to his post, but a combination of personal reasons caused him to decide to retire from the diplomatic service." Treat, 78. He left on April 28, 1865. Notehelfer, 600.

[59] Notehelfer, 600. Pruyn arrived in autumn of 1865. Edwin Lee, 136.

[60] *National Cyclopaedia*, 440.

[61] R. H. Pruyn was appointed Chairman in 1872. "Portraits of Presidents," 5.

[62] He also served as vice president of the Albany Savings Bank and trustee of the Metropolitan Trust Co. of New York City. *National Cyclopaedia*, 440. He served as director and trustee of educational and philanthropic institutions, as well as commercial enterprises.

[63] Republican Governor John A. Dix had known father Robert H. Pruyn as Assembly Speaker.

[64] Thomas Williams came from England between 1645 and 1656, settling in Connecticut. *National Cyclopaedia*, 226.

[65] Martha Andrews was daughter of Rueben Hough of Whitesboro (later Utica, N.Y.). *National Cyclopaedia*, 226.

[66] Chauncey Pratt Williams retired as president of the National Exchange Bank of Albany in 1887 but continued as treasurer of the Albany Exchange Savings Bank until his death. *National Cyclopaedia*, 226.

[67] Charles Lansing Pruyn received his B.A. from Rutgers in 1871 and his M.S. in 1874. *National Cyclopaedia*, 225.

[68] Charles became a trustee or director of Albany Savings Bank, New York State National Bank, and the Union Trust Company. *National Cyclopaedia*, 227.

[69] Robert Hewson Pruyn died on February 22, 1882.

[70] R. H. Pruyn's successor was Daniel Manning, owner of the *Albany Argus* newspaper and president of the State Democratic Committee. Manning, who is credited with securing Grover Cleveland's Democratic nomination for the presidency, resigned from the bank in 1885 and followed Cleveland to Washington to head the Treasury Department. Years later, Pruyn eulogized Manning, saying that "in the Secretary of the Treasury . . . was centered the greatest power held by any human being." Editorial, *Frank Leslie's Illustrated Newspaper*, clipping undated (c. 1887), Pruyn Papers. It is a statement,

commercial bank only four years after his first professional experience with banking, but he proved to be an effective and durable leader. For forty-six years, he served as president or board chairman.[71]

## Banker Pruyn

Albany, although a small city, was capital of the State of New York, located at a juncture of major transportation routes, and was the financial center of an industrial area that included important mill towns such as Troy and Cohoes. During Robert Pruyn's long tenure, his bank grew exponentially. When Pruyn became president, the bank's assets stood at $3.5 million. In 1901, National Commercial acquired the assets of its Albany competitors, Merchant's National and Albany City National, and in 1920 merged with the Union Trust Co., becoming National Commercial Bank and Trust Co. By 1921, assets had soared to $36.8 million.[72] (After consolidating many other institutions, the name became "Key Bank." Now based in Cleveland, it became one of the largest banks in the United States.)

Pruyn's professional stage was larger than Albany. The bank's growth under his leadership mirrored not only the nation's financial surge, but also reflected a growing public trust in the American banking system. Between 1897 and 1907, bank investments in the United States quadrupled.[73] It was during Pruyn's years at the helm of National Commercial that the country's banking system took on its modern form, including the establishment of the Federal Reserve, and in this development Pruyn was a key player at the state and national levels. When the public trust faltered in 1893 and financial panic threatened the very structure of the American banking system, Pruyn stepped forward to organize his colleagues for a united response. Arguing that the solution to the crisis was to stabilize the system, not tear it down, Pruyn founded the "Group of Six," an association of upstate bankers that later became the New York State Bankers' Association.

Randall J. LaBoeuf of Albany lauded the Group of Six in a 1927 speech, for having calmed investors' fears during the dark days of panic. "This old guard . . . had their fighting pluck up. They insisted that the country was sound, that its natural resources were hardly scratched, that the structure of credit could be restored." That night LaBoeuf lionized the aging Pruyn as "the dean of the Albany banking community."[74]

One factor which accounted for Pruyn's influence in the world of banking was the long string of young, hand-picked male secretaries whom Pruyn mentored much in the way that promising young law school graduates today clerk for federal appellate judges, and much in the way his own father had taught him. Pruyn was a good judge of men and a good teacher, and became noted nationally for the number of his protégés who became leaders of industry or finance.[75] Choice of aides revealed the tightness of his elite network. Of twenty secretaries who served him during his career, twelve had attended Yale University and four went to Harvard (only one graduated from Rutgers); fourteen were varsity athletes; and eight came from two fraternities, Delta Kappa

---

which attests to Pruyn's belief that it was the financiers who controlled progress in America.

71 *National Cyclopaedia*, 226.

72 *The National Commercial Bank and Trust Company of Albany, N.Y.: Improvements and Additions with a Brief History* (Albany, 1922), 32.

73 William J. Shultz and M. R. Caine, *Financial Development of the United States* (New York: Prentice-Hall, 1937), tables 35, 37.

74 "Lauds Old Guard Bankers for Help in Panic of 1893," clipping from unknown newspaper, February 13, 1927, Pruyn Papers.

75 Harold Stanley became a senior partner in Morgan Stanley; his brother Clarence Stanley also became a partner at Morgan Stanley and a vice president of General Motors. Joseph Rockwell Swan became a senior partner at Smith Barney; Frederick Adams, an executive for several major railroads; Carl Adams, president of the Air Reduction Co.; Lawrence Murray, president of Mellon National Bank and Trust Co.; and Frank Wells McCabe, president and chairman of the board of National Commercial Bank and Trust Co. "Secretaries of R. C. Pruyn" (National Commercial Bank and Trust Company, Albany, undated).

Epsilon and Psi Upsilon.[76] The network was close-knit.

Robert C. Pruyn was well connected in national financial circles.[77] In later years he would receive an honorary doctorate of law from Rutgers, "in recognition of his services and importance in the world of finance."[78] Robert C. Pruyn was said to be "one of the most widely known bankers and industrialists in the East."[79]

The Pruyn fortune accrued not only from banking. Robert C. Pruyn was a developer of public utilities and of railroad equipment companies.[80] He was a director of the Chase National Bank, the Delaware and Hudson Railroad and many other companies.[81] No mere passive investor, he was active in management.[82] For many years he maintained an office in Manhattan to keep up with his many businesses and directorships. Like his father before him, he was director and trustee of philanthropic as well as commercial and social institutions. Like his father, he also was dedicated to public service.[83]

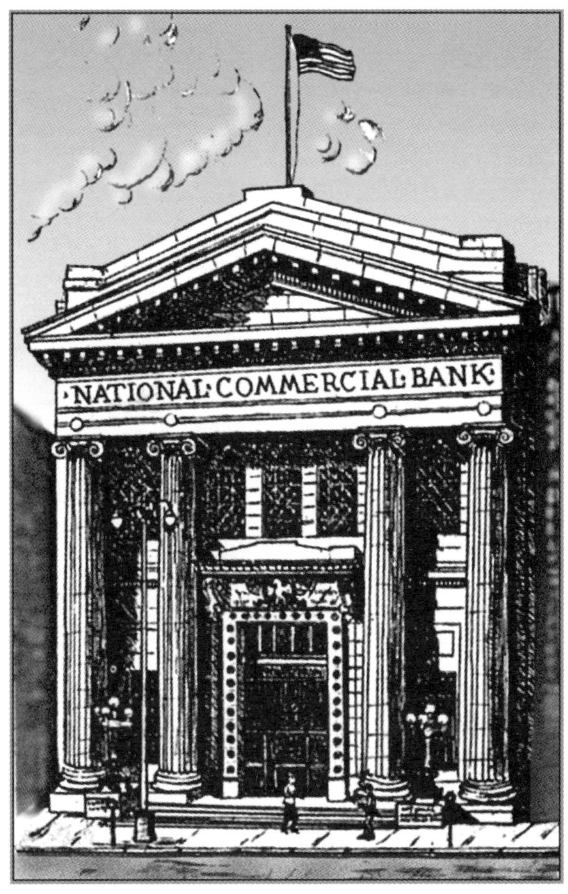


National Commercial Bank, Albany
York and Sawyer, Architects[84]

76 "Secretaries of R. C. Pruyn."

77 Not only did his predecessor at the bank Daniel Manning become Secretary of the Treasury but in 1898 Charles Sumner Hamlin, a future architect of the federal reserve system, longtime Federal Reserve board member and Assistant Secretary of the Treasury under Presidents Cleveland and Wilson, married Pruyn's favorite cousin, Huybertje (Huybertie) Pruyn. The Hamlins spent their honeymoon at Santanoni in June 1897.

78 "Rutgers College Degree for Robert C. Pruyn," undated newspaper clipping, Pruyn Papers, Box 11, Folder 10.

79 "Portraits of Presidents," 7.

80 Pruyn "aided in the development of many companies, including the Municipal Gas Company, United Traction Company, the Air Reduction Co., and the Consolidated Car Heating Company in Albany." "Portraits of Presidents," 7.

81 Pruyn served as director of the Mohawk Hudson Power Corp., North American Cement Co., Mechanics and Metals National Bank of New York, and other corporations. *National Cyclopaedia*, 226.

82 In a letter to the powerful Walter Oakman, president of the Guaranty Trust Co., Pruyn complained that his Consolidated Car Heating Co. was being shut out of bidding on a contract to supply parts for eighty-five Long Island Railroad cars. Oakman intervened. R. C. Pruyn, letter to Walter G. Oakman, January 14, 1899; R. C. Pruyn, letter to Frederick W. Kelley, General Manager, Consolidated Car Heating Co., January 24, 1899. An April 1902 letter to Robert M. Burnett, receiver for New England Gas & Coke Co. (and brother of Edward Burnett, designer of Santanoni's farm) is icily firm in posting a claim for a $90,000 debt, on which company stock and bonds had been pledged as collateral: "This is to notify you that unless the moneys due as above specified, together with the interest thereon, are paid, I propose to offer the said securities at public sale in the City of New York, and if there is a deficiency on any such sale, I will hold the New England Gas & Coke Co. responsible therefor." Both letters in collection of Susan Pruyn King.

83 Robert C. Pruyn served as member of the New York State Legislature and the State Board of Regents, as Albany Comissioner of Parks, and as financial advisor to the National Council of the Protestant Episcopal Church. "Robert C. Pruyn, 87, Financier, is Dead." Obituary, *New York Times*, October 30, 1934, 19.

84 Drawing by Alice Pauline Schafer, "Portraits of Presidents," cover.

## The Cultured Pruyns

The Pruyns were a cultured family in a cultured city that "had its own group of painters and sculptors in the mid-19th century."[85] An artistic trait ran through generations of Pruyns; Robert's father had been a collector of art who "made literary and art collections, which became noted."[86] He is believed to have introduced to America a species of Japanese tree.[87]

Son, Robert C. Pruyn, "was a scholarly man, well read, and very sociable."[88] "As a person, he was described as 'naturally warm-hearted and polished in both personal appearance and manner,' suave and kind."[89] Like his father, Robert C. Pruyn was a collector of art. He gave many paintings as gifts to others.[90] He amassed an important collection of Japanese art objects. His wife Anna "was some-thing of an artist" as was their daughter Ruth Pruyn Goodrich, who was a potter.[91] Their eldest son, Edward Lansing Pruyn, became a painter.

Robert Clarence Pruyn

With this interest in the arts, it is not suprising that three generations of Pruyn men are themselves memorialized in fine portraits: Robert H. Pruyn by Eastman Johnson, Robert C. Pruyn by William Merritt Chase, and Edward L. Pruyn in a self-portrait.[92]

Albany was noted for its interest in architecture. "Few, if any, cities its size could display such a bouquet of the flower of the American architectural profession. The city had good architecture because its citizens hired good architects."[93] Like his prominent uncle, John V.L. Pruyn, Robert C. Pruyn was interested in public as well as his private building projects.[94] Robert was "long . . . involved in important architectural events in Albany."[95] Early in his business career, perhaps because his family was growing with the birth of a second child, he commissioned New York City architects, Potter and Robertson, to design an Albany town house at Willett and Lancaster

---

85 Bennett, 116; also, Jeanne Winston Adler, *Early Days in the Adirondacks: The PhotographS of Seneca Ray Stoddard* (New York: Abrams, 1997), 152.

86 *National Cyclopaedia*, 440.

87 Interview, July 1992 with Merle Melvin, Jr., who recalled that it might have been a Cork tree or "Katsura." John Winthrop Aldrich, *Santanoni Preserve: Source Book #1* (Albany: New York State Department of Environmental Conservation, 1992-1993), 157.

88 *National Cyclopaedia*, 226.

89 Wesley Haynes, "Farm Complex," 70-71.

90 Cynthia Pruyn Green, Aldrich, 139.

91 Aldrich, 20-21.

92 The Eastman Johnson painting was in the collection of Susan Pruyn King until sold; the William Merritt Chase portrait is in the collection of Key Bank, Albany. Reproductions appeared in "Portraits of Presidents," an exhibition and catalogue (Albany: The Bank, 1970). The Edward L. Pruyn self-portrait is in the collection of Susan Pruyn King.

93 Eugene J. Johnson, *Style Follows Function: Architecture of Marcus T. Reynolds* (Albany: Washington Park Press, 1993), 3.

94 John V.L. Pruyn was author of the program for the state capitol, judge of the entries, and worked closely with the selected architects. He was demanding, but the results were not entirely satisfactory, so another architect, H.H. Richardson, supplanted the original designers. Cecil R. Roseberry, *Capitol Story* (Albany: Office of General Services, State of New York, 1964), 7-25.

95 Johnson, 95.

Willett Street House, Robert H. Robertson, architect

Streets.[96] The architect Robert H. Robertson was his college friend, whose own distinguished career was beginning. Robertson's elevation drawing for the Willett Street house, reproduced here, was published in a national journal and has appeared in a recent architectural exhibition and publication.[97]

The Potter and Robertson firm also designed an office building for Pruyn's father and a house for his brother.[98] Robert Robertson soon would design the Santanoni villa, far different in character. Robert C. Pruyn also owned an 1885 row of houses designed by Albany architects, Fuller and Wheeler.[99]

Pruyn selected New York City architect Robert W. Gibson in 1887 to design a building for the National Commercial Bank building at 38–40 State Street.[100] After having the bank's offices remodeled, Robert Pruyn, "resolved to procure the best," in 1902 engaged New York City architects York and Sawyer, "who had achieved a great reputation as designers of bank buildings," to design imposing, neoclassical bank headquarters at 60 State Street.[101] Pruyn also commissioned prominent Albany architect Marcus Reynolds to design two important structures: headquarters of the Albany Railroad Company (1899) and the Municipal Gas Company (1915).[102] Robert C. Pruyn served as a member of the commission that engaged the capitol architect, H. H. Richardson, to design the Albany City Hall (c. 1883), a building that was voted at the time to be "the seventh most beautiful building in America."[103] Its tower contains the Pruyn memorial carillon.[104] Richardson also designed a Pruyn cemetery monument.[105]

96 Diana S. Waite, *Albany Architecture: Guide to the City* (Albany: Mount Ida Press, 1993), 180.

97 *American Architect and Building News*, August 18, 1877; the drawing was reproduced full-page as Illustration 10, Steven M. Bedford, "Country and City: Some Formal Comparisons," *The Long Island Country House, 1870-1930* (Southampton, N.Y.: Parrish Art Museum, 1988), 44. That Pruyn house at the corner of Lancaster Street was extant, "hardly altered," and illustrated in a 1993 guide, *Albany Architecture*, Waite, 87, 104, 180.

98 The R. H. Pruyn Building, a mercantile apartment structure, was built 1879-1880 at 70 North Pearl Street. It is illustrated in Waite, *Albany Architecture*, 89. Robertson's designs for both Pruyn brothers' houses were published in *American Architect and Building News*; the Robert C. Pruyn residence appeared in the issue of Aug. 18, 1877.

99 Waite, 142.

100 The earlier bank building, designed in 1887, became the Hampton Hotel. Johnson, 93, 95.

101 *The National Commercial Bank and Trust Company of Albany, N.Y.: Improvements and Additions with a Brief History* (Albany, N.Y, 1922).

102 Johnson, 95-96.

103 An 1885 poll of readers of the *American Architect and Building News* ranked buildings. Kennedy, illustration 44, caption, f.p. 175.

104 Kennedy, illustration 27, caption, f.p. 132. The carillon was "donated as a memorial to Dutch patrician civic leader and statesman John V.L. Pruyn by his daughter and her husband. . . ." Kennedy, 270.

105 The R. H. Pruyn monument is in the Albany Rural Cemetery. Henry-Russell Hitchcock, *The Architecture of H.H. Richardson and His Times* (Cambridge, Mass.: MIT Press, rev. ed., 1966), 227, note. The R. C. Pruyn monument is also in that cemetery.

The Robert Pruyns lived in their Robertson-designed town house on Willett Street for over a decade. Some of their Willett Street neighbors would become regular visitors at Santanoni.[106] In 1889 Robert, Anna, and their four children moved into a grand house on Englewood Place, at "one of the most desirable locations in Albany," situated on a large, landscaped lot overlooking Washington Park.[107] The twenty-two-room house had fourteen bedrooms and seven baths. Several rooms were finished in teak and leather. The house was twice featured in *American Architect and Building News*.[108] The carriage house itself was an imposing structure. At Englewood Place regal Robert and Anna Pruyn lived in a manner that was "very formal, complete with a butler and all," recalled a granddaughter, "[but not] unpleasantly so."[109]

The state had abolished the feudal patroon system, but esteem for landed families like the Van Rensselaers and Coopers survived. Robert C. Pruyn shared their culture. After coming into his inheritance, following the prosperous decades of the 1880s (but prior to the financial depression of the 1890s) he and Anna Pruyn began to acquire land for a vast country estate. We may understand that they wanted rural property for a country house—but why not a conventional estate, reasonably accessible from town, with social peers as neighbors? Instead they assembled some thirteen thousand acres deep in the Adirondack wilderness, creating the Santanoni Preserve.

Pruyn Residence, 7 Englewood Place, Albany
Robert W. Gibson, Architect

Pruyn Carriage House
Robert W. Gibson, Architect

[106] Edward Bowditch, an Albany stove manufacturer, lived at 40 Willett Street. General Robert Shaw Oliver's family occupied 42. Robert Pruyn's brother, Charles Lansing Pruyn, lived at 44 Willett Street.

[107] The *Albany Knickerbocker News*, 1942. Robert W. Gibson, the New York City architect who had designed All Saints Episcopal Cathedral at Albany and later the National Commercial Bank building for Pruyn, designed the Englewood Place House about 1884 for George Evans. Waite, 170.

[108] The Pruyns were new owners when the house was published for a second time in the *American Architect and Building News*. When the main residence was demolished in 1941, the carriage house was retained, remodeled to become itself a grand residence. Waite, 170.

[109] Beatrice Pruyn Thibault. Aldrich, 154.

Newcomb Lake in the Santanoni Preserve

##  2. A Wilderness Estate 

In acquiring country estates and practicing gentleman farming, [they] defined what it meant to be members of an American elite. Rural pursuits turned out to be a powerful means of self-characterization.

*Tamara Plakins Thornton*

Reasons for life's important choices are many and complex; they are difficult to isolate. Our personal motives may reflect the values of our friends and of the larger culture around us. These values in turn may be integral to broad historical trends. Cultural determinism should be tempered, however, by awareness that our actions may be less than historically significant. As Freud commented, "Sometimes a cigar is just a cigar."

Basic to the Pruyns' motivation was Anna Martha Williams' love for the outdoors. As a youngster the call of the wild had been imprinted at the Williams' own retreat in the southern Adirondack hills where "fishing and tramping were [her father's] favorite sports."[1]

Chauncey Pratt Williams was a Connecticut Yankee of old family who became a financier, moving in 1835 to Albany where he became interested in lumbering, an interest that may have attracted him to the north woods before they became widely popular as a resort. Like the Pruyns, Chauncey Williams was also a prominent Albany banker, perhaps better known in larger financial circles than were the Pruyns. He "achieved a wide reputation as a writer on financial topics" and was a reform activist who, at his own expense, carried a bank-tax suit to the U.S. Supreme Court. Williams was not only a scholar of political economy but an avid gardener.[2] From her father Anna acquired her deep interest in nature.

After her marriage to Robert Pruyn, Anna "did not go in for the social whirl of Albany" but wanted to escape to the woods that she had come to love as a child.[3] Anna "used to go out and get all kind of mushrooms and stuff and she knew what she was doing—nobody ever died from eating them. She used to make terrariums; she was really into the flora part of the Adirondacks."[4]

According to family lore, Robert preferred conventional country living but Anna wanted the wilderness.[5] Tradition also has it that

1 Chauncey Pratt Williams owned property in a section of the Jerseyfield Patent and died in the Adirondacks (Hamilton County). Cynthia Pruyn Green, interview, February 1993, in Aldrich, 134; *National Cyclopaedia,* 226. Jerseyfield Mountain and Lake are near the juncture of Hamilton, Herkimer and Fulton Counties, southwest of Piseco Lake.

2 *National Cyclopaedia,* 225-226.

3 Beatrice Pruyn Thibault, Aldrich, 23. Green, letter, August 1992.

4 Cynthia Pruyn Green, Aldrich, 134. Planting terrariums and dish gardens was "a tradition passed down to all the granddaughters." Susan Pruyn King, manuscript note to authors.

5 Cynthia Pruyn Green, letter, August 1992; also interview, February 1993, Aldrich, 134.

Anna's inclination to live privately, deep in the woods, might be attributable to the Williams' strain of Native American blood, which could account for Anna's dark coloring and other physical attributes that were not common to New England Yankees but which ran in the Williams family.[6]

Anna Pruyn was not one to retreat demurely into the wife's separate sphere, the role commonly approved for proper ladies of her time. Although "she was a very private person," Anna was not the genteel Victorian spouse who would recline on her divan while the men of the house enjoyed pursuits of woods and water.[7] Her granddaughters described her as an active outdoorswoman. "She had a great deal of guts, . . . a great deal of courage." Anna was "very much bowlegged" from a horseback riding accident, and in private walked with a carved ebony stick reputed to have belonged to a Philippine revolutionary.[8] After breaking her hip at age eighty, she "walked without a cane on polished floors with small oriental rugs. She was that kind of person."

Anna Williams Pruyn

Anna's attraction to the wilderness was not the only reason for purchasing land in the sparsely settled town of Newcomb. The Pruyns both enjoyed outdoor life; they also appreciated traditional values of their particular culture. A great estate might identify them with Dutch and English aristocracy. The Adirondacks were becoming a vacation place favored by wealthy New Yorkers who adopted the elite English taste for hunting and fishing. Sportsmen here and elsewhere were becoming important proponents of the growing conservation movement. Given these conditions, a chance event apparently triggered their decision; a close friend introduced them to the Santanoni property.

## Aristocratic Traditions

It is no coincidence that, when Robert Pruyn visited his new Adirondack holdings to select a house site, he was accompanied by two friends, Howard Van Rensselaer and James Fenimore Cooper, both scions of great Yorker landed families.

6 Anna was "very short and dark," according to Beatrice Pruyn Thibault, Aldrich, 23. Susan Pruyn King thought that the Native American in the family line was the second wife of Thomas Williams, "Rebekah (of no last name)." Williams had been kidnapped by Native Americans and married a native woman. Susan Pruyn King, letter to Howard Kirschenbaum, January 15, 1999. Beatrice Pruyn Thibault recalled being informed by an orthopedic surgeon that her bone characteristics were those of Native Americans, as were those of her three brothers. Beatrice Pruyn Thibault, Aldrich, 23. Furthermore, a family tendency to place body weight on the outside of their feet likewise was characteristic of Native Americans. Susan Pruyn King, letter to Howard Kirschenbaum, January 15, 1999.

7 Cynthia Pruyn Green, letter, August 1992; Delilah West Bissell, "My Memories of Pruyn's Preserve at Newcomb." Unpublished manuscript, June 12, 1991.

8 Cynthia Pruyn Green, Aldrich, 119; Cynthia Pruyn Green, September 1992, Aldrich, 119.

The Pruyns were familiar with grand country houses and landscaped parks of Hudson River estates, not only of Dutch patroons, such as the Van Rensselaers, but of prominent British families such as the Livingstons. Dutch and English cultures had merged into a regional subculture by the last decade of the nineteenth century. As the Revolution receded into distant history, emulation of aristocratic English traditions became more acceptable among elite Americans. Being "landed" characterized patrician families like the Van Rensselaers and Coopers; being landed distinguished "old' from "new money," at a time when rapid economic change was producing many new industrialists of great wealth. As a banker, the "new men" were Pruyn's clients. As a host of a great estate, he could convey to them his old family's distinctive prestige.

The English country estate provided a ready model for the Pruyns as they sought to establish a rural manor of their own. For British aristocracy, a country property typically consisted of a "country house"—a grand home, princely in its proportions and appointments—surrounded by a large hunting park. In addition, the estate had its "home farm," the name indicating the farmstead that provided products for the owner's country house, as distinct from other farms, rented by tenants for their own use. The gentleman farmer, who made a personal hobby of estate agriculture, became common among the eastern elite of the nineteenth century.[9] An aristocratic rural estate was generally identified by imposing entry gates or gate lodge structure. All of these features would be incorporated into the Pruyns' woodland estate, where their country house would require the most ambitious house-building campaign of the forest region at the time. Santanoni would be a timber and game preserve of some thirteen thousand acres, incorporating a model agricultural facility.

In this sense, Santanoni Preserve may have been envisioned as a family seat, to serve future generations. The notion of identifying a landed family with its own *place* was traditionally aristocratic, and very British. The Brandreths, who inaugurated this patrimonial notion in the Adirondacks, had made their fortune originally in Britain.[10]

Another feature of this aristocratic heritage was an emphasis on sport, particularly hunting or "shooting." Although he was the very antithesis of a rough-and-ready woodsman, Robert Pruyn, like his wife, was an outdoorsman. His model, however, rather than the mountain trapper, the hunting guide, or tough lumberjack, was the English country gentleman. Robert and Anna both fancied riding and driving horses. Hiking also was popular. They both hunted on occasion, but their favorite outdoor sport was fresh-water angling.

For those fond of the outdoors, the Newcomb area has always been attractive for its forests, abundant game, and several lakes and ponds. It was not, however, very suitable for a gentleman's estate on the English model. Hardscrabble Adirondack Mountain terrain hardly would be attractive to an aspiring farmer.

In retrospect, Robert Pruyn's determination to cultivate the wilderness seems quixotic. Why did he endeavor to make productive the rocky, thin soil that other farmers had largely abandoned?

"Camp Santanoni was, I understand, the result of a compromise between my grandparents. My grandmother was fond of the Adirondacks and my grandfather favored farming, so they had both at Santanoni. . . ."[11] But the Pruyns could have found closer to home

9 Tamara Plakins Thornton has provided an exemplary study, *Cultivating Gentlemen: The Meaning of Country Life among the Boston Elite, 1785-1860* (New Haven: Yale University Press, 1989).

10 Brandreth Park of 26,000 acres was established in 1851, decades before others followed their example. Dr. Benjamin Brandreth was wealthy when he arrived in the United States in 1835. Alfred L. Donaldson, *A History of the Adirondacks*, (New York: Century, 1921), I: 60.

11 Green, letter, August 1992; also interview, February, 1993, in Aldrich, 134.

the mixed forest and field of the "middle landscape" that was more favored in the nineteenth century, and was characteristic of much of upstate New York. Why did they seek isolation in vast reaches of forest instead of joining social peers who had established landed estates in the Hudson Valley or nearby Hudson Highlands?

The innovative aspect of Santanoni was its combination of a pastoral model of rural life, an older European ideal, with the wilderness experience that was then becoming valued as a novel aspect of American culture. Pruyns brought to the Adirondacks the model of the large country house on a domain made relatively self-sufficient by a farm.

## Adirondack Great Camps

Change of attitude toward nature was pivotal to the history of the mountain region. An early developer, Sir William Johnson in 1770 deemed the northern wilderness "so verry [*sic*] mountainous and barren that it is worth nothing."[12] It was largely *terra incognita,* inhabited only temporarily by Native Americans, and considered hostile by European settlers before the Civil War.

Romantic writers and other artists by the mid-nineteenth century had transformed attitudes toward wilderness, transmuting aversion into attraction. The Adirondacks became a place offering escape, if only briefly, from crowded cities, post-War industrialization, and from cultural change. There one might retreat to the newly rediscovered, romantic, restorative world of nature. No longer forbidding, many remote and once hostile places lured literate and affluent urban families. City dwellers ceased to see the forest through the eyes of the pioneer farmer who sought a livelihood from this largely unproductive land. Nineteenth-century exurbanites took up rod and rifle and advanced intrepidly into the wilds of the Adirondacks.

Outdoor enthusiasts who could afford to come to the Adirondacks for extended hunting and fishing trips typically would camp with their guides or sojourn at the growing number of boarding houses and hotels springing up in the mountains. Expansive private camps and estates were rare in the northern wilderness until the late 1870s, when William West Durant introduced the luxury camp along the shores of remote Raquette Lake.[13]

Durant, heir to a railroad fortune, a compulsive builder, and visionary developer, sensed a market for grand retreats of woodland character. He transformed the logger's cabin, the trapper's shanty, into the rustic villa.[14] A taste for Japanese culture was widespread at the time. Like Rikyu, who evolved the rustic or *wabi* style in Japan, Durant converted "the beauty he found in peasant life into an aesthetic form."[15] His seminal Camp Pine Knot, evolving over many years, beginning in the late 1870s, served as a model for other log or rustic vacation homes nearby.

The "Great Camp" has since become an icon of the region. While the term was not coined until much later, the style served as model for national and state park buildings, as well as for private retreats elsewhere.[16]

---

[12] Sir William Johnson, letter to Goldsboro Banyar, April 6, 1770, in *The Papers of Sir William Johnson* (Albany: University of the State of N.Y., 1921-1962), XII, 814-815.

[13] Craig Gilborn, *Durant: The Fortunes and Woodland Camps of a Family in the Adirondacks* (Blue Mountain. Lake, N.Y.: The Adirondack Museum, 1981).

[14] "Villa" is the term, in use since Roman times, for a large, typically seasonal country house and its supporting facilities.

[15] Sen no Rikyu was the "best-known tea master" of Japan who developed the *wabi*, or rustic style in Japan. Yasuhiro Ishimoto in Gropius and Tange, 27, 30.

[16] The term "Great Camps" may have been first employed by Arnold Lehman, "Great Camps of the Adirondacks." Unpublished manuscript. (Blue Mountain Lake, N.Y.: Adirondack Museum, 1970). Eight years later the term was given wider recognition by Mary Ellen Gadski, "Research Report on the Great Camps of the Adirondacks." Unpublished manuscript. (Albany: Preservation League of New York State, 1978). Subsequently Howard Kirschenbaum described the prototypical Great Camp as a complex of many buildings, utilizing rustic materials in an artistic style, with a high degree of self-

Brandreth Park was progenitor of the great Adirondack preserves. By the 1890s summer residents of the region favored the sort of rustic décor then seen at Camp Comfort.

A Durant-inspired colony of camps, executed with rustic artistry and craftsmanship, developed around Raquette and nearby Blue Mt. Lakes.[17] The style quickly spread to other areas. Wealthy patrons at Paul Smith's Hotel in the northern Adirondacks purchased lakefront parcels in the St. Regis Lakes area, often for use as tuberculosis cure compounds. The camps they built were initially compounds of tent platforms and rustic shelters, which later were elaborated into larger, permanent buildings in the rustic style. Other lodges were built on the Saranac Lakes, and another summer colony developed around Keene Valley.

The era of the Adirondack Great Camps already was well underway in 1892 when the Pruyns began to develop their Newcomb property. Earlier Adirondack camps had been rustic cottages rather than expansive country houses on the English model; the signature log and bark-covered cabin at Camp Pine Knot had indeed been called the "Swiss Cottage." The Pruyns probably knew of these rustic retreats; they were related to the Ten Eycks, another prominent Albany family of Dutch descent, and probably visited the Albany mayor's rustic summer home, from which vantage point they viewed other notable camps around Raquette Lake.[18]

In other regions, many achievers with new money and even some inheritors of great fortunes acquired large land holdings and the grandiose trophy houses of the Gilded Age. In the Adirondacks this propensity to self-indulgence found expression in the Great Camps, sometimes established in large hunting preserves. To be identified with the likes of the Brandreths, who had bought an entire township, had cachet.

Santanoni was radically different from other Great Camps of the time. Brandreth Park, with its family enclave of rustic lodges, had been a hunting preserve for generations, but the Pruyns' new camp conformed more to the agrarian model of the family seat on a self-

sufficiency, built for a single family, typically along a lake shore. "Thirty-Four or More?" *Adirondack Life*, (May/June 1985), 9-12. In popular usage, properties with *several* of these qualities have been called Great Camps.

17 Camps included Durant's Camp Pine Knot (1876-1890), Colonel Stott's Bluff Point Camp (1877), Charles Durant's Camp Fairview on Osprey Island (1879-85), Albany Mayor James Ten Eyck's camp on North Point (after 1882, when the property was acquired according to deed), Connecticut Governor Phineas Lounsberry's Echo Camp (1883), all on Raquette Lake, and the Durant-built Lilienthal Camp Kla-How-ya on nearby Blue Mountain Lake (1882).

18 Subsequently Ten Eyck family members would visit Camp Santanoni.

sufficient estate. The Pruyns' main camp, moreover, was the first truly large complex planned and erected in a single campaign. In the Adirondacks, Santanoni was the first important country house built on such a great land holding. The remote, rustic villa, independent amid thousands of acres of wild preserve, became the Great Camp prototype. Other notable estates—of William West Durant, William Seward Webb, William C. Whitney, Edward Litchfield, William Rockefeller, and Alfred and Frederick Vanderbilt—soon followed.

By the 1890s the Adirondacks had become fashionable; attitudes toward wilderness had changed. To enjoy country life in company of social peers, a prominent Albany family could look northward to the mountains as well as southward to the Hudson Valley. The Pruyns might have bought lakefront property from Durant, however, or from Paul Smith, and could have built their camp on relatively few acres. An appreciation for nature and enjoyment of active, outdoor life does not require acquisition of thirteen thousand acres. Pruyn, who later became a member of the Tahawus Club, might have stayed there to give his family access to the wilderness; he did not need to acquire such a large amount of it. Visitors could also hike, canoe, hunt and fish on ample State land elsewhere. Furthermore, the sociable Pruyns had many friends with summer homes to visit. Much of the land they purchased had been lumbered recently, so there was little prospect of immediate gain from their investment. Why did the Pruyns launch a major campaign of land acquisition?

The precedent of the English hunting preserve provides an important, but only a partial explanation. There was still another precedent, closer at hand, which helps account for Santanoni Preserve. This was the conservation movement just coming into being in New York State, a movement that would soon exercise a profound influence on national values and land management policies.

## Private Preserves and Public Conservation

As the nineteenth century waned, it became evident to the public, as widely reported in the press, that rampant lumbering was despoiling the Adirondacks—not merely as a scenic recreational area, but as a watershed for downstate cities and state canals. "Cut and run" was the rule of the day. After logging, flooding, or burning, properties of thousands and tens of thousands of acres had become largely valueless, so often reverted to local governments for unpaid taxes. These lands contained lakes, ponds, streams, forests, fish and wildlife with potential for timber management and outdoor recreation.

The region was too vast and the problem too great for the state to solve expeditiously, so the government turned to landowners for help. In 1871 New York State enacted legislation for "the protection of private parks and grounds." Private preserves were encouraged as a means to save a natural resource for the people of the state—including, not incidentally, sportsmen. Their preserves served ". . . to encourage the propagation of fish and game."[19] The State Forest Commission observed that interests of preserve owners were "identical with those of the State." The Forest Commission assessed a deplorable situation: "It is evident also, that owing to the persistent refusal of the Legislature to appropriate money for the purchase of Adirondack lands, the preservation of its forests, outside those owned by the State, is dependent largely on the existence of these private preserves."[20]

---

[19] Chapter 831, Laws of 1871, quoted by Edward Comstock, Jr., "The Role of Private Preserves in the Adirondack Park," *Adirondack Journal of Environmental Studies* 2(2), Fall/Winter 1995: 33-39.

[20] "Private Preserves in the Adirondack Forests." *Annual Report of the Forest Commission of New York for the Year 1893* (Albany: James B. Lyon, 1894), 1: 153, quoted by Mary Ellen Gadski, "Research Report on the Great Camps of the Adirondacks." Unpublished report. (Albany, N.Y.: Preservation League of New York State, 1978), 52.

Newcomb Lake and islands seen from site of the main camp, Moose Mountain in the distance

Groups of business and professional men joined together in clubs to purchase large mountain holdings. By 1904 there were sixty private reservations in the Adirondacks.[21] Among these was the Tahawus (formerly the "Adirondack") Club, which leased thousands of acres in the central Adirondacks adjoining the property on which the Pruyns built their Adirondack camp.

The proliferation of private preserves coincided with widespread resort development during the latter decades of the century, a movement related to emergence of an urban middle class. The rapidly rising standard of living made the two-day weekend, vacation travel, resort hotels and country clubs, as well as second homes more widely available to Americans.

The newly wealthy often followed the lead of patrician families, who generally favored the sporting tradition of the English gentry but disdained association with the upwardly mobile at public hostelries, and even at private clubs, in the Adirondacks. Withdrawing into private estates, some families conducted scientific forestry on their large game preserves.[22] These retreats provided occasional recreation for the owners, so were improved with seasonal residences that usually were visited by wealthy proprietors for only a few weeks of the year. In America hunting had been regarded as a necessity for less affluent rural folk. Landed families, however, continued a European sporting tradition. In the growing upper-middle class, hunting was adopted largely as a male pastime, introduced widely through popular sporting journals that conveyed the image of the sporting gentleman. In more elite families sport with rod and gun was not so restricted by gender. At Brandreth Park ladies hoisted their shooting pieces alongside the men.

It is a paradox that while some wealthy Adirondack property owners were popularly

[21] New York State Forest, Fish and Game Commission, *Eighth and Ninth Annual Reports*, 37-43.

[22] Brandreths, Webbs, and Whitneys were patrons of scientific forestry.

regarded as "robber barons" and "malefactors of great wealth," many of the large land holders and members of land-owning clubs comprised the nucleus of the wilderness preservation movement. At the time, few Americans favored preserving wilderness; even those who were most concerned with the natural environment, like the Pruyns' guest, Theodore Roosevelt, more regularly advocated conservation of natural resources for future use, rather than preservation of wilderness in perpetuity. The more typical view was that of President Roosevelt's advisor, Gifford Pinchot (who also served as the Webbs' forest consultant). Pinchot advocated forest management for commercial use.

Enlightened commercial foresters as well as sportsmen condemned the rapacious lumbering practices of the era. Both groups advocated state protection of woodlands in the Adirondack and Catskill regions. Legislation of 1885 created "the first state forest preserve in the nation," now commemorated as a National Historic Landmark.[23]

The Forest Preserve was dedicated solely to land preservation for various public benefits—initially for watershed protection, but as many soon recognized, also for wildlife conservation, outdoor recreation, even spiritual renewal—although some of the conservationists would have preferred provision for controlled forestry as well. The state then undertook a concerted program of land acquisition to expand the Forest Preserve.

Large landowners who influenced wilderness-preservation and wildlife-conservation policy of New York State benefited in return. State acquisition of neighboring lands protected their property from unwelcome commercial activity while affording increased hunting and fishing terrain. During more than a century, as large tracts of land have become public domain, the decreasing number of large private tracts has increased their market value. Advocacy of state wilderness preservation and wildlife conservation policy has not been altogether self-serving, however. In 1902, some major landowners formed the still-influential Association for the Protection of the Adirondacks. Robert C. Pruyn was a founding trustee, charter member, and life member of the organization.[24] Several national leaders of the conservation and wilderness movements have been identified with the Adirondacks.[25]

Coincidence of public and private interests accounted for the nationally influential development of wilderness policy in New York State, accomplishing the initial Forest Preserve (1885) and subsequently the Adirondack Park (1892), followed by adoption of the pioneering but much-debated "forever wild" provision of the New York State Constitution (1894).[26]

"The land, the land, always the land," was a favorite saying of Robert Pruyn.[27] He spoke, not merely as a banker considering real property a sound investment, or as a sportsman appreciating wilderness for wildlife conservation, or even as a gentlemen farmer who regarded the land as a creative challenge and its produce a satisfaction, but as we shall see, Robert and Anna Pruyn shared a reverence for the land

[23] The "Adirondack Forest Preserve" [*sic*] was designated in 1963. Robert Sandoval of the National Historic Landmarks Survey, letter to Paul Malo, April 6, 1999.

[24] Association for the Protection of the Adirondacks, *Special Report No. 11: Organizational Proceedings of the Association for the Protection of the Adirondacks in 1901 and 1902*. Schenectady, NY, 1977.

[25] Theodore Roosevelt, as mentioned subsequently, was an Adirondack sportsman. He visited the Adirondack (later Tahawus) Club, Paul Smith's Hotel, and the Pruyns' estate. As Governor of New York Roosevelt was involved in the vigorous state conservation campaign. As President of the United States he made history by dramatically expanding the national role in land and wildlife conservation, as well as by preaching from his "bully pulpit" a conservation ethic to the world. Robert Marshall and Howard Zahniser both enjoyed camps here.

[26] Several excellent studies of the state's Adirondack policy and practice include those by Graham, Terrie, and VanValkenburgh, mentioned in the bibliography.

[27] Related to the Pruyns' granddaughter Susan Pruyn King by her guardian Frank McCabe. Susan Pruyn King, manuscript note to authors, January 1999.

and for nature as having, beyond mere utility, an intrinsic value.

It may be more than coincidence that Santanoni Preserve and the Adirondack Park share the same anniversary—or that the Forever Wild provision of the State Constitution was drafted during the inaugural season of Camp Santanoni—for they are indeed kin.[28] As one of the first great private estates of the Adirondacks, Santanoni both represented and contributed to the conservation movement and the wilderness ethic then evolving in the Adirondacks—developments that would affect not only the public policy of New York State, but of the nation.

## Newcomb

It was not happenstance that the Pruyns selected a sparsely settled corner of Essex County to create their private sporting preserve and family retreat. Throughout the region other property was offered at a reasonable price. With his business contacts in Albany and northern New York, Pruyn easily could have located available land in any of the most desirable lake and mountain areas of the North Country. The Pruyns chose this particular, remote township in the heart of the Adirondacks Mountains because of one man—Robert Henderson Robertson.

Robertson's family was engaged with this part of the Adirondack wilderness for much of the nineteenth century. In the early 1800s, after the Indians and the trappers, and before the loggers, a few pioneers had settled near today's hamlet of Newcomb. A Vermonter, Joseph Chandler, cleared a patch of land at the foot of Rich Lake in 1816. Two years later Nathaniel Pendleton came and with several other settlers formed the hamlet of Pendleton in that location. Still others followed, including Daniel Tobias Newcomb who in 1822 cleared a farm two miles east of Lake Delia—later renamed Newcomb Lake, which would become center piece of the Santanoni Preserve.[29] Daniel Newcomb helped to incorporate Newcomb Township in 1828 and was its first elected supervisor.

In 1837 Robert Robertson's father, Archibald, bought a large percentage of the fledgling MacIntyre Iron Works, six miles northeast of Newcomb Lake.[30] The other owners were Archibald's uncle Archibald McIntyre, his brother-in-law David Henderson, and state senator Duncan McMartin.[31]

The four Scottish-American partners had stumbled upon one of the richest iron ore deposits yet discovered. Situated, however, in a rugged, virtually unmapped wilderness, the mine was extremely remote from an accessible market. So, in 1828, McMartin used his influence to pass legislation commissioning a road that would link the iron works eastward to Cedar Point (now Port Henry) on Lake Champlain.[32] The Cedar Point Road continued westward from the iron works, past Daniel Newcomb's farm, then to Newcomb Lake, where it crossed a bridge over a narrow portion of the lake at its southern end (at the present Duck Hole bridge) and continued to the Pendleton Settlement. There it joined the Carthage Road, completed in 1841, that connected Crown Point on the east to Carthage on the west of the mountains.[33]

28 The "Forever Wild" amendment was introduced "at the request of a group of New York City business men . . . ." Louis Marshall, father of wilderness advocate, Bob Marshall, was "most active in formulating the amendment and in securing for it what was practically a unanimous vote . . . ." James M. Glover. *A Wilderness Original: The Life of Bob Marshall* (Seattle: The Mountaineers, 1986), 12.

29 Arthur H. Masten, *The Story of Adirondac* (Syracuse, N.Y.: Syracuse University Press, 1968), 171.

30 Robert Robertson's paternal grandparents, Peter Robertson and Catherine McIntyre, emigrated from Scotland in the 1780s. Archibald, their eighth child, and Elizabeth Henderson, Robert's parents, settled in Philadelphia. The family name McIntyre is spelled without the "a", while the names of the company and its mine are spelled with the "a."

31 Harold Hochschild, *The MacIntyre Mine: From Failure to Fortune.* (Blue Mountain Lake, N.Y.: Adirondack Museum, 1962).

32 Masten, 34.

33 Barbara McMartin, *To the Lake of the Skies: The Benedicts in the Adirondacks.* (Canada Lake, N.Y.: Lakeview Press, 1996), 21-22.

Daniel Newcomb's farm on the Old Cedar Point Road with the High Peaks in the distance, sketched by David Henderson, from Ebenezer Emmons, *Geology of New-York, Part II*, 1842.

These roads were essential to the development of the area, which by 1850 had 277 residents in the Town of Newcomb and a thriving village of miners and their families around the MacIntyre Iron Works, known as Tahawus.[34] Timbering soon became the second major industry in the region.

Important though the older Cedar Point Road and newer Carthage Road were for basic transportation and commerce, they still were too rough for shipping the heavy pig iron produced by the mine. A railroad initially was proposed in 1839, but was not completed for another century.[35]

Difficulties culminated in disaster. David Henderson, project innovator and most active managing partner, was killed in 1845 by an accidental discharge from his own pistol at a remote spot near the mine—the event memorialized by a monument at the place, renamed Calamity Pond. Thereafter, despite compelling business interests in Philadelphia, Archibald Robertson increasingly spent time at the mine, assuming an active role in management.[36]

In 1856, a flood destroyed much of the works. The unresolved transportation problem, a nation-wide financial crisis in 1857, and discovery of the rich and accessible Mesabi ore beds in Minnesota precluded any plans to rebuild. McIntyre and Robertson both died in 1858, and for a time the mine was abandoned. Thereafter the road from Tahawus and Newcomb Lake to the hamlet of Newcomb was largely unmaintained.

34 Fennessy, 25.

35 After several starts, tracks were completed in 1944, when required for the second world war. Hochschild, 6; Michael Kudish, *Where Did the Tracks Go?* (Saranac Lake, N.Y.: Chauncy Press, 1985), 58.

36 Masten, 111-112.

The thousands of acres of the mining company's property went to heirs, among them Robert Robertson, then nine years old. Seven years later Robertson entered Rutgers College where he met Robert C. Pruyn. They graduated together in 1869 and remained fast friends for thirty years; both enjoyed hunting and fishing.

Robertson was an organizer in 1876 of the Preston Ponds Club, probably the first fish-and-game club with its own Adirondack preserve. The club leased lands from the MacIntyre Iron Company, of which Robertson would later be president.[37] The next year the organization expanded, renaming itself the Adirondack Club. In 1897, the club was reformed once again, becoming the present Tahawus Club, of which Robert Robertson, Robert C. Pruyn and his eldest son Edward were among the founding members.[38]

We are virtually certain that Robert Robertson introduced Robert Pruyn to the Newcomb area and to the lands adjacent to the iron mine property which would become Santanoni Preserve. Pruyn probably visited his friend at the Adirondack Club in the 1870s and 1880s. Sportsmen easily hiked from there to Lake Delia or Newcomb Lake (it was still known by both names) on the old Cedar Point Road, no longer maintained as a public thoroughfare but still readily passable.[39] Anna may have joined the two Roberts on a hike (more likely a horseback ride) to the lakeshore, where the Pruyns and their architect friend Robertson may have envisioned Camp Santanoni.

While Robertson's friendly suggestion may have triggered the Pruyns' settling in this particular locale, other factors might also have contributed. Robert Pruyn's business made him privy to prospective investments. His family connection to a major lumbering company, Finch, Pruyn & Company, may have informed him of opportunities in this area.[40] The Pruyns probably knew mountain developer William West Durant, and may have visited his rustic camps on Raquette Lake. Durant later established three preserves in the Newcomb area and sold land to the Pruyns.[41]

The Pruyns probably liked to think that they had ventured into unknown territory, where they tried farming and continued to live in primitive isolation for a half-century. Newcomb, however, already was a well-established community when they arrived. Agriculture had been established in the locale much earlier. Old photographs indicate substantial farmsteads. Buildings stood on some parcels when acquired by the Pruyns. Before reverting to woodland there were more open fields that provided panoramic views.[42]

Newcomb had long been a tourist destination. "Aunt Polly" began innkeeping in a log building about 1830. An Albany guest mentioned the place (also know as "Bissel's") in 1849. Apparently it operated into the Pruyn era. The larger Wayside Inn was owned by local lumbermen John Anderson and Dennis Moynehan, who also operated one of

37 Alfred L. Donaldson, *A History of the Adirondacks* (New York: Century, 1921) I:148. Masten mentions Robertson as president, 129.

38 Masten, 179.

39 Lake Delia was beginning to be called "Newcomb Lake" by 1876. O.W. Gray, *New Topographical Atlas of Essex County, New York* (Philadelphia: O.W. Grady , 1876) map of Township 27, but Wallace still called it "Delia" in 1895, 377-380.

40 Jeremiah Finch and Samuel Pruyn sold 763 acres to expand the Santanoni Preserve. Essex County Grantee Book 116, Page 414, March 2, 1898.

41 Durant did not promote this area until 1898, after Pruyn had acquired much land, but may have had the notion in mind much earlier. The three estates were Arbutus Lake Preserve, sold to Archer Huntington, who called it "Mossy Camp," Zack Lake Preserve, and Goodnow Mountain Preserve. Durant also planned a subdivision of the north shore of Rich Lake into forty-two lots of several acres. Gilborn, 137. Pruyn acquired a parcel of 798 acres from Durant. Essex County Grantee Book 108, Page 206, October 9, 1894. Mrs. J.V.L. Pruyn and daughter Huybertie were entertained at Durant's Pine Knot in 1894, the same year that Pruyn purchased the 798 acres from Durant. Huybertie Pruyn Hamlin. "In the Days of the Doanes at Bishop's House, 29 Elk St., Albany, N.Y." Typescript, 28.

42 Information in this and the following two paragraphs is derived from Lana Fennessey, *The History of Newcomb, Essex County, New York* (Elizabethtown, N.Y.: Denton Publications, 1977); and Raymond D. Masters, *A Social History of the Huntington Wildlife Forest (Which Includes Rich Lake and the Pendelton Settlement),* (Utica, N.Y.: North Country Books, 1993).

The entry drive at the Duck Hole bridge in 1990s, the road at this point probably a vestige of the old Cedar Point Road

the general stores and the post office.[43] Among other hostleries and club houses was the Lake Harris House, an elegant lakeside resort. "Among the best known hotels in the Adirondacks," it was built in 1903.[44]

John Anderson erected a remarkable round barn, which housed eighty-five horses. This feature alone says something about Newcomb, as does Anderson's Newcomb Snow Plow factory (already operating when the Pruyns arrived). There was also the Cough and Lung Balm Company. The *Adirondack News* began publishing at Newcomb in August, 1893, the year that the Pruyns arrived. Lana Fennessy observed that "Newcomb was in its prime in the 1890s."[45]

Robert and Anna Pruyn both were drawn to nature—in its pastoral state, as cultivated by the practical farmer, and also as wilderness, revered romantically by nineteenth-century artists like the Hudson River painters and writers such as Emerson and Thoreau who reacted to the radical change of modern life. In these attitudes the Pruyns were not unlike many others who were attracted to the region. Their estate at Santanoni, however, would be unlike any other in the Adirondacks.

[43] The Anderson-Moynehan lumbering operations were headquartered in their hotel.

[44] Fennessy, 38.

[45] Fennessy, 12.

Lake and Little Minister Island, right, from boathouse, 1929

#  3. Santanoni Preserve 

It is said that a private club is contemplating the purchase of a large tract of land of P. Moynehan in the town of Newcomb, and the erection of a club house.

*The Essex County Republican, February 23, 1893*

The Pruyns took their first step toward assembling an Adirondack estate in December 1890, when Robert Pruyn purchased 6,500 acres of land in the Town of Newcomb at a state tax sale in Albany. Known as the "parallelogram parcel," the property was divided into three parts which for twenty-five years, on and off, had been owned by Albany lumberman Lemon Thomson.[1] Thomson would cut the timber on a portion of it, stop paying property taxes so it would revert to state ownership, then years later would buy it back at a state tax sale when a new crop of timber had matured. Although Robert Pruyn paid the delinquent taxes at this time, Thomson had two years in which to redeem the property. During this period, Thomson agreed to sell his interest to Glens Falls timber magnate Patrick Moynehan and Elizabeth Moynehan, who then agreed to sell Pruyn their interest in the property, plus several small adjoining lots, for $18,000. Thus in July 1892, the Moynehans sold Pruyn some 6,975 acres around Newcomb Lake, and Santanoni Preserve began.[2]

Thereafter, the Pruyns moved quickly, constructing the main camp and steadily acquiring additional parcels of land. Six years later, the 12,900-acre preserve was virtually complete. Robert Pruyn was characteristically methodical. Twenty-two contracts, some covering multiple small parcels, were entailed. In 1894, for example, the Durant parcel added almost 800 acres on the western side of the

[1] The succession of early transactions is reported in Haynes, "Farm Complex," 30-33.

[2] Agreement between Moynehans and Pruyn dated June 4, 1892, Essex County Grantee Book 103, 396. Deed from Moynehans to Pruyn dated July 9, 1892, Book 103, 449. Title was cleared the following year with a tax sale deed from the Comptroller of the State of New York to Pruyn dated February 24, 1893, Book 104, 527.

preserve; a purchase from the MacIntyre Iron Company added about 1000 acres to the east, giving Pruyn complete control of Newcomb Lake and Duck Hole, and three parcels totaling some 300 acres southwest of the original purchase secured the area of what was to be the working farm portion of the estate. Many of these purchases were smaller ones. With several in the southwest section, surrounding the old road to Newcomb, the Pruyns' southern boundary steadily approached the hamlet. One parcel along Harris Lake, just east of the current Gate Lodge, once had been owned by Mitchell Sabbatis, the famous Abenaki guide.[3]

In 1897, another state tax sale secured a 1,046-acre parcel he had first purchased from the Moynehans in 1893.[4] In 1898, the Finch and Pruyn parcel of 763 acres and another 1300-acre acquisition just about completed the estate.[5]

When the campaign ended, the consolidated Santanoni Preserve was roughly rectangular in shape, about two-and-a-half miles wide, beginning at the hamlet of Newcomb on the southern end and extending northwesterly about eight miles toward the Adirondack High Peaks.

## The Name *Santanoni*

One of those peaks gave Santanoni Preserve its name. At 4,607 feet, Santanoni Peak is the fourteenth tallest mountain in the Adirondack range. Situated on State Forest Preserve lands, it stands alone and dominates miles of uninhabited forests on all sides. Pruyn's land lay at the southern slope of the mountain, which is prominently visible from the main camp site. Viewed from a canoe on Newcomb Lake, Santanoni's mile-wide ridge resembles an enormous wave, about to crash down on the landscape.

David Henderson gave the first recorded explanation of the mountain's name in an 1837 letter to the *Albany Daily Advertiser*. Henderson related that on his exploratory expedition with the state geologist Ebenezer Emmons, "The party were desirous to ascertain from the individuals of the nearest settlements, whether the Indians, who occasionally frequented these mountains on hunting expeditions, ever gave them any name." He noted that "to the Indians coming from the West to these hunting grounds, this mountain would appear the most prominent and conspicuous of the whole group. . . . We were informed that the large mountain to the west of the Great Notch [Indian Pass] the Indians invariably gave such a name to, as *San-ti-no-ni*, or *Antonini*, strongly accenting the third syllable; but that they gave no name to any other peaks of the group. As these Indians were of Canadian tribes, we conceived that this word was only a corruption of St. Anthony."[6]

Thus "Santinoni" remains the earliest recorded name for the mountain, a name thought by early settlers to have been used by Algonquins of the north. An 1858 map showed the name as "Santanon*a* or St. Anthony," although most mapmakers of the later eighteenth century rendered it as "San*t*a*n*oni."[7] Not everyone accepted the theory that "Santanoni" was derived from "St. Anthony," however. In fact, the origin of the name has been the subject of serious study. Henderson went on to venture a theory of his own, while other early Adirondack writers Charles Fenno Hoffman, Joel T. Headley, and Alfred Billings Street explored other possible derivations, as did twentieth century historians Alfred Donaldson, Warder Cadbury and Native

[3] The deed for Lot 10 of Township 27 (Essex County Grantee Book 113, Page 26, March 20, 1897) is from Bissel to Pruyn. Sabbatis was an earlier owner, as shown on "Whitlock's Map of Essex Co., NY," 1858.

[4] Moynehan deed dated April 7, 1893, Essex County Grantee Book 104, Page 173. State Comptroller's deed dated February 5, 1897, Book 113, 340.

[5] Sellers were the Andersons, Hunters, and Dennis Moynehans. November 16, 1897, Essex County Grantee Book 115, 443.

[6] Letter from Henderson to James Hall, September 1, 1837, James Hall Papers, New York State Library. Written under the pseudonym "Z," the letter was later ascribed to Henderson, Masten, xvi, fn. 10. Masten thanked, and we also thank, Warder Cadbury for this insight.

[7] *Whitlock's Map of Essex Co., NY*, 1858.

American expert John Fadden.[8] At one point Russell Carson of Glens Falls, an authority on Adirondack place names, researched the origin of Santanoni's name for Robert Pruyn.[9]

All this scholarship has produced no consensus for derivation from a particular Native American name or term. Hence, based on Henderson's original explanation, we are left with the popular theory that the name derived from the Abenaki (who spoke Algonquin) pronunciation of the name that French Canadian trappers gave to this mountain—Mont St. Antoine—near which both groups hunted.[10] However, the name is not the French "St. Antoine," but merely the English "St. Anthony," rendered with a French accent, the "th" dropped for convenience.[11]

Taking the name of the mountain, the Pruyns referred to the entire estate as "Santanoni Preserve," and to their residence there as "Camp Santanoni." The latter name appeared on camp stationery and bookplate.

Later correspondents were often confused as to the spelling. Pasted in one of the Pruyn scrapbooks are numerous variations clipped from business and personal correspondence, ranging from close approximations like Camp Santonini, Santonani, Sananoni, and Santanosci to the far more creative Lieutonini, Lantonnani, Dentemoni, Frantanini, Camp Sanitorium, and Cramp's Sanitarium.

## Natural Features

Robert Pruyn assembled a vast preserve virtually surrounded by wild lands, and they remain wild today. On the east were timber lands of Finch, Pruyn & Company and thousands of acres of the Tahawus Club.[12] To the north was state land, now known as the High Peaks Wilderness. On the west were lands of W. W. Durant and the Caughnawauga Club of sportsmen, of which Pruyn became a member.[13] On the south, state and private land, Harris Lake, and the hamlet of Newcomb bordered the estate, much as it does today, although the state has acquired more land at the southern end of the preserve.

Newcomb Lake shorelines, painting by Edward Lansing Pruyn

[8] A much more detailed description of the scholarship surrounding Santanoni's name may be found in the archival edition of this work, on disk, available from Adirondack Architectural Heritage, Keeseville, N.Y.

[9] Russell M. L. Carson, letters to R.C. Pruyn, January 3 and November 15, 1923. Pruyn Collection, Adirondack Museum.

[10] Carson letters. The Abenakis were a tribe of Algonquins from Vermont. It is not known which of history's two St. Anthonys, the third-century Egyptian ascetic or the eleventh-century Italian cleric, that Santanoni commemorates. Both led lives of solitude and self-denial.

[11] Unlike English, French pronunciation stresses no syllable. The traditional Pruyn and Newcomb residents' pronunciation has always been "Sant'noni," dropping the middle "a." Susan Pruyn King, manuscript note to authors.

[12] The MacIntyre Iron Company leased land to the Adirondack (later Tahawus) Club. Now owned by the National Lead Company, the State is considering acquisition of the property.

[13] Durant's lands were property of his Forest Land Company. Both the Durant and club properties were acquired by railroad magnate-heir Archer M. Huntington and now comprise the Huntington Memorial Forest of the State University of New York's College of Environmental Science and Forestry at Syracuse University. Raymond D. Masters, *A Social History of the Huntington Wildlife Forest (Which Includes Rich Lake and the Pendelton Settlement)* (Utica, N.Y.: North Country Books, 1993), 95.

Centerpiece of Santanoni Preserve is Newcomb Lake. The main part of the lake is about a mile-and-a-half-long by one-half-mile wide. Ringed by enormous cedar trees, it contains seven islands, the two more sizable in its center and west end. The larger island was called "Long Island." The small island in front of the boathouse was called "Little Minister."[14] The expansive portion of the lake closest to the main camp runs to a depth of ninety feet. The camp compound stretches across a broad point on the eastern shore. To the north, about three-hundred yards by trail, is a lovely sand beach. From this end of the lake, one looks westward toward the islands. Above the largest towers a one-acre stand of old-growth white pine, trees as old as the nation.

A mile-long appendage at the southeast corner of the lake is named the "Duck Hole." Its mucky bottom is never more than a few feet below the surface. The largest stream within the Preserve is the outlet at the southern end of Duck Hole, called the Newcomb River. It runs into the Hudson River about a mile after leaving the Preserve. Four other ponds dot the preserve. Moose Pond is about three-quarter mile long. Ward, Shaw, and Black Ponds are smaller. The two miles of Santanoni Preserve between Newcomb Lake and Moose Pond is the divide between two great watersheds. While Newcomb Lake drains south toward the Hudson, the outlet of Moose Pond feeds northwest to the Raquette River, which flows north to the St. Lawrence River.

Fred Kelley's map

The land contains four mountains tall enough to be named on maps: Baldwin (2,837'), Moose (2,980'), Wolf Pond (2,484'), and the southern knob of Little Santanoni (2,580'). Seventy per cent of the land is sloped, mostly covered with hardwoods.[15] The land is strewn with glacial deposits, with a

[14] Cynthia Pruyn Green and Susan Pruyn King. Aldrich, 105. "The small island that does not show on the topographic map that is right in front of the boat house was known as 'Little Minister' because *The Little Minister*, a play by J. M. Barrie, was popular in the late nineteenth century and was published in book form. One house party weekend in the late 'nineties, all coming were asked to bring a book to read aloud, and they all—coincidentally—brought exactly the same book, *The Little Minister*, and the island was so named." Aldrich, 105. This is a charming story, but on Fred Kelley's sketch map of Newcomb Lake in 1892, before the camp was ever built, he calls the island "Little Minister." Pruyn collection, Adirondack Museum Library.

[15] Sixty percent of the land was characterized as "hardwood slope," ten per cent as "spruce slope," and 30 per cent as "spruce flat." D. B. Cook, "Part I, Softwood Logging on the R. C. Pruyn Tract, 'Santanoni Preserve,' Newcomb, N.Y., Summer of 1923." Typescript, 1923. "According to the timber survey by Fisher and Bryant in 1910, the tract contains 11,900 acres of timber, 881 acres of water, 106 acres of marsh, 75 acres of cleared land, 18 acres of brush and 10 acres of burn." "History of the Robert C. Pruyn Tract, Essex Co., N. Y.," n..d., handwritten note: "1939," 1.

number of small, boulder-laden creeks draining the ponds into the two major watersheds.

A spring above Newcomb Lake had attracted noted visitors since the mid-nineteenth century. Richard Henry Dana, author of *Two Years Before the Mast* and noted authority on international law, reported his visit to the spring in 1849.[16] The water of Delia Spring was purported to have marvelous restorative powers.[17] Lake Delia and its spring were a short hike from the Adirondack (Tahawus) Club. Possibly the Pruyns were among many visitors who made the trek to try the remarkable waters. One may readily imagine a scenario whereby Robertson suggested a walk to the spring, setting off the whole chain of events that has become our saga. The Pruyns' belief in curative properties of the water may account for its being bottled and delivered throughout the year to their residence in Albany. In the 1920s visitors still came to drink the water at the spring.[18] Purported "restorative power" may have been a factor in the Pruyns" selection of their country house location. This spring apparently became the water source for the main camp. That supply was abandoned in later years when the pipe under the lake disintegrated, but the water still flows through a hillside cistern.[19]

Of several clearings in the forest, Montgomery Clearing, between the base of Moose Mountain and the marshy headlands of Newcomb Lake, is of interest because it is identified by family lore as a station on the Underground Railroad. According to another version, the clearing was made by black freedmen.[20] National abolitionist leader Gerrit Smith owned all of this and surrounding properties prior to the Civil War.[21] He provided blacks with plots of land to the north of the Preserve, at North Elba, and invited abolitionist John Brown to settle there to assist the black community. Brown's farm is a state historic site today. There is no record of a black settlement at Santanoni Preserve, but there may have been a route to North Elba through the property.[22]

[16] Richard Henry Dana, "How We Met John Brown," *Atlantic Monthly,* July 1871.

[17] Richard Henry Dana, *The Journal, 1815-1882* (Cambridge: Belknap Press of Harvard University, 1968).

[18] Masten, 171.

[19] Merle Melvin recalled that during his family ownership the old water system failed. Since pipes were buried in forgotten location, the Melvins thereafter relied on lake water for all purposes. Aldrich, 100-101. Merle Melvin recalled, "This spring is located a couple of hundred feet up a hillside, along the north shore of Newcomb Lake between Sucker and Santanoni Brooks, but closer to Sucker Brook than Santanoni Brook. A little square house, three or four feet high with a shingled roof, covered the spring. A pipe carried the water to lake shore. Then under the lake to the shore by the Camp and right up into the kitchen. Because the spring was considerably higher than the kitchen, there was no need for pumping, and gravity did the work. Sometime during the late 'fifties or early 'sixties, the flow of water gradually lessened until this source of drinking water was abandoned for lake water. The lessening of the water flow was not due to a diminishing output from the spring, but rather from holes developing in the pipe caused by corrosion, we assumed. . . . I feel quite confident that the spring referred to by Mr. Dana in the 1850s and the one I have described here are one and the same." Aldrich, 102. In the 1990s Aldrich found the spring and cistern open and hazardous, but water still flowed into the lake (J. W. Aldrich to Paul Malo).

[20] Letter from Susan King to Patrick Noonan, November 19, 1971. Also Crandall Melvin, Jr., interview with J. Winthrop Aldrich, July 1992. Aldrich, 157.

[21] Gerrit Smith had purchased the "Parallelogram" tract, which included Lake Delia (Newcomb Lake) and Montgomery Clearing, in several parcels between 1834 and 1853. In 1855 he sold the entire Parallelogram to Benedict, Sherman, and Cronkhite, who transferred the property the same year to one of the three, Augustus Sherman of Glens Falls. Sherman and his wife sold the property after the Civil War, in 1866. Any Underground Railroad activity on the property probably would have occurred during the Smith and Sherman tenures. Wesley Haynes has provided a chronology with citations of deeds. *Farm Complex*, 29.

[22] The "Cold River Tote Road," indicated on the 1910 Fisher and Bryant Map, provides a route to North Elba, parallel to the Indian Pass route, via Preston Ponds and Averyville. Lyman Epps, a black resident of North Elba, built a "famous trail" southward to Indian Pass, which led to Henderson Lake (Tahawus). Lake Delia (Newcomb Lake) lay about six miles farther to the southwest. Sandra Weber, *The Finest Square Mile: Mount Jo and Heart Lake* (Fleischmanns, NY: Purple Mountain Press, 1998), 14. "An interesting walk" from Camp Santanoni "leads to the ruins of an old village, built by Gerrit Smith in pre-Civil War days to house the Negro slaves which he spirited up from the South by the 'underground railway'...." Guy H. Lee, "Estates of American Sportsmen: Santanoni, the Adirondack Camp of Robert C. Pruyn, Esq. of Albany, New York," *The Sportsman*, VI, No. 4, October, 1929, 92. North Elba is more than twenty-six miles distant—hardly a casual "walk." Lee, who visited Santanoni while Robert Pruyn was

Montgomery Clearing was not so remote as it seems today. Prior to the Civil War, major routes converged nearby.[23] The earliest road came up the Hudson and went by the present Santanoni Preserve en route to the outlet of Long Lake; by 1834 this road had been extended to Canton, New York.[24] From there to the border would have been an easy trip for escaped slaves. Like many other clearings in the region, Montgomery Clearing probably was named for an early settler who cleared the land for a farm. A cabin may have survived through the pre-Civil War period. The clearing was at a juncture of routes from the south to both the black settlement at North Elba and to Canton and Canada. Its situation makes the notion of some sort of "station" at Montgomery Clearing seem more plausible than may be suggested by its present isolation.

## Country Roads

> Newcomb, October 17: Work is progressing finely on the new road from the village to Newcomb Lake Club house. It is a difficult task as it is through a rough country, and is intended to be fitted for carriage driving.
> *The Essex County Republican, October 20, 1892*

As suggested above, although sparsely settled, Newcomb was not isolated. By mid-nineteenth century, the Town of Newcomb sat at the crossroads of three state highways traversing the Adirondacks.[25]

The "first highway through the mountains," a so-called "Old Military Road" between Chester in Warren County and Russell in St. Lawrence County, was authorized in 1807. Finally completed in 1834, the route generally followed the Hudson from Chestertown, Pottersville, and Minerva to Lake Harris at present-day Newcomb. It followed today's Route 28N briefly, then crossed the outlet of Rich Lake, passing through the settlement of Pendleton, and continued on the north side of Rich Lake. It then turned northward to reach the outlet of Long Lake, where the road crossed the Raquette River and proceeded north toward Canton.[26]

The second highway was built in 1828 at the initiation of Duncan McMartin, partner in the MacIntyre mining operation, in a manner that would be considered scandalous today. While serving in the New York State Senate, Judge McMartin "secured passage of an act to appoint a commission" to build a road to provide direct access to the Tahawus mine from Cedar Point (now Port Henry) on Lake Champlain.[27] The act authorized a road, not merely to Tahawus, but on to the western boundary of Essex County. Accordingly, about 1830, this "Cedar Point Road" was extended westward beyond the iron works, past Daniel Newcomb's farm and across what is now Santanoni Preserve.[28]

Log cabin, probably at Daniel Newcomb's farm on the Cedar Point Road (Pruyn album page dated 1907)

---

alive, may have been referring to some other site, perhaps Montgomery Clearing.

[23] Barbara McMartin provided a helpful map of old roads in this area in her book, *To the Lake of the Skies: The Benedicts in the Adirondacks* (Canada Lake, NY: Lake View Press, 1996), 21.

[24] Donaldson II, 72, 123.

[25] A more detailed discussion of the early roads in the Newcomb area is contained in the archival edition of this work, available on disk from Adirondack Architectural Heritage.

[26] Donaldson, II, 123-124.

[27] Hochschild, *The MacIntyre Mine*, 3.

[28] The segment of the Old Cedar Point road east of the Santanoni Preserve was known as the "Old Newcomb Farm Road" on Fisher and Bryant's map, 1910.

The Cedar Point Road crossed over the foot of Newcomb Lake (at the north side of the Duck Hole) and continued southwesterly for about two more miles.[29] It did not turn south then, like the Pruyns' entry drive which leads to the present Newcomb village. Instead, at the location of the present Honeymoon Bridge, where the entry drive now turns southward, the Cedar Point Road continued southwesterly, climbing over the spur of Baldwin Mt. that rises above the farm. It led to the earlier Pendleton settlement located farther west, on Rich Lake, where a dam at the foot of the lake served a grist and sawmill.[30]

The MacIntyre associates, contemplating construction of works and housing at nearby Tahawus, apparently had prevailed upon the state to build the road between the site of the subsequent Honeymoon Bridge and of the Pendleton Settlement, where they bought Pendleton's saw mill.[31] This extended Cedar Point Road joined the older Chester-Russell Road at Pendleton, less than four miles from the county line, prescribed terminus of the authorized road. So the site of Santanoni's main camp, now remote from the public highway, was built virtually on what was once a principal thoroughfare through the region.

Still a third highway, another east-west route known as the "Carthage Road," was initiated in 1841 and was built across four counties over several years. Its route ran parallel to the Cedar Point Road, generally less than ten miles to the south in the segment between Blue Ridge and Newcomb.[32] The Carthage Road, which connected Crown Point on Lake Champlain in the east to Carthage on the Black River west of the mountains, passed through the hamlet of Newcomb following a route south of Rich Lake to the village of Long Lake.[33] It became the present main highway through Newcomb. Following construction of the Carthage Road, the portion of the Cedar Point Road east of Tahawus fell into disuse.

When settlement migrated eastward from Pendleton at the outlet of Rich Lake to the hamlet of Newcomb south of Harris Lake, the segment of the Cedar Point Road that climbed over the spur of Baldwin Mt. also ceased to serve much purpose, and a more direct route from the Honeymoon Bridge to the new village supplanted it. Even this newer route did not seem to follow the path of the present entry road, however, for an earlier road from the Honeymoon Bridge may have run partway along Roaring Brook to the narrows at the head of Lake Harris, where there may have been a crossing.[34] An 1876 account said that "Lake Delia or Newcomb" was "3 m. by path N.E. of Newcomb," probably by the Roaring Brook road.[35] The present entry road is closer to five miles long.

When Robert Pruyn acquired his Santanoni holdings, then, there was a public thoroughfare through his property that linked Tahawus and Newcomb. As Pruyn steadily purchased the land through which it passed, he improved the road at his own expense, regarding it as his private drive. In 1893 he

[29] David Burr, *Map of the County of Essex* (Ithaca, N.Y.: Stone & Clark, 1840), based on earlier Burr maps.

[30] Benson J. Lossing, *The Hudson: From the Wilderness to the Sea . . .* (New York: Virtue & Yorston, 1866), 21. David Burr, on his 1840 map, showed the Cedar Point Road and a parallel route, indicated as a county road, the latter running in a virtually straight line between the Duck Hole crossing and a mill at the foot of Rich Lake. Possibly the line that Burr had originally shown on his 1829 map was merely the route proposed for the Cedar Point road, authorized the year before, whereas the parallel road, shown on the 1840 map as built by the county, may have been the only road actually constructed, the publisher neglecting to erase the earlier line.

[31] Masten mentions purchase of a sawmill at Pendleton, 41. On the Burr map, the mill was indicated not as a sawmill, but as a "flouring mill." Source of grain in 1841 is puzzling. Perhaps the MacIntyre company carted whole grain from Lake Champlain to be milled at Pendleton for local use.

[32] Roger Mitchell "2. Adaptation from David H. Burr's 'Map of the County of Essex' 1839" [*sic*], showing both roads. Roger Mitchell, *Clear Pond: The Reconstruction of a Life* (Syracuse, N.Y.: Syracuse University Press, 1991), 69.

[33] Barbara McMartin, *To the Lake of the Skies* (Caroga Lake, N.Y.: Lake View Press, 1996), 21-22.

[34] It is not clear whether the earliest crossing from Newcomb hamlet to the current Santanoni Preserve was near the present bridge site or much farther to the east across the narrows between the small westerly part of Harris Lake and the main part of Harris Lake.

[35] E. R. Wallace, *Descriptive Guide to the Adirondacks (Land of the Thousand Lakes)* (New York: American News Co., 1876), 176.

even paid to have a major iron bridge built over the river between Rich and Harris Lakes on the public right-of-way to improve access to his lands.[36] He wished to close the access road altogether, building a gate house to limit entry, but there were two problems. The existing road from Duck Hole to the Honeymoon Bridge crossed state land at one point, and the state was not about to give Pruyn exclusive rights to it. In fact, the state initiated a trespass action against Pruyn for his unauthorized road building activities on state land.[37] Second, the Roaring Brook road from Honeymoon Bridge to the head of Harris Lake also crossed private and state-owned land. The Village of Newcomb, as it was known then, had the right to use and maintain this road and the bridge Pruyn had built to the village. They too did not want to cede the right-of-way and bridge to Pruyn, thereby cutting the town off from the old Cedar Point Road. Although the town no longer maintained that stretch of road, it still provided public access for hunting, fishing, hiking, or travelling from Newcomb to Tahawus.

To solve the first problem, Pruyn relocated much of the route from Duck Hole to Honeymoon Bridge, so it was all on his own property. A later edition of the earlier guidebook mentioned in 1895 that Newcomb Lake could now be reached by "a fine carriage-road through a primeval forest; distance about four miles," instead of the earlier three.[38] So two years after Pruyn's camp was completed, the public was still able to travel freely through his estate and, apparently, even fish in Newcomb Lake.

While relocating the road was an engineering challenge, solving the problem of access required real estate and legal solutions. Pruyn continued purchasing properties south of the Honeymoon Bridge in order to bypass the Roaring Brook route to the east. This approximate two-mile stretch south of Honeymoon Bridge probably had a passable road developed over the nineteenth century to serve one or more farms in the vicinity.[39] Additional purchases in 1897 brought land on the north side of the river running between Rich and Harris Lakes (site of the present Gate Lodge complex) under Pruyn's control. This gave him virtually continuous ownership of this route from Newcomb Lake to the river, just a few hundred feet from the state highway (now 28N).[40] The next year he purchased a right-of-way from John and Mary Anderson, allowing passage across the stream and over their land to the highway.[41]

Now he had assured access from the state highway into the Santanoni Preserve, but it was not yet exclusive access. The Village of Newcomb had its original access from the hamlet across the Andersons' land, across the Pruyn-built bridge, up along the Roaring Brook route to the old Cedar Point Road to Newcomb Lake and Tahawus. The village also had access by the two-mile stretch that Pruyn had improved as his main entry road from the river to Honeymoon Bridge. It took him another few years to prevail upon the town to discontinue these routes as public roads, but eventually he

---

[36] "The iron bridge spanning the Hudson on North Main Street is being pushed to completion. It is quite an imposing structure, and a valuable adjunct to Mr. Pruyn's excellent road. *Adirondack News*, December 15, 1893. The river between Rich and Harris Lakes was still sometimes referred to as the Hudson River then, although it is a tributary of the nearby Hudson. The "North Main Street" road still exists today, providing access to several properties fronting on the western portion of Harris Lake.

[37] Santanoni real property file, Department of Environmental Conservation, Albany, N.Y.

[38] E. R. Wallace, *Descriptive Guide to the Adirondacks (Land of the Thousand Lakes)* (Syracuse, N.Y.: 1895), 377-380.

[39] Helen Tummins, wife of Santanoni's last caretaker, remembered seeing foundations of homes along the road between the farm and the hamlet, where many of these landowners had lived. H. Bond. "Notes Taken During a Trip Into Santanoni on July 29, 1986." Typescript, 1988, NYSDEC. The history of earlier farms on Santanoni Preserve is discussed further in Chapter 6, but deeds to Pruyn clearly indicate this road existed.

[40] Transactions included: Williams to Pruyn, Essex County Grantee Book 113, Page 110, and Wallis (Wallace) to Pruyn, Box 113, 111.

[41] Essex County Grantee Book 116, Page 507. The right-of-way crossing location was a short distance west of the town-owned bridge that Pruyn had replaced at his own expense in 1893.

succeeded. In 1902 the town abandoned as a public highway the road from "the Village of Newcomb to the outlet of Newcomb Lake." It approved "also the discontinuance of the *old* branch of said highway" and the sale of its interest in the bridge across the river connecting Harris and Rich lakes.[42] The "old branch" probably was the Roaring Brook road, which crossed Forest Preserve land.

The next year Pruyn purchased Anderson's land south of the river between the crossing and the state highway. Now the estate was truly complete and private, and Pruyn could begin plans to relocate the bridge on his own land, slightly upstream, and erect a massive gate lodge guarding the entrance to his property.[43]

Unfortunately, his attempts at road closure led to a falling out in 1899 with his old friend and architect Robert Robertson, and strained relations with neighbors, as did subsequent posting of the preserve.[44] The road had provided access from the public highway at Newcomb village to former mining company land east of Santanoni Preserve, of which Robertson was the principal owner, and to other properties to be lumbered. If inaccessible, these lands would diminish in value. Robertson and others sued Pruyn, but lost.[45] Perhaps the friendship had been strained earlier, for Robertson never signed Pruyn's guest book. The altercation may also explain why Pruyn selected other architects for later projects. Newcomb residents no doubt also resented being cut off from hunting and fishing areas used for generations. All over the Adirondacks in the 1890s, resentments abounded as absentee owners took advantage of the new New York State posting law by making their lands off limits to hunters, anglers, berry pickers, and other recreational users. But Pruyn was a major employer of local workers and eventually the town adjusted to the new status quo.

Honeymoon Bridge

## Estate Road and Bridges

Even before owning all the land fronting on his entry roads, Pruyn undertook extensive road rebuilding. This began almost immediately upon purchase of the parallelogram tract and continued in stages when new portions of road came under Pruyn's control and old portions were relocated. As mentioned previously, the new route required construction of a

[42] Pruyn paid the town $3,008 to abandon their rights. Town of Newcomb, Resolution, October 4, 1902, Essex County Grantee Book 127, page. 481, italics added. While the "old branch" probably was the Roaring Brook road, shown as still extant on Fisher and Bryant, "Topographic Map of Santanoni Preserve," 1910, the reference might have been to the Old Newcomb Farm Road or some other spur.

[43] The evidence only suggests that the bridge was moved from its original location a short distance upstream to the current bridge location. It is also possible that the 1893 bridge was removed and a new one built upstream, or that Pruyn's iron bridge was always in the current bridge location.

[44] Aldrich, 65. In 1909 Pruyn posted the Santanoni Preserve as a private park. "Notice of Laying Out a Public Park, July 30, 1909." The term "public park" is misleading. As mentioned in Chapter Two, it referred to State legislation of the early 1890s that encouraged posting of private game preserves, paradoxically defined as "public parks" from which the general public thereafter would be excluded.

[45] In addition to Robertson's own Tahawus partners, the Finch-Pruyn lumber company joined in the suit (J. W. Aldrich to Paul Malo).

Entrance drive at Harris Lake, with Ned's guardrails and boat house beyond

substantial bridge over the river at the entrance to the preserve. Apparently metal trusses were prefabricated, for the bridge was "shipped to its destination."[46] Eventually, six other streams had to be crossed, entailing construction of three masonry bridges—Honeymoon Bridge (the largest) and the Twin Bridges—plus a new bridge over the Newcomb Lake outlet by Duck Hole, and numerous culverts.[47] Honeymoon Bridge was completed around the time that Charles Sumner Hamlin and Pruyn's young cousin Huybertie spent their honeymoon at Santanoni in June 1897 and was named in their honor.[48]

The 1893 Forest Commission report described the Santanoni road as "an object lesson in road building, . . . a well-graveled drive, smooth as a park road, affording a delightful ride through a grand old forest, with charming views here and there of the lofty mountains of the Marcy Range."[49] It proved that "the hard-pan found in a part of the Adirondacks is an admirable road material. The road is built entirely of this, the secret being thorough ditching." Another writer, probably commenting on later improvements, reported, "The Pruyns were fortunate in finding a pit of superior red-brown road gravel on the place, and although building of the road offered one of the most difficult problems, it [was] done with great success."[50] The same writer reported that "The last half of [the original road] was relocated to avoid passing over a steep hill"—probably not realizing (some thirty years after the fact) that the primary reason for relocation was not the gradient, but the location of a portion of the old road on state land.[51] "The engineering work [was] done by Mr. Edward Pruyn." This, again, probably referred to a later stage of road building, as eldest son Edward ("Ned") was nineteen

[46] "Newcomb, Aug. 31." *Adirondack News*, September 1, 1893.

[47] Fisher and Bryant. Topographic Map, 1910.

[48] This, at least, is the most popular of several family stories for how the bridge was named.

[49] NYS Forest Commission, *Annual Report,* 179

[50] Guy H. Lee, 72, also the source of the following two quotations.

[51] The original route and relocated road were both shown on Fisher and Bryant's "Topographic Map of Santanoni Preserve," 1910. The map suggests that virtually the entire route between Newcomb village and Newcomb Lake may have been relocated at different times, except probably the present segments at the Honeymoon and Duck Hole bridges.

years old when the first road improvement was completed.[52]

In 1915 Robert Pruyn commented that "about one hundred thousand dollars ($100,000) has been expended on the roads which are good for motors and not too hard for saddle horses."[53] That was a significant sum in pre-1915 dollars. The result was a road of almost five miles length (not counting other roads within the preserve) which rarely failed to impress visitors as they traveled from the hamlet to the main camp on Newcomb Lake.[54] The Gate Lodge was arranged so the great entry portal would frame a vista of Lake Harris and the mountain beyond. Between the farm and main camp, an overlook provided " a superb view" of Santanoni Peak beyond the lake.[55] The last half-mile of the drive skirts Newcomb Lake. The last of the bridges, over the Duck Hole outlet of Newcomb Lake, in effect becomes an inner gateway to the main camp compound. Family oral history has it that Ned devised the low, log guardrails running alongside Santanoni roads for long distances, and his design became a prototype for road building in state and then national parks.[56]

Despite the favorable impression of summer visitors and connoisseurs of road building, families living on the estate knew different conditions in the spring. "You can't imagine the mud on those dirt roads in those days. . . . The road was like quicksand. We all wore rubber boots, and if we weren't careful, we'd get stuck and walk right out of our boots" when walking over a mile to school in the spring, because the road was impassable for vehicles.[57] Automobiles used it only in summer and fall. In the spring a team of horses and wagon would try to avert becoming mired in mud; in the winter children went to school in a sleigh.

## Flora and Fauna

> I remember . . . heading out with little round tin pails to pick blueberries.[58] . . . There were lady slippers, violets, adder-tongues and many other beautiful flowers and trees to be found all over the place. We looked for each as it bloomed. "[59]

Thirteen thousand acres provided material sufficient to engage a naturalist for a lifetime. Anecdotes vividly recall the natural character of Santanoni Preserve, especially the wildlife.

"It was raspberry time, and we decided to go and pick some. . . . We started walking along one of the logging roads. We picked berries as we went along. . . . Suddenly we saw this bunch of animals going every which way. One went up a tree, another went behind a rock. I don't remember where the other one went. They weren't bobcats, because these had long tails. They were mountain lions, young ones! We studied them very carefully, because we knew no one would believe us. They had rounded ears, and their coats were spotted and tawny in color. The one behind the rock would peek at us and 'meow.' They didn't seem afraid at all. Then we heard the mother coming. She made a call like she was coming back with food. That's when I got scared. You've heard of people's hair standing on end—well, mine did! We got out of there in a hurry. We were right. No one believed us."[60]

---

[52] The 1893 project was "under the directions of Mr. E. Gilmore, overseer." "Newcomb, Aug. 31." *Adirondack News*, September 1, 1893.

[53] [R.C. Pruyn] "Santanoni Preserve/Adirondack Mountains," typescript of general description, c. May, 1915, versions #1 and 2. Cited in Haynes, *Farm Complex*, 44-45.

[54] Our preferred figures are 4.9 miles from Rt. 28N to the main camp, and 4.7 miles from the Gate Lodge to the main camp, although other measurements have varied slightly.

[55] Guy H. Lee, 72.

[56] Aldrich to Kirschenbaum. This would be an interesting avenue of further research. The topic is resumed in Chapter 8, fn 12.

[57] Recollection of Rowena Putnam. David Garrison, "A Working Dairy in the Middle of the Mountains," *Snow Times*, February 3, 1988."

[58] Beatrice Pruyn Thibault. Aldrich, 52.

[59] Delilah West Bissell, "My Memories of Pruyn's Preserve at Santanoni." Unpublished manuscript, June 12, 1991.

[60] Helen Tummins quoted in David Garrison, "Former Resident Recalls Life in Area Preserve," Glens Falls *Post Star*, December 1, 1987.

"I remember one morning when we got up, the path across the road was covered with dead sheep and lambs. . . . Less than a week passed when a large cat was seen between the house we lived in and the farm a mile away. Henry and I were chased by probably the same cat when we went to put screens on a lean-to by the river. Mom said she could tell we were gaining as I screamed louder than the animal."[61]

The caretaker's wife recalled that the owner "asked if we were still being bothered by bears. It had been quite a while since one had raided our trash, and I told him just that. I had to go out to the kitchen for something, and as I passed by the window, I saw a bear right in the yard. [He] couldn't get over that."[62]

"[Sis'] mother shot the bear that was mounted in the Camp, and Dad was not happy as it was too far to drag." "There was another smaller one that was a rug in front of the fireplace."[63] "My first husband shot a bear and brought it back in a guide boat and had it propped up with a hat on, and holding the oars."[64]

Cynthia Pruyn Green recalled how "once, luckily I had a flashlight because I went to take my dog out . . . and when I got . . . here, the light reflected in a big pair of eyes. There was a [black] bear right there! . . . I don't think you'll find any other kind around here, just black bear. They are supposedly harmless unless you get between them and their cubs, [but] if you leave food . . . they'll take everything apart. But the worst trouble really is the raccoons because they can get in everything and eat everything, too. . . . Had to put hooks on [the ice boxes on the kitchen porch because] the coons learned that we kept blueberries there." They even learned how to unlatch the hooks.[65]

"In the pantry the mice used to get into the flour and make tracks all over the shelves. . . . And we use to have porcupines under the porch. . . . You could hear them gnawing the porch every night. But the creatures I loved were the loons. At first I was scared of them, when I was a little girl, but they make the most marvelous sound."[66] "Porcupines were so often heard chewing at the Main Camp's underpinnings at night that a general collapse was always believed to be imminent."[67]

"[Dad] shot me a red fox which he had made into a fur stole. In those days, they were very fashionable and I felt like a queen with my rare red fox from the family preserve."[68]

"The preserve affords excellent shooting. . . . Deer are plentiful, and in summer often appear on the lake shores or among the cows and sheep in the pasture. There are also bear in the woods, and ruffed grouse, and plenty of woodcock in the alder coverts beside the streams and about the lakes."[69]

"When they were lumbering at Santanoni, the deer used to hang around the horses [employed to haul logs]."[70] Deer swam to and from the islands regularly. "They used to come to Sand Beach, the swimming beach; a doe and her fawns would play on the sand."

"There was a pet deer, 'Harriet,' that came to the kitchen steps to eat saltines fed by hand. Nearby was a salt lick where rock salt was dumped, after making ice cream."

"When [Mrs. Dunham] had to do a lot of baking—maybe twenty-four or twenty-five pies—the deer would smell the spice and they would come in and stick their heads right in the bake house, right in the window. [Caretaker] Buster [Dunham] had a radius from the Camp within which he would allow no hunting for miles around, so that the wildlife was protected and comparatively unafraid.

[61] Delilah West Bissell, 1991.

[62] Helen Tummins. Garrison, 1987.

[63] Cynthia Pruyn Green. Aldrich, 14, 190. Sis' mother was Beatrice Morgan.

[64] Beatrice Pruyn Thibault. Aldrich, 69.

[65] Cynthia Pruyn Green. Aldrich, 117-118.

[66] Beatrice Pruyn Thibault. Aldrich, 64, 48.

[67] Susan Pruyn King, handwritten notes, August 1992.

[68] Beatrice Pruyn Thibault. Aldrich, 14.

[69] Guy H. Lee, 92.

[70] This and the following quotations are Beatrice ("Sis") Pruyn Thibault. Adrich, 17, 29, 46, 148, 32, 54, 29, respectively .

Entry road at Honeymoon Bridge

"The moose was in the water eating the lilies, drooling, and we startled him in his dead calm. We were down wind, so he didn't smell us. Dad paddled like an Indian, very easily, very quietly with the J stroke, and the moose took off towards us. I guess we threatened him." The bull moose almost tipped over the canoe.

"Buster [Dunham] loved animals. He found a skunk once that had got his head caught in a tomato can and . . . reached down and picked up the skunk, put it under his arm (tail pointing away, of course) and he worked that tomato can off his head very, very carefully; when he got it off he put the skunk down, and it ran off. [Buster and his son Stan] once met a bear on the trail when they were out in the woods pretty close to where we used to camp, but [they] never harmed it—[Stan] wouldn't hunt or even fish. So this bear comes down the path and Buster took off his hat and put it in front of that bear and he circled that hat round and round, talking all the while, and the bear just turned around and ambled off."[71]

"Dad and I were on the trail along the east side of the lake one day, and he stopped me and said, "Be quiet . . . ssshhh—and pointed ahead. All I could see was a log; then I noticed a movement. We walked up and it was a deer's ear. She was lying behind the log. He had an eye for the woods. Farther along, he pulled me off a fallen tree and pointed down. I didn't see anything. He took a stick and moved the grass and there was a bird's nest. He was amazing, a real woodsman."[72]

"Red squirrels used to get into the corn bin and eat the corn. The boys would pop the lid up and shoot them with 22's when they ran out. We didn't like red squirrels as they steal birds' eggs but we had gray squirrels as pets. They were a barrel of laughs, slept and traveled in our coat pockets. Lots of funny stories about them. . . ."

---

[71] Marian Dunham to Robert Engel, August 17, 1992. Aldrich, 167.

[72] Beatrice Pruyn Thibault, referring to her father, Frederic. Aldrich, 51, 4 , 11.

Frederic Pruyn used to "blow up the beaver dam," probably to keep the stream flowing, and he "played a game with one beaver, throwing snowballs at him—he seemed to enjoy it so he challenged him by popping up and ducking back in! His name was Sam!"

"The lake before the house abounds with brook and lake trout and beyond is Moose Lake, providing, if possible, even better fishing of the same sort. In addition, the river crossed just before reaching the gate lodge is full of small-mouthed bass and the great blue pike or pickerel of the North, not to mention the more humble yellow perch, bullheads, and other pond fish."[73]

"There used to be landlocked salmon in the lake. Mother caught one. It was a rare event to boat one. We used copper line and a big copper spoon along the bottom. The lake is so deep that when you catch a fish and bring it up its bladder bursts from change in pressure. When you swim the surface of the water is warm but when your feet go down, it's like ice!"[74]

In the 1930s fish were plentiful. "When I wanted fish for supper, I would stop at the bridge at the narrows. I could lie down on the rocks and watch the trout take my worm. They were beautiful speckled trout."[75]

Idyllic though it may seem, Santanoni Preserve remained a relative wilderness, sometimes hostile. "A man came in one afternoon starved and terrified—he was out of it. Dad always said that a man who claims he cannot get lost is either a damned fool or has never been in the woods."[76]

The incident was ominous.

## Lumbering the Land

Pruyn's land was not unspoiled wilderness when he purchased it. Lemon Thomson and Patrick Moynehan had heavily logged much of it.[77] However, as was sometimes the practice in the Adirondacks, loggers had spared the area immediately surrounding Newcomb Lake.

Area residents spoke for years about the great swindle Moynehan pulled off in managing to sell property that he didn't own at a forty-four-percent profit. The story has become family lore.[78] Moynehan had been logging the land under contract with its Albany owners, Lemon Thomson, Augustus Sherman and William Weed. Moynehan, the story goes, arranged to buy the land for $12,500 only hours before selling it to Pruyn for $18,000. In addition, Moynehan retained the right to cut softwood timber for two years within a specified zone around Moose Pond.[79]

Moynehan also held on to hundreds of wooded acres north of the land he sold to Pruyn. Spring runoff from Pruyn's Moose Pond provided the only practical means for transporting softwood logs from this land to the nearby Hudson. For this reason, the July 9, 1892 deed also entitled Moynehan to dam and raise the level of Moose Pond four feet every spring for the next six years. This allowed his workmen to skid felled softwood logs onto its frozen surface and wait until the thaw to release the dam and float the logs a short distance to Shaw Pond, then via Newcomb Lake down to the Hudson and thence to the mills at Glens Falls.

Since the spring log drive was always complete before camp was opened, Moynehan's logging activity hardly affected the Pruyns or their guests. After denuding this land of its marketable softwood, Moynehan sold all of his remaining thirteen-hundred acres to Pruyn for $2,574. This inverted T-

[73] Guy H. Lee, 92.

[74] Beatrice Pruyn Thibault. Aldrich, 31.

[75] Helen Tummins. Garrison, 1987.

[76] Beatrice Pruyn Tibault. Aldrich, 50.

[77] Barbara McMartin concluded from documentary evidence, a century later, that the tract had not been lumbered. "Santanoni Preserve," undated typescript, NYS Dept. of Environmental Conservation. However, this does not appear to be consistent with the ownership, tax sale and oral history.

[78] Sam Scranton, step-son of Frederic Pruyn, Jr., letter to J. Winthrop Aldrich, September 1992. Aldrich, 156.

[79] *Essex County Land Grantee Book 103*, Office of the County Clerk, Essex County, New York, 449.

shaped section tops off the remote northwest reaches of Santanoni Preserve.

Local stories of how Moynehan got the best of the deal may be questioned because of some factual errors and by recognition that banker Pruyn probably had no less business acumen than his Newcomb neighbors.[80] Thirty years later, Pruyn contracted with International Paper Co. to log sections of the estate, and earned almost $730,000 over a five-year period.[81] Pruyn must have been sufficiently astute to foresee this potential. Or maybe he just didn't care. A few years and a few thousand dollars would mean little to him when putting together an estate meant to be in his family for generations.

Sand beach near the main camp, Newcomb Lake, painting by Edward Lansing Pruyn.

## The Campaign Begins

> Newcomb, June 13: There are a few sporting people in town. A party recently from Albany were here with a view of organizing a reserve at Newcomb Lake. It is understood they contemplate erecting a three-story house near the lake.
>
> *The Essex County Republican, June 16, 1892*[82]

In June 1892, a few days before signing the contract with Moynehan to purchase the main parcel that would become Santanoni Preserve, Robert Pruyn visited his new domain with Howard Van Rensselaer and James Fenimore Cooper, who would be frequent guests.

Not only were Pruyn's two friends born with famous names, they were conscious of their family identities. James Fenimore Cooper III, fourth generation of a Yorker landed family, was regarded as "a zealous caretaker of the family reputation and history."[83] Intimates at Santanoni teased Howard Van Rensselaer (whose family had been more extensively landed, for more generations, than Cooper's) as "the Black Patroon," presumably because of his dark features.[84] Van Rensselaer, strikingly handsome and of patrician mien, was the Pruyns' physician who visited Santanoni Preserve thirty-one times over the next three decades. Jim Cooper was Robert C. Pruyn's attorney and Albany neighbor, two doors down Willett Street from the Pruyns. He would notarize the deed to Santanoni two

[80] Sherman and Weed had not owned the property since 1873. The right to cut timber was not for two years, but six.

[81] "Santanoni Preserve Receipts from Lumbering Operations," undated (ca. 1924) handwritten document in R.C. Pruyn papers, KeyCorp, Trust Company archives, Albany. "The soft woods were lumbered between 1921-1925, under a contract which required the Lumber Company to leave soft woods standing along the lakes, roads and trails. The firs reproduced very well in the parts lumbered." "Santanoni Preserve, Newcomb, Essex County, New York," n.d., typescript in National Commercial Bank records. By another account, "soft wood timber removed in operation, 1920-1923. No timber has been removed from area less than 100 yards from any trail, road or lake." "Santanoni Preserve," n.d., typescript in National Commercial Bank records.

[82] Like the report that opened this chapter, from the same newspaper but written the following year, this news item does not recognize that the ambitious project was intended for a single family.

[83] William Cooper, the great land owner and founder of Cooperstown, N.Y., was great-grandfather of James Fenimore Cooper III (1858-1938). "He first published the family tradition in his introduction to the republication of William Cooper's *A Guide in the Wilderness*. The great-grandson repeated that tradition in two eclectic collections of family papers and antiquarian observations: *The Legend and Traditions of a Northern County* (1921) and *Reminiscences of Mid-Victorian Cooperstown* (1935). Alan Taylor, *William Cooper's Town: Power and Persuasion on the Frontier of the Early American Republic* (New York: Vintage, 1995), 365.

[84] Anonymous poem, stanza ten, in Santanoni scrapbook, Adirondack Museum library.

The Shanty, 1892

weeks later and be an annual guest at Santanoni Preserve for fifteen years.

The three friends intended to explore the shores of the large lake to select a site for the main camp. It was an inauspicious beginning. The unpredictable Adirondacks provided a heavy snowfall on May 29, when they arrived at Newcomb after a half-day ride from the railroad terminus at North Creek. The trio had to remain at the modest Newcomb Hotel for a few days.[85] The friends then camped in a canvas tent on the shore of Newcomb Lake.

The party was not the first to camp here. As Lake Delia was accessible by the public road from Newcomb to Tahawus, guidebooks had informed visitors about the attractive destination.[86] A lakeside "shanty" had been built by previous owners for camping or by Moynehan for his logging operation. Even before Pruyn received the deed, his surveyors and other workers may have occupied the shanty. The three city gentlemen preferred the more romantic tent.

The shanty was located on the north shore of the lake, west of the sand beach.[87] Photographs show a curious log structure with bark cladding and a very large porch, its roof steeper in pitch than that of the enclosed portion—virtually an enlarged Adirondack lean-to. If not used by visitors during construction of the main camp, the shanty may have provided workers' housing or served as a workshop during bad weather. A short distance

[85] Entry for June 1, 1892, *Santanoni: A Record of Fish and Some Other Things*. The Adirondack Museum Library.

[86] Wallace, *Descriptive Guide to the Adirondacks*, various editions.

[87] According to family tradition, "there was a temporary camp near what later became the bathing beach." Cynthia Pruyn Green, handwritten notes, August 1992; also Aldrich, 127-128. The Shanty site as pictured conforms to Location 2 in Fred Kelly's map, "Newcomb Lake, July 15, 1892." The Shanty was not at the beach, which was shown on the scaled Fisher & Bryant 1910 map as site of the bath houses, and also shown on the Otto Jantz 1936 map that accompanied his appraisal inventory (untitled).

beyond this encampment, on the next point of land was another campsite and shelter, known as "Poplar Point Camp," likewise shown on the 1892 map (page 36). [88]

For the main camp, the Pruyns did not choose the most the conveniently accessible site, on the southern shore of the lake. Probably they thought that this area, where the access road arrived at the water, then used by the visiting public, might be a better location for a service complex. For their summer home, the Pruyns preferred a more remote point of land on the less frequented eastern shore. The favored location required additional access road, and probably reconstruction of the Duck Hole bridge. Perhaps the primary factors were privacy and attractive setting. It was not then certain that Pruyn would succeed in closing the road to the public, and the eastern site had a grand outlook across the length of the lake, toward the islands and the setting summer sun. The prevailing western breeze may have been considered, as well as proximity to the spring and sand bathing beach. There may have been still other factors. For reasons to be demonstrated, a traditional form of Japanese architecture faced west. Moreover, "a Japanese will never sleep with his head towards the north . . . nor will they build a house fronting to the north, else it will soon be destroyed."[89]

The following month, eighteen-year-old Ned Pruyn and his cousin, Fred Kelley, set up camp on the Preserve with their guide Elbert Parker for some fishing at Moose Pond. In the "Moose Lake Chronicle," a whimsical diary of the trip, Kelley and the younger Pruyn related their adventures in building a bark shanty, catching dozens of trout, getting soaked in a thunderstorm and, most important, guiding "the architects" around the lake in a river boat.[90] Work on the main camp began immediately.

[88] Location 3 on Fred Kelley's map. The Poplar Point shelter might have been the simple, unidentified cabin on Newcomb Lake pictured in several photographs in the Pruyn collection.

[89] Margaret Tate Kinnear Ballagh, *Glimpses of Old Japan, 1861-1866* (Tokyo: Methodist Publishing House, 1908), 70.

[90] "Moose Lake Chronicle," Santanoni Scrapbook, Adirondack Museum Library.

Twin log repositories,
Toshodi-ji[91]

The log storehouse (*azekura*), relatively fireproof, was a common feature of the Japanese temple. Probably it was known to Pruyn, who had resided in Japan at Zempukuji Temple. Twin repositories often were paired, placed a short distance apart for fire separation.

Connected twin repositories,
Kofu-zo, Horyu-ji[93]

A single roof often connected paired storehouses, sheltering the planked floor of a breezeway and protecting access doors. All repositories were raised high off the ground on vertical log supports. All extant storehouses have hipped roofs.

Twin log repositories connected,
Shoso-in, Todai-ji[92]

The area between storehouses might be enclosed with a light screen wall, different from the two log-cabin store rooms.

Santanoni villa,
kitchen wing[94]

The distinctive kitchen block, seen first on arrival, announces the Japanese aspect, recalling the storage facilities (*shoso-in*) of Japanese temples known to Pruyn.

## From Japanese Temple to Adirondack Great Camp

[91] Treasure repository (right) and *sutra* (sacred text) repository. Kakichi Suzuki, *Early Buddhist Architecture in Japan* (Tokyo: Kodansha, 1980), 130. Image reversed.

[92] Suzuki, 113.

[93] Suzuki, 112.

[94] Harvey Kaiser, *Great Camps of the Adirondacks* (Boston: David Godine, 1982), 171.

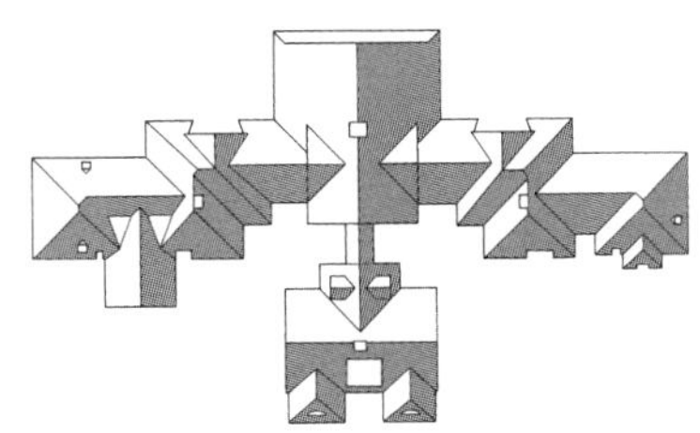

The great roof: bird in flight

#  4. From Japanese Temple to Adirondack Great Camp 

> To the Japanese mind . . . the roof is the part . . . essential in a building—it is the house itself as the primordial form of the tent makes plain.
>
> *Werner Blaser*

Robert H. Robertson was the Pruyns' first architect at Santanoni. Like his client, he was scion of an old and respected family. There were not yet any architectural schools in America so after graduating from Rutgers in 1869, Robert Robertson went to his ancestral Scotland to study architecture. He returned to his native Philadelphia to work for an architect, then moved to New York City to work for more prominent architects.[1] In Manhattan he developed a private practice, then began a prolific five-year partnership, designing churches, collegiate buildings, suburban homes and town houses.[2] Robertson designed several Albany buildings for the Pruyns, including Robert and Anna's town house at 38 Willett Street, one of four Queen Anne town houses facing the new Washington Park. The row today is considered an Albany landmark.[3]

Independently again, Robertson continued his very successful New York City practice. At age fifty, with two productive decades still ahead, Robertson was honored by the American critic, Montgomery Schuyler, and the national journal, *Architectural Record*, with a thirty-seven-page retrospective of his work.[4] He was then designing the Park Row Building for New York City—the building that briefly would be the tallest in the world. "Mr. Robertson has done quite his share of 'skyscrapers,' from the comparatively modest altitude of eight stories to the unquestionably immodest altitude of twenty-one, and even, in a project in course of execution, to the 'record' of twenty-seven."[5]

In the Adirondacks, Robertson designed the Webbs' Adirondack villa, Forest Lodge at Nehasane Park, in the early 1890s.[6] He also designed all the major buildings at the Webbs'

---

[1] In Philadelphia Robertson worked for Richard Sims, designing churches. Robertson moved to Manhattan in 1873 and worked with architects Edward T. Potter and George B. Post.

[2] Robertson formed a partnership with William A. Potter in 1875, when President Grant appointed the latter supervising architect in Washington. *National Cyclopaedia*. Montgomery Schuyler, "The Work of R. H. Robertson," *The Architectural Record*, 6 (October 1896), 184-219.

[3] The Potter and Robertson row houses were begun in 1877. Robertson also designed a store and apartment building at 70 North Pearl Street for R.C. Pruyn's father, which survives, converted to office use. (Robert Pruyn and brother Charles also built houses on Hudson Street as an investment.) Diana S. Waite, ed. *Albany Architecture* (Albany: Mount Ida Press, 1993), 104, 141, 142, 180.

[4] Montgomery Schuyler, "The Work of R.H. Robertson," *Architectural Record* 6 (October, 1896): 182-219.

[5] The Park Row Building, extant across from City Hall at 15 Park Row, between Ann and Beekman Streets, was completed in 1899. Schuyler included a rendered elevation of the building in his article. Schuyler, 219.

[6] Nehasane is pronounced Ne-ha-sa-nee, with accent on the second syllable. Kaiser says Forest Lodge was constructed in 1894, 182, 186. Mary Hotaling believes it was designed "around 1890." "Robert H. Robertson, Architect of Santanoni," *Adirondack Architectural Heritage Newsletter* 5, No. 1 (June 1996), 3. Webb's Adirondack Railroad, which traversed Nehasane Park, was completed in 1892.

landmark estate, Shelburne Farms, Vermont.[7] The architect died of a heart attack while visiting Nehasane Park in 1919, where he was fishing with Seward Webb.[8] According to Webb family lore, when the host found his guest lifeless, he sat his congenial friend's body in a chair near the fireplace, poured him a cognac, and continued the visit for another day or two.[9]

Architects H. H. Richardson and Richard Morris Hunt were preeminent in America during the later nineteenth century, until McKim, Mead and White became dominant. Robertson was a prominent and socially well-connected architect whose work, like many of his contemporaries, evidenced Richardson's influence.[10] He adapted Richardson's early "Queen Anne" style, then his solid, relatively simpler mode, now known as the "Shingle Style."[11] Forest Lodge, the Webb villa at Nehasane, represented the latter species of country house. Forest Lodge was more characteristic of Robertson's residential practice than was the log villa at Santanoni Preserve. For reasons being explored here, the latter was an anomaly. If not so well known today as work of the leading architects of his time, Robertson's has not been forgotten. It continues to appear in works of architectural history.[12]

Robert H. Robertson was "tall, well built, . . . with a well-developed physique, having given no small attention to athletics, and is a most enthusiastic hunter and fisherman."[13] In this, he had a bond with the Webbs and Pruyns. Like them, moreover, he was cultured, "a fine musician, being a highly prized member of the Mendelssohn Glee Club, of which he has for many years been the president." He married Charlotte Markoe, daughter of a

---

[7] Joe Sherman, *The House at Shelburne Farms* (Forest Dale, Vt: Paul S. Eriksson, 1992), 29. Plans for Webb's office at Shelburne were published in *American Architect and Building News*, December 8, 1888.

[8] Seward Webb was son of Dr. W. Seward Webb. Hotaling, 3.

[9] J. Watson Webb, interview by Julie Bressor, Shelburne Farms archivist, handwritten notes, Shelburne Farms, 1993.

[10] John Burchard and Albert Bush-Brown, *The Architecture of America: A Social and Cultural History* (Boston: Little, Brown, 1961). William H. Jordy and Ralph Coe, Editors, *American Architecture and Other Writings by Montgomery Schuyler* (Cambridge: Belknap Press, 1961), 35.

[11] The contemporary term "Queen Anne" referred to its British origin, represented by the work of the English architect, Richard Norman Shaw. Richardson's Watts Sherman villa at Newport (1874-6) derived from Shaw's eclectic manner. Potter and Robertson were quick to adapt the mode, employed for villas at Oyster Bay, New York. *American Architect and Building News*, November 3 and December 21, 1878. The architectural historian, Vincent Scully, coined the term "Shingle Style". *The Shingle Style: Architectural Theory and Design from Richardson to the Origins of Wright* (New Haven: Yale University Press, 1955).

[12] Sarah Bradford Landau illustrated two of his works in *Edward T. and William A. Potter: American Victorian Architects* (New York: Garland, 1979), 70-79. Drawings for three houses by Robertson appeared in an exhibition catalogue of the Parrish Art Museum, *The Long Island Country House, 1870-1930*, 42-44.

[13] This and following quotation from *National Cyclopaedia of Biography*, 98.

distinguished New York City physician.[14] The Robertsons moved in elite circles and were at home with other established families. Robertson's letters to friend and client, Robert Pruyn, convey something of his character and their relationship. Robertson, two years Pruyn's junior, seems to have been the more ebullient of the two.[15] The architect concluded one letter, largely concerned with technical problems of building the Pruyns' Albany house, "My brain is on fire. My reason wavers. I swoon! I swoon! Farewell as Ever."[16]

While working on the house, Robertson described to Pruyn his visit to Herter Brothers of New York, one of America's most prestigious interior design firms and manufacturer of fine furniture. "My visit to Herters' this morning was not a success," he wrote. "I found in waiting a very high-toned young man with a great many good clothes on, who in a very condescending manner approached me and waited for an order. I told him I came to look at a brass bracket fixture which Mr. Pruyn had liked. . . . He smiled sweetly and said that Mr. Pruyn had been in a number of times and looked at a great number of things. . . . I lost my temper and walked out without knocking him down." Herters' showroom catered to professional designers working for wealthy clients more than to the designers' clients themselves. It may be telling that Robert C. Pruyn "had been in a number of times." This attention to detail confirms the "just so" characteristic recalled by a granddaughter. It suggests Robert Pruyn's personal involvement in design of the log villa at Santanoni.

What did Pruyn and Robertson have in mind when they planned the main lodge at Camp Santanoni? What models occurred to them? From our subsequent vantage point, Santanoni appears to be one of many grand camps of the Adirondacks—distinctive, to be sure, but generic as one of a type. In 1893, however, most of these establishments did not yet exist in the Adirondacks. Only William West Durant's seminal Camp Pine Knot at Raquette Lake was recognized as a gentleman's villa of consequence. Virtually "a small village," it alone might have qualified as a grand country house.[17] Despite Pine Knot's rustic charm, that casual aggregation of small cabins, evolving without benefit of architect, was comparatively naïve. As suggested earlier, other Adirondack summer homes of the 1880s were cottages, not country houses and, as mentioned, possibly the Pruyns were familiar with Camp Pine Knot. They surely knew the nearby, rustic camp at Raquette Lake of their relatives, the Ten Eycks. According to one account, the Pruyns' initial notion was to have a place more like the Ten Eycks' or Durants'—a casual assemblage of rustic cabins.[18] Instead, architect Robertson and client Pruyn evolved a new concept for the villa at Santanoni Preserve, qualifying it not only as unique, but also as a significant work of architecture.

## Significance in Architecture

Architecture that is "significant," as the term literally denotes, serves as a "sign" to convey meaning. A significant form is more than merely pleasant or theatrical, for conceptual content underlies perceptual appearance. The image of the famous mountaintop castle of mad King Ludwig of Bavaria is so arresting as to be a familiar icon. It is superbly picturesque, effective as romantic theater (and was in fact designed by a theatrical set designer). What the mock-medieval fantasy achieves, it

[14] The Robertsons had one child, Thomas Markoe Robertson. *National Cyclopaedia.* 98. Thomas M. Robertson, an architect like his father, had no children. Markoe is pronounced "Markoo." J. Winthrop Aldrich conducted an extensive search for Robertson architectural records or family papers, finding only those at Shelburne Farms. (J. W. Aldrich to authors).

[15] Robert H. Robertson was born in 1849. *National Cyclopaedia.*

[16] This and following quotation from Robert H. Robertson, letter to R. C. Pruyn, July 9, 1877. Pruyn Papers.

[17] Craig Gilborn is quoted. *Durant*, 23. See also Donaldson, II, 92. The Pruyns may also have been aware of Henry VanHoevenberg's Adirondack Lodge, the well-known, large, log guest accommodation completed in 1880 near Lake Placid.

[18] Origin of the form was mentioned in Chapter (page 24).

achieves with panache. But architecture is not merely theater, and Ludwig's Schloss Neuschwanstein, model for the castle at Disney World, is not widely regarded as art.

Looking at buildings, we may associate familiar aspects with previous experiences, and consider an effective building to have "character." This is an important quality of architecture, but it does not suffice for a work to attain the highest level of architectural achievement. To be distinguished as art, a work must convey an intention not merely to the eye, but to the mind's eye—not merely recalling visual memories, but engaging active intellect. A great work of architecture, like any work of art, rewards those who penetrate beyond initial appearance.

*Form* is conceptual, not perceptual. Formal organization may not be readily perceived, for it is visible only by a sort of mental x-ray. Why, if something is invisible, is it relevant? Beyond levels of sensory stimulus and associational fantasy, revelation of hidden relationships entails discovery. Moreover, a work of art has a unity and completeness; nothing may be added or removed without impairing satisfaction. Ludwig's folly, intriguing though it is, might have one more or one less tower, to no great consequence. One ought not, however, to remove a minaret from the Taj Mahal.

The controlling concept—the Greek *schema*, or (as we will see) the Buddhist *mandala*—is what determines the relationship of parts to whole. When pieces fit together, we find the result satisfying. The parts should add up to something, a whole that is more than the sum of the parts.

The Great Camps of the Adirondacks invariably have "character." They were consciously integrated to the locale by use of native materials and traditional craftsmanship. They were intended to be nostalgically antimodern, and succeeded in being charmingly quaint as well as picturesque, given their splendid natural settings. All of this is fine, but has little to do with architecture as an art.

## The Great Log Villa As a Work of Art

A "work of art" requires more than a designer's innate taste or acquired style, although those qualifications may yield products that are "artistic." The great log villa at Santanoni Preserve is both artistic *and* a work of art.

Robertson was regarded in his time as more a master of fine detail than of larger design.[19] This concern is evident at Santanoni in numerous details, such as a simple, but richly developed, exterior doorway.

Exterior door, Santanoni villa

Superimposed images provide multiple readings. The primary figure is the light door, startling in the context of the dark-stained log wall. Within the door's main rectangle are two panels, different in size and proportion, within which split saplings of two diameters and two colors alternate to provide striking patterns of

[19] Montgomery Schuyler, 202 and subsequently.

light members superimposed on a dark ground. Diagonal and vertical stripes contrast boldly. It is something of an optical illusion, for we quickly see a perceptual inversion of reality; black slashes appear on the larger light field.

Three frames, expanding like concentric rings caused by a pebble tossed in a pool, ambiguously define the rectangular figure of the door. The light shape of the literal door, with its cedar frame, expands into a vibrant red stripe, part of the wall that becomes perceptually part of the door. The ambiguity, uncertainty about what is door and what is wall, is effective in blurring the elemental simplicity of door and wall. An echo—the outer, shadow figure of the dark log door frame—follows this second iteration of the rectangular figure.

Although this is but a simple door, one of many, constructed out of natural materials found at hand, the deftness of the architect in employing formal devices to provide ambiguity—multiple readings and figure-ground reversals—evidences Robertson's dexterous command of formal technique. Most generally, what Santanoni demonstrates is invention disciplined by consistent intention. Although bold, his design recalls the elegant Japanese minimalism.

The log villa is not "rustic" in the same sense as are many Adirondack buildings and furnishings. In Japanese terms, its character is *shibui*—"tasteful in a rustic manner"—but not *wabi*; the latter is more consciously primitive.[20] At Santanoni there are few contorted roots and branches, few rough bark finishes, no bizarre conceits. Occasional introduction of unfinished elements recalls similar use in Japanese teahouses, where natural elements are intentionally juxtaposed with refined work. Balance (*gyô*) between the formally rigid (*shin*) and the naturally fluid (*sô*) is a Japanese ideal. "It is the secret of a life of good sense and its expression in all the necessary objects and works of practical living."[21]

According to an 1893 account, "pains were taken to avoid city effects [and] although built of logs, [the camp is] well designed, and offer[s] a remarkably fine example of what can be done with rustic work in architecture."[22]

Robertson contributed much artistry to the lodge at Santanoni, but as a work of art it is atypical of Robertson's designs. Why did it attain a quality absent from his other works? The answer may entail an accident of history—the meeting of architect and client at Rutgers University.

The achievement at Santanoni Preserve was collaborative, attributable in large part to the cultivated taste of the client. Most importantly, the unique quality of Santanoni's main camp derived from Robert Pruyn's opportunity, virtually unprecedented for an American at the time, to spend impressionable formative years in Japan, living in a historic building built as a Buddhist temple.

Japan provided the conceptual diagram for the main camp at Santanoni Preserve. It was a *schema* of a Japanese temple, which nobles subsequently adapted for important villas. It might be more aptly called an "ideograph," like a character of oriental script that conveys a concept—or even more aptly (as we shall propose) a *mandala*.

Had Robertson's design for the Santanoni villa been mere replication of an exotic model, the result might have been a local curiosity. It is, however, a creative synthesis; Japanese precedent was reinterpreted, translated into a different vernacular language, transformed by integration into a different culture. As other architects, such as Frank Lloyd Wright, Greene and Greene, and Richard Neutra absorbed influence of the Orient, producing innovative architecture that was American, so Robertson created a building distinguished by its novel

[20] Clay Lancaster, *The Japanese Influence in America* (New York: Rawls, 1963; New York: Abbeville Press, 1983), 276. Yasuhiro Ishimoto, "Tradition and Creation in Japanese Architecture," in Ishimoto, 27.

[21] Werner Blaser, *Japanese Temples and Tea Houses* (New York: F.W. Dodge, 1956), 28.

[22] New York State Forest Commission, 179.

identity. The Santanoni villa is not Japanese; it is an Adirondack building, constructed of native materials, built by local craftsman using woodsmen's skills.

Camp Santanoni is more than a generic Adirondack structure, however. Its fusion of cultures has yielded a universal quality. There is more to the log villa than distinctive character. Other camps, likewise built of logs, similarly are integrated into a natural setting, and convey regional distinction. Other camps may be charming, but rarely are so moving. Many of those who annually visit the Pruyns' vacant country house have commented on its singular quality. Very few have perceived any Japanese character, yet most have recognized something different. Some have commented on a mysterious or haunting aspect.[23]

What touches the observer at Santanoni is what is unseen; the invisible is what contributes the aspect of mystery. There is more than meets the eye; it is the hidden *form* of the work, a ghost of ancient Japan—perhaps what Robert Pruyn's classmate, orientalist William Elliot Griffis, called "the soul of Japan."[24]

## Buddhist Iconography of the Villa

Buddhism provided a *mandala*, a symbolic figure, for Santanoni.[25] The shape of the plan represents a bird in flight.[26] This image signified a pantheistic concept: "All things in nature are . . . embodiments in reality of the spiritual world."[27] The bird form represents ascending flight toward "paradise, or, at least, a world better than this one."

Pantheism had become American; Emerson wrote, "Behind nature, throughout nature, spirit is present."[28] The precedent for Santanoni, however, was nine centuries old. The model was no single historic building, but rather a type of building that had evolved according to the same basic plan, the *mandala* of the mythical bird in flight, the Phoenix, ". . . believed to transport souls to the Western Paradise of Amida Buddha."[29]

The "most wonderful bird is the Japanese phoenix. Have I ever seen one? No, its visits are rarer than angels' since it appears on earth only at millennial intervals or at the birth of some great man. This, like the Chinese dragon, is a fabulous creature, and all representations of it seen to be combination of the pheasant and peacock. As it flies, so graceful are its movements that a host of birds follow it."[30] The form of Santanoni is difficult to convey in photographs, or even on the ground, because the *mandala* of the Phoenix was conceptual, not perceptual. The image was seen in the mind's eye—or, (prior to the airplane) only the bird's eye could have perceived this

[23] Steven Engelhart, Executive Director of Adirondack Architectural Heritage, who has conducted many tours of Santanoni Preserve, recalled that "the visitor's experience there is usually so profound. . . . I wonder if the visitor, in some intangible way, doesn't feel the power of that concept through the architecture. I know I do." Letters to Paul Malo, December 4 and 7, 1997.

[24] William Elliot Griffis' dedication to Pruyn in *Japanese Fairy Tales* was mentioned in Chapter 1.

[25] A *mandala* is "a diagram of the type particularly associated with esoteric Buddhism," not invariably geometric but often representing a natural form that was symbolic, such as the phoenix. Sherman E. Lee, *A History of Far Eastern Art* (New York: Abrams, n.d.), 266.

[26] The most famous Japanese example of the bird-shaped plan is the *Hoo-do* (the "Phoenix Hall") or the "Amida Hall" of the Byodo-in, originally built as a villa in 1053 at Uji, subsequently converted to serve as a temple. Symbolism is made more explicit by gilt-bronze representations of the phoenix adorning the ends of the roof ridge. Kakichi Suzuki, *Early Buddhist Architecture in Japan* (Tokyo: Kodansha International, 1971), 139; Sherman E. Lee, 300-303.

[27] Teiji Ito, The *Japanese Garden: An Approach to Nature*. (New Haven: Yale University Press, 1972), 159.

[28] Ralph Waldo Emerson, "Nature," *Works*, I.

[29] The name, "Amida", referring to the "Buddha of the West," derived from the Sanskrit, "Amitabha," reflecting origin in India, which was the "West" to China and Japan. The Western Paradise was *Jodo*, or "Pure Land." Sherman Lee, 299.

[30] Ballagh, 71.

Phoenix ascending

heavenly apparition.[31] A Japanese scholar has observed that ". . . the ideal view was from above, and so an ideal building should be designed as though to be viewed from the air."[32]

The Japanese did not see a temple or villa, such as the Phoenix pavilion, as an isolated object, but required that it be essentially integrated to a pond-garden, toward which it was oriented. Arranged before a Phoenix pavilion was an artfully design landscape that represented the heavenly goal, paradise. Here the great bird is aligned so that the main gable frames a wilderness vista, terminated in the west by mountains beyond the lake.

[31] Mary Hotaling observed that "...the idea that this concept was designed to be seen from the air—and in particular relation to the landscape—finally gave me a physical basis for my feelings about the place. . . . Photographs do not convey what is so special about it. Now I feel as if I finally understand why that is." Letter to Paul Malo, December 23, 1997.

[32] "The compositions from eye-level are accidental; those from a hypothetical and unrealizable view from above are planned. . . . The ideal of the Japanese mind is metaphysical. Just as one perceived the structure of the [building] through an interpretation of its mandalistic intention, so one perceived with the inner eye of understanding its ideal view from above." Ito 161-3.

## Japanese Villa Precedents

The symmetrical bird *mandala* served not only temples, but also residences of nobles, in an eleventh-century villa of a type called *Shinden-zukuri*.[33] Tetsuro Yoshida observed that the model "was clearly based on the principle that the individual parts of the building should be merged as much as possible into the garden. . . . The main wing, *Shinden*, comprising the master's living and reception rooms, opens . . . into the garden. Corridors running [in three other directions] connect . . . symmetrically arranged subsidiary build-

[33] *Shindenzukuri*: "consisting of a series of oblong houses systematically arranged and joined by corridors, with a garden laid out on the southern side in which was a big pond...." Jiro Harada, "Japanese Architecture," *Encylopaedia Britannica*, v. 12, 955.

ings."[34] In contrast to the more compact, more practical ordinary house, aristocrats broke conventional buildings apart, scattering elements throughout a contrived landscape, linked by covered walkways. "The fusion of [internal] space with natural setting—in other words, the openness of Japanese buildings—is rightly considered one of the most distinctive qualities of Japanese architecture."[35]

A historically conscious aristocrat adapted traditional, more vernacular forms for his seventeenth-century villa, probably the Japanese residence most admired in the West, and indeed one of the most famous houses of the world. The Katsura villa, situated on a river of that name that provides water for its famous garden, was built in the early seventeenth century southwest of the Imperial city of Kyoto. Like Santanoni, the Katsura villa was consciously nostalgic in architectural association. Prince Toshohito, instead of adopting the conventional aristocratic *shinden-zukuri* villa, returned to a still older, simpler type.[36]

A *Shinden-zukuri* villa

Whereas a *shinden-zukuri* villa had been approached frontally, on axis through the garden, subsequently the sequence was reversed so that the garden became the final destination. Nature became not something to pass from, but rather to go to, as the object of contemplation. The Katsura Detached Palace, as a major Imperial villa, was of this later type.[37] The royal retreat evidenced an elite Japanese taste for disciplined informality—the "calculated tea-ceremony taste in architecture."[38]

Like Katsura, the Santanoni villa is not approached frontally, on the main axis, but from the back, off the axis, and is entered obliquely.[39] There is no grand entry frontispiece; in fact "the front" is difficult to locate. As in the typical Japanese house, there is "no display of an architectural front; indeed, there is no display anywhere. The largest and best rooms are in the back of the house.... Here all the rooms open directly on the garden. Along the verandah are . . . rooms *en suite*. . . . The verandah is quite spacious."[40] A Japanese writer commented that "the veranda . . . is indispensable and must be regarded as one of the most important living rooms. It forms the transition from the inside of the house to the gardens. . . . It is in its best position when it is built round the corner of the house."[41]

Like Katsura, the Santanoni camp becomes not the ultimate destination, but the whole building serves merely as a portal to the ultimate paradise towards which the great bird

[34] Edward Hyams, *A History of Gardens and Gardening* (New York: Praeger, 1971), 59, 60.

[35] Kenzo Tange observed that "buildings in the *shinden-zukuri* style were not merely open but were completely integrated with the gardens surrounding them." Tange in Ishimoto, 20, 22.

[36] Katsura has been regarded less as representing the aristocratic *shinden-zukuri* style, but rather as the second major form of Japanese house, *shoin-zukuri*, which evolved from the more compact farmhouse. Tange in Ishimoto, 23. To have visited Katsura, Minister Pruyn and his son would have required special dispensation. Not only was it a property of the xenophobic Emperor, but foreigners were not ordinarily allowed to travel to the Imperial city of Kyoto, near which the villa is situated.

[37] Although often called the "Katsura Imperial Villa" in the West, the Japanese now call it *Katsura no Rikyu*, or "Katsura Detached Palace." Tange in Ishimoto, editor's note, 36.

[38] Sherman Lee, 463.

[39] Referring to Katsura, Gropius said, "It conforms to the favorite Zen approach, which is rarely direct, axial, and symmetrical. This is a decided distaste for the imposing straight avenue; instead, there is a preference for the intimate and casual but carefully planned approach which supplies surprises at every turn and leads up to the main objective in a human, natural, unimposing manner. Gropius, "Architecture in Japan," in Ishimoto, 8.

[40] Edward S. Morse, *Japanese Homes and Their Surroundings* (Boston: Ticknor, 1886), 55.

[41] Tetsuro Yoshida, *The Japanese House and Garden* (New York: Praeger, 1956), 103.

points and flies—here the Adirondack wilderness.

Again, like Katsura, the bird's wings are swept back, creating the figure of an arrow. The wings similarly are formed of several blocks of building, linked by an open gallery along the garden side. This was a common Japanese plan.[42] The stepped arrangement provided "an increased number of corner rooms with broad views. . . ."[43]

Finally, like Katsura, Santanoni's main lodge is flanked on either side by a satellite pavilion. The Katsura's Geppa-ro and Shoi-ken become Santanoni's boathouse and studio.[44] The arrangement is not perfectly symmetrical. In seventeenth-century Japan, aristocrats cared less for predictable formality than had that of the earlier eleventh century. The Katsura Villa evidenced "a return to Japanese artistry, after centuries of being deluded by foreign imitations, brought about by the stabilizing force of Zen ideals that eschewed extraneous ornamentation and abnormalities of proportion."[45]

Katsura Imperial Villa

## Recognition of Santanoni's Japanese Origin

According to a well-known guidebook, shortly after Camp Santanoni was constructed it presented "the appearance of a rambling old English manor-house."[46] That may strike us as an odd characterization. Surely no British country house ever looked like this. A more perceptive observer might have thought the villa to be what William Randolph Hearst told his architect he wanted at San Simeon, " a Jappo-Swisso bungalow."[47] That may be the way the Santanoni log villa appears in retrospect, a century later. The commentator of 1895 saw it through different eyes, or a different conceptual lens. Probably he was persuaded that Santanoni *Preserve* was a country place on the English model and erroneously applied that preconception to the architecture of the main camp.

Did Anna Pruyn, like Alice Vanderbilt, returning from Europe to behold the Breakers, her stupendous new summer home at Newport, sit down on the steps and cry, sobbing, "It's not what I wanted at all"?[48] Probably not, for the log villa is no grandiose, mock-Renaissance palazzo, but a rustic camp perfectly suited to the Adirondacks. Nevertheless, it is more than a hunting camp. More than an attractive caprice, it is serious architecture.

Were the real source of inspiration for the great log villa not so evident, one might suspect that the architect had prevailed upon his client to adopt the *avant garde* bungalow mode. The low house with extensive verandahs, purportedly adapted from British colonial models built in India, was a novelty on the east and west coasts of America in the 1890s.[49]

42 Another prominent landmark evidencing a stepped plan with circulation by means of external verandahs is the complex at Nijo Castle comprised of the Tozmurai, Shikidai, and Ohiroma.

43 Arthur Drexler, *The Architecture of Japan* (New York: Museum of Modern Art, 1955), 127.

44 Akira Naito, *Katsura: A Princely Retreat* (Tokyo: Kodansha International, 1977).

45 Lancaster, 166.

46 Wallace, 1895, 377-380.

47 David Nasay, "Earthly Delights." *The New Yorker*, May 23, 1998, 66. What his architect, Julia Morgan, gave him was neither Jappo, Swisso, nor bungalow.

48 Louis Auchincloss, *The Vanderbilt Era: Profiles of a Gilded Age* (New York: Scribners, 1989), 37 ff.

49 Clay Lancaster, *The American Bungalow, 1880-1930* (New York: Abbeville, 1985). Dell Upton and John Michael Vlach, *Common Places: Readings in American Vernacular Architecture* (Athens, Georgia: University of Georgia Press, 1986), 79 ff.

The few examples that appeared in national architectural journals prior to 1893 bore little resemblance to Santanoni.[50] The form of the log villa, although not Indian, is indeed Asian. Its inspiration, however, was Japanese.

In 1929, a landscape architect, Guy H. Lee, after visiting Santanoni and taking a series of fine photographs, published in a national journal an article describing the estate.[51] Robert and Anna Pruyn were spending one of their last summers together there at the time. Certainly the visitor had come by invitation and had permission to photograph and describe the camp. The level of knowledgeable detail suggests he spoke with Robert Pruyn himself for background information. This is relevant, because Guy Lee was the first to recognize, or at least to comment in print on, the Japanese character of the great log villa:

> The galleries take the place of hallways . . . all the rooms giving on them. It is interesting to recall that the Japanese always employ this method of getting to and from the various rooms in the rambling structures which are typical of their architecture; and as Mr. Pruyn spent many years of his youth in Japan, it is possible that his experiences there influenced him in the design of Camp Santanoni. In the method of arriving at the final grouping of the different units this influence is also felt. The Japanese first locate the important rooms of their houses and then connect them up and roof them in; at Camp Santanoni all the units were placed to command pleasant outlooks or to be thrust back out of the way as their use suggested, and brought under one roof and connected with galleries." [52]

Lee's detailed account of the farm as well as the villa suggests intimate familiarity with

Santanoni porches, 1895

"The veranda . . . forms the transition from the inside of the house to the gardens. . . . best . . . when it is built round the corner of the house."

Santanoni Preserve. Apparently he had limited knowledge of Japanese building practice, however; otherwise, he would not have thought that this sort of log construction was alien to Japan, but would have recognized that Japanese log treasure houses were the evident precedent for the kitchen block.[53] Probably some comment by one of the family, perhaps Robert Pruyn himself, suggested the Japanese connection.

Albany society called the Robert Pruyn family "the Japanese Pruyns," referring not only to the Japanese sojourn, but to the Pruyns' collection of Japanese art.[54] Family members have recognized the importance of Japan to Robert Pruyn and to Santanoni. "His house in Albany was filled with Japanese furniture, and he had the second largest collection of netsukes in the world, Japanese ivory figurines, and we accused him of admiring everything he saw because in Japan in those days custom required that anything you admired

[50] The sort of "California bungalow" designed by Green and Green in the mid-'nineties was not representative of the more common bungalow type that evolved in the early twentieth century.

[51] The author was identified as "Member American Society of Landscape Architects." Guy H. Lee, "Estates of American Sportsmen: Santanoni, the Adirondack Camp of Robert C. Pruyn, Esq. of Albany, New York." *The Sportsman*, October 1929, 71.

[52] Guy H. Lee, 72.

[53] Five examples of temple storage buildings (*kura*) remain, all with hipped roof (Todai-ji, Hombo, Tamukeyama, Hokke-do, Kanjinsho). Twin storage buildings (*narabi-kura*) when connected, as at Santanoni, formed a "triple store house" (*mitsugura*). Kakichi Suzuki, *Early Buddhist Architecture in Japan* (Tokyo: Kodansha, 1980), 211.

[54] In contrast, the John V. S. L. Pruyns were the "Chinese Pruyns" because of their famous collection of Chinese export porcelain. Aldrich, 68.

you were given."[55] Granddaughters recalled bedroom wall coverings of Japanese tea paper. Interior shutters on the windows derived "from Grandfather's years in Japan."[56] "The big antique iron gong . . . out on the front porch, on a red wooden stand . . . was used to call everyone in from the lake, woods, etc." Around the rim was inscribed: "This gong was the gift of Hisano Kahiye Masahide to the Ten Ryuzan Dainichi Tera Temple of Kojima Mura Village in the County of Imizugan, in the Province of Etchu No Kuni, in March of 1782."[57]

## Japanese Values

Whereas, in the West, ethics and aesthetics had become polarized during the nineteenth century, Japanese culture remained more integrated. Principles of Buddhism contributed to the "singular life-esthetic of [Japanese] aristocracy."[58] Aesthetics were not merely a matter of Fine Art, relegated to museums; life was regarded as an aesthetic issue. The German-American architect, Walter Gropius, a leader of the modern movement in architecture, observed, "I have never seen a better . . . integrated culture than Japan. . . . Beauty, for instance, a cultural factor of great importance more and more lacking in the Western world, is still a basic requirement of life for the Japanese."[59] Anglo-American critics found in Japan an attractive alternative to industrialized culture and the fragmentation of modern life. The Pruyns had lived in Japan at the end of an era, before the Meiji Restoration initiated the emergence of modern Japan. On the Pruyns' return, the contrast between a traditional, integrated culture and the rapidly modernizing one, in upheaval and ferment after the Civil War, was striking.

Cultivated taste for the rustic evolved as conservative protest against change, in reaction to Victorian elaboration and in opposition to Edwardian opulence. Simplicity of natural material and hand-crafted treatment, favored by reforming English aesthetic theorists like William Morris, introduced in the Adirondacks by William West Durant at his prototypical Camp Pine Knot, attained a quality of *shibui*—"an unassuming quality in which refinement underlies a commonplace appearance, perceptible only to a cultivated taste."[60] Understatement, in contrast to the ostentation of the newly successful, has appealed to patrician families in East and West.[61] Surely Robert Pruyn appreciated *shibui*; his Santanoni villa evidences a "deeply rooted Japanese taste for simplicity in architecture."[62] A scholar observed, "From the earliest times, the Japanese people have consistently chosen the plain and simple over the highly elaborate. Particularly in the planning of country retreats, or *besso*, the Japanese have tended to build unornamented informal environments, quite distinct from their urban homes."[63]

## The *Ho-o-den*

Pruyn and Robertson may have been influenced not only by the historic buildings of Japan, but by another Japanese example, closer at hand. In January of 1892, probably several months before construction commenced—but probably about the time Roberston undertook design of the Santanoni villa—an American

[55] Beatrice Pruyn Thibault. Aldrich, 42.

[56] Beatrice Pruyn Thibault. Aldrich, 42.

[57] Susan Pruyn King, Aldrich, 43, and letter to Howard Kirschenbaum, January 15, 1999. In the Pruyn scrapbook in the Adirondack Museum library, the inscription is written somewhat differently: "Gong dedicated by Hisano Kahioye Masa-hide to the Temple Dainichi-ji, Monuk Tenrin, Village of Kojima, Province of Yetchin, Dated 1st year of Tenisei period (1780)" [Tokugawa, Late Edo period]. This appears on an undated form headed "J. B. Wooley, dealer in Japanese, Chinese, Turkish and India Goods, _____ , 189__," suggesting the gong was a later acquisition, not brought back with the Pruyns from Japan.

[58] Torao Miyagawa, *Modern Japanese Painting: An Art in Transition* (Tokyo: Kodansha, 1969), 11.

[59] Gropius in Ishimoto, 1.

[60] Harada, 956.

[61] "The whimsical Japanese habit of concealing prestige and wealth behind a humble front has remained unchanged down to our time." Rudofsky, 116.

[62] Sherman E. Lee, 463.

[63] Michio Fujioka, *Kyoto Country Retreats: The Shugakuin and Katsura Palaces* (Tokyo: Kodansha, 1983), 33.

The *Ho-o-den*, the Japanese Pavilion at the World's Columbian Exposition at Chicago, 1893

architectural journal, reviewing projects underway at the Chicago World's Fair, forecasted, "From an architectural point [of view] the exhibit from Japan promises to be extremely interesting." Extensive descriptions and illustrations followed in subsequent issues of journals. By April of 1893, more than a month prior to the Pruyns' house warming party, the Japanese pavilion was "quite completed."[64]

The 1893 World's Columbian Exposition, or "Chicago World's Fair," as commonly called, had a profound effect on American culture and industry. The Japanese pavilion influenced not only Robertson but other architects such as Frank Lloyd Wright, who likewise adapted its traditional plan, based on the phoenix *mandala*.[65] Given Pruyn's affinity for Japan and Robertson's professional contacts, it is probable that they were aware of Japanese plans and moreover is plausible that they might have seen drawings for the pavilion prior to its construction. Inasmuch as the painstaking but slow handcrafting of the pavilion began many months before work commenced on the Santanoni villa, Robertson or Pruyn may even have visited the Chicago project during construction.[66]

The Japanese have had a long, and probably the world's most accomplished, tradition of timber construction. Japanese workmen in Chicago assembled components of the *Ho-o-den* that had been crafted in Japan virtually at the same time Adirondack woodsmen cut the

[64] *American Architect and Building News* 35, no. 836, Jan 1892, 10; also 40, no. 905, April 1893, 67; also 41, no. 927, September 1893 (the latter an extensive article). J. B. Wight provided drawings and critical commentary, serialized in two installments, "Japanese Architecture at Chicago," *The Inland Architect and News Record* 20, no. 5, December 1892.

[65] Clay Lancaster discusses influence on architects such as Green and Green and more generally on the Chicago School. *Japanese Influence*, 96 and elsewhere.

[66] ". . . Early in 1892, a company of odd, merry and industrious Japanese artisans made their appearance in Chicago, with innumerable packages and timbers." *The Dream City: A Portfolio of Photographic Views of the World's Columbian Exposition with an Introduction by Prof. Halsey C. Ives* (St. Louis: N.D. Thompson, 1893), n.p.

trees to build the great log villa at Santanoni Preserve. Both buildings were virtually complete in May, when the Pruyns' house warming at Santanoni coincided with public opening of the World's Columbian Exposition at Chicago.

The Japanese pavilion received critical acclaim. "From an architectural standpoint it is perhaps the most interesting contribution to the Exposition."[67] The building was no replica of any single historic monument; rather, the government's architect, Masamichi Kuru of Tokyo, adapted styles of several periods for portions of the pavilion. The basic arrangement, however, like that of Santanoni, was that of a building type, a *Ho-o-den*, "a palace whose ground plan bears a general conformity to the outline of a flying bird."[68] Santanoni was more of a *Ho-o-den,* however, than was the Chicago example. Pruyn remembered that the bird had a tail, which was omitted at Chicago.[69]

In fact, the log villa at Santanoni Preserve replicated neither the Katsura Villa nor the Chicago *Ho-o-den*. Whereas the fair pavilion was really three distinct buildings connected by covered walkways, the Santanoni villa is six buildings, but is less articulated because the parts are consolidated by a more continuous roof.[70] The Pruyn-Robertson work represents a synthesis of eleventh- and seventeenth-century villa forms. That composite Japanese model in turn was translated into the Adirondack loggers' mode of construction. The result of this creative mix is unique. Surely there is nothing like it elsewhere in the Adirondacks or, probably, in the world.

As the great Japanese architect, Kenzo Tange, remarked, "The dialectical synthesis of tradition[s] . . . is the structure of true creativeness."[71] The lesson of Japan, apparently absorbed by young Robert C. Pruyn, demonstrates the vitality of creative synthesis. Tange observed at Katsura the tension between the aristocratic *Yayoi* culture, "a definite, formal aesthetic, quiet, well-balanced, and dominated by a subjective, lyrical frame of mind," and the *Jamon* principle, "the primitive life force, . . . an irrepressible vitality that invariably threatens to destroy formal aesthetics."[72] It is precisely this tension between the refined and the primitive, the sophisticated and the primeval, the cultivated and the natural, that makes the architecture of the great lodge at Santanoni as alive today as when built more than a century ago.

The Chicago Fair opened just as the nation sank into a long economic depression, but with return of prosperity at the end of the decade the architectural influence of the exposition became widely evident, even in the Adirondacks. William West Durant, the premier Great Camp builder, apparently modeled his well-known main lodge at Sagamore on the fair's Idaho State pavilion. The Idaho pavilion, admired as "the handsomest log house ever

---

[67] Wight, p. 50. One of the many publications devoted to the Exposition was not so complimentary, commenting in unmistakably xenophobic terms, ". . . Modern architects have not wrought with the grace of their ancestors. These little buildings were erected in the Japanese manner by Japanese, and gave to Americans a sharp reminder of the superiority of Caucasian ideas." *The Dream City*, n.p.

[68] Wight, p. 50. The Japanese term, *Ho-o*, refers to a sacred bird, the Phoenix, while *den* means "villa." The historic temple model was called *Ho-o-do*, as the term, *do*, means "temple."

[69] The *Ho-o-den* remained after the Fair, and was restored in 1935, but burned in 1946. Lancaster, *Japanese Influence,* 83. Noted for its "structural honesty," among other things, the building had great influence on the Chicago architect, Frank Lloyd Wright.

[70] The kitchen wing was not incorporated under the main roof, probably for reason of fire isolation. Virtually a separate building, the service block is connected by a narrow, covered verandah link. The large, unitary roof is more characteristic of the later model, the Katsura villa.

[71] Tange is paraphrased; as a modernist, he referred to synthesis of "tradition and anti-tradition." Tange in Ishimoto, 35.

[72] Tange in Ishimoto, v. Tange added, "...The dichotomy is parallel in some ways to that between the Dionysiac and Apollonian elements in the life of ancient Greece." (18). Walter Gropius concurred: "Perhaps it is the aristocratic tradition on the one hand and the more earth-bound, elemental feature of the plain farmhouse on the other which, combined in this unique design, have earned it [Katsura] its fame." Gropius in Ishimoto, 8.

A temple guesthouse like the Pruyns' home in Japan, integrated into garden by the typical corner verandah. The *irimoya* roof would be recalled at Santanoni.[73]

The Pruyns' Adirondack country house, similarly related to the landscape by corner porches. Painting by Edward Lansing Pruyn.[76]

erected," was replicated not only in the Adirondacks but as far off as England.[74]

Similarities between Santanoni and Japanese precedents resulted not from imitation, but from similar intentions. The great log villa at Santanoni Preserve is a *ho-o-den*, not so much because of conscious Japanesque style, but because that model of *shinden-zukuri* villa served the Pruyns' objectives. The Japanese precedent had been "completely integrated" into surroundings, becoming "a prime example of the interpenetration of building and setting—a quality typical of Japanese architecture in general. Interpenetration of this sort is usually considered to result from the Japanese love of nature in its ever-changing aspects."[75]

Thinking of Japan, Tange observed that contemplation of nature was a common trait of aristocratic culture. We may make the same generalized observation in the Adirondacks, Here as well, perhaps, reverence for wilderness is less likely to be the attitude "of people who have labored to subdue or harness nature. [Contemplation of nature] shows no determination on the part of man to make himself master over the elements, but merely a passive appreciation of nature's beauty. Left to himself, a farmer, forever battling with the wind, the rain, and the perverse changes of the seasons, develops a more aggressive concept. . . . Farmers, unlike aristocrats, are concerned with the actualities of nature rather than its romantic aspects. . . . Not so with the aristocrats who created the *shinden-zukuri* mansion. They had no quarrel with nature. Indeed, to them it was no more than a reflection of their inner selves."[77]

### American Interest in Japan

An earlier fair, the Centennial Exhibition of 1876 at Philadelphia, had first introduced Americans to novel Japanese buildings. Interest in Japan was growing at the same time that the Great Camp style was evolving. Robert C. Pruyn, when twenty-nine years old, probably saw these earlier Japanese buildings at Philadelphia, perhaps visiting them with his father, ex-minister to Japan. Probably architect Robert Robertson saw these exotic pavilions as well, for his family was Philadelphian.

---

73 Saoin-in, Horyu-ji, image reversed. Minoru Ooka, *Temples of Nara and Their Art* (Tokyo: Weatherhill/Heibonsha, 1973), 172. The *irimoya* roof is mentioned in Chapter 4, footnote 14.

74 Seattle architect Kirtland Cutter designed the Idaho State Pavilion. Lucy Carnegie soon thereafter commissioned Cutter to design new structures at North Point, Raquette Lake, where Cutter employed the less rustic Swiss construction of squared logs, likewise used by Durant at Eagle's Nest. The Idaho pavilion was acclaimed in *The Dream City*, n.p. Henry Matthews presents the subject more fully in *Kirtland Cutter: Architect in the Land of Promise* (Seattle: University of Washington Press, 1998) 89-95 and elsewhere.

75 Tange in Ishimoto, 20.

76 A lower portion of roof on this and one other guest cabin was removed after construction to admit more light.

77 Tange in Ishimoto, 20, 23.

In decades following the Philadelphia fair, Japanesque oddities appeared improbably in the Adirondacks, such as Dr. Gerster's floating tea house on Raquette Lake and the Frederick Vanderbilts' pagoda on Upper St. Regis Lake.[78] While these were curiosities, more pervasive were the paper lanterns and fans, without which an Adirondack rustic interior would have been incomplete. The rage for things Japanese was not merely American; England likewise was entranced. Many a late-nineteenth-century camp retains not only fans and lanterns, but bamboo furniture and pieces of brown-and-white china with oriental motifs—Anglo-Japanese transfer ware imported in vast quantity from England. Similar designs appeared on wallpaper, book covers, lamps and elsewhere, the fad peaking in the 1880s.

Other Japanese precedents were well known by 1893. Popularity of Japanese decorative wares had stimulated interest in Japanese buildings. Books as well as magazine articles appeared, most notably *Japanese Homes and Their Surroundings* by Edward Morse, who "was the first to make a sustained effort to try to understand [Japanese architecture] from the Japanese viewpoint."[79] The popular work appeared in at least four editions, including eight or more printings prior to 1895.[80] Undoubtedly Robertson was familiar with the book. The national professional journal, *American Architect and Building News,* serialized a review in five issues, calling the Morse work " a noble and unique book [that presents] indigenous art absolutely free from affection [*sic*] or masquerade."[81]

Pruyn's sense of Japanese culture ran deeper than the Japanesque fashion of the period. He became a long-standing member of the Japan Society and collector of many Japanese works of art. We recall that Japanese scholar William Elliot Griffis thanked Robert Pruyn, who "first told me about the soul of Japan."[82]

The Pruyns' intent in building a remote villa, isolated in the wilderness was antithetical to the social motivation that attracted others to fashionable American resorts. The impulse for Santanoni was rather what the Japanese call *suki*, literally "taste" in the general sense, but more particularly "a way of life in which one abandoned everything except that which one liked and lived, 'supported by the wind and the moon.' It meant to retire to a hermitage where one could do whatever one pleased without being hindered by social obligations. . . . By outwardly adopting poverty one gained freedom from the vanity of aristocratic life. . . . To go and live in a little hut, away from everybody, was a lot to be envied by a king. What, indeed, could be more luxurious?"[83]

## Nature in East and West

More than decorative fashion linked Japan and the Adirondacks. "There are only two attitudes toward nature," observed a Japanese scholar. "One confronts it or one accepts it."[84] Another writer noted that "the difference between Japan and the West is between willing adaptation to and absorption in nature and a heroic attitude of seeking to breast and conquer it."[85]

---

78 Paul Malo, "Nippon in the North Country: Japanese Inspiration in Form and Philosophy," *Adirondack Life* 29, no. 7 (Collectors' Issue 1998-99): 50-55.

79 Edward S. Morse, *Japanese Homes and Their Surroundings* (Boston: Ticknor, 1886). A paperback edition was reprinted in 1961. The work was again reprinted (Rutland, Vt.: C.E. Tuttle, 1972). Morse's book was substantial, containing about 400 pages and 307 illustrations.

80 Lancaster, *Japanese Influence,* 66-67.

81 "The book proved to be the definitive study on Japanese residential architecture for at least three-quarters of a century." Lancaster, *Japanese Influence,* 68-9. During 1889 and subsequently *Scribners Magazine* presented articles by Sir Edwin Arnold, later published as the book *Japonica* (London: Osgood, McIlvaine, 1891). Rudyard Kipling had been writing articles about Japan since 1889, including four pieces about his 1892 trip.

82 The Japan Society was founded in 1907 at New York City. Lancaster, *Japanese Influence,* 263. Griffis, "A Forward of Dedication," n.p.

83 Tange in Ishimoto, 30.

84 Ito, 138.

85 Kenzo Tange, quoted by Charles Cleaver, *Japanese and Americans: Culture Parallels and Paradoxes* (Minneapolis: University of Minnesota Press, 1976), 66.

William Seward Webb, also a client of Robert H. Robertson, evidenced the latter of these opposing attitudes towards nature. The story of his building the Adirondack Railroad would be titled aptly *Conquering the Wilderness*.[86] Webb had Robertson build Forest Lodge at Nehasane Park as a very large, but otherwise conventional, suburban house (with little Japanese about it). Mown lawns surrounded the Shingle-style villa; the green carpet extended to a tidy but artificially edged lakeshore.

More intentionally harmonious with the wilderness had been several of the camps built earlier, during the 1880s, at Raquette and nearby Forked Lakes. These logs structures and their surroundings were less cultivated. Probably these campers of the late 1870s and early eighties were not yet conscious of their properties as landscape gardens in the Japanese manner, but Yorker appreciation of the wilderness was akin to Japanese reverence for nature—the Japanese close reading of nature as a sacred text.[87]

The Japanese arrangement of the Santanoni villa, with backswept wings comprised of separate buildings, provided an extended verandah. During rainy weather, the extensive porch provided a promenade 265 feet long—not in a monotonous straight line but, because of the stepped plan, broken into eight segments with varied outlooks, particularly fine from many external corners that provide encompassing views into the natural environment. Traverse of the verandahs reveals constantly shifting compositions, as slivers of lake appear and disappear through a colonnade of trees, the forest garden dappled with sunlight. The Santanoni villa becomes a veritable wilderness museum, a shrine to nature.

[86] Charles Howard Burnett, *Conquering the Wilderness: The Building of the Adirondack & St. Lawrence Railroad by William Seward Webb, 1891-92* (Norwood, Mass.: Plimpton Press, 1932). Charles was brother of Edward Burnett, farm design consultant at Santanoni Preserve.

[87] The aspect of nature in Japan is such as to influence the mind of the people to an extent but faintly realized by one born in a foreign land." Ballagh, 74.

The campaign begins, 1892–1893

##  5. The Main Camp 

Newcomb, August 8: Mr. Pruyer [*sic*] of Albany, President of the Newcomb Lake Reserve, is in town. Work is being rapidly pushed on the new buildings and ground [*sic*].

*The Essex County Republican, August 11, 1892*

When completed, the great log villa at Santanoni Preserve was considered a marvel, not merely for its ambition, but for its construction by local workmen with materials found at hand on the isolated estate. "The work was done almost entirely by men from the neighboring Adirondack villages."[1] Quarried on the site, native granite, "beautiful with its pockets of garnet, tourmaline and mica," was used for seven chimneys and nine fireplaces. Spruce trees of appropriate size were selected, felled from a large area, so that no major clearing was required. Robertson inserted the camp into the forest adroitly.

Between the preparation of drawings in the architect's Manhattan drafting room and realization of the great log villa deep in the wilderness there occurred a remarkable process, about which no record is available. Surely the busy architect did not supervise construction of the remote project, yet probably the size and complexity of the great lodge was beyond the capability of most local woodsmen to construct. The roof plan is formidable, even to an architect. There must have been a contractor or some intermediary between the architect and the craftsmen, someone who knew how to read the architect's complicated drawings and understood his design intentions.

That intermediary may, in fact, have been one or more other professionals. Architects

[1] This and following quotation from New York State Forest Commission, 178.

Van Wormer and Reynolds were on the site in July 1892 as construction was commencing.[2] Perhaps this was Albany architect Marcus T. Reynolds, who in 1892 was at the beginning of his career and who would do work for Robert Pruyn several years later. Robertson and Pruyn visited the work site in September, but throughout the construction period it may have been Reynolds and others who mostly supervised the project on the ground.[3]

Few architects or trained builders knew the woodsmen's skills, however, knowing for instance the season in which a spruce tree's sap flow would allow its bark to be removed most easily. Someone had to engage and organize a large work crew. More than 1,500 spruce trees were logged remote from the building site, in order to preserve its natural environs.[4] All end-trimming, limbing and saddle notching was done with hand tools, and done with such skill that after more than a century there is hardly a gap between log and notch wide enough in which to probe a pine needle. The lodge was carefully placed on the irregular terrain. The ground floors and surrounding porches are built on a single plane, about twenty feet above the lake's surface. The ground itself, however, slopes downward from north to south, resulting in virtually no crawl space under the northernmost cabin and a substantial space under the southernmost. The kitchen block has three stories because the ground slopes about ten feet from a lakeside ridge to the rear service area.

We remember the names and admire the accomplishment of architect and client, who collaborated on the remarkable project; but we are unable to know or adequately acknowledge the indispensable contribution of the local craftsmen who actually built the great log villa at Santanoni Preserve.

[2] Fred Kelley and Edward Pruyn, "Moose Lake Chronicle," July 1892, 3,4. Adirondack Museum Library.

[3] Pruyn and Robertson signed the guest register at the nearby Adirondack Club on September 1, 1892.

[4] New York State Forest Commission, 178.

## Design Features and Building Craft

It is difficult to connect logs end-to-end. If a building is to be larger than a simple cabin with four sides, it might require an exterior wall that is longer than the length of one log. Rather than butting logs end-to-end in a straight line, the wall may be broken into segments, arranged at right angles to each other. Some portions may project outward a short distance, offsetting the line of the wall for the length of a log, before returning to the original line. The bay-like projection on the exterior provides an alcove on the interior. Other segments of wall may turn inward rather than outward from the original line, forming recesses on the exterior, located where entry or sitting porches may be useful. Each turning of the wall allows typical notched-corner connection of logs, and the perpendicular segments of wall provide lateral bracing. Each of these corners requires labor-intensive notching of logs, so a complicated footprint of a large log structure entails costly construction. Well-built log buildings never were a bargain, even if trees supposedly were "free."

Alternately, where interior space is to be divided into several rooms, the partitions between them (if likewise built of logs) may brace the exterior wall, allowing it to continue unbroken for more than the length of a single log. If the notching method requires extension of log ends beyond the notch, in usual "log-cabin" manner, the projecting log ends appear (rather oddly) on the exterior, interrupting the continuous wall.[5] For this reason, designers usually prefer to adjust the plan at these points, breaking the exterior wall inward or outward.

[5] Although this arrangement is not familiar in the Adirondacks, the Stokes cabin at Upper St. Regis Lake provides an illustration. Mildred Phelps Stokes Hooker, *Camp Chronicles* (Blue Mountain Lake, N.Y.: Adirondack Museum, 1964), 30. At Santanoni, the side walls of the kitchen block are longer than a single log, but are neither broken in plan nor have such projecting ends of logs where the interior partitions brace the long exterior walls. How the exterior wall is tied to the interior partitions is not evident.

The kitchen block, left, is connected to five cabins by breezeways or "dog-trots," 1895.

Internal partitions of large log houses may be built of logs, not only for bracing purpose, but to provide matching wood surfaces on all sides of the rooms. Each room becomes virtually a separate log cabin, as in the "saddle bag" house type, where two log-walled rooms are covered by a single roof, but separated by a common chimney.[6] A variant is the "dog-trot" type, where two cabins are connected by the open "dog trot" or "breezeway" under the single roof. The main lodge at Santanoni Preserve is a combination of saddle-bag cabins linked by breezeways in the dog-trot manner, but with five rather than the usual two cabins under the single roof. The kitchen block is virtually a separate log building, linked only by a narrow, covered walk.

There are different explanations of how the particular plan for Santanoni originated. "It was my grandmother who devised the idea of a central building for kitchen, living room, and dining room, with an upstairs for both guests and over the kitchen servants—and cabins on both sides for sleeping." The family also credits Anna with "the idea of the cabins on a porch."[7] But by another report, "Mr. Pruyn had originally planned to have a group of separate log cabins [like Durant's Camp Pine Knot] but was persuaded to modify this idea by his architect. . . . The idea of separate cabins was maintained, but these were all tied together under one great rambling roof . . . ."[8] Robert Robertson probably had less

[6] Log compartments are technically "pens." The English term, "pen . . . represents an individual room," according to John B. Rehder, who provides an illustration of a dogtrot house, Fig. 6-8. "The Scotch-Irish and English in Appalachia," in Allen G. Noble, ed. *To Build in a New Land: Ethnic Landscapes in North America* (Baltimore: Johns Hopkins University Press, 1992), 105. Allen G. Noble also discusses and illustrates saddlebag and dog-trot houses. *Wood, Brick & Stone: The North American Settlement Landscape*, v. 1: Houses, (Amherst, Mass.: University of Massachusetts Press, 1984), 115-118. The main lodge at Durant's Camp Uncas, like the major buildings at Camps Fairview, Cedars, and Echo, mentioned previously, might be termed a "multi-pen" structure.

[7] Cynthia Pruyn Green, handwritten notes, August 1992.

[8] Guy H. Lee, 73.

familiarity with Japanese precedent than his client, and because many characteristics of Japanese practice appear at the log villa, it seems probable that this aspect may be attributable to Pruyn himself. Probably it was Anna who insisted on a woodland character. "Pains were taken to avoid city effects, and to make the place picturesque rather than elegant."[9]

A continuous verandah connected the five lakeside units, as well as the service wing to the rear. Large intervals between the solid blocks provided room-sized outdoor sitting areas under the great roof. "There is so much rain in the Adirondacks, and life indoors is so unnatural, that provision against confinement was made by adding 5,000 square feet of piazzas." There is about as much exterior porch space as there is interior space under the main camp roof.

Robertson employed at Santanoni the same technique of log construction that the Durant workmen had initially used at the Pine Knot chalet, the prototypical Great Camp. Saddle notches connect horizontal logs, laid with broken rather than continuous coursing. This was the typical log-cabin mode, but the log villa at Santanoni was more finely crafted than usual for the vernacular practice of the region. Very tight joints were chinked with oakum and lime, the latter made in pits near the boathouse.[10] Santanoni differed from Pine Knot and all other earlier work of the Adirondacks by being more refined; at Santanoni, bark was stripped from spruce logs, which were varnished.[11] While the log exterior was light in coloring for the first two decades, eventually the logs darkened. By 1929, writer Guy Lee recounted how "The walls [were] treated from time to time with crude Cabot's creosote without any coloring matter. In the course of years they have taken on a rich brown color shading to black where smoke has settled in the corners."[12] In Japan, "the houses, if of wood, are painted black; or else, as is more usually the case, the wood is left in its natural state and this gradually turns to a darker shade by exposure."[13]

The roof slope of the large, central gable at Santanoni may recall that of Durant's Pine Knot chalet, as does the decorative truss work inserted into the gable—a familiar Adirondack motif probably introduced by Durant, subsequently developed by other architects, most notably with virtuosity by Coulter at Knollwood Club (1899) on Lower Saranac Lake. The diagonal fret work is not so ornate or whimsical as is the gable adornment of many other camps. Less apparent than its Swiss or Adirondack character is the Japanese aspect of the central feature. Although employing a similar roof slope, the Japanese likewise inserted a screen in the gable, more generally made of wooden lattice. Unlike other Adirondack examples, the main gable of the Santanoni villa has a skirt of sloping roof extending across the bottom of the truss. This is not an alpine feature, but characterizes the Japanese *irimoya* roof.[14] This sort of gable appears

---

[9] This and the following quotation from New York State Forest Commission, 178, which added, "In the construction, every detail was studied with reference to insuring comfort and health. . . . A fine spring furnishes a constant water supply and enabled the architect to add a complete system of modern plumbing."

[10] Cynthia Pruyn Green, handwritten notes, August 1992. Guy Lee, 92, mentioned spruce logs. Joints were chinked with oakum. New York State Forest Commission, 178.

[11] In 1893 the camp's logs were "stripped of their bark, and caulked with oakum and deck varnish [*sic*] like a ship's deck." New York State Forest Commission, 178.

[12] Guy H. Lee, 92. In later years, pigmented oil was used regularly on the villa, which progressively darkened the logs. As a youngster, Newcomb resident Tom Dillon painted the buildings with "the recipe," linseed oil, turpentine and brown paint. Tom Dillon, interview by Robert Engel, handwritten notes, Santanoni Preserve, August 1991. Merle Melvin recalled having some exterior creosoting done on the Gate Lodge. J. Winthrop Aldrich, Memorandum to File, May 7, 1996, recording oral commentary of Merle D. Melvin. A former caretaker told Howard Kirschenbaum (about 1991) that he had applied creosote to the main camp for the Melvins.

[13] Morse, 51.

[14] The Japanese term, *irimoya,* refers to a combination roof form, with gable over hip. Robertson used it elsewhere, as at Forest Lodge and Keepawa Station at Nehasane Park, illustrated by Kaiser, 182, 187. Later Japanese builders employed this sort of roof for the boat shelter at Pine Tree Point. Kaiser, 125. At Santanoni, the decorative truss replaces the lattice traditional in the Japanese *irimoya* gable.

Katsura Imperial Villa with *irimoya* roof

Santanoni, the bird's beak with *irimoya* roofs

on the Old Shoin of the Katsura villa, which bears other similarities, mentioned previously. At both villas the great prow is the dominant exterior feature seen from the waterfront.

Typically the Great Camp, like the lumber camp, was a casual arrangement of small cabins, one reason being the constraints of log-construction. Santanoni, however, is not merely a forest campus of rustic cottages—even though the main villa is comprised virtually of independent structures—for here they cohere under one vast roof. The great roof is the dominant element of Japanese architecture.[15]

Comparison of roof and floor plans strikingly reveals a Japanese priority of roof, which at Santanoni is colossal, covering about sixteen-thousand square feet.[16] Its solid mass is particularly striking in contrast to the fragmented plan below.[17]

In contrast to the open verandahs on the lake side is the monumental solidity of the approach side. Massive log treasure houses of eighth-century Japan served as models for the tail of the bird at Santanoni, which recalls the *narabi-kura* (double storehouse) style.[18] Although utilitarian, the service wing was to be first seen on arrival, hence it warranted the architect's special attention. Representing the forked tail of the Phoenix, two striking log pavilions, raised on massive plinths, are lidded with hipped (or, in Japanese, *hogyo*) roofs, like Japanese farmers' hats—graced by eyebrow dormers that recall a Japanese roof form.[19] An open gallery, centered overhead by a larger, rectangular roof dormer linked the fortress-like corner masses.[20]

Very small panes of glass in all windows contrast in scale, emphasizing mass of the log

[15] Margaret Ballagh remarked, "The most imposing feature of a Japanese temple is the roof." Probably this was Bertie's impression on first seeing Zempukuji Temple.

[16] The combined area of the six buildings and porches measures 10,834 square feet according to 1971 appraisal data. Aldrich, Memorandum, 3. Of this, about five thousand square feet are covered verandah areas. New York State Forest Commission, 178. Large overhangs around the several hundred feet of perimeter account for larger area of roof.

[17] Gropius notes the Japanese taste for strong contrasts, as "against the light, transparent house construction, the heavy, sculptural roof." Gropius, in Ishimoto, 8.

[18] The *Shoso-in* of the Todai-ji monastery at Nara, as illustrated previously, similarly is tripartite in composition, with the main floor likewise raised above the ground. Massive end pavilions, each with a single opening, less massive connecting bay and hipped roof are recalled at Santanoni. The motif of paired log cabins appeared elsewhere, as at Toshodai-ji where the Treasure Repository and Sutra Repository are two distinct buildings, while at Horyo-ji the Kofu-zu is more like Santanoni, for one roof links two storehouses. Kakichi Suzuki, *Early Buddhist Architecture in Japan* (Tokyo: Kodansha, 1980), figs. 92, 111. It is not of log construction, however. The Shoso-in at Nara is said to be the only extant example of the double log-cabin repository. Minoru Ooka, *Temples of Nara and Their Art* (New York: Weatherhill/Heibonsha, 1973).

[19] This sort of secondary roof of double curvature was employed in the Momoyama and Tokugawa Periods. Sherman E. Lee, 461-4. The dormers are not original, as evidenced by the early photograph on the next page.

[20] An exterior flight of service stairs once gave access from ground to kitchen porch. In later years Crandall Melvin, Jr. removed the stairs for fear that his son might fall down them. J. Winthrop Aldrich, Memorandum to File, May 7 1996.

Arriving visitors passed along the massive walls of the kitchen block before disembarking

structure, while recalling Japanese *shoji* screens. A remarkable composition is crowned by a stone chimney at the apex of the roof. Although this is but the kitchen wing, the dark masses, highlighted by red windows, strike the arriving visitor as a powerful and memorable form—indeed, one of the most arresting images of Adirondack architecture.[21]

## The Interior

Within the six sections of the great log villa were at least twenty-four rooms, seven bathrooms, and nine fireplaces.

Opening onto the gabled prow was the lofty main "hall" (or "living-hall," as sometimes termed at the time) centered by a massive, freestanding stone chimney that incorporated back-to-back fireplaces. Like a tent pole, the granite chimney is the element that both anchors and supports the structure. Hewn cross beams rest on cut blocks that protrude high above the hearth. The masonry chimney was the first thing built and, if the wooden architecture were to burn, it would be the last thing standing. The dominance of the

[21] Santanoni's trim color of the late twentieth century has been called "Chinese red." While the oriental connotation seems appropriate, this color was not original. Sis Pruyn Thibault recalled that in the late 1920s "it was a quieter red, not so bright, soft and muted." Rob Engel reported that she remembered "the more muted red tone, more like the color of port [as] the original color of all the trim at both the Lodge and the Camp. This is now to be discerned underneath the roof of the arch [at the Gate Lodge], and you can see that it's very different from the very bright red found elsewhere." Beatrice Pruyn Thibault concurred, "—almost burgundy." Engel added, "Also, it should have a flat finish, not a shiny enamel like what seems to be on the trim now." Aldrich, 81-82. A paint analysis of the Gate Lodge for Adirondack Architectural Heritage by George Lyons in 1998 revealed the original color, indeed, to be the deeper, more muted red. This was the traditional color of trim for rustic log buildings of the Adirondacks. William West Durant apparently introduced the color at his Camp Pine Knot. The State applied the current bright red paint in the 1970s.

spine as a vertical element in a horizontal composition, as well as the symbolism of the primal hearth, would become recognized features of Frank Lloyd Wright's work in coming years.[22] He, too, would recognize the fireplace as the spiritual center from which home life radiated, and to which it eventually returned. The fire's warmth, sight and sound, and that of old friends, after a typical ten hours' sporting in a cold Adirondack drizzle, was the reward that rendered the day's discomfort acceptable.

According to family lore, Robert Pruyn engaged a stone carver to work a massive boulder into the mantelpiece. After working an entire summer, he showed the result to Mr. Pruyn, who decided he preferred the uncarved surface of the boulder. It was installed with the natural surface exposed; no one has seen the carving, hidden within the chimney, in more than a century.[23]

In this "free plan," as modern architects subsequently would call it, the central masonry element separated the hall into implied areas. The lake or front side of the great room was for lounging or, on occasion, for dancing. The opposite or rear portion was subdivided into two areas. The corner by the stairway served as the library and den and contained a round poker table with movable top.[24] The southeast corner became the dining area. A second fireplace opening in the back of the center chimney warmed these latter two spaces.

[22] Frank Lloyd Wright was an innovative architect but naturally absorbed many prevailing notions of his time. The fireplace was a feature of the entry (or "living") hall of large houses in the last decades of the nineteenth century.

[23] Sam Scranton, stepson of Frederic Pruyn, Jr., letter to J. Winthrop Aldrich, September 1992. Aldrich, 156.

[24] Susan Pruyn King owns the poker table.

In library and dining areas, original woven matting, recalling Japanese grass cloth, still covers the walls.

Broad multi-sash windows surround the living hall on three sides above continuous, cushioned window seats. These low, horizontal bands contrast with the pronounced verticality of the central chimney, which rises to a lofty ceiling, sixteen feet above the floor. On the lake side of the room, a second, higher range of similar windows extends across the front wall, through which late afternoon light angles downward across the space to highlight the granite chimney.

A detail of the main hall reveals inventive use of natural materials and fine quality of joinery. The branches that project from the vertical cedar logs served as brackets for curtain rods.

Wainscoting of small, split logs backed continuous seating around three sides of the sitting area. Running both vertically and diagonally, the rustic wainscoting forms a bold pattern some seven or eight feet in height. Upper portions of walls and the entire ceiling were clad with large sheets of birch bark, joints covered with half-log battens. The silvery birch bark, resembling Japanese rice paper, reflects light into shaded corners. The grid of half-saplings, applied as battens, recalls linear patterning of Japanese interiors, later adopted by Frank Lloyd Wright. Interior door lintels, made from unpeeled cedar logs, project in elevation two inches beyond the supporting members, a device that recalls familiar Japanese forms such as the *torii* gate. Throughout, natural materials were selected, finished, and arranged to attain a refined rather than primitive character—more characteristic of the Japanese teahouse than the Adirondack log cabin. A Zen-like minimalism attains refinement rather than quaintness, like a Japanese *Sumi-e* painting, where a few brush strokes suggest much. Although the interior, like the exterior, was not intended to replicate those of houses on the other side of the world, references to Japan are consistent throughout.

Ascending from the dining and library area is a fine stairway that evidences Robertson's artistry with detail. The design also evidences the Japanese quality of *shibui*, or artfully elegant simplicity. It is not "rustic" in the same sense (*wabi*) as a remarkable stairway at the Walter Hochschilds' Eagle Nest, where tree stumps serve as balusters—or as the grand flight of steps rising to the great hall at Mrs. Post's Camp Topridge, framed with an agony of contorted roots and branches (very wabi). Rather, at Santanoni, neat tree trunks and saplings were carefully selected with the converse intention, to be without irregularity. Matched, peeled and polished, they become natural, but disciplined balusters. The subtle rusticity is akin to that of Japanese rustic furniture, more refined than most American rustic work.[25]

Robertson invented an artful screen containing the stairs, to imply separation from the great hall. The permeable plane preserves the definition of the main space while it provides

[25] *An Example of Japanese Villa (Mountain Villa of Baron Kita-Mitsui)* (Tokyo: Meiji Shobo, [1936]).

visibility of the stairs in an alcove. The architect wanted to have it both ways; attainment of this sort of multiple readings is a measure of architectural skill. Although the arrangement is simple and natural, Robertson adroitly provided spatial enrichment of three receding planes. The foreground plane serves primarily as semi-transparent wall of the room, only incidentally as stair railing. An ingenious and deft move reinforced this perception; Robertson extended the screen, flipping upside-down that portion that serves as stair railing, transforming it into a spindled transom over the entry to the stairwell—a device the Japanese called a *rama*.

Difference in diameter of two main posts evidences the thoughtful subtlety of the design. A lesser architect might have routinely made both posts the same size. Hierarchically they are different, however, for one is more important. The large post terminates the stair and marks the portal to the stair well, whereas the other post is merely part of the stair itself. The window sash enhances the Japanese quality, for the tiny panes of glass, set in a web of muntins, create a lattice effect, recalling the paper *shoji* screens of the Japanese house, as does placement of the windows, at different heights. At the time, double-hung windows sometimes were glazed with small panes, but here more distinctive casement sashes were employed for a more Japanese effect.[26] The stairs lead to two large, guest bedrooms and a bathroom. When the weather was cool and the second floor bedrooms unoccupied, material was unrolled across the stairwell to prevent heat from escaping up the stairs. A large, canvas-backed map of the Adirondacks may have served this purpose.[27]

Near the foot of the stairs, leaving the dining area, there is a door that leads into a foyer between the butler's pantry and a large, lead-lined cistern. Piped from its hillside spring half a mile across Newcomb Lake, drinking and cooking water trickled year-round so that it would not freeze, thus providing a winter supply.[28] "We got a big bang out of it because we would go in the kitchen and the water would just be running all the time."[29]

A local craftsman forged iron door hardware, probably in the blacksmith shop on the estate.[30] Wrought iron andirons and fireplace

[26] The small-paned, double-hung window characterized the "Queen Anne" style. H. H. Richardson used similar windows on his Shingle-style houses, as did many architects of the last three decades of the nineteenth century. Rarely were casement sash employed, however. Probably Pruyn and Robertson preferred the vertical proportions because they recalled the *shoji* panels of Japan.

[27] Verbal recollection of a family member to Robert Engel. Susan Pruyn King retains such a very large map from Santanoni.

[28] Beatrice Pruyn Thibault. Aldrich, 35. "There probably is an unlocated second cistern at a higher elevation . . . to make the system work. . . ." There was also an attic gravity tank, filled by automatic electric pump. Aldrich, Memorandum. The spring was mentioned previously, in Chapter 3, "Natural Features."

[29] John Thibault. Aldrich, 101.

[30] A blacksmith shop would be used to shoe horses as well as to forge hardware.

tools from the main camp are now at the Adirondack Museum.[31]

The decor, like the architecture, was not intentionally Oriental in overall character, but reflected the Pruyns' taste for Japanese arts and crafts, some collected during young Robert's sojourn abroad. Perhaps refined Japanese decorative objects seem incongruous in a rustic Adirondack lodge; conspicuous were a three-panel standing screen between dining and library areas, an enormous, floor-standing ceramic vase, and a smaller porcelain vase on the mantelpiece.[32] "Oddly contrived book cases, ingeniously placed in all unoccupied nooks and corners," recalled irregular, staggered Japanese shelves artfully arranged in an alcove, a central feature of villa interiors.[33] On a felt-covered card table might be found a fine chess set with Japanese figures.[34]

Decor was eclectic, however, as was often the case in Adirondack camps. Much furniture was considered by the family to be "department-store type—nothing extra except the walnut wardrobes, which were cabinet quality."[35] "My family never had any of that custom-made rustic furniture in here. It was chiefly Department Store cheap—my Grandmother was that way."[36] Today the Pruyns' mission oak pieces from the early twentieth century might be appreciated more. Many camps have museum-quality Stickley pieces.

Floor and table lamps with pleated and fringed shades lighted the spaces. On the mantel, with the Japanese ceramic vase, was a tall, stuffed great blue heron. A large brass telescope served to seek distant canoeists. A bronze bust of "Chief Black Bird - Ogallala Souix" [*sic*] and two Native American bowls lent a cosmopolitan note.[37] A Chippendale-style wall-clock hung among mounted game heads and paper silhouettes of choice trout.[38] For the fireplace, the caretaker "made these beautiful 'fans' of cedar kindling wood by working them with small hatchet or other tool so they had curlicues on the end."[39]

On the north side of the chimney was an Albany-made Marshall & Wendell oak piano, shipped by sleigh in time for the first spring party. Huybertie Pruyn wrote: "I often think of the evenings in the big living room with the huge logs burning so cheerily, and Uncle Neddy [Bowditch] standing at the piano."[40]

Behind the central cabin of the log villa, connected by a short, covered walkway, is a virtually independent, three-story building, itself larger than most Adirondack camps. It housed the kitchen (where one of three enormous stoves still remains), a staff dining room, and ancillary rooms on the main level: wine storage, wood cellar, tackle room, two pantries and linen room.[41] The porch at the rear of the main level originally was connected to the ground by an exterior flight of wide steps, on the east side, along the wall. Below, in a mostly-open-air basement, was originally a large, walk-in cooler, "a Wickes' refrigerating room." On the top floor were seven staff bedrooms and bathroom.[42]

---

[31] Accession Record, Numbers L7. 1988. 1a-c and 2 a-d, Descriptors HF 190, Adirondack Museum.

[32] Susan Pruyn King now owns the enormous Japanese ceramic vase, where Beatrice Pruyn Thibault once hid liquor bottles from her father, a problem drinker. Frederic Pruyn's alcoholism is mentioned in Chapter 8.

[33] The alcove in Japanese is called a *tokonoma*, the shelves *chigaidana*. Quotation is from "Bits of Fact and Fiction For All," Pruyn albums, Adirondack Museum Library.

[34] Beatrice Pruyn Thibault had her grandfather's chess set, which she showed Paul Malo at her home in Clayton, New York.

[35] Cynthia Pruyn Green, handwritten notes, August 1992.

[36] Cynthia Pruyn Green. Aldrich, 118.

[37] Susan Pruyn King, Aldrich, 33, and notes on manuscript. "The bust was by A.J. Weinmann, who did the 'Buffalo' nickel."

[38] "Record of Fish. . .," entry for November 2, 1917. Hamlin, "Four Spring Parties," 5.

[39] Cynthia Pruyn Green. Aldrich, 90. This practice was often employed at well-staffed Adirondack camps.

[40] Hamlin, "Four Spring Parties," 7.

[41] These ancillary rooms were listed in "Santanoni Preserve," undated typescript, Bank Records. There were two wood-burning stoves and, in later years, one gas stove, "a giant restaurant-sized Vulcan." Susan Pruyn King. Aldrich, 35.

[42] Beatrice Pruyn Thibault remembered that the lower level served as the wine cellar and for storage of maple syrup and other items. Aldrich, 148. The New York State Forest Commission, 17, called the cooler a "Wickes' refrigeration room" and said the upstairs bedrooms were "guides and servants quarters [with] accommodation for eight or ten servants."

Even at Great Camps, much family life gravitated to the back door (here the kitchen steps).

Flanking the central cabin in a symmetrical, setback pattern are four one-story dependencies, again virtually independent, but here linked under the huge roof. They were primarily sleeping cabins. The southernmost cabin had two bedrooms, each with fireplace and adjoining bathroom. The two cabins on either side of the main hall each had two bedrooms, two fireplaces sharing a common chimney, and a shared bathroom. The northernmost cabin had a large bedroom with fireplace, plus bathroom. With the two bedrooms above the central cabin, family and guest sleeping rooms in the main complex totaled nine. On some occasions cabins might be used as bedroom-sitting room combinations.

Cast iron "back-breaker beds" (recalled with little nostalgia) had "no good springs." Family and guests "slept on very simple metal bedsteads with horsehair mattresses."[43] But, in Adirondack style, beds were covered with Hudson Bay blankets, bright red with black stripe at the top. Linens were embroidered with the camp name.[44] Bathrooms had cast iron tubs, plus bowls and pitchers on wood wash stands.[45] Hot water originally was hand carried by staff to the bathrooms as required.

The southernmost sleeping cabin was dubbed "Scylla" and the northernmost, "Charybdis." In Greek mythology, Scylla is a sea monster and Charybdis a whirlpool. To be caught between the two meant that escape from one would only incur peril from the other. In the early years at Santanoni, the boys stayed in Charybdis and the girls in Scylla.[46] The message was clear. When the nest was empty, Robert and Anna Pruyn moved into Scylla, the cabin closest to the boathouse and lake. One room was their bedroom, the other their sitting room. It became their private camp within a camp; they added a separate porch on the south side, with its own stairway.[47]

---

43 Susan Pruyn King. Aldrich, 84.

44 In addition, "At the [Gate] Lodge there were linens with embroidery . . . that said 'The Lodge'." Susan Pruyn King. Aldrich, 17.

45 M. Lee Pruyn, letter to Charles A. Ten Eyck, August 6, 1953; Cynthia Pruyn Green, handwritten notes, August 1992.

46 Hamlin, "Four Spring Parties," 5.

47 Cynthia Pruyn Green, Aldrich, 108. Years later, one of the bathrooms was removed and a small kitchenette installed.

The Studio

## The Main Camp Compound

Nearby, augmenting the main lodge, were the studio, boathouse, and at least eight other buildings that comprised the camp compound at the east end of Newcomb Lake.

The studio, sometimes referred to as the "Artist's Studio," contains one large room with a stone fireplace. It was built a few feet from the shoreline some hundred-and-fifty feet north of the main lodge. The studio has been attributed to New York City architects Delano & Aldrich and was constructed no later than 1904.[48] Its grand, stone arch on the lake side related the studio to two other Delano & Aldrich buildings at Santanoni that also featured stone arches, both built in 1904–05. The large arched window overlooks the lake. Its large panes of glass, divided with a few metal mullions, is strikingly different in character from the tiny panes set in a lattice of wood muntins employed by Robertson—and as well by Delano & Aldrich—elsewhere at Santanoni.

The studio possibly was built about the same time as the log villa, for its log construction is similar, and the window treatment on the southeast elevation resembles Robertson's earlier work.[49] Moreover, the interior walls, with Japanese style rush matting (still partially intact today), are similar to portions of wall in the dining area of the main lodge.

If the studio was original, Delano & Aldrich probably added the lakeside stone arch with its different fenestration (although it is possible that the studio arch was original and became the model adopted by the later architects for other buildings on the estate). In any case, the window design is the most dramatic feature of the building whether viewed from

[48] Aldrich, 183. A winter photograph dated March 1905 in the Pruyn collection clearly shows the present building with stone-arched window.

[49] The logs are smaller, the hardware is different, and the notching is less finely crafted than seen on the villa. The studio is not mentioned in early accounts, when son Edward was young. On the other hand, the symmetry of the two flanking buildings, studio and boathouse, recalling ancillary structures at Katsura, suggests an architectural intent from the outset.

inside or lake side. The building is striking when viewed from the lake.

The different lakeside window arrangement probably represents the preference of the client, given the use of this particular structure. The Pruyns' son Edward was an artist who used the building for half a century. A considerable degree of northern light, high ceilings, and beautiful view made the building a fine studio for the artist.[50]

The mate to the studio, flanking the villa on the opposite side, was the boathouse. Also constructed of logs, it was a large, hipped-roof pavilion with two wide slips for boats to enter while in the water, and a broad, wooden ramp, for small skiffs and canoes to be hauled out of the water. While large, plank doors provided access for carrying boats in and out, the side door and windows were characteristic of the small-paned fenestration of the main camp.

The Pruyns never had a motor boat—testimony to their conservative taste—but there were many other kinds of boats in the three boathouses at Newcomb Lake, Harris Lake and Moose Pond. At one time there were eleven guide boats, seven canoes and two magnificent sailing canoes, the "Wanderer" and the "Idler," both now at the Adirondack Museum. The fleet also included "Grandmother's two unsinkable jobs," flat-bottom rowboats.[51]

Little Minister, the tiny island a short distance off shore, creates a narrow inlet and shelteres the boathouse. Two enormous floating pine logs, connected by smaller log braces, were positioned between island and shore as a breakwater. By the boathouse remains a pit lined with masonry, believed to have been used to fire brick which lined the fireplaces, or to make lime for mortar.[52]

The Boathouse

[50] Edward began studying art right after leaving Harvard around 1896. Susan Pruyn King, notes on manuscript. If he was old enough to engineer Santanoni roads in the 90s, as Guy Lee asserts, Ned may have been old enough for a studio, which also may have been his drafting room when working on Santanoni road improvements.

[51] Helen Tummins recalled the inventory, interviewed by Robert Engel, Newcomb, New York, July 1991. Cynthia Pruyn Green recalled grandmother's boats. Aldrich, 103. Susan Pruyn King has some of the other boats, as well as a cedar Rushton canoe. Aldrich, 34.

[52] Susan Pruyn King. Aldrich, 106. Cynthia Pruyn Green thought lime rather than brick was fired in the pits, of which there had been more than one. Aldrich, 107.

A red-painted, cedar post-and-screen structure stands on an isolated knoll about twenty paces north of the main camp. It recalls a "little screen house on the way to my father's studio. . . . I was always told it was Aunt Ruth's screen house but we never went up there. So she could sit in the woods without being bothered by bugs."[53] Three nieces of Ruth Pruyn, visiting Santanoni together after many years, still expressed foreboding at approaching "Aunt Ruth's gazebo," unaware that the modern pavilion was a reconstruction of their formidable aunt's retreat.[54]

A few feet from the kitchen block is a small, concrete building with shingle siding, built about 1935, used to house a new generator. The main camp never had outside electrical service, but by the late 1930s electricity generated by a Kohler Plant illuminated many buildings.[55] A granddaughter recalled, "After Grandfather died, Dad [Frederic Pruyn] wanted Grandy [Grandmother Anna] to have electricity, so he put it in. She brought her conveniences to camp, including a toaster. The butler would put in a slice of bread. For one piece, the engine would turn over and grind away, burning up gallons of gas which Art [Tummins] had to tote in from the village." "It made a lot of racket, so it would come on only every so often."[56] The Kohler plant sent electricity through a six-fuse box located in the butler's pantry, indicating enough output for a few light bulbs per camp building—and a toaster. None of the staff houses had electricity.[57]

There is also a shingled pump house on the lake shore that still contains a Gould pump.[58] The pump turned on when water in the attic tank fell below a set level and drew lake water for washing, toilets and fire protection.

Directly behind the kitchen block are the ruins of an unpeeled-log icehouse and behind that a deteriorating, stone "ash house" or "oil house" used to store fuel for kerosene lamps and later the generator.[59] Next to that are the larger ruins of a building used as a storehouse and shop.[60] An earlier wood shed has long since disappeared.[61]

The camp's beach is less than a quarter-mile from the main lodge, north of the studio. The bathhouses there, still existing, have four changing rooms.[62]

## The Service Complex

About a quarter mile from the main camp compound, just across the bridge separating the main part of Newcomb Lake from the Duck Hole, the Pruyns built a substantial caretaking complex to serve the needs of the main camp and the growing estate. Located

---

53 Aldrich, 8.

54 Robert Engel, "A History of Camp Santanoni," 56. The screened pavilion extant today is not Ruth Pruyn's original pavilion; that gazebo apparently disappeared prior to the Jantz or National Register inventory. Otto Jantz. Appraisal, 1934, typescript. Raymond W. Smith and Richard C. Youngken. National Register of Historic Places Inventory-Nomination Form, 1986. The existing screen house was constructed (or possibly reconstructed) by Crandall Melvin, Jr. as a playhouse for his son. Aldrich, 126-127; Aldrich, Memorandum.

55 Beatrice Pruyn Thibault, July 1992. See also Aldrich, 49. Ethel Bissell recalled, probably from conversation with Art Tummins, that R. C. Pruyn bought a 5,000-kilowatt generator at Old Forge, N.Y. in 1928, identical to that used by Admiral Byrd at the South Pole. It served until 1967 or '68, when the Melvins installed a new plant. Aldrich, 158.

56 Cynthia Pruyn Green. Aldrich, 114.

57 Notes, Aldrich, 183.

58 The journal "Record of Fish and of Some Other Things" mentions the pump house in a May 1912 entry. The remaining pump may not be the original.

59 It was identified by Smith and Youngken as an "ash house" for the National Register nomination in 1987. Smoldering embers may have been stored there for fire protection and ashes possibly collected to make lye for soap. Otto Jantz called the building "the oil house". Appraisal, 1934, typescript. Susan Pruyn King recalls kerosene stored there in the late 1940s. Notes on manuscript, January 1999.

60 This was the "original boat house" on the National Register nomination. It may have been the boathouse from the nearby service complex, moved in later years to this location. Cynthia Pruyn Green remembers it from the 1920s as a staff retreat. "I never went in it, that was the servants' private space." Cynthia Pruyn Green, September 1992. Susan Pruyn King, 1992, remembers the same building from the 1940s and '50s as a storage shed. Howard Kirschenbaum examined it in the early 1980s, just before it collapsed, and it was clearly a workshop.

61 Identified in the 1936 inventory, it had disappeared by the time of National Register nomination in 1986.

62 Beatrice Pruyn Thibault, Aldrich, 46.

adjacent to the southern end of Newcomb Lake, the service complex was situated along the public road from Newcomb to Tahawus. During his first few years of ownership, Pruyn developed this site while he endeavored to attain exclusive rights to the road and adjoining properties. Probably the group of service buildings was substantially complete by the end of the century.

None of the buildings and only two foundations at this site remain today, making it difficult to establish the plan and evolution of the service complex with certainty. But with a combination of early photographs, maps, building inventories, and interviews with staff families, a reasonably reliable picture of the compound emerges.[63]

After crossing the Duck Hole bridge from the main camp, immediately to the left along the Duck Hole lake shore was a building that has been described as an icehouse.[64] The foundation, still visible, appears divided into two sections.

Coming uphill from the bridge, the first building on the right was a staff residence. Initially, it would have housed the preserve's head caretaker and his family. Described in successive years as "Bissell's House," "Old Caretaker's House," "Guide's House," "large caretaker house," and "staff boarding house," the two-story building contained twelve rooms, two baths and a cellar.[65] Like other buildings of the lakeside service complex, the caretaker's home was clad with "dark-stained shingles, with dark red trim."[66] A small laundry building was located adjacent to the caretaker's house.

The next building on the right had an unusual evolution. Initially, in 1893, it was a simple, rectangular stable with single, steeply-pitched gable roof. Before the turn of the century, Pruyn engaged Edward Burnett to expand the building into a larger, more versatile barn. Burnett was a leading farm designer of the period who would soon come to play a major role in Santanoni's development. If the original rectangular building was about 20x30 feet, as judged from photographs, plans for the new building show its length extended to fifty feet. With large, double, sliding doors on ei-

Caretaker's House

Wagon Barn and Stable

[63] Sources include Pruyn photograph collection, Adirondack Museum; Fisher and Bryant's "Topographic Map of Santanoni Preserve," 1910; Dunham and Schuyler family photographs from around 1928; "Santanoni Preserve, Newcomb, Essex County, New York." Typescript. Undated, but post 1925; "Santanoni Preserve: Approximately 12,500 acres. . . [etc.]. Typescript, 2 pp. Undated, but 1953, as it contains "Auction Details"; David Garrison, "Former resident recalls life in area preserve." (Helen Tummins Interview). *Post-Star*, December 1, 1987; Interviews and notes in Aldrich, 25, 178-9, and other references following.

[64] Fisher and Bryant's map shows a "Spring House." Madeline Dunham Covert identified foundations at the Duck Hole as those of the icehouse, which is consistent with the 1934 inventory. Interview with Robert Engel, Aldrich, 172.

[65] "Bissell," the name of an old Newcomb family, is probably the difficult-to-read name on the 1910 map. On the back of a Dunham family photograph, it was called the "way-in house," meaning way in from the entrance to the Preserve.

[66] Cynthia Pruyn Green, Aldrich, 26.

ther end, the long open area had ample room for carriages and wagons. A new 17x48-foot wing was added for the stable, containing seven horse stalls on the first floor and a hay-loft above.[67] Its two gables facing south, with rooflines perpendicular to the original roof-line, and cupola added architectural interest.

The building was described successively as a "barn," "stables," "large horse, barn and carriage house," "large horse/wagon barn," and "horse barn." Susan Pruyn King re-membered as a little girl in the late 1940s pulling the old carriages out and playing with them.[68] In a 1953 inventory, the building was described as a "3-car garage" with "stable and 6 stalls," carriage storage having given way to automobiles.[69] There was also a sub-stantial addition on the lake side of the build-ing, looming two full stories high above a basement level.[70]

Garage

Still farther from the Duck Hole bridge, another building was located beyond the barn on the right side of the road. It may have originally served as a carriage house when the barn was primarily used as a stable, but from 1910 on it was consistently referred to as the "garage." It would have stored the Pruyns' Lincoln limousine and other vehicles.[71] As the 1928 photograph suggests, this large building may have served other purposes as well, per-haps as additional staff quarters, accounting for the porch.

Beyond the garage, still on the lake side of the road, another staff residence was described over the years as "Lodge," "Chauffeur," "cottage for help," "2-story Chauffeur's House" with nine rooms, bath and cellar, "Chauffeur's House" and possibly "Team-ster's Home" with three bedrooms. The building appears in an undated but early Pruyn family photograph of a handsome, shingle-sided dwelling labeled "Stable-men's house at camp."[72] Stablemen of the early years would be replaced by the Pruyns' chauf-feur(s).

Chauffeur's House

Apparently there were other service buildings (or versions of these structures) at different times.[73] There was a boathouse at the service complex. It may have been moved at some point to become the storage building-workshop at the main camp. The foundations remain.

[67] Untitled, undated, unsigned plans, Adirondack Architectural Heritage archive.

[68] Susan Pruyn King, Aldrich, 26, and e-mail to Howard Kirschenbaum, May 9, 1999.

[69] The adjacent garage may have disappeared by 1953.

[70] The use of this portion of the building is unknown. but may have provided additional staff quarters. The design may have been by Burnett, for the addition appeared in a photograph dated 1901.

[71] Madeline Dunham Covert, interview with Robert Engel, and "Notes," Aldrich, 178-9, 184.

[72] A photograph of the same building was identified as the "Chauffeur's House," "Newcomb, New York in the Adiron-dacks," brochure No. 43030, 2/50 (New York: Previews), n.p.

[73] The succession of building inventories suggests that these par-ticular versions of structures may not have been present si-multaneously.

When completed, the main camp compound and service complex comprised an enclave of some twenty structures along the lakeshore. There were nine bedrooms for family and guests and at least fifteen for staff, spread over a half-mile—the Adirondack version of the English country house. The log villa at Santanoni Preserve became the centerpiece of a truly Great Camp, at the time alone in a class with Durant's Camp Pine Knot. Soon these two estates were joined by a third and fourth Great Camp, Webb's Nehasane and Durant's Uncas, and then many more. By the end of the nineteenth century luxurious Adirondack camps were becoming familiar possessions of wealthy families.

As large camps and estates proliferated around the region, Santanoni continued to expand. The first decade of Santanoni's development was centered on Newcomb Lake. The second decade saw Camp Santanoni enlarged to include two more, grand building complexes, reaching almost five miles back toward the outskirts of Newcomb village.

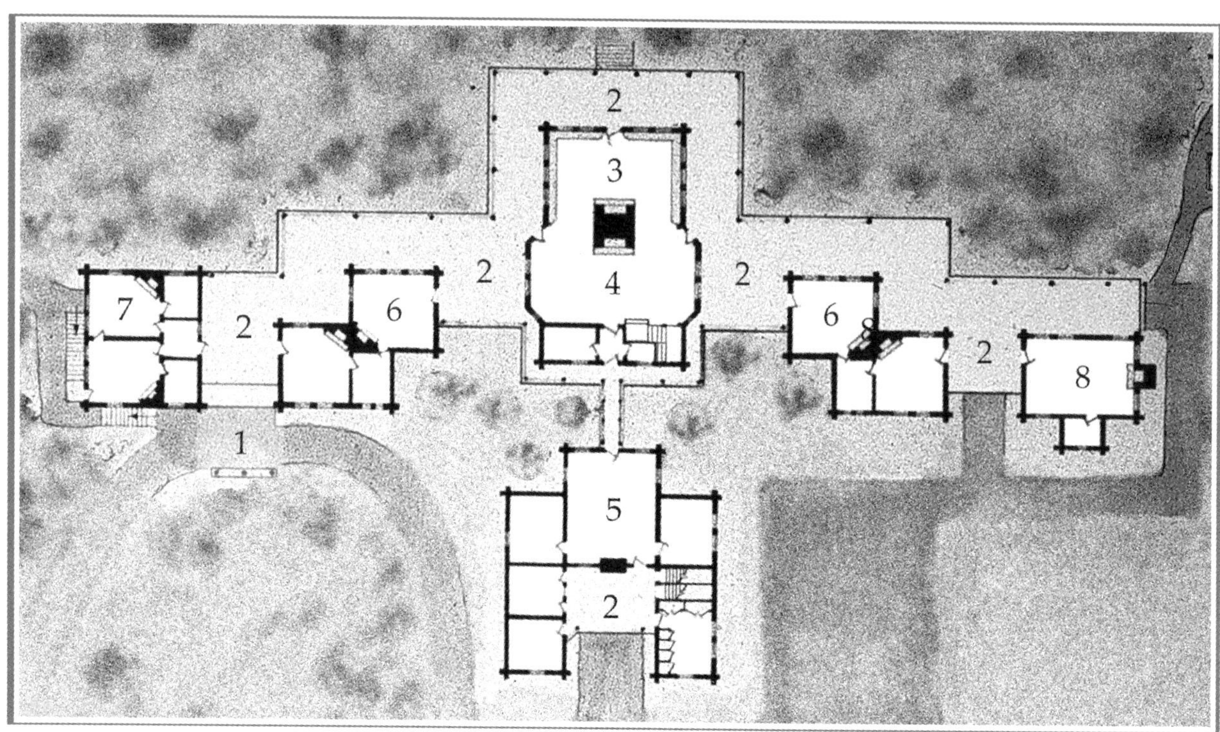


Santanoni Villa, Main Floor Plan

1. Entry drive with porte cochère
2. Verandahs
3. Main Hall
4. Dining and Library Area
5. Kitchen
6. Guest Cabins
7. "Scylla," later the owners' apartment
8. "Charybdis," the bachelors' cabin

A portion of the farm complex, looking southward across the upper Hudson River valley toward Vanderwhacker Mountain.

# 6. The Farm and Gate Lodge

The farmer, it was believed, was the uniquely ideal republican type.

*Tamara Plakins Thornton*

In addition to assembling almost thirteen thousand acres near Newcomb and building a major country house in the woods, Robert C. Pruyn established a rural manor, containing a model agricultural facility and an impressive entrance complex. By 1915 he was able to write, "There are about forty buildings on the preserve, large and small, and they are mostly designed by eminent architects."[1]

Some twenty of those buildings were arranged in the two compounds previously described—the main camp and the service complex on Newcomb Lake. When Pruyn and Robertson developed the Newcomb Lake facilities, however, Pruyn did not own all the property between the lake and the hamlet of Newcomb. It took several more years for him to secure the land and exclusive right-of-way along the entry road. Thus the four building complexes evolved in reverse order from the way one approaches them today. Completion required some fifteen years. When finished, all four areas were arrayed along the almost-five miles of entry road through the forest: the Gate Lodge complex, the farm, the lake-side service complex, and finally the main camp compound.

## Santanoni Farm

From their first conversations about building at Newcomb Lake, Pruyn and Robertson must have recognized that a farm would be needed for the remote camp to succeed. While trout and venison were to become staples, a stew needs onions and potatoes, and cakes require

[1] [Robert C. Pruyn,] "Santanoni Preserve, Adirondack Mountains," typescript, May, 1915. A 1934 inventory and appraisal identified forty-three structures. Otto Jantz, Appraiser.

milk and eggs. In less remote locations, such provisions could be imported from nearby farms, but in the central Adirondacks then, there were no farms nearby that could reliably be counted on to supply the new camp with ample and safe dairy products and produce. In fact farming in this part of the Adirondacks, undertaken by hearty settlers earlier in the century, had all but disappeared, as one family after another gave up trying to secure a living out of the unforgiving climate and unresponsive soil.[2] When Pruyn pieced together his large preserve, a number of the parcels contained old abandoned farms or ruins, testifying to the futility of Adirondack agriculture.[3] Local residents recalled that Pruyn had some of these old structures moved when he bought the preserve.[4]

Wesley Haynes, in his consultant's report on Santanoni's farm (a report virtually as large as this book) reconstructed the development and operation of the farm in great detail. He speculated that one old farmhouse, dating from the mid-nineteenth century, still remained along the entry road when Pruyn made his initial purchase.[5] Pruyn did not yet own this farmhouse, however. Huybertie Pruyn remembered how at the house-warming party of 1893, "everyone poured their own tea or coffee or milk, for even at that early date there were cows browsing on the stump lands—the farm was developed later."[6] Due to the preserve's remoteness, by another account, "even milk was unprocurable, and so the first season Mr. Pruyn bought a cow, and from that cow . . . the present farm, complete in every detail, has developed."[7] According to the Annual Report of the Forest Commission, describing Santanoni in 1893, "small clearings, hidden in the woods, furnish a supply of vegetables, and pasturage for cows."[8] Apparently farming that first year or two was a makeshift affair, located around the Newcomb Lake facilities in the wake of construction.

Once the main camp was finished and the lakeside service complex well along, Pruyn could turn his attention to developing a real farm, without which a gentleman's estate would be incomplete. His first step was to procure the property for the farm, which was not included in the original purchase around Newcomb Lake. Three acquisitions in September 1894 transferred about 300 acres in Lots 12 and 13 to his control.[9] These properties included the old farmstead along the entrance road, located about three-and-a-half miles from the main camp and one-and-a-half miles from the Newcomb hamlet. It was a south-facing, sloping site overlooking a large, open marshy area, with a view of surrounding mountains. While he may have begun rehabilitating the old farmhouse (map #7), serious work on the farm awaited one more purchase—a twenty-five acre parcel across the road from the farmhouse. This was acquired

[2] The New York State Forestry Commission's *Report* for 1885 described how "All attempts at settlement on the Adirondack plateau by an agricultural population . . . have resulted in disastrous failure. Abandoned homes and fields are scattered everywhere along the borders of the forest, while the scanty population which still struggles to compel the inhospitable soil to yield its miserable existence too plainly shows the hopelessness of the task." Assembly Document 36, Albany: Weed Parsons, 1885. Quoted by Wesley Haynes, "Farm Complex: Santanoni Preserve, Newcomb, New York: Historic Structure Report," prepared for Adirondack Architectural Heritage, 1996, 32.

[3] "The base survey of the property commissioned by Robert C. Pruyn in 1892 suggests the presence of several unidentified buildings along the route of the present road, located in parcels 12, 13 and 24 in Township 27, where Pruyn established his farm complex around 1895." Haynes, "Farm Complex," 18. Helen Tummins, who lived at Santanoni from the 1930s-70s, recalled seeing a number of cellar holes and ruins of abandoned farms on the preserve. H. Bond, "Notes Taken During a Trip Into Santanoni on July 29, 1986." Typescript, 1988, NYSDEC. Deeds to Robert C. Pruyn refer to extant farmhouses.

[4] Haynes, "Farm Complex," 18.

[5] Haynes, "Farm Complex," 137. This is based on Haynes' physical inspection of one of the extant farm houses (later called the "Old Farm House") as well as on an 1892 surveyor's plat of the preserve on which "what appears to be a building is indicated near the farm complex." Haynes, "Farm Complex," 33.

[6] Huybertie Pruyn Hamlin, "Four Spring Parties," 7.

[7] Guy H. Lee, 71-72.

[8] NYS Forest Commission *Annual Report*.

[9] Ward parcel, Essex County Grantee Book 107, Page 184. Cox parcel, Book 107, Page 185. Anderson and Moynehan parcel, Book 107, Page 585.

Barns and Creamery from New Farm House, *The Sportsman*, 1929

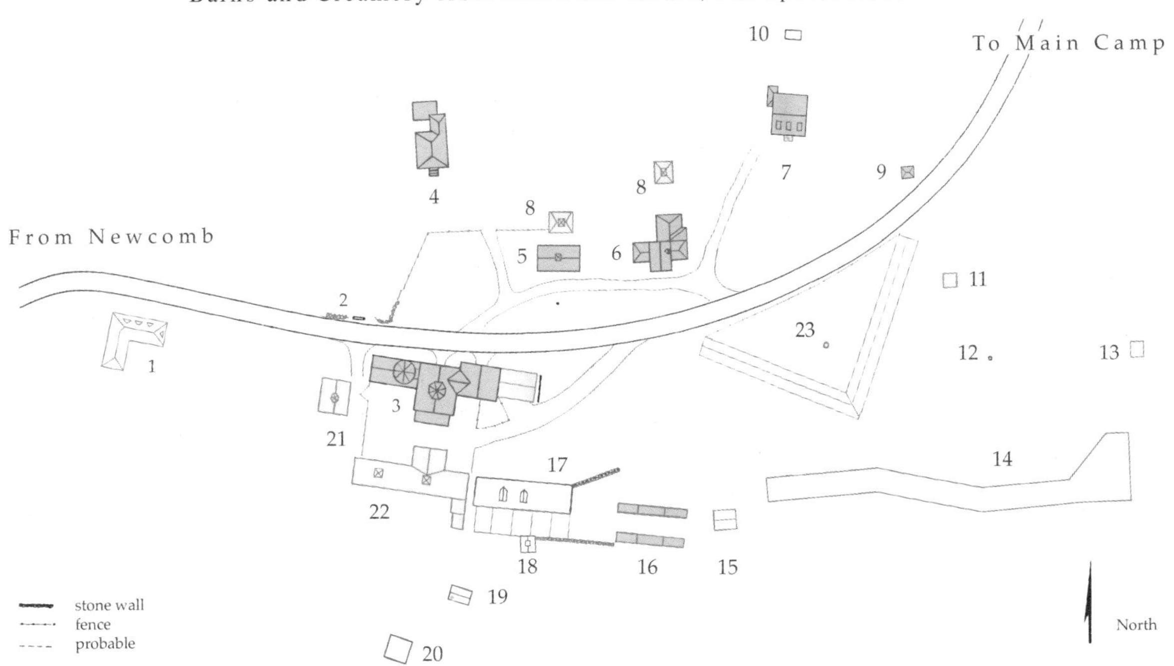


The Farm Complex: extant buildings (1999) indicated darker

1. Garage-Shop
2. Gate
3. Barns*
4. Farm Manager's Cottage
5. Creamery
6. New Farm House
7. Old Farm House
8. Refrigeration and Ice Houses*
9. Smoke House
10. Shed
11. Hen House*
12. Spring Box
13. Shed (Hen House?)*
14. Turkey Run and Poultry Coops*
15. Seed House*
16. Cold Frames
17. Piggery*
18. Unknown Building*
19. Slaughter House*
20. Duck House
21. Sheep Barn
22. Chicken and Pigeon House
23. Poultry Coops

* ruins or foundation remains

in the spring of 1896, which was when the first stage of Santanoni Farm's development under Pruyn really began.[10]

The Old Farm House

He immediately had a barn built on the new property across the road, close to older pastures.[11] The new barn was likely "a multi-purpose structure used to house early farm activities including dairy operations, feed and equipment storage, and probably cows and draft horse stables."[12] Other horses—carriage horses for access and riding horses for recreation—would have been stabled at the lakeside service complex. Most of the Pruyns were avid horse people who enjoyed recreational horseback riding.

An active farm would of course necessitate a larger staff. Expanding and totally remodeling the nineteenth-century farmhouse on the site was a beginning. The work suggests an architect's hand. A new roof was built to incorporate the front porch into the main volume. Haynes suggests that this rendered the building more of a newly fashionable bungalow; it also increased useful space on the second story, under the roof.[13] The steep pitch is not characteristic of the original bungalow model, but is typical of vernacular Adirondack building.[14] Like the main camp, rustic log posts appear on the porch and railing. The doubled columns and design of the railing, like the roof dormers, suggest a skilled designer's hand. Its interiors, all walls and ceilings clad with beaded wooden boards, were not to everyone's taste. One resident recalled, "The homes were beautifully built, but the inside of ours was totally finished with wainscoting—ceiling, walls, everything. It was all varnished, which made it so dark and gloomy. All winter, from three o'clock in the afternoon on, we had to light lanterns. There was no electricity."[15]

Even with the expansion of the "Old Farm House," as they sometimes called it, a second staff dwelling was needed, so in 1896, the "New Farmer's Cottage" was constructed closer to the barn, a bit lower on the slope and westerly of the first house.[16] The design again suggests the hand of an architect. Not only its symmetry, but its combination of hipped and gable roofs, and particularly the rather eccentric bracketed eaves, surely do not suggest a local builder's design. Rustic logs, rarely used in the farm complex, here appear as eaves brackets, as well as porch posts.[17] This sort of affectation, on a building otherwise of ordinary frame construction, clad with shingles like the other farm buildings, probably would

[10] Chase to Pruyn, May 27, 1896. *Essex County Grantee Book* 111, Page 315.

[11] Wesley Haynes suggests 1895 as date of the barn's construction, although the following year seems more likely, after the property was acquired. However, a 1929 article states, "The nucleus of the group [of farm buildings] was an old barn beside the road on a steep hill, and the buildings to house the farm teams, the cows and calves, poultry and pigeons, were grouped around the sides of a court below the barn, the court forming the barnyard." Guy H. Lee, 92. It is ambiguous as to whether "old " means being extant in 1902, when the other portions were added, or the barn being extant on the property when acquired by Pruyn. Haynes, 87, notes that the barn is of the New England type, common in this region.

[12] Haynes, "Farm Complex," 87.

[13] Haynes, "Farm Complex," 137.

[14] The bungalow was a tropical building type, originally one story with low-pitched roofs. Paul Malo notes the characteristic Adirondack steep pitch in "A Home to Call Our Own," *Adirondack Life*, November-December, 1997: 56-61.

[15] Rowena Putnam in Garrison, "A Working Dairy . . .," 8A.

[16] Haynes gives 1904 as the construction date, but various photographs, including two dated 1896 in the Santanoni scrapbook, Adirondack Museum Library, suggest the earlier date.

[17] Haynes notes that the rustic railing was added at a later date. Caption, "Farm Complex," illustration 94, f.p. 150.

not have occurred, except to an architect enchanted by the natural context.

The building of the new farmer's cottage and remodeling of the Old Farm House, both completed only two or three years after construction of the main camp, may have been the work of Robert Robertson. The unusual, exaggerated roof brackets on the newer structure are similar to the office building Robertson had designed for William Seward Webb at Shelburne Farms.[18] Haynes also suggested that Robert Robertson might have contributed at least some design features to the farm project; the detail of the original barn windows, for instance, is similar to that of the main camp.[19]

Although their original names were appropriately generic, the two staff residences at the farm complex changed names over the years, as occupants sometimes moved from one house to another around the preserve. The Old Farm House was later referred to as the "Farm House," "hired man's house" and finally the "Herdsman's Cottage." The New Farmer's Cottage was also called the "main Farm House," more simply "farmhouse," and eventually "Gardener's Cottage." For the sake of clarity, we refer to them as the Old Farm House and New Farm House.[20]

[18] *American Architect and Building News*, December 8, 1888. Architectural historian John Deming, Jr. writes, "I have to believe that Robertson designed the [Santanoni] farm group. In looking at . . . Robertson's work for Dr. W. Seward Webb . . . at Shelburne Farms and . . . at Camp Nehasane, I see too much of Robertson in the farm group to think that Delano & Aldrich had a hand in those buildings." Letter to Steven Engelhart, September 30, 1998.

[19] Haynes, "Farm Complex," 87. This earliest portion of the barn comprises less than a quarter of the whole, but projection forward in plan of the steep-roofed gable from lower-roofed elements makes the initial segment the most prominent. Steep roofs are characteristic Adirondack vernacular forms. They appear on two of the farmhouses, as well as on the Creamery. Architects Delano and Aldrich subsequently recognized the appropriate regional character of the steep roof, which Robertson had not employed on the villa because of a Japanese intent–but Robertson (we suppose) used the steep roof on the original portion of the barn, possibly adopting that form from the extant farmhouse across the road.

[20] Wesley Haynes, in his definitive study of the farm complex, called these residences the Herdsman's Cottage and the Gardener's Cottage, respectively.

This first stage of the Santanoni farm was undertaken during the grave depression of the mid-1890s; perhaps for this reason the project was not ambitious in scope. The larger farm campaign awaited return of prosperity. Nevertheless, Santanoni was one of the first relatively self-sufficient Great Camps.[21]

New Farm House and hunters, head gardener Charlie Petoff and sons, George and Roger

The Great Bull Market began in 1897, no doubt yielding a bounty to financier Pruyn. As elsewhere in the region and nation, affluent

[21] Pruyn's initial farm was on a similar scale to Durant's modest farm at Camp Pine Knot, which preceded Santanoni. Camp Uncas was developed between 1893 and 1895, so its farm would have been established about the same time as the farm at Santanoni Preserve.

families celebrated the return of national prosperity at the turn of the century with construction of grand estates. The original farm had sufficed for nearly a decade. Now Pruyn was ready to create a gentleman's farm worthy of his aristocratic tradition. In the first decade of the new century, he would expand his earlier facility into the most extensive farm operation associated with an Adirondack camp.[22] To do this, Robert Pruyn engaged one of the leading agriculturists and "farm experts" of the day.

### Edward Burnett, Farm Designer

Edward Burnett (1849–1925) was the eldest of eleven children of Joseph and Josephine Burnett of Southborough, Massachusetts.[23] Joseph Burnett (1820–1894) was a chemist who made a fortune by being the first person to produce liquid vanilla flavoring. He soon acquired a national reputation for other flavor extracts.[24] Financial success enabled purchase of large land holdings in Southborough and his retirement there as a gentleman farmer, philanthropist, and leader in the Episcopal Church.

Like many wealthy businessmen of the nineteenth century, Joseph Burnett created a rural seat, "Deerfoot," with a country house on five hundred acres and a working farm. The year Edward was born Burnett constructed the large villa on the estate established the previous year. Joseph actively managed Deerfoot Farm and was a member of the Middlesex Agricultural Society, boasting at a meeting about the pears he had grown.[25] Joseph reflected the attitude of many large estate owners of the period who believed that by operating model, experimental farms they would provide good examples that would elevate the quality of American agriculture.[26] Joseph Burnett was "a pioneer in scientific farming."[27]

From life on a gentleman's farm, Edward Burnett moved to begin his formal education at age thirteen at the prestigious St. Paul's School in Concord, New Hampshire. Recognizing that he had five more sons to educate, Joseph Burnett followed the suggestion of St. Paul's Rector and founded his own academy, St. Mark's School, in Southborough in 1865.[28] Edward completed his education at St. Mark's, as did his brothers after him. "Edward and his classmates (with well known Boston surnames like Abbott, Abercrombie, Howe and Russell) were invited to the family mansion regularly by Joseph and his wife."[29]

Edward entered Harvard College in 1867, where he spent the next four years pursuing a rather undistinguished academic career. His neglect of classes and church services, his hazing of Freshman, his defacing seats in the university auditorium, and his other acts of rebellion earned him several reprimands and ultimatums; nevertheless, he completed his Bachelor of Arts degree in 1871, the same year Robert C. Pruyn was working on his master's degree at Rutgers.

After graduation Edward returned to Deerfoot Farm at Southborough. Apparently his wild oats were fully sown, for Burnett married Mabel Russell Lowell (daughter of James Russell Lowell) and devoted the next fifteen years to managing Deerfoot. While at Harvard, Edward had taken courses in chemistry, botany and other sciences and had "been exposed to the newly formed school devoted to agricul-

[22] There were larger farms in the Adirondacks, but they were either commercial operations or were associated with country houses that would not be considered "camps." There were still much larger and more important estate farms beyond the Adirondacks.

[23] The two main sources for this section are: Taya Dixon, "Edward Burnett: An Agricultural Designer on Gentlemen's Estates" (unpublished master's thesis, University of Pennsylvania, 1998) and Haynes, "Farm Complex," 71-74.

[24] Haynes, "Farm Complex," 71-72.

[25] Nick Noble Presentation to the Southborough Historical Society. Dixon, 36.

[26] Dixon, 27, quotes one influential author, apparently taking umbrage at the charge that such an attitude might be condescending. "It is not a condescending effort of the high [the gentleman farmer] to exalt the low [the common farmer], nor of the peculiarly cultivated to elevate and benefit the less refined and privileged of men." Rev. John D. Blake, D.D., *Home in the Country* (Auburn, NY: Derby & Miller, 1854).

[27] Haynes, "Farm Complex," 71.

[28] Albert Emerson Benson, *History of Saint Mark's School* (Southborough, MA: Alumni Association, 1925). In Dixon, 32.

[29] Dixon, 32-33.

tural sciences."[30] The lessons apparently took hold, for Edward soon transformed Deerfoot from a gentleman's farm into a major commercial operation that demonstrated some advanced practices in American agriculture. With employment expanded to more than five-hundred persons, Deerfoot Farm became the largest business in the area. Its sausage factory was a steam-powered facility that "slaughtered about 1,500 pigs a year, most weighing one hundred and seventy five pounds." Its Deerfoot Dairy handled over three tons of milk a day.[31]

The ability to process such a large amount of milk was made possible by the newly invented Weston Centrifugal Machine for separating milk and cream, which Weston and Burnett improved through experimentation at Deerfoot Farm. Much faster and far more space saving than the old pan-settling method, the centrifugal separation method enabled Deerfoot Farm to process more raw milk than the farm's own herd could produce. Burnett saw this as an opportunity to adopt the "factory system" of farming, which had recently been promoted at the 1876 Centennial Exhibition in Philadelphia. Under this system, Burnett contracted with farmers from the surrounding region to sell their raw milk to Deerfoot Farm, which did the processing and distribution.[32] "The forty-quart milk containers were loaded in refrigeration cars and shipped to Boston twice a night arriving at two thirty and ten thirty in the morning when it was sold to customers." Burnett set up his own stores in the Boston area to sell Deerfoot Farm products. Between one hundred and one hundred-fifty pounds of butter were sold daily, along with skim milk, "family milk," buttermilk, and cream.[33]

Burnett's success at Deerfoot Farm attracted national attention. A U.S. Department of Agriculture report about Deerfoot was distributed to farms around the country.[34] Excerpts were reprinted in England where Burnett, "the boy farmer from Deerfoot," was invited to attend the Royal Exhibition at Derby in 1881. A book on dairy farming at the time described the "famous Deerfoot Dairy."[35]

Two particular innovations that Burnett emphasized at Deerfoot and promulgated throughout his career were the strengthening of farm stock and the practicing of good hygiene in all aspects of dairy operation. (Both practices would be visible at Santanoni.) Burnett was an early importer of fine breeds and a pioneer in breeding stronger American stock, weakened by decades of inbreeding. He experimented with the most suitable feeds and gave his animals meticulous care. "With three-hundred acres of land available for grazing, Burnett had a large herd of Jersey cattle imported from England for use on his farm."[36] By the mid-1880s he was trading through cattle clubs his own and other farmers' Jersey and Guernsey cattle.[37]

Another prominent concern of Burnett was managing the dairy operation in the cleanest, most hygienic means possible. This included the efficient handling of manure and liquid waste, proper grooming of cattle, and especially moving the milk processing operation

[30] Dixon, 37.

[31] Dixon, 38, 42.

[32] In another form of the "factory system," farmers created their own cooperative factory to produce and distribute the dairy products. Dixon, 38-41.

[33] Dixon, 44-45, citing information given by Edward Burnett in an address to the New York Farmers' Club, December 18, 1882.

[34] E. Lewis Sturtevant, M.D., "Deerfoot Farm Centrifugal Dairy," in Annual Report of the Committee of Agriculture for the Year 1880, *United States Department of Agriculture Report, 1880* (Washington, D.C.: Government Printing Office, 1881), 629-638.

[35] J.P. Sheldon, *Dairy Farming.* (New York: Cassell, Petter, Galpin & Co., 1883-5), 440. Cited in Dixon, 51.

[36] Dixon, 46.

[37] Dixon, 51, citing *The Cultivator and Country Gentleman*, vol. L (Albany: Luther Tucker & Son, 1885-1892). For example, "Of the seventy Guernseys imported to the United States in 1898, forty-five were selected by Burnett." Haynes, "Farm Complex," 72. Haynes says Joseph Burnett, even earlier than Edward, was "a pioneer" in importing Jersey cattle. "Farm Complex," 71.

Robert C. Pruyn and young visitors at the farm

out of the barn to a separate facility. Tuberculosis was a scourge at this time, and scientists were beginning to understand that improper handling of milk and dairy products was linked to the disease. At Deerfoot Burnett invented special refrigeration tanks for storing the milk and patented or co-patented four inventions for transporting milk more safely and efficiently to market.[38]

As a successful businessman and the largest employer in the region, Edward Burnett entered public life, winning a seat in the United States House of Representatives in 1886 when Cleveland became President. An active member of the House Committee on Agriculture, Burnett was considered the "farmer's representative." Congressman Burnett traveled to England, where he met the Prince of Wales while touring agricultural facilities.[39]

As he was not re-elected, Burnett returned to private life. In the interim his brother Robert had taken over management of Deerfoot Farm. Edward then entered the third phase of his career, which he or others described alternately as "farm expert," "farm designer," "farm architect," "agricultural designer," and "agricultural expert." For the next thirty-six years, until his death, Burnett would

[38] With Alexander Browne he developed patents for a "Stopper for Liquid Containing Vessels" and two other devices for properly sealing milk cans. Burnett's own invention was a special "truck" for transporting milk cans which enabled the cans to be tipped for pouring without removing them from the truck or requiring undue handling by the driver. Dixon, 61, 47-50.

[39] Donald C. Bacon, ed., et al. *The Encyclopedia of the United States Congress*, vol. 1, "House Reports of the 50th Congress" (New York: Simon and Schuster, 1995), 31-34.

design, equip, and sometimes manage farms for some of America's wealthiest families.

The new career made sense. Burnett had the experience, the expertise, the reputation, and the contacts to succeed. He had known and socialized with elite families from his youth at St. Paul's, St. Mark's, and then at Harvard. He was a member of the Union Club of Boston and the University Club in New York City.[40] He also became a regular guest speaker at the "New York Farmers' Club." The "Fifth Avenue Farmers," as they jocularly called themselves, were men of wealth and position who, as gentleman farmers, met regularly to discuss advances and best practices in agriculture. Odd as it might seem today, on a weekday evening after leaving their offices, J. Pierpont Morgan, William K. Vanderbilt, Frederick Vanderbilt, architect Richard Morris Hunt, and other prominent members would gather for dinner at Sherry's followed by a lecture and discussion on "The Feeding of Cattle" or some other agricultural topic. Edward Burnett was a frequent speaker between 1888 and 1903, and later became a member of the club, addressing the millionaires on "Pigs," "Hay," "Weeds," "Farm Structures and Fences," "The Reclamation of Waste Lands," and other bucolic subjects. On one occasion Burnett was featured on the program with Gifford Pinchot, leader of the scientific forestry movement and founder of the Division of Forestry of the U.S. Department of Agriculture.[41]

Thus when Edward Burnett was ready to offer his services to wealthy gentleman farmers, he needed no introduction to a long list of potential clients. One of his first clients was George Vanderbilt, who sought advice about designing his notable estate, Biltmore, in Asheville, North Carolina. From 1889--1892 Burnett served as Biltmore's agricultural planner, chief purchasing agent, and then head of the Agricultural Department.[42] There he combined talents with Frederick Law Olmsted, integrating the farm into the estate's landscape. The farm was acclaimed for its "scientific drainage, the improved machinery, the importation of fine stock, the judicious and lavish use of fertilizers, and the most up-to-date and scientific methods of farming."[43] Burnett was part of this grand project from the start. He traveled to the site with Vanderbilt, Olmsted, architect Richard Morris Hunt, Hunt's son, and Gifford Pinchot on Vanderbilt's private railroad car, the *Riva*. "While maintaining a professional relationship with these men, he seemed to get along well with all on a personal basis. Vanderbilt wrote to Burnett in familial terms," while Pinchot confided in Burnett about the "gay time" he had with two women after Burnett left Ashville.[44]

Burnett's next major position, beginning in 1892 and lasting several years, was as designer and general manager of H. McKay Twombly's Florham Farms in Madison, New Jersey. Twombly was George Vanderbilt's brother-in-law, and the Twombly brothers had attended St. Marks and Harvard.[45] Burnett probably developed as well Twombly's Adirondack farm, now called Asplin Tree Farms, near the St. Regis Lakes. Vanderbilt and Twombly were but two of Burnett's many prominent clients.[46]

---

[40] Dixon, 84.

[41] Citations for all of Burnett's known talks to the New York Farmers' Club are given both in Haynes, "Farm Complex," and Dixon.

[42] John Bryan, *Biltmore Estate: The Most Distinguished Private Place.* Washington, DC: Rizzoli, 1994. Cited in Dixon and Haynes, "Farm Complex," 73.

[43] "Farmer Vanderbilt," *Ashville News and Hotel Reporter,* February 20, 1897, quoted in Haynes, "Farm Complex," 21.

[44] "You may have thought there were lively times at the Brick House before you left. . .," wrote Pinchot. Bryan, *Biltmore Estate.* In Dixon, 63.

[45] Haynes, "Farm Complex," gives the dates as 1892-95, the title as Director of Agriculture, and the connection as Burnett's Harvard classmate. Dixon says 1892-1900, the title of General Manager, and the St. Marks-Harvard connection with the Twombly *family.*

[46] Other clients for whom he designed major agricultural facilities included Frederick Vanderbilt at Hyde Park; Tracy Dows of Rhinebeck, New York; F.B. Lord of Cedarhurst, L.I., and Harry J. Fisher of Greenwich, Connecticut. He imported select cattle and horses for the Vanderbilts, J. Pierpont Morgan, former New York Governor and Vice President Levi P. Morton, F. Lothrop Ames, E.F. Bowditch, and many others.

Edward Burnett, left, and distinguished professional associates: (left to right) architect Richard Morris Hunt, landscape architect Frederick Law Olmsted, kneeling, with client George Vanderbilt at his estate, Biltmore, 1892. Reclining at right is Hunt's son, Richard Howland Hunt.

Some of these projects were Burnett's sole commissions, while others were collaborative efforts, for around the turn of the century Burnett established a more formal practice in New York City. He employed architects and landscape architects, most notably architect Alfred Hopkins who was associated with Burnett for many years. In addition to private farms, he and his firm also designed the International Garden Club in New York City, commercial dairies on Long Island and in New Hampshire, as well as other projects.[47]

In 1905, following the death of his wife, Burnett married Ethel Raymond Mason, widow of his brother Charles and granddaughter of the founding publisher of the New York *Times*. Ethel's father gave them Four Winds Farm in Peterborough, New Hampshire as a wedding present, which they owned until 1915. Edward Burnett died at his home in Milton, Massachusetts in 1925, at age seventy-five. He left "ten children, countless grandchildren, a wife, and a legacy of exceptional

[47] Dixon's thesis presents the fullest, published enumeration and descriptions to date of Burnett's work. She points out that as Burnett's work is more fully appreciated and studied, more examples will no doubt come to light. Edward's Burnett's grandson, John B. Vaughan of Bristol, RI, has also compiled an extensive listing of Burnett's work.

and productive work on gentlemen's estates."[48]

His legacy was more than the farms themselves. The agricultural facilities he developed at Deerfoot Farm and for many prominet clients, attracted a great deal of national attention and set an example for other gentlemen farmers and commercial dairies of the period. Edward Burnett was a major influence in the American dairy industry and farm design due to his importation of new breeds, his breeding, care and feeding of livestock, and his hygienic dairy practices. Burnett's stature in scientific agriculture has been compared to that of Gifford Pinchot in forestry.[49]

### Burnett at Santanoni

There are innumerable ways that Robert C. Pruyn might have known of or been acquainted with Edward Burnett, if not by reputation alone, then through many mutual acquaintances, such as Pruyn's banking colleague Pierpont Morgan. Some of Burnett's fellow members of the New York Farmers' Club signed the Santanoni Guest Book: Frederick and William Vanderbilt, James Fenimore Cooper and Gifford Pinchot. Burnett imported Guernsey cattle in 1883 for Pruyn's friend Edward L. Bowditch, who had an estate at Framingham, Massachusetts.[50] With so many connections, Burnett could be considered the obvious choice to help Robert Pruyn realize his vision of a country manor in the Adirondacks.

Burnett had designed the expanded horse and wagon barn at Santanoni's lakeside service complex in the late 1890s. Now with the full return of prosperity, he designed the new farm complex at Santanoni from 1901-1904.[51] Following the Burnett plans, the new facilities were built "between 1902 and 1908. This farm grew to include more than twenty structures capable of producing and processing meat, poultry, dairy and wool products."[52]

*The Barn and Dairy Herd.* Burnett typically located his barns on a hillside so gravity could facilitate drainage and waste removal, and farm vehicles and equipment could have easy access to the upper story at grade level. There the hay could be unloaded and stored conveniently along with wagons and equipment. The lower level, reachable from the rear, provided stables and stalls for animals. The earthen bank around the lower level provided natural insulation in the winter when the animals were inside. Moreover, if the barn were sited on a south-facing slope, windows on the south side provided natural lighting and heating in the colder months. In the summer, the cattle would be out to pasture. Such was the arrangement of the 1896 barn Burnett inherited at Santanoni, and such was his plan for expanding it between 1902–04.

The Santanoni main barn became an accretion of five connected elements, collectively 144-feet long and 18 to 40-feet wide. Most of the barn survives. The original section has an upper level entered from the road, while the sloping site allows a lower level containing horse stalls to be entered at grade from the rear. A one-story annex, a wagon shed, once extended to the left, as viewed from the road.

Attached to the right of the oldest section, as viewed from the road, is another front-gabled segment of two stories, recessed three feet back from its twin and extending fifteen

---

[48] Dixon, 67, 84.

[49] Haynes, "Farm Complex," 22.

[50] Dixon, 89, tells us the Vanderbilts, Cooper and Gifford Pinchot were Club members. Haynes tells of Burnett's connection to Bowditch, "Farm Complex," 72.

[51] Dixon, 90, says the Burnett plan was "instituted in 1901 and completed in 1904," but provides no evidence. We know that Burnett signed the Santanoni Guest Book on October 20, 1901, October 19, 1902 and October 22, 1904. The regularity of these dates suggests that, in addition to professional reasons for visiting Santanoni, he may have been a social guest at Robert Pruyn's annual fall hunting party; although two letters from Pruyn to Burnett in 1902 suggest a more formal relationship. Haynes, "Farm Complex," 37. Burnett also may have visited the work site on other occasions when he would not have signed the guest book.

[52] Haynes, "Farm Complex," 5. Henceforth, dates given in this section will follow Haynes' chronology, unless otherwise noted. Haynes also cites contemporaneous Burnett drawings for expanding the horse stable at the Newcomb Lake service complex, 38.

feet to the rear. This major addition of the Edward Burnett period was well designed to provide an integrated ensemble. Almost a twin of the original barn, the Burnett barn is actually larger but cleverly set back to defer to the earlier portion.

Burnett's upper floor served as the haymow. To ventilate the hayloft under the steep roof he provided a rooftop cupola. On the lower level, likewise accessible from the rear, he installed a concrete floor and two rows containing fifteen Louden cow stanchions.[53] Surmounting each stanchion was a framed glass plate that held a card bearing the name of the cow that occupied the stall. A bullpen stood alone in a corner. Rowena Ross Putnam,

Stanchions with name frames, c. 1990

daughter of herdsman George Ross, has on display in her Newcomb home a placard that reads:

FERN OF SANTANONI
Registered Thoroughbred Guernsey

The cows stood in their stanchions on a soft pavement of cork bricks. When thirsty, a cow could push its nose into a ceramic bowl to activate a valve that filled the bowl with spring water. Milking was done by hand, twice a day. Mrs. Putnam remembers her father leaving the house with a lantern every morning before first light and in all seasons to milk the cows.

"The white tails of the Guernseys were kept clean and bleached. When the herdsman George Ross knew that Mr. Pruyn was coming north, the cows' tails were braided and then curry combed," said his daughter Mrs. Putnam. "It seemed as though every time a cow had a passage my father was right there with a shovel and a water hose."[54] The best cows got an annual ride to the Essex County Fair at Westport. "There was a case on the dairy wall with blue ribbons and other awards won at the fair."[55] The lone Guernsey bull was a ribbon winner at the State Fair in Syracuse.[56]

Again viewing the barn complex from the road, to the right of the cow barn rises an imposing silo. Clad with cedar shingles, it proved to be more picturesque than useful. In Newcomb, warm weather after the harvest generally is too brief to allow silage to ferment properly. Vertical ensilage was not fully understood by scientists then, and the climatic factors were still being discovered. An early photograph confirms that the silo was loaded at least once with corn.[57] Reluctantly, the experiment was abandoned. As a child, Mrs. Putnam would "go in there and hoot and holler." Subsequent photographs show heavily loaded hay carts, for the barn has a large loft for storing winter hay.[58]

Still farther to the right, next to the silo, again as seen from the road, is a cow shed, now in poor condition. To the rear of the cow barn was attached a manure shed, of which only the pit remains. In the winter, cows would move between the milking room, the barn yard and the cow shed. Located south of the barn, the yard captured the short winter sun and was

[53] These were installed in the 1920s. "The original head stalls for the cows have recently been removed, and Louden equipment substituted throughout." Guy H. Lee, 92, writing in 1929.

[54] David Garrison, "A Working Dairy. . .," 8A.

[55] Delilah West Bissell.

[56] Garrison, "A Working Dairy . . ." 8A.

[57] Haynes, "Farm Complex," Illustration H.12.

[58] "A silo proved impractical, on account of the shortness of the season, and has been abandoned," Guy Lee wrote of Santanoni in 1929, 92. Improbably, Kamp Kill Kare, in densely forested terrain, likewise has a silo appended to its remarkable barn complex, as does Camp Uncas nearby.

Guernseys in uphill pasture

shielded from the wind by surrounding buildings. In summer, the cattle grazed on the fenced hillsides above the farmhouses.

Burnett selected the best imported stock for Pruyn's herd. Haynes suggests that the earliest herd at Santanoni consisted of Brown Swiss cattle, a hardy alpine breed that could thrive in the harsh Adirondack climate. However, "Guernseys were the principal dairy cattle at Santanoni through most of the farm's active years. . . . It is likely that the introduction of the breed had prompted the expansion of the barn in 1902."[59] Following Burnett's recommended mode of operation and Pruyn's own, fastidious, banker's style, Robert Pruyn had his farm manager keep careful records of all aspects of the farm's operation. Thus we know the names of many members of the Santanoni herd: Blanche of Edgewater 1, Castelpolly of Rockledge, Beatrice of Santanoni, Rosemary of Santanoni, and many others. We also know their registration numbers, dates of birth, tenure at Santanoni, breeder, and eventual disposition.[60]

*Dairy*. A major feature of the Burnett improvements was the stone dairy building, the "Creamery," built in 1904. Vying with the larger barn complex, the masonry structure was the centerpiece of an array of buildings across the road, at the base of a steep hill that had been cleared for grazing. The Creamery is a side-gabled rectangle, constructed entirely of rough-cut and uncut fieldstone. Massive piers and stone arches of the front portico recall the masonry arch in the artist studio at the main camp and the arched entryway at the Gate Lodge (illustrations pp. 89 and 110). The design is reasonably attributed to Delano & Aldrich, the architects who were working on other Santanoni projects for Pruyn at the time (to be discussed shortly), as well as the talented stonemason executing the architect's plan.

Thick exterior walls provided good insulation from summer heat. Cold spring water ran constantly through a network of iron pipes fabricated by the Consolidated Car Heating Company, which Pruyn controlled. Milk would be carried from the barn in five gallon cans and "poured into pans in the deep set method of immersion into ice cold water."[61] Cream rose in the tinned pans until a mechanical separator was installed.[62] "One of the most original features is the method of disposing of the buttermilk. This is poured into a tank from which it is piped underground downhill

[59] Haynes, "Farm Complex," 76. "The dairy herd is of registered Guernsey stock inspected and certified as for a commercial herd." Guy Lee, 92.

[60] For example, Blanche of Edgewater 1, No. 75,101, "dropped" on 1/11/17. Her breeder was Ernest R. Parmlee of Greenfield Center, NY. She remained at Santanoni from 1923-30, when she was sold. Beatrice of Santanoni, No. 177,175, dropped on 6/17/24, was bred by "RCP" and was sold from Santanoni in 1930.

[61] "The empty cans were returned to the washroom, where they were sterilized and stored until the next milking." Dixon, 99.

[62] Delilah West Bissell. It is puzzling that Burnett did not install one of his mechanical separators originally. The operation may have been too small to justify one of these machines; perhaps a smaller model subsequently became available.

to the pigpen where it is drawn from a tap, as occasion requires, and fed to the pigs."[63] Farm workers made butter by hand with vitrified churns from the Sanitary Churn and Manufacturing Company of Albany.

Directly behind the Creamery was a refrigeration house in which containers of milk, cream and butter would be immersed in cold water from a nearby spring, awaiting transfer to the main camp, shipment to Albany, or sale. Several Newcomb residents still display glass milk bottles with "Santanoni" in raised lettering.[64] Nearby was an ice house, filled with ice cut from Newcomb Lake or from Harris Lake, which is closer to the farm.

At a time when epidemics of tuberculosis and influenza were killing hundreds of thousands of people in America's cities, the Santanoni dairy provided safe milk and dairy products for the Pruyns and their guests, their employees on the Preserve, and when available, their Newcomb neighbors and Albany friends. Following Burnett's plans, the Santanoni farm conducted hygienic dairying two decades before such practices were required by state regulation.[65]

Of all the farm operations, "The dairy was first established. Next came the vegetable garden, and following in quick succession, the hens, the pigs, the ducks, the pigeons and all other necessities."[66]

*Sheep.* While the barn constituted the northern side of the barn yard, the sheep fold occupied the western side. Also known as the "sheep house" and "sheep barn," it provided shelter for the flock in winter. Only the roof, with octagonal cupola like that of the cow barn, is visible in historic photographs. A later inventory indicated the sheepfold was a one-story, shingle-sided structure. It was rectangular, "measuring about 30 feet north-south by 24 feet east-west."[67]

The stock consisted initially of "one of the very few flocks of Black-faced Highland Sheep in this country," according to Robert Pruyn.[68] This hearty breed was particularly suited to surviving in cold, mountainous regions where food was scarce. Later Southdown sheep and Shropshire sheep augmented or replaced the original flock.

Black-faced Highland Sheep

The sheep grazed on the cleared hillside behind the Creamery and on the hillside above the Gate Lodge. They provided meat for the table and Anna Pruyn knitted with Santanoni wool.[69] "Everything was used," recalled her granddaughter Sis Thibault. She remembered gathering tufts of wool from the floor of the sheep shearing building (probably the sheepfold) where she played as a child. Her mother, Beatrice Morgan Pruyn, also knitted sweaters from Santanoni wool.[70]

---

[63] Guy Lee, 92.

[64] Dave Garrison provided a photograph of a milk bottle belonging to Helen Tummins. "Former resident recalls life in area preserve." *Post-Star*, December 1, 1987.

[65] Haynes, "Farm Complex," 22.

[66] Guy Lee, 94.

[67] Haynes, "Farm Complex," 189.

[68] "Santanoni Preserve: Adirondack Mountains," May, 1915, version 1, p. 3.

[69] Hallie Bond, "Notes Taken During a Trip Into Santanoni on July 29, 1986," with Helen Tummins and Andy Blanchette. Typescript, 1988.

[70] Beatrice Pruyn Thibault, letter to J. Winthrop Aldrich, August 1992.

Poultry Yard

*Poultry*. Along the southern side of the barnyard was a large poultry house, about ninety-feet in length and containing nine sections for coops, plus a feed room. Built into the still-descending hillside, the southern and taller side of the building had a long row of windows along the upper wall capturing light and heat in the winter months. On the northern side there was a small wing, probably used as a killing room, that extended into the cow yard.[71] The poultry house was placed strategically, following a typical Burnett plan, sheltering the cows in the adjoining yard from the wind and cold, which might adversely affect milk production.[72]

In 1915 the poultry house housed one thousand Wyandotte chickens. "Mr. Pruyn selected these breeds for their appearance as much as for their other sterling qualities. The generous runs behind the coops [on the south side] are shaded by huge old pine trees." In separate compartments, "Mr. Pruyn keeps the large French pigeons—great brown birds with slightly iridescent necks, forty to a pen—and kills only the full-grown, six-months-old birds, finding them tender and delicious."[73] These Carneau pigeons produced squab for the Santanoni table.

---

[71] Building description based on photographs and Dixon, 104-105. Dixon provides "proposed plans" and further details for most of the major farm buildings, based on historic photographs, extant ruins at Santanoni, and documentary evidence of other Burnett farms.

[72] Dixon, 104.

[73] There were 800 to 1000 chickens in 1924. Figures based on farm records. Haynes, "Farm Complex," 83; quotations by Guy Lee, 94.

> At the foot of the hill, below the farmyard, is a pond, and here live the white Brazilian quackless ducks selected more for their silent quality than for any other reason, although they are fine birds in all other ways. The guinea hens, which make up the balance of the feathered flock, are not of a soundless variety, however, and their persistent cry of "Buckwheat buckwheat" pervades the farmyard. Various cottages for the farmer and his men rise from the side hill overlooking the farm buildings, and about these in the summer are the pens for raising innumerable broods of small chickens and baby ducks.[74]

A small building to house the ducks was also constructed near an artificial duck pond. In summer the chickens were moved to smaller coops within a large triangular area about two-hundred-feet east of the poultry house, up along the road, where they could feed outside.[75] Another hen house sat just east of this coop area.

*Pigs.* East of the poultry house was the "piggery," built into the hillside and entered through a twelve-foot-high masonry wall. Located opposite the barn's wagon shed addition, the piggery further extended the farm yard enclosure. It was about eighty feet long and "composed of eight pens inside the stone structure and an additional eight exterior runs."[76]

The black Berkshire pigs kept at Santanoni were large animals, weighing about one-hundred-seventy-five pounds at six months and three hundred pounds at one year. Wesley Haynes states that there were typically about seven registered breeding adults and twenty or more piglets.[77] They spent winter in the piggery and summer days in open pastures. It was a good pig's life, but ultimately the hide went into one of the two large, iron boiling kettles that remain.[78] A cobblestone smoke house is situated across the road, at the edge of the farm complex. Sis Pruyn Thibault retains a label on which is printed, "Santanoni Bacon."[79] Pruyn wrote that the farm could produce annually "fifty hams of rare quality . . . cured each year, and over a hundred sides of bacon."[80]

Black Berkshire Pig

Beyond the barnyard were arrayed varied agricultural facilities, including hot beds, potting shed, slaughter house, spring house and root cellar.[81] Nearby was a workshop, called "Shops and Tool House" on one photograph, containing shop area, parts and equipment storage, and a blacksmith shop. The latter was used for shoeing horses, fixing wagons, and possibly repairing decorative iron work. Sheep sheds and at least one cow shed stood on the cleared hillside above the farmhouses.

---

[74] Guy Lee, 94. Haynes says the "Brazilian ducks" have also been known as Guinea, Musk or Barbary Duck and are known as Muscovie Duck today, "Farm Complex," 82.

[75] Although these coops and a building beyond them, presumably a hen house or storage barn, are visible in a 1908 photograph, Dixon, 113, suggests that the coops probably were not designed by Burnett, as there is no evidence that he ever designed chicken coops and yards like these.

[76] Dixon, 102.

[77] Haynes, regarding size and number of pigs and quoting Pruyn, "Farm Complex," 79. Guy Lee, 94, wrote, "A gate leads from the farmyard down some steps to the pigpens, where from twenty to thirty black Berkshires are housed. . . ."

[78] Boiling removed coarse hair from hides before smoking. At this writing the kettles appear on the Gate Lodge lawn.

[79] Aldrich, 3.

[80] Quoted in Haynes, "Farm Complex," 81.

[81] Howard Kirschenbaum saw the root cellar entrance around 1980, but it has not been mentioned or documented since.

Lower barns with piggery in foreground, poultry house behind left, and main barns above right.

Garage-Shop

A dog kennel, housing wire-haired fox terriers, added to the farm's interest, as did "sugar-house, beehives, and other appurtenances to the perfectly appointed farm."[82]

*Fields and Gardens.* About seventy-five acres of forest had been cleared as farmland in the early days. In later years the estate had "two or three hundred acres of cleared land" for pasture, hay fields, orchard and cultivated garden.[83] An eight-foot-high deer fence enclosed a half-acre, hillside vegetable garden together with a nearby fruit orchard, three minutes' walking distance northeast of the barn. Photographs attest that the garden bore both quantity and variety, despite the short growing season. Lettuce heads the size of beach balls covered the foreground. Even celery sprouted from the hardscrabble soil, potent evidence of the gardener's skills. Concrete hot beds near the piggery, once topped with framed glass, tell of the gardener's efforts to defeat the inevitable May frosts. Escaped asparagus and rhubarb plants still provision knowing hikers.

Cornell University tested fruit from surviving apple trees in October 1992. They were found to be "Duchess of Oldenburg" (or "Dudley"), a Russian variety highly resistant to frost and infestation, perhaps introduced by gardener Charles Petoff.

## The Farm Completed

"Although minor improvements were made in the interim, Pruyn did not again substantially change the farm complex until around 1919, when the . . . farm manager's cottage was constructed, and the stanchions in the cow stable were updated."[84] This was the third stage of the farm's development under Robert Pruyn's ownership.

The "New Farm Manager's Cottage," later called the "Main Farm House," was built in 1919 and subsequently enlarged. This was a more typical "bungalow" than the remodeled Old Farm House. Although cobblestone piers of the porch and parapets of the entry steps recall masonry elsewhere, the building is different in period character, having the low, hipped roof common to the type, and wood clapboard siding, rather than shingles employed elsewhere on the farm buildings. Wesley Haynes observed that "the core appears to have been a prefabricated house purchased from Sears', Roebuck and Co. [which] offered plans and materials for complete dwellings between 1909 and 1934."[85] He notes that hardware, furnace, and other appliances were standard for such Sears' houses.[86]

Although the great log villa was considered a marvel after its completion, Santanoni's model farm also attracted attention. *Sportsman* magazine described the facility in glowing detail in 1929, only a month before the stock market crash ended an era:

> Although the place [Santanoni Preserve] is essentially a camp to provide the owner with facilities for fishing and hunting, for tramping or riding over the lovely Adirondack trails, and for enjoying the solitude of the wilderness, the farm

[82] Guy Lee, 92. These would not have been Burnett features. A sugarhouse was common in the Adirondacks. The beehives and kennel would have been preferences or hobbies of the owner.

[83] Robert C. Pruyn, "Santanoni Preserve/Adirondack Mountains," typescript. Haynes, "Farm Complex," fn. 110, 51. Elsewhere Haynes gives the figure as 190 acres of cleared pasture and 10 acres tillable, "Farm Complex," 24.

[84] Haynes, "Farm Complex," 5.

[85] Haynes, "Farm Complex," 167.

[86] Although only three houses at the farm complex are known to have existed (Old Farm House, New Farm House, and Farm Manager's Cottage, in that order), on an unidentified, undated, hand-written list of buildings, a fourth house appears: a "residence by pond (3 br)." The pond could have been the duck pond, situated below the sheep barn, or the marshy pond below the farm complex, or the writer may have been mistaken.

Vegetable Garden

> nonetheless remains one of the most interesting features of the establishment. . . . None of these pleasures could be enjoyed . . . without the farm.[87]

This utilitarian rationale may have been relevant during the early years of the preserve, but as the century unfolded and as roads from Albany to Newcomb improved, the Pruyns could have ordered provisions delivered from Albany far less expensively than continuing to operate the Santanoni farm. Instead, the produce went in the opposite direction. ". . . There was a real effort by the family to use every aspect of Santanoni that you could. . . . One of Art Tummins' jobs early in his career here was to bring the dairy products and poultry products and spring water down to Albany and of course you had maple sugar and maple syrup and I suppose firewood and the vegetables from the garden."[88]

Robert Pruyn's delight was *having a farm.* Pruyn genuinely loved farming. Pride of ownership enhanced his pleasure when showing others around the fine facilities. The Pruyns relished eating their own home-grown meat, dairy products, vegetables and fruit, both at camp and in town. This joy sustained the gentleman farmer for almost four decades.

Robert Pruyn represented contradictory impulses toward nature. At the main camp, he was a contemplator of unspoiled nature, who enjoyed wilderness for its own sake. At the farm, he was an improver, driven by a desire to control nature. He realized his vision of a country manor while savoring the challenge of a place relatively inhospitable to horticulture. Rugged terrain and brutal climate, famous for driving North Country farmers into early, boulder-strewn graves, was for Pruyn a challenge. The farm never was a rational economic enterprise, but the Pruyns loved working with nature and were fond of animals. No doubt it gave them satisfaction to employ local folk and to provide homes on the estate for many families. The impractical farm was a labor of love.

[87] Guy Lee, 92.

[88] Beatrice Pruyn Thibault. Aldrich, 3.

Farm Manager's House, c. 1920

See how he sits deep wrapped in thought
Thinking great thinks as sachems ought
If you could peer into his brain
You'd see it working might & main
His tribal problems to explain
at Santanoni

Are my white hens, (he thinks), the beauties,
Aware of their maternal duties
And does that red Swiss bull I bought
Whose life is with such romance fraught
Attend to business as he ought
at Santanoni?

And then there's Silo, and string beans
Tomatoes, cabbages and greens
Churns, piggeries and road repairs
And catching poachers unawares
These are but small part of his cares
at Santanoni

His business methods come in well
In ways too various to tell
He makes his hens lay by the clock
Instead of salaries, tails he'll dock
He's far best, though, at watering stock,
at Santanoni[89]

[89] Undated tribute by a Camp Santanoni guest, Pruyn Papers, Box 11, Folder 10, Albany Institute of History and Art.

## The Gate Lodge Complex

In 1897 Robert Pruyn purchased most of the property providing entrance to the Preserve, on the north side of the river between Rich and Harris Lakes.[90] At least two old farmsteads were acquired here, which Pruyn integrated in the first phase of his developing farm, centered a mile farther into the Preserve. At the time the road passing through his new lands was still public. Not until 1902, when the town ceded all rights of way to Pruyn giving him exclusive access to Santanoni Preserve, could he make plans to erect a dominating Gate Lodge which marked the entrance to the estate. Although other buildings came later, the Gate Lodge, built in 1905, was Pruyn's last major architectural addition to the Preserve.

The English precedent for Santanoni Preserve is immediately evident at its entrance, where the Gate Lodge and an imposing, stone gateway arch recall the entry lodges of English estates. By the late nineteenth century in America, a commanding gate lodge was fre-

[90] Williams to R.C. Pruyn, dated April 28, 1897. Essex County Grantee Book 113, Page 110. The deed conveyed all the land in Lot 3 north of the river, except for a one-acre parcel and two previous exceptions, which presumably Pruyn acquired later.

quently found at the entrance to large estates, clubs and other exclusive developments. In addition to intimidating unwanted intruders, according to *Architectural Record*, a gate made an important architectural statement.

> The initial approach to the country estate of the summer home should be in harmony with the atmosphere of the place to which it offers access. It should be something more than a mere architectural ornament mounting a name plate. Like an outstretched hand of greeting, from which radiates the personality of a welcoming host, the entrance gate should hold some definite suggestion of the character of the environment to which it opens. . . . The utilization of the keeper's lodge as an entrance archway is not a common [i.e. plain] way of introducing one to a country place. . . . Beyond such an entrance one would expect to find not only an elaborate mansion but well appointed barns for blooded horseflesh, and fancy, registered dairy cows. Farming de luxe can well be imagined to be the hobby of one who must need drive through the side of a house to gain access to his broad acres.[91]

The arch and rustic masonry of Santanoni's entry complex recall the well-known Ames Gate Lodge, designed in 1880 by H. H. Richardson.[92] Pruyn would have been familiar with Richardson's work, particularly Albany projects.

## Delano & Aldrich, Architects

Architects for Santanoni's grand entrance and Gate Lodge were Williams Adams Delano (1874–1960) and Chester Holmes Aldrich (1871–1940). Delano & Aldrich were of a different generation from Robertson and Pruyn.[93] They were educated at the École des Beaux-Arts in Paris, at the time the preeminent school of architecture in the world.[94] They both had worked for one of the nation's most prominent architectural firms, Carrère and Hastings, on the New York Public Library. Robert Pruyn engaged the two architects relatively early in their career, shortly after they formed their partnership in 1903. They had just completed the Egerton L. Winthrop, Jr. house in Syosset, Long Island and the Walters Art Gallery in Baltimore. While working on Santanoni projects they were also designing Kykuit for their most difficult client, John D. Rockefeller, Sr.[95] The classical taste of the young architects was demonstrated in many elegant designs including the noted studio building at Westbury, Long Island, designed about 1915 for Gertrude Vanderbilt Whitney. Many of their New York town houses have been regarded as outstanding examples of Italian and English Renaissance styles. "Well connected socially and well trained [the architects] achieved prominence by producing reserved and stately homes for the extremely wealthy."[96] A characteristic favored by their clients was understatement. They made palatial residences appear relatively unassuming.[97]

Less formal than their usual town houses, country houses by Delano & Aldrich might be in the English manor or American Colonial

[91] Orin Crooker, "The Personality of the Entrance Gate: Notes and Comments," *Architectural Record*, January, 1919, 93-96. Quoted by Wesley Haynes, "Gate Lodge Complex, Santanoni Preserve, Newcomb, New York: Historic Structure Report," Prepared for Adirondack Architectural Heritage, 1998, 8. Haynes also suggests Pruyn would have known Richardson's work.

[92] The gate lodge of the F. L. Ames estate, at North Easton, Massachusetts, was built in 1881. Wayne Andrews, *Architecture, Ambition and Americans: A Social History of American Architecture* (New York: Free Press, 1947), 162.

[93] Delano's family home in the New York City was one of the early landmark town houses on Washington Square. Sarah Bradford Landau, "Delano," *Dictionary of American Biography*, Supplement Six (1956-60), 1980.

[94] Delano graduated from Yale, then attended Columbia as a special student in architecture before going to Paris. Subsequently he was awarded a second baccalaureate degree, B.F.A., from Yale. Aldrich attended only Columbia, before going to Paris. Adolf K. Placzek, editor-in-chief. Steven McLeod Bedford, "Delano and Aldrich," in *Macmillan Encyclopedia of Architects* (New York: Free Press, 1983), 538.

[95] J. Winthrop Aldrich, manuscript note to authors.

[96] Richard Guy Wilson, "Picturesque Ambiguities: The Country House Tradition in America," *The Long Island Country House, 1870-1939* (Southampton, NY: Parrish Art Museum, 1988), 69.

[97] Mark A. Hewitt, "William Adams Delano and the Muttontown Enclave," *Antiques* 132 (August 1987), 316-27.

veins.[98] Architectural historian Richard Guy Wilson noted, "from about 1910, Delano & Aldrich was *the* quality country-house architectural firm in the United States."[99] "By 1935, the firm's portfolio listed 243 individual commissions of which 111 were for country houses.

Why were these architects selected? Rustic work typical of the Adirondack genre decidedly was not their métier. Delano & Aldrich were, however, noted for their sensitive adaptation to existing site conditions.[100] William Delano commented, "I avoid thinking of the new job until I have seen the site and examined it carefully. . . . You must see a place in all its aspects before you can have an adequate idea of its possibilities. A glimpse of a vista here or a tree there or even the roll of the ground may give you the inspiration. . . ."[101] His design of the Gate Lodge at Santanoni evidences this penchant for realizing the potential of a natural setting.[102]

The entrance road was arranged intentionally so that the great entry portal would frame a vista of Harris Lake and distant mountains.

An extending stone wall deflected all movement into the entry arch.[103] As Richard Guy Wilson observed, such skill in planning the approach to a building was the architects' "most outstanding accomplishment."[104]

Most striking to visitors at Santanoni is the recurrence of the stone arch in three important structures: the frame and stone Gate Lodge, the masonry creamery at the Farm, and the artist studio, built of logs and stone, at the main camp.[105] If the arch of the artist studio existed prior to Delano & Aldrich's involvement at Santanoni, then Delano & Aldrich incorporated the arch design in the stone creamery in 1904 and in the Gate Lodge in 1905.[106]

---

[98] "Delano and Aldrich . . . were among the foremost designers of white-on-red Neo-Georgian houses, clubs, and churches.". Walter C. Kidney, *The Architecture of Choice: Eclecticism in America, 1880-1930* (New York: Braziller, 1947). Caption for illustration of the Willard Straight house, fig. 109.

[99] Richard Guy Wilson, "Delano and Aldrich," in Robert B. MacKay et al., eds., *Long Island Country Houses and Their Architects, 1860-1940* (New York: W.W. Norton, 1996), 127, quoted in Haynes, "Gate Lodge Complex," 10-11. Following statistics on Delano and Aldrich's work also from Haynes, "Gate Lodge Complex," 11.

[100] Richard Guy Wilson. *The Long Island Country House*, 71.

[101] Quoted by Richard Guy Wilson, "Delano & Aldrich," 127.

[102] Original blueprint reproductions of seven sheets of drawings, signed and stamped "Delano and Aldrich, August 9, 1905," for "Gate Lodge for R. C. Pruyn, Esq., at Camp Santanoni," remained in the Gate Lodge until acquired by the State. They were removed to files of the New York State Archives and Records Administration, Albany. Drawings were number one through eight, with number five missing. J. Winthrop Aldrich noted "I am pretty certain that the handwriting seen on the drawings is that of Chester H. Aldrich [his great-uncle], but from reading the Pruyn papers and press accounts it is evident that William A. Delano was the partner-in-charge. (He signed the Santanoni guest book in late 1904 and May 1905.)" Letter of J. Winthrop Aldrich to Ms. Janet Parks, Avery Architectural and Fine Arts Library, Columbia University, November 30, 1992.

[103] Period photographs testify to the adroitness of the arrangement, not apparent in later years, when the entry road was diverted, the curved stone wall removed, and the vista obscured by forest growth. Such a major aspect of the site plan ideally ought to be restored.

[104] Richard Guy Wilson, "Delano & Aldrich," 127.

[105] These arches, in turn, are reminiscent of the masonry arch bridges along the entrance road, including the "Honeymoon Bridge" constructed in 1897.

[106] Pruyn attributed the Creamery to Edward Burnett; as consultant for the entire farm complex, he apparently providing designs for some of the buildings. Wesley Haynes observed that "architectural treatment was more likely left to William Adams Delano and the anonymous stone mason, who were engaged by Pruyn for other Santanoni projects at the time." "Farm Complex," 120.

Gate Lodge and Rich Lake outlet, with village of Newcomb beyond

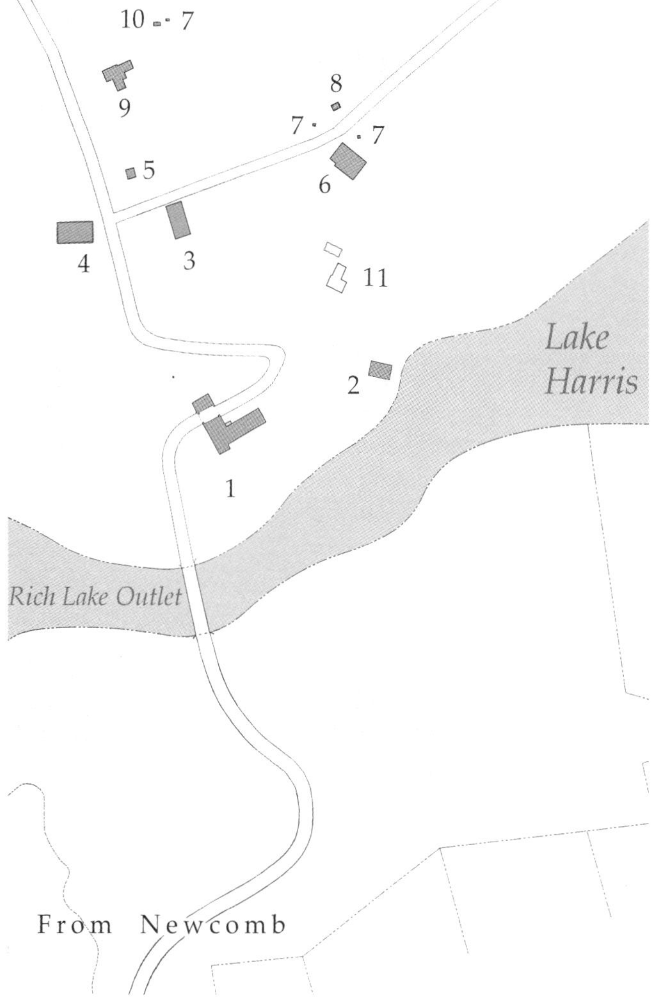


## Gate Lodge Complex

1 Gate Lodge
2 Boathouse
3 Carriage house/garage
4 Barn (burned c. 1990)
5 Gasoline tank (1990s)
6 Garage (1990s)
7 Outhouses
8 Sheep shed
9 "West" Cottage
10 Chicken coop
11 Approximate site of an earlier farmhouse

Alternatively, if the artist studio did not include the stone arch from an earlier construction phase, or the artist studio did not yet exist, then Delano & Aldrich built all three stone arches concurrently. Either way, they deserve credit for integrating the three main complexes of the Preserve in this understated, yet artful manner.

Creamery Arch

## The Gate Lodge

What is a gatehouse for? Such a facility might discourage intruders; it might serve other practical functions, such as providing all-season housing for the gatekeeper, or as a residence for a caretaking family, or for other male employees. Pruyn may have had these considerations in mind, but above all he probably intended to provide a fine architectural frontispiece. A monumental gate would announce to visitors their arrival at his domain. The portal conveyed a sense of arrival, a momentary rite of passage between two worlds and their divergent states of mind.

The site chosen for the Gate Lodge is at first glance curious. Its portal does not address the entry directly, so is not apparent from the public highway. The access bridge was located on the line of the road from the village to one of the two old farmhouses on this part of the property, but the gatehouse was not placed on this path; rather the road was deflected and the gate turned ninety degrees so that the lodge is only partially visible on approach. This may have been done to attain a more gradual incline up the slope from the river, but as the deflection entailed a difficult hairpin turn, probably the motivation was visual—the entry arch would frame a mountain vista and the new road overlook would provide a superb view of Lake Harris. Possibly there was another factor: the second of the existing farmhouses on this part of the property, shown in old photographs, was located only a short distance uphill from the gate lodge site. Rather than have this dwelling detract from the artfully designed siting and architecture of the Gate Lodge, the farmhouse was removed.

Adjoining the impressive entrance arch to Santanoni Preserve, the Gate Lodge is itself a commodious house providing six rooms on the lower floor and six bedrooms and two baths on the upper floor.[107] On the lower floor are living room, dining room and office, all with fieldstone fireplaces, plus a kitchen, pantry, and woodshed-storage room.[108] On the eastern side of the building a porch overlooks Harris Lake and the mountains beyond. On the other side of the entry arch from the residence is a small building formerly used as a paint shop and tool room.[109] Except for the stone driveway portal, the building was of frame construction, clad with cedar shingles like the farm buildings. Originally the trim

[107] "Santanoni Preserve," undated typescript, National Commercial Bank Records. The 1971 appraisal indicated that the 2660 square-foot Gate Lodge had twelve rooms, and two bathrooms. J. Winthrop Aldrich. Memorandum to File, May 7, 1996, 3.

[108] "Santanoni Preserve," undated auction notes, apparently 1953. This source mentioned only the first five rooms.

[109] Beatrice Pruyn Thibault. Aldrich, 75.

was a wine-red color, similar to the trim of the log villa.[110]

Robert Pruyn referred to Gate Lodge as "a very fine Superintendent's house, with a huge stone archway at the entrance."[111] As Pruyn's description implied, the first use of the building was as residence and office of Santanoni's first superintendent Ellis Baker. For the first decade or more, caretaker Elbert Parker had been able to manage the Preserve's business and still have time to serve as hunting and fishing guide for the Pruyns. By 1905, however, Santanoni's acreage, number of buildings, and expanding farm and forest operations had grown to such proportions as to require the services of a full-time, professional manager.[112]

Pruyn probably knew Ellis Baker from the Jekyll Island Club in Georgia, where Pruyn was a member and where Baker was "a good accountant."[113] Whether Pruyn had the Gate House erected with Baker in mind or, more likely, built the Gate Lodge for its own merits and then found a superintendent to occupy it, Baker moved to Santanoni around 1907 to take over the affairs of the estate.

## The Gate Lodge Compound

Above the Gate Lodge, several hundred feet farther into the Preserve, is one of the old farmhouses that Pruyn acquired with the property. Haynes suggests that this dwelling was built after 1876.[114] It is a two-story house of common form, with a main two-story section with front gable, connected to side wing of one-and-a-half stories.[115] The building represents a vernacular type of the region, characterized by a steep roof of forty-five-degree slope and two-over-two windows. The three-bedroom dwelling was called a "caretaker's home" on an unidentified handwritten list of buildings and called the "West House" in the 1934 inventory and appraisal.[116] The West family last occupied the residence, accounting for the name generally used today, although sometimes it is called the "Guide's House."

The West Cottage

In addition to the Gate Lodge and farmhouse, the entrance complex also contained a small barn, a carriage shed, a boat house on Harris Lake, plus sheep shed, chicken coops

[110] Paint analysis by the consultant George Lyons (Chapter 5, fn. 21) is inconclusive due to long exposure of the available sample. George Lyons to Steven Engelhart, September 1, 1998.

[111] "Santanoni Preserve," undated typescript, Bank Records; and "Santanoni Preserve/Adirondack Mountains," typescript, May 1915, NYSDEC, Haynes, "Farm Complex," fn. 98, 45.

[112] Haynes notes that Parker left the Pruyns' employ in 1906. "Gate Lodge Complex," 11. Aldrich, 77, noted that the Gate Lodge was identified as the Baker residence on the 1910 Fisher and Bryant map.

[113] Robert C. Pruyn, "Santanoni Preserve: Adirondack Mountains," typescript, version 1 [c. 1915], quoted in Haynes, "Gate Lodge Complex," 11. Haynes speculates that Ellis Baker may have been a relative of the nationally prominent banker, George F. Baker, a co-owner with Pruyn of the San-Souci apartment building at Jekyll Island. His father was George Ellis Baker, according to J. W. Aldrich, manuscript note to authors, July 1999.

[114] Haynes also suggested that the building was built prior to 1897, "Gate Lodge Complex," 6.

[115] The two farmhouses pictured in this vicinity have similarities which suggest the present West Cottage might have been the house originally located nearer the Gate Lodge. This house may have been relocated to the new site a few hundred feet uphill. Rural buildings often were moved in the nineteenth century. If so, several changes were made. Photographs show not only different orientations of the fronts, but different roof heights of the side wings, different chimney locations, and different porch arrangements. Possibly the moving process resulted in some changes, and others may have been made subsequently. Further investigation may be productive.

[116] This building, apparently the "Caretaker's Cottage" on the 1953 auction list, was described: "5 rooms and bath, 2-story shingle dwelling with porch and cellar." "Santanoni Preserve," typescript, n.d., National Commercial Bank Records. According to another inventory, the "caretaker's cottage is about 200 yards up a hill from the Gate Lodge. This is a two-story building of six rooms." "Santanoni Preserve," typescript, n.d., National Commercial Bank Records.

and other farm dependencies.[117] This, the fourth major building complex within Santanoni Preserve, was completed by 1906, almost a decade and a half from the estate's inception.

After a long mountain drive, on crossing the bridge to finally arrive at Santanoni Preserve, new visitors would first see the commodious Gate Lodge, announced by the imposing stone entry portal. New guests might have supposed this to be their awaited destination,for beyond the expansive lawns appeared a large lake with boat house, while upon a nearby slope there was a farm with sheep grazing around the farmhouse. Here, the visitor might have thought, was a complete Adirondack camp.

But this complex was merely overture; a mile ahead lay the *real* farm, and more miles-beyond awaited the great log villa on Newcomb Lake. With little idea of what lay ahead, the new guest, after passing through the great stone arch, might be surprised soon to leave the gatehouse with its tidy lawns. One then re-entered the forest, anticipating in the surrounding wilderness promised fishing and hunting—good times coming.

Entry bridge and Gate Lodge

[117] The extant carriage shed probably was erected later.

On the road to "another kind of life": "Bertie" Pruyn and her friends

# 7. Camp Life

It would be hard to express all I feel about those Santanoni parties. In fact, I do not think I possibly could. They were a very bright spot in our lives, not only giving greatest pleasure but also showing us another kind of life—that to me at least was absolutely new.

*Huybertie Pruyn Hamlin*

The Pruyns were meticulous. They planned activities carefully. Likewise they recorded and reported events diligently. In addition to many photograph albums and recent oral histories, three different kinds of records of camp life survive, amplified by recent oral histories.

The *Guest Books* were registers of visitors. The three volumes contain names of four hundred and thirty-four visitors during more than forty seasons between 1893 to 1937. The *diary*, titled "Santanoni: Record of Fish and of Some Other Things," is a report of camp activities, the weather, and the fish or hunting catch for each day. With characteristic thoroughness, the Pruyns itemized not only the total catch, the size, weather conditions, and the fly or lure used, but specified who caught which fish, at what location. Several *scrapbooks* complete the collection.[1] One titled "Bits of Fact and Fiction By All" contains miscellaneous inscriptions and sketches by family and guests. The larger scrapbook, untitled, is filled with photographs, letters, telegrams, comments and observations. It in-

[1] Two scrapbooks are at the Adirondack Museum. Family members retain others.

cludes four pages of letters and telegrams that contain ingenious misspellings of "Santanoni."[2]

Anna Pruyn shared her husband's attention to detail. Many of the diary entries are in her hand. She became the camp photographer because, her granddaughters suspect, she was extremely camera-shy. Indeed, when she does appear in photographs, she typically is staring down, looking away from the camera, or covering her face. Anna's consistent interest in documenting camp life suggests her devotion to Santanoni.

### Getting There

A prize is more savored for a difficult challenge.[3] It is hard to imagine today the marvel of Santanoni's luxury, achieved in wilderness that seemed almost inaccessible. Merely traveling to Santanoni was an adventure, as the 1893 house-warming party discovered.

Prior to the first expedition each spring, Robert Pruyn informed the caretaker that the family would be arriving, presumably with servants and luggage, and provided instructions:

> Please send both buckboards to North Creek on Wednesday, and also a large baggage wagon, and ask Abner to look for the luggage and express matter on the train arriving Wednesday evening, and have the baggage wagon start right off that night, with instruction to try to make the camp in the early afternoon, so that you may unpack the things that go by express before we arrive. Please have all the rooms in readiness for use. [4]

The era of the weekend had not yet arrived. In the early years, the better part of two days were spent just getting to Santanoni. Rigors of the journey encouraged extended sojourns. ". . . The whole family, the servants, and the necessary luggage had all to be moved together, and once arrived at camp they had to stay there for the whole period of the vacation."[5]

By 1900 Adirondack roads were much improved. Leaving North Creek after lunch, Robert Pruyn arrived at camp with three guests at 6:15 p.m. The ten-hour trip had been cut almost in half. "Roads very good," the diary notation reads.[6]

The automobile further expedited the trip.[7] By 1913, the Pruyns could climb into their car at 7 Englewood Place after breakfast and step out in the shade of the porte cochère at Santanoni in time for lunch. The time was noted with characteristic Pruyn care, to the half-minute: "Albany to Santanoni—4 hours, 32.5 minutes, Edward L. Pruyn and Langdon P. Marvin in E.L.P.'s Fiat."[8]

A Newcomb resident remembered that Mrs. Pruyn "was always driven by a chauffeur and usually took her little lap dog along. One day we got on a ledge so we could look down into the car and really see what she looked like and the dog was very little with a pug nose."[9]

### Fishing

Fastidious diary entries confirm the seriousness of fishing: "Clear. Water 46 degrees, air 45 degrees, 7 a.m.," reads an entry, which continues: "Gov. and Mrs. Roosevelt left. Mr. and Mrs. Elkins and Mr. and Mrs.

---

2 The "Santanoni Photograph Albums," "Guest Books," "Santanoni: Record of Fish and Some Other Things, 1893-1931" ["diary"], "Bits of Fact and Fiction by All: 1893-1915," and "Santanoni Scrapbooks" are included in the Bibliography. The untitled scrapbook is listed and hereafter referred to as "Santanoni Scrapbook."

3 Paul Malo recalled A.N.B. Garvan's observation regarding motivation for Great Camps, "Adirondack Architecture and the Culture of Exurbia," *Forever Wild: The Adirondack Experience* (Katonah. N.Y.: Katonah Museum of Art, 1991), 23.

4 The party was to arrive on May 17. R.C. Pruyn, letter to Elbert Parker, May 3,1900, collection of Susan Pruyn King.

5 Guy H. Lee, 71.

6 The buggy ride from North Creek took five hours and 20-minutes. "Santanoni: Record of Fish and of Some Other Things, 1893-1931," entry for May 17, 1900.

7 Santanoni Preserve in the early twentieth century was "126 miles from Albany by motor." The distance from the "nearest railroad station—North Creek—[was] 25 miles." "Santanoni Preserve." Newcomb, Essex County, New York," n.d., typescript in National Commercial Bank records.

8 "Santanoni: Record of Fish. . . ," entry for August 24, 1913. The trip would take under two-and-a-half hours today.

9 Delilah West Bissell, "My Memories. . . ."

Embarkation in full regalia

Richmond arrived. Seven trout."[10] A fish got more attention than Roosevelt—a ten-ounce landlocked salmon caught "on a Yellow Jungle Cock."[11] The salmon was small but of interest because it had been stocked as fry the previous year.[12] Like others with private or group preserves, the Pruyns stocked their waters, employed fish weirs, and utilized pisciculture to manage and improve their stock.

Fishing was not merely a man's pastime. The young women were avid and accomplished. "We have fished hard these last two days. Mabel and I have been off alone in the mornings just to see if we could not beat the others and we have. We got several splendid trout and a lot of ordinary ones."[13] A teenage guest, Bessie Oliver, ". . .talked about minnow gangs, casts and baited buoys as easily as if they had been frills and furbelows."[14] When Bessie landed a two-pound, fourteen-ounce brook trout, it was chronicled as "the largest trout ever taken on Santanoni Preserve."[15]

Weather did not deter dedicated anglers; in fact rain is good weather for fishing. "It rained pretty steadily all day, most of the time with a west wind, and we fished both morning and afternoon." Another day, more succinctly: "Showers. Everyone fished."[16] Fly-fishing was favored, although small children engaged in still fishing from shore.

In these accounts few complaints appear about black flies breaking up picnics or swarming about boats. The Pruyns did their spring fishing in May, before the winged

[10] William L. Elkins. Jr., son of the prominent western Pennsylvania oilman, was active in public utilities promotion and investing. The Elkins were frequent guests, as were Mr. and Mrs. Charles Alexander Richmond.

[11] Edward Bowditch caught it. "Santanoni: Record of Fish . . .," entry for May 22, 1899.

[12] Beatrice Pruyn Thibault recalled that the lake had been stocked with salmon at one time, Aldrich, 47.

[13] Huybertie Pruyn [Hamlin], letter to her Mother, May 20, 1894, "Santanoni Scrapbook." "Mabel" was Mabel Sard.

[14] Cornelia Kane Rathbone, "A Dethroned Ideal," *Godey's Magazine*, September 1893, 335. See fn. 55 for more on this fictionalized account of the 1893 summer party. While in her teens, Elizabeth "Bessie" Shaw Oliver was one of the most adept anglers in camp.

[15] "Santanoni: Record of Fish. . .," May 24, 1900 entry.

[16] "Santanoni: Record of Fish. . .," entries for July 1893 and May 1894.

The house-party ritual included the obligatory group photograph on the porch steps. Vivacious "Bertie" appears in the top center, next to the host, flanked on her other side by young and bored Ned Pruyn, unsmiling as usual, while Anna Pruyn, as usual, faces away from the camera.

scourges appeared in full force. Typically the Pruyns were not seen again at Santanoni until July, when the black flies were gone. Although the best fly-fishing season had waned, still they fished. Santanoni was less a hunting lodge than fishing camp; it was less a place to luxuriate in comfort than to rise at dawn and go out, even if raining, to cast flies into the mist.

### Spring and Fall Parties

The Pruyns invited about sixteen guests, young and old, to Santanoni for annual spring parties that lasted from one to two weeks."[17] May occasionally can seem like winter in the mountains. "The fishing has been very poor as the water is too cold for the fish to rise. Even Uncle Neddy and Mr. Cooper have gotten discouraged, although they got a good catch, as they went over [to Moose Pond] at 6 a.m. this morning and are still there." Moose Pond is a four-mile paddle and hike, one way.

A little later in the season, the fishing was less arduous:

> In the afternoon all fished and as a result, a total of sixty to seventy trout were ready for export [to Albany]. The event of the day was the catching of three trout at one cast by Miss [Bessie] Oliver, the same fisherwoman also securing a double. The flies used were Brown Hackle, Montreal and Queen of the Waters. [18]

[17] Huybertie Pruyn Hamlin chronicled the first four of these outings in a life-long journal that includes "The Four Spring Parties." Letters home to her mother add texture and detail. Pruyn Papers, Albany Institute of History and Art.

[18] "Santanoni: Record of Fish. . . ," June 1, 1893.

For one week between mid-October and early November, Robert Pruyn hosted an annual hunting party. In the thirty-two seasons between 1897 and 1928, twenty-nine autumn hunting parties of three or more people registered in the guest book. Women rarely attended. The average party numbered nine men in addition to the host. For several of these parties, Pruyn chartered a private railroad car to deliver his guests from Albany to North Creek.[19]

Most of the fall regulars were members of Albany's business and banking community.[20] The fall trip usually coincided with Robert Pruyn's birthday, celebrated with a banquet. The "Natal Day" celebration inspired songs and rhyming toasts, some of which were preserved in the scrapbook:

> Of all the months of all the year
> That bring us health and sport and cheer
> We love October most.
> The leaf puts on her gorgeous hue
> The buck grows bold, the bird flies true
> The wildfowl seeks the coast.
> The best of all these autumn days
> In glee we hail, in song we praise
> The birthday of our host.
> Then pour the old October ale
> Let jest go round and merry tale
> And hunter's jovial boast.
> That's why the blest who gather here
> And joy in Santanoni's cheer
> Of all the months of all the year
> Love brown October most. [21]

The fall party notwithstanding, Camp Santanoni was not primarily a hunting lodge. At designated hunting parties, while the men surely did some hunting, "most of the time Buster [Dunham, the caretaker] got up early in the morning they were to return to New York and he would go out and hunt and bring back their game trophies and put them on their cars for them. That's the way it was. I've often heard tell of how he would have to get up and get a few trophies and tie them on the cars so they could each go back with a trophy."[22]

## Outings

Between the spring fishing party and the fall hunting party, family and guests were concerned less with serious sport than summer entertainment.

The sandy bathing beach to the north of the villa naturally served as a gathering place; the boathouse to the south was another major focus of activity. Hiking was a favorite pastime on the estate, which provided "about fifteen miles of good [walking] paths."[23]

Picnics were major affairs. Staff prepared side dishes, which were packed in jars, tins and boxes from the storeroom; it was assumed that the cool waters of Santanoni Preserve would provide the main course.

---

19 Helen Tummins interview, 1991.

20 Guests included: Nicholas Brady, son of utilities tycoon Anthony Brady; Grange Sard, partner in Rathbone, Sard & Co. stove manufacturers and also a vice-president of National Commercial Bank; and David Marvin Goodrich, son of the rubber tycoon and husband of Pruyn's daughter Ruth. Twenty-one men, nearly all of them associated with R. C. Pruyn through business, attended three or more fall parties. Twelve of these twenty-one attended ten parties or more. Edward Bowditch was present for twenty-six. While Howard van Rensselaer attended the fall party only once, his brother William Bayard van Rensselaer, also a lawyer, participated nine times.

21 Anonymous verse dated October 23, 1901, "Santanoni Scrapbook," 23.

22 Marion Dunham to Robert Engel, August 17, 1992, Aldrich, 167.

23 [Robert C. Pruyn], "Santanoni Preserve: Adirondack Mountains," version 1, May 1915. Haynes, "Farm Complex," 19.

A lovely trail leads in three miles from the head of Newcomb Lake, over a spur of Moose Mountain, to the jewel-like, mountain-surrounded Moose Lake. At the end of this trail is a lean-to with a soft bed of balsam twigs, facing a great open fireplace. Near by is a boathouse with four or five Adirondack skiffs and canoes, and all the paraphernalia for cooking and sleeping in comfort in the open.[24]

The all-day trips to Moose Pond were an annual excursion to which we all looked forward, and we rowed and fished from a boat kept there in a locked boathouse and where were also stored kettles and other necessaries for a most galumptious repast cooked by the guides over a campfire. Forked sticks held the trout if any had been caught in time. . . . Cousin Anna [Pruyn, who walked with difficulty] came on these excursions, on a sure-footed horse named 'Magog,' so everyone was on hand.[25]

We came in about half an hour ago after a day at Moose Pond. It is about three miles of hard walking with a grand lunch at the end and a snooze at the open camp over there. We came home in time for five o'clock tea and I feel peaceful and at home with the world after a bath and clean clothes. [26]

When inclement weather prevented rowing to the Duck Hole or packing lunch into Montgomery Clearing, then a game of ping-pong or quiet reading on the verandah sufficed. Rain kept the mosquitoes in the woods, under leaves.

Although Santanoni was luxurious for the wilderness, guests did not spend their time in indolence, served by staff. The "strenuous life" advocated by the Pruyns' friend, Theodore Roosevelt, was the rule. Both men and women, if not otherwise inclined to plunge into the outdoors, would be motivated by the example of their host and hostess.

An arbiter of etiquette, Emily Post, enjoined ladies to take to camp sewing or knitting "to 'work on' in unoccupied moments, such as the hour of sitting silent in a canoe while husbands fish."[27] At Santanoni, however, Anna Pruyn's love of the outdoors, and her example, despite her handicap, must have encouraged more active participation, even by older women. Anna had passions for fishing and horseback riding, as well as gardening.[28] Assisted by her cane, she enjoyed walking in the woods to collect mushrooms and plants and, on rainy days, often strolled the porches around the main camp. Twenty times around made a mile. Anna also liked to be rowed about the lake in one of the heavy, metal, flat-bottomed rowboats.[29]

My grandmother [Anna] couldn't swim, so I, aged fourteen, got elected to take her all the way down the Duck Hole in one of the 'untippables.' And that's just like rowing the Queen Mary. And I guess I got all the way down, and was trying to come back up and a breeze had come up and it was against me. I wasn't progressing at all. I was just about dying. My father [Edward Lansing Pruyn] came down in the cedar canoe, saw that I was all right, spun around and went back.[30]

What made him confident? "Cynthia wasn't drowning and therefore she had to conquer this," her stepsister explained.[31] The result: "You'd never get me to paddle one of those again."[32]

"All were taught how to shoot and how to respect guns," Susan Pruyn King recalled.[33] "There were lily pads in front of the boathouse and Dad and I sat with a rifle and popped the buds."[34]

---

[24] Guy H. Lee, 74.

[25] Huybertie Pruyn Hamlin, "Four Spring Parties," 8.

[26] Huybertie Pruyn [Hamlin], letter to her Mother, May 20, 1895.

[27] Emily Post, *Etiquette* (New York: Funk and Wagnalls, Co., 1923), 441.

[28] Anna had an extensive garden and conservatory at the Englewood Place residence in Albany, as well as a collection of gardening books and notebooks. Ned Pruyn painted the garden. Cynthia Pruyn Green and Susan Pruyn King. Aldrich, 135.

[29] Cynthia Pruyn Green, Aldrich, 134.

[30] Cynthia Pruyn Green, Aldrich, 103.

[31] Susan Pruyn King, Aldrich, 103.

[32] Cynthia Pruyn Green, Aldrich, 103.

[33] Susan Pruyn King, Aldrich, 71.

[34] Beatrice Pruyn Thibault, Aldrich, 71.

Moose Pond Picnic

Daughter Ruth and her young women friends and cousins understood that camp was a place where certain, but only certain, social conventions could be set aside. Dress was hardly casual. Visitors who became regulars doubtless appreciated and respected the Pruyns' patrician tastes. Suffragettes offended the conservative Pruyns, but active sportswomen, like Anna, were roundly embraced and encouraged. The 1890s were liberating years for American women. Outdoor athletics became an acceptable activity, even for proper young ladies in elite families. Ruth Pruyn was not a field-and-streamer, however. "The long trek in the woods from the end of the Camp to the studio was her wilderness experience."[35] Otherwise, Ruth retreated to her screened gazebo.

Outdoor recreation and a woodland mystique were consciously cultivated at Santanoni Preserve, but it would be misleading to suggest that guests were totally immersed in the wilderness. On the contrary, at the outset the great stone entry arch had announced that this place was a human artifact, the domain of a proud man and his family. Guests could not spend all of their waking hours away in the wild; the farm was their host's hobby and the appreciative visitor (if he or she cared to return) had better indulge his host's interest. "Mr. Pruyn loved the place and enjoyed

[35] Susan Pruyn King, Aldrich, 8; also source of next sentence.

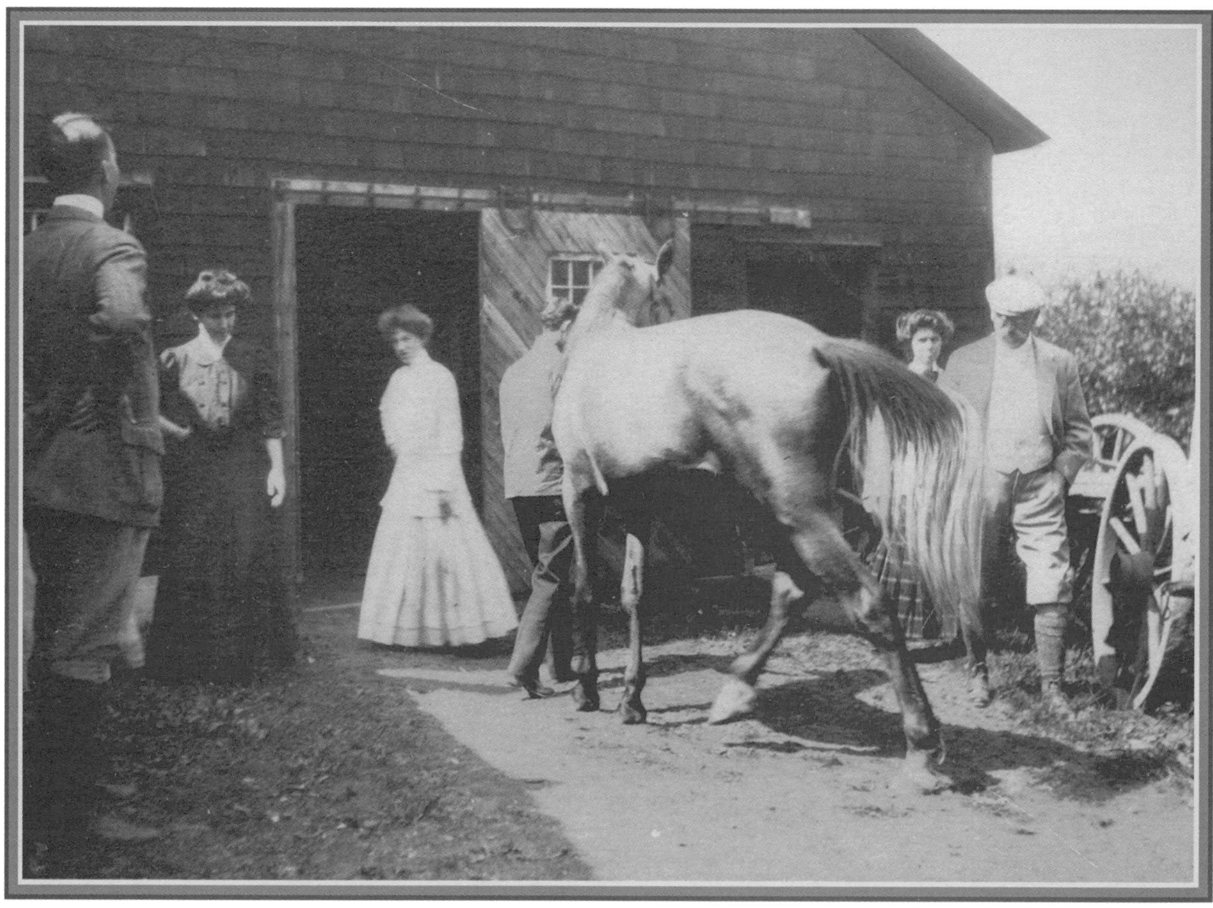

Tour of inspection to admire the Santanoni stock, an obligatory ritual

showing it off."[36] Surely a tour of the farm, to admire the stock and the facilities, was an obligatory rite.

## Pastimes

Life at Camp Santanoni reflected the genteel quality of the Edwardian era, tempered by the relative informality of life in the woods. Some amusements at Santanoni may seem boring today, when social customs differ and popular taste has become attuned to commercial entertainment. At the time, guests invited to a house party were asked to bring a book, to read aloud.[37] Robert Pruyn often read to his grandchildren from the *Japanese Fairy Tales* which had been dedicated to him.[38] Conservative tastes of the elder Pruyns perpetuated old ways, although younger generations probably favored more modern pastimes.

Interaction between young people was properly chaperoned and the sexes were carefully separated, but "there was a continual amiable warfare between the two."[39] Competition pervaded many activities.

> An exciting ball game took place in the morning between the girls and men, the latter playing left handed. The girls led until the last inning, when the men gauged Miss Cooper's curves and won the game 9–7. The evening being stormy, a game of 'It' was played, the host being the victim.[40]

In the evenings family and guests savored the "delicious tired feeling of having been out all day."[41] Music sometimes was imported

[36] Edward Johnson, letter to Ethel Bissell, October 29, 1982.
[37] Aldrich, 105.
[38] Beatrice Pruyn Thibault, Aldrich, 155. Griffis' dedication is mentioned in Chapter 1.

[39] Huybertie Pruyn Hamlin.
[40] "Santanoni: Record of Fish. . . ," May 31, 1893.
[41] Hamlin, "Four Spring Parties," 16.

from Newcomb, but most often the guests made it themselves as they gathered around the fireplace or a campfire.

> We have had stunning camp fires every night and Uncle Neddy sings all sorts of things. . . . We have no end of music with his singing and Pauline's playing [piano], Mr. Meneely's flute and Bessie's violin.[42]

Porch Polka

On occasion the Pruyns arranged an "Adirondack reel." "'Noe' (guide Noah LaCasse) called the steps and a young boy from Newcomb fiddled into the night," Bertie reminisced. "None of us ever will forget Bill's breakdown danced with all his colossal energy—in hob-nailed boots—and the holes he dug in the wooden floor."[43]

Life at Camp Santanoni certainly would have been more staid, were it not for the young people and their pranks—escapades that never would have been tolerated back in Albany. Irrepressible cousin Huybertie Pruyn was a culprit, often an instigator. She explained with mock remorse in her 1895 journal, "We were idle and Satan laid his hands on us."

The pattern of mischief was set in the first week of Santanoni's occupation. Amazed to find bathtubs in the wilderness, cousin Bertie succumbed to temptation:

> Yesterday afternoon Bessie, Ruth and I caught about twenty shiners and minnows and I built an aquarium in the men's tub—made an island of rocks with moss and sticks and dumped the fish in. You never saw anything funnier and we nearly died. So did the men when they came home. We thought they would burst laughing.[44]

Adults might be recruited for the fun, even the aristocratic Howard Van Rensselaer. "The doctor caught a horrid bull frog and put it in. They took it very well, I must say."[45] Anticipating her mother's pained reaction, Bertie added, "I can see your face over all this and I hear you say, 'Do remember to be a lady.' But if you were here, you would see it all as we see it. . . . It is very hard to write as there is such a noise all the time."

"One night we [girls] rigged up a heavy tic-tack on the stove pipe outside of Charybdis [the bachelor quarters] and the Doctor was heard to remark, "These girls are Hell."[46]

Not everyone was amused. At the second spring party, Bertie's proper cousin, Lewis Rathbone Porter, lost no time in telling her that she was making "a jackass" of herself. Word spread to Albany and Huybertie's horrified Mother wrote that she had asked Lewis not to write anyone else about these doings so the

---

[42] Hamlin, "Four Spring Parties," 24.

[43] Hamlin, "Four Spring Parties," 25. Previous and subsequent quotations from pp. 26 and 18, respectively.

[44] Huybertie Pruyn [Hamlin], letter to her Mother, May 20, 1894, Hamlin papers, McKinney Library.

[45] Huybertie Pruyn [Hamlin], letter to her Mother, May 20, 1894.

[46] Hamlin, "Four Spring Parties," 20; quotations in next paragraph, 15.

performance could die "a natural death." But Lewis evidently caught the Santanoni spirit as the week wore on. "Yesterday Lewis caught a wonderful trout . . . so he is happier," Bertie wrote.

A bedtime ritual quickly evolved:

> Every night when we took our candles to go to bed, we would make a line—each one with his left hand on the shoulder of the one in front, while with the right we grasped the candlestick. And with Uncle Neddy as leader, we sang at the top of our lungs. . . . Each squad of us was conducted to their cabin and then, the procession growing smaller and smaller, wound its way along the dark piazza while the black forest all around us looked uncanny, and as if bears might be laughing at our antics.[47]

The antic tradition continued. "Those [Pruyn] boys were awful cut-ups. That story . . . about them sawing a guide boat in half, and putting it back together to hold just long enough after coaxing a guest into it, is true. They would climb up onto the roof of the lodge, tie a dead fish to a string, and then lower it down the chimney and let it dangle there until their mother or father spotted it. They drove their parents crazy."[48]

A granddaughter recalled how, "We used to try to hit bats under the [Gate Lodge] arch at night with brooms, but scarcely ever hit them."[49]

"Ned—I don't remember what he did except fall out of a tree house and break his collar bone. Then we were told we couldn't go there anymore. Last I knew the wood cleats were still on the tree way up high but the lower ones were removed."[50]

Although the Pruyns were relaxed at camp, family tradition recalls their "fairly large house parties" there as "not riotous."[51] The horseplay notwithstanding, a sense of upper class propriety seems pervasive. The general impression of gentility, even innocence, in an uncorrupted Arcadia may, in the main, be apt. The idyllic image needs to be tempered, however, by realism. If Victorians often were staid about social behavior, they consumed alcohol as widely and copiously in the nineteenth century as did subsequent generations—sometimes more so. While Robert Pruyn's Calvinist father had been opposed to overindulgence, son Robert, becoming Episcopalian, was less averse to social drinking.[52] There was a wine cellar at Santanoni Preserve.

> The Sachem has called all the nations,
> And gathered lots of liquid rations,
> And soon there will be great elations
> At Santanoni.[53]

Spirits were not reserved for dinner:

> When other braves for game make hunt,
> They merely [with] derision grunt.
> They sit all day and watch the lake
> And try their sudless thirst to slake
> With the "big medicine," they make
> At Santanoni.
>
> One dram will make a brave quite happy,
> While two will make him rather scrappy,
> But when they get to "fours" or "fives",
> Should any last till that arrives,
> All fear is gone—even of wives
> At Santanoni.

---

[47] Hamlin, "Four Spring Parties," 6-7.

[48] Helen Tummins, in Dave Garrison. *Post-Star*, December 1, 1987. Mrs. Tummins referred to the three sons of Robert and Anna, but she married caretaker Art Tummins in 1933 when these boys were in their fifties. Probably the culprits were son Frederic's three sons.

[49] Beatrice Pruyn Thibault, Aldrich, 73.

[50] Delilah West Bissell.

[51] Cynthia Pruyn Green, handwritten notes, August 1992.

[52] "This good Calvinist [had noted a] horrible amount of drunkenness" among expatriates in Japan. He was contemptuous of "my worthy predecessor here [Townsend Harris, who] had some desperate attacks of the delirium tremens" and for periods was incapable of work. Edwin B. Lee, 130.

[53] Anonymous twenty-four-stanza poem, probably by a guest, n.d., in R. H. Pruyn Correspondence, CH 532, Box 11, v. 10.

Robert and Anna Pruyn with Ned, Ruth and friend

## Attire

All this outdoor activity was accomplished by men and women in full dress—costumes that may strike us as ludicrous today. But dress was serious business for both men and women in the 1890s, as it often is today. Bertie's impulse, on receiving the "coveted invitation" to visit Santanoni, sounds familiar more than a century later: "Mabel Sard, May Cooper, and I talked incessantly on the telephone and in person as to our outfits."

> Bessie got terribly excited about shoes and leggings and we went down together to find suitable ones on Broadway or Pearl Street. But only spats or high rubber boots could be found to protect our legs from brambles and flies. I finally ended with a horrible pair of long black cloth leggings found in Troy—they had shiny black buttons that had to be hooked with a patent button hook, and they generally twisted off in the process–also they were horribly hot. . . .[54]
>
> Then the skirt problem was serious. To be a real sport, the skirt should not touch the ground. And yet, some considered that was rather shocking. We held up the telephone system of Albany discussing how many inches off the ground it would be decent to wear them. . . . Bessie [Oliver] had on a real street sweeper, and May [Sard] one almost as bad.
>
> Our shirt waists had high choking linen collars with ties, and then came the hat question—it never occurred to us to do without them. Mabel had a very becoming tricorne while Bessie had a squash felt with her fish flies caught around the hat band, and I had an orange felt called a "Land and Water Hat" presumably because it was good for any time or place.
>
> I had a dress of Tyrolean green cloth made at Munich the previous summer, and which was considered excellent for such an occasion. Lida Mulcahy was called in to make a short skirt of striped denim but it was never finished—she became interested in bloomers, and so I tried to finish the hem in Camp but Mabel came to the rescue and lent me an extra skirt of Gertrude's to wear with a red flannel shirt or cotton ones.

[54] One young woman wore leather leggings borrowed from her uncle; the others wore heavy black silk leggings. Huybertie Pruyn Hamlin, "Four Spring Parties," 1-3.

## Romance

Where there were young people together, there was bound to be romance, or romantic fantasies. One regular woman guest, an author, wrote:

> It was a perfect day, clear, bracing and sunny. The air had an effect on us like champagne. We scrambled laughingly up the trail. . . . Once, though, we stood still to listen to the solemn silence of the woods. The wind lowered its voice, too, as if it knew that reverence behooved the place. It was God's acre of the forest, a burying place for kings. . . . The hush of the place stole over me like a spell. I looked at Mr. Brown to see if he understood. He took my hand to help me over the rocky path, and we went on in silence.[55]

High drama in the wilderness, in the 1890s. That was genteel, romantic fiction, of course. In reality, life was less poetic:

> Then Pauline sprained her knee and we accused her of doing it on purpose so as to have Dr. Bowditch look after her, as she was completely gone on him.[56] We also told her never to ask him to sing, "Oh, Genevieve, my Genevieve . . . ." We said the girl to whom he had been engaged was named Genevieve. She had been burned by his cigar ash, and of course he never could forgive himself. He had always remained single and this song made him weep onto her picture in the back of his watch. Pauline fervently promised never to speak of it and thanked us for tipping her off—and—promptly that evening she asked for the song . . . adding that she was sorry for his disappointment. He was the most puzzled man I ever saw—polite but bewildered. He said he would love to sing Genevieve if only he had the music. . . . Pauline blurted out the whole story. Poor Genevieve became the joke of the Camp.[57]

Bertie and her friends were irrepressible:

> Bessie and Cora and I made up our minds that May Cooper and Dick Meneely must make a match somehow. We pledged ourselves to refuse any invitations to fish or canoe or do anything else with Dick—we must scorch him out so that he would finally come to May and they would go off together. This led to one or another of us being well left on invitations, but we felt so virtuous. I remember the bewildered and concerned looks of [our host,] poor Cousin Robert [Pruyn] one moonlight evening when he found me all alone in the large room, reading, while the rest were paired off. He even offered to take me out himself as he worried for fear I might feel slighted. I did not like to give away the plot and as he was busy with mail, he was relieved to have me decline.
>
> Later the astute Dick gently suggested to one of us, that he wished we would not place him in awkward positions—that he had great respect for his good neighbor Miss May, but could assure us it would never take another form, so the old game was up.

[55] Huybertie was not the only one taking notes at Santanoni. Cornelia "Nelly" Kane Rathbone, who signed the guest book twenty-eight times between 1893 and 1929 and apparently was a friend of Anna, published a short story fictionalizing the 1893 summer party. "A Dethroned Ideal" appeared that September in *Godey's Magazine*. The story was largely autobiographical; the first-person character is a genteel society dame, woefully unmated, like Nelly. An attentive, soft-spoken bachelor is provided. The heroine recounts this passage. Rathbone, "A Dethroned Ideal," 335.

[56] Dr. Vincent Bowditch, probably related to the Albany Bowditch family, was from Boston.

[57] Hamlin, "Four Spring Parties," 19-20, and the following quotation, 22-23.

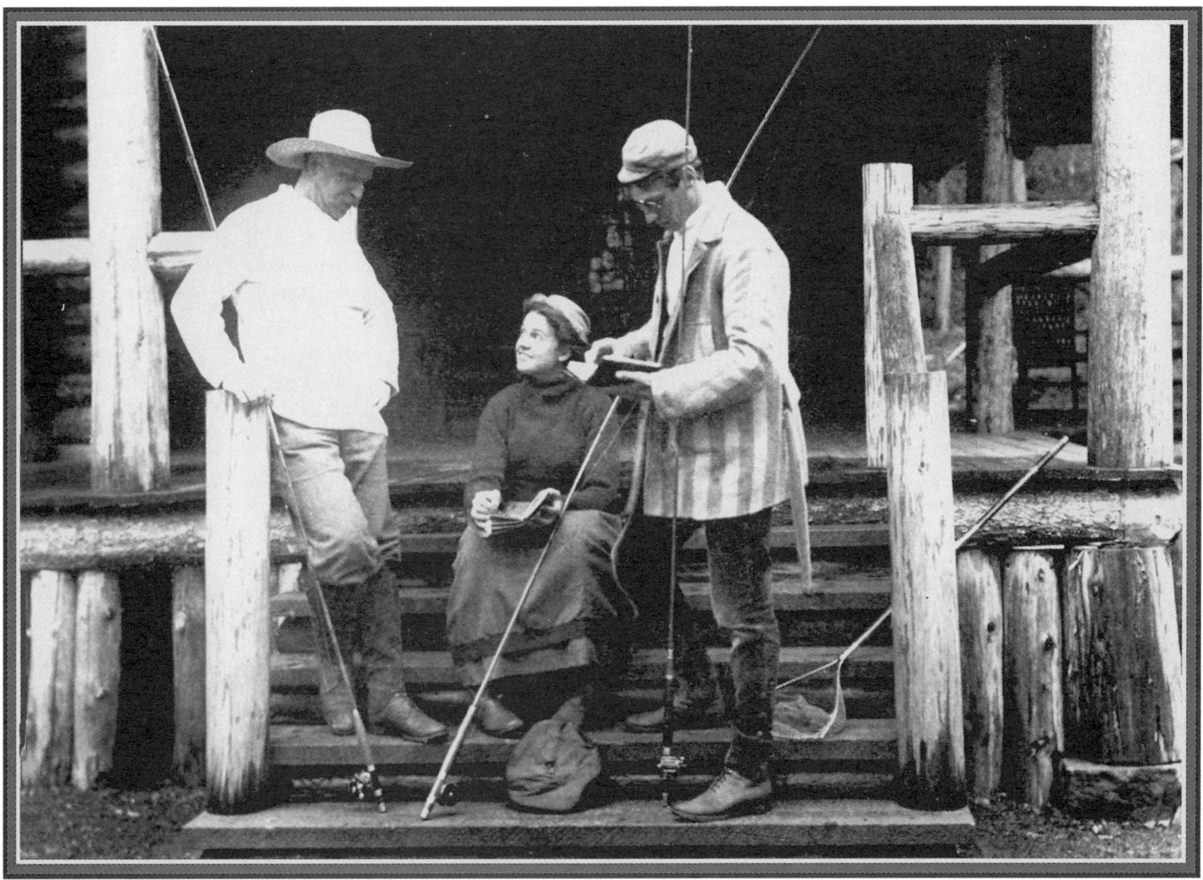

Checking the record books: Edward Bowditch, Huybertie Pruyn, and James Fenimore Cooper III*

Bertie happily recalled:

> We acted like birds let loose—what a riot it was. . . . Billy Sheldon undertook to show me how to walk correctly, so he ran me all the way uphill to Lake Andrew and back in record time. We were considered very *Fin de Siecle* to have gone without a chaperone. He overheard one of the party remark to another, that it was time to go home with such things happening. This amused us greatly. . . ."[58]

## Guests

The Pruyns, like other patrician families who established Great Camps, did not go into the woods to socialize with neighbors. Although the Pruyns joined the Tahawus Club, within hiking distance of Santanoni, and occasionally visited there and at other nearby camps or clubs, they typically came to Santanoni to stay.[59] A Great Camp provided its own society.

Of the Pruyns' hundreds of guests, many were notable. A good number were relatives; some were business associates and Albany friends, together with their families. The Pruyns had not the social ambition of some Adirondack hostesses, such as Margaret Emerson of Camp Sagamore or Marjorie Merriweather Post of Camp Topridge, both of whom favored national celebrities. The Pruyns' preferred social milieu was conservative. Many of their friends represented families of the Yorker establishment, like the Van Rensselaers, Coopers, Morgans, Roots, and Roosevelts.

* Bertie Pruyn seems evident by her familiar appearance, although a recent, photo album note identified Bessie Oliver

[58] Hamlin, "Four Spring Parties." First sentence, 5; remainder of quotation, 25.

[59] R.C. Pruyn was a trustee of the adjoining Caughnawauga Club.

## Theodore Roosevelt

Scanning an old Santanoni album, a granddaughter commented casually, "That's Teddy Roosevelt."[60] She pointed to a portly figure high in a tree, improbably menacing a porcupine as it retreated out on a limb.

Theodore Roosevelt probably had met Robert Pruyn in Albany when Roosevelt came to serve as State Assemblyman from Manhattan.[61] Less than a year after he captured the imagination of the American public with his fabled charge up San Juan Hill, now Governor Roosevelt visited Pruyn at his "delightful mountainous retreat."[62] The Guest Book entry for May 20, 1899 duly registered signatures of Theodore and Edith Roosevelt. In tiny lettering between their names appears an inscription in the Governor's hand that echoed the wartime motto, "Remember the Maine":

"(remember the porcupine!)"[63]

May 20th/1899
Theodore Roosevelt
(remember the porcupine!)
Edith K. Roosevelt
Lucy B. Bowditch
Edward Bowditch
Elizabeth Shaw Oliver
Gertrude Sard

Treed by Theodore

Governor Roosevelt was supposed to be spending his weekend in the Adirondacks drafting a message to a special session of the Legislature—not pursuing porcupines up trees. Newspapers told readers that while in the woods he would work on amendments to the Ford franchise tax bill, a reform bill opposed by entrenched interests.[64] The fight was bitter, and Roosevelt had refused to sign an earlier, watered-down version. Before going to the mountains, he spent Friday in Manhattan where he met with political leaders but failed to win agreement on language that would strengthen his bill.[65]

The issue was politically critical for Republican Roosevelt because big business inter-

[60] Susan Pruyn King to Howard Kirschenbaum, 1991.

[61] Roosevelt was Assemblyman between 1882 and 1884.

[62] The Roosevelts visited from Saturday, May 20 to Monday, May 22, 1899. "Roosevelt in the Adirondacks," *The Essex County Republican*, Vol. LIX, No. 39, May 25, 1899, 3. New York State Library

[63] Roosevelt was a life-long naturalist whose first published work at age 18 was *The Summer Birds of the Adirondacks in Franklin County, NY* (1877). He may have been investigating the porcupine because of scientific curiosity. J. Winthrop Aldrich, manuscript note to authors, January 1999.

[64] Roosevelt favored a franchise tax on public service corporations for their use of public streets. "Roosevelt in the Adirondacks," *The Essex County Republican,* May 25, 1899, 39.

[65] "They Did Not Agree," *Albany Times Union*, May 20, 1899, 1.

ests vigorously opposed him, as did the powerful Republican boss Senator Thomas Platt.[66] Roosevelt's persistence was a signal to the public that the hero of San Juan Hill was his own man. It would be a milestone to mark his political career.

Probaby Roosevelt was so confident that he did not reschedule this weekend visit to Santanoni Preserve. Did he work on his address to the special legislative session? Photographs show Roosevelt standing on the dock preparing to go boating, rowing a guide-boat, posing with other guests for the requisite front-porch portrait, and chasing a porcupine along a tree limb.

"I do not know when I have enjoyed forty-eight hours more," Roosevelt wrote Pruyn one week later.[67] Meanwhile, in Albany, he had prevailed. His reform legislation passed, despite the opposition.

The Pruyn family and longtime Newcomb residents talk of Roosevelt as a "regular" at the camp. The guest book documents only the one visit. Roosevelt's papers at the Library of Congress show that the following April, he wrote Pruyn thanking him for a shipment of maple syrup, presumably harvested from the Santanoni sugar bush. And in June, he wrote, "I am genuinely disappointed not to be able to visit your lovely Adirondack place this year."

Roosevelt's next recorded visit to the Adirondacks, in September 1901, made history.[68] His destination was the Tahawus Club, where now Vice-President Roosevelt met his family for some hiking in the High Peaks. The whole family was there but one, Roosevelt's daughter, Alice, who was at Santanoni visiting her friend Ruth and the three Pruyn sons.

On September 14, while the Vice President and his hiking party descended Mount Marcy, a messenger ran up with a telegraph report that President McKinley, who had been recovering in Buffalo from a professed anarchist's bullet, had taken a turn for the worse and that Roosevelt should return. By the time he descended to the Club, word had arrived that McKinley was dying. A third message came, urging Roosevelt to return immediately.

Thus began Roosevelt's famed midnight buckboard ride over thirty-five miles of treacherous road. Three sets of horses and drivers were required, so arduous was the unlit journey. McKinley died during Roosevelt's ride. Roosevelt arrived on the North Creek train platform at 4:30 a.m. to learn that he had become the 26th President. He boarded a waiting train for Buffalo, where he was administered the oath of office.

The following summer, Alice again visited Santanoni as the daughter of the President.[69]

## Camp Regulars

While family comprised the core of the Santanoni community, some close friends were regarded as family.

"Uncle Neddy," who visited Santanoni Preserve fifty-seven times, more often than anyone outside the family, was businessman Edward Bowditch, no actual relation. The Bowditches were among the Pruyns' closest friends and were at one time next door neighbors. Ned and his wife Lucy often came with their family. Bowditch, a partner in Rathbone and Sard stove works, for thirty-five years attended many of the spring fishing parties and most of the fall hunting parties. The Rathbones and Sards likewise were regular visitors.

The frequent visits of Pruyn's close friends James Fenimore Cooper and Howard Van Rensselaer have been mentioned earlier.

[66] Platt had an Adirondack camp on Raquette Lake.

[67] Theodore Roosevelt, letter to Robert C. Pruyn, May 27, 1899. Theodore Roosevelt Papers, Library of Congress, V8-P399, Washington, DC.

[68] One of many accounts is provided by Masten, 182.

[69] On her trip back to North Creek to catch the train south, the carriage stopped at Aiden Lair Lodge, which had been the starting point for the final leg of her father's journey the previous year. The innkeeper, Mike Cronin, had been his driver. After urging Cronin to tell the story one more time, Alice asked whether he had any horseshoes from the ride to serve as a memento. Cronin, who over the years unabashedly gave away dozens of commemorative shoes from the two-horse team, happily obliged.

Albany artist Walter Launt Palmer visited with his wife, Zoe. Palmer, son of sculptor Erastus Dow Palmer, had been a student of Hudson River School painter, Frederic Church. Palmer was mentor to eldest son, Ned, and painted with him in his Santanoni studio.[70] During a mid-summer party one year, another frequent guest, Abby Seldon, commissioned Palmer to paint a group portrait of the family gathered around the fireplace in the main room of the camp. Palmer made the picture for sixty dollars and presented it to the Pruyns. Its whereabouts today is unknown. Several other Palmer paintings also hung in the Pruyn house at 7 Englewood Place.[71]

Another regular mid-summer guest was Frederick Kelley, a nephew of Anna Pruyn, who by 1899 was general manager of Robert Pruyn's Consolidated Car Heating Co. of Albany. Kelley logged into the Santanoni guest book thirty-three times between 1893 and 1928. Kelley was one of two friends who joined brothers Ned and Robert Pruyn to ring in the new year at Santanoni, an event recorded whimsically by an illustrated entry in the guest book.

Many visitors represented Boston society—a connection reinforced when the Pruyns' three sons attended Harvard. The Pruyn youngsters brought college friends to Santanoni, some of whom continued to visit after their Harvard years. A few of this Boston contingent were invited to join the fall hunting party.

"The guests had to pass muster to be invited back," a granddaughter remembered. "If you had a beau who didn't fit in, you found out fast."[72]

Many decades later, Bertie recalled:

> The generous hospitality and thoughtful provision of the host for so many varieties of recreation—their amused tolerance of our endless jokes and tricks, the "understanding hearts"—all are still, after the lapse of a generation, talked about whenever two or three members of the old parties are gathered together.[73]

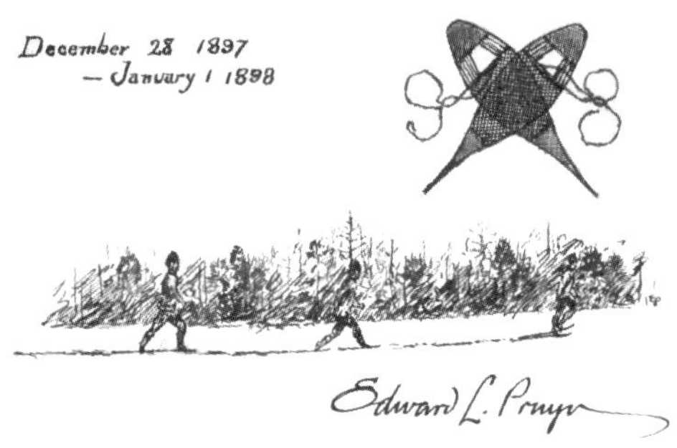

[70] Palmer signed the guest book six times between 1903 and 1919.

[71] J. Winthrop Aldrich searched extensively for Palmer's Santanoni paintings. The family portrait and a landscape of Newcomb Lake were among the Palmer paintings at Englewood Place. Both are lost (J. W. Aldrich to Paul Malo).

[72] Beatrice Pruyn Thibault, Aldrich, 52.

[73] Hamlin, "Four Spring Parties," 26.

I.

"For ten years, 'Pruyns,'
We have drunk your wines
And cast for your speckled fish.
We have rowed your boats
And wore your coats
And obtained our slightest wish.

II.

We have warmed our toes
And forgot our woes
By your friendly and cheering fires.
We have lost your hooks
We have read your books
But your kindness never tires."

III.

Ten springs have gone
Like our idle song
Happiness moves by stealth.
It seems a sin
That it's only ten
But God bless you here's your health. [74]

[74] "Santanoni: Bits of Fact and Fiction By All," undated entry (ca. 1903).

## Staff

Guests appreciated Robert and Anna Pruyn as both meticulous and considerate hosts.[75] The Pruyns astonished first-time visitors with the unexpected luxury of their country house in the forest. At the initial house-warming party it was not the grandeur of the great log villa that impressed young Bertie; it was the sound of a piano playing deep in the wilderness and discovery of her bath tub filled with hot water.

A piano tuner had to spend days traveling in and out of Santanoni to keep that instrument in tune. Hot water had been prepared out of sight, to appear magically on demand. Adirondack weather can be disagreeable, but wet, gamy clothes would return cleaned, dried and folded for each day's venture. After ten hours of fly-casting in cold and windy May or hunting in snowy October, chilled guests would return to a hot bath, a sumptuous meal of game and farm produce, a musical evening by the fire, afterwards to retire to their own cabin with roaring fire, to a bed turned down with fresh linens under a Hudson Bay blanket.

The Pruyns maintained the illusion of an idyllic, simple life. In reality, behind the scenes, the illusion was being maintained by a complex institution, not only of forty buildings, but also of numerous employees. A skilled, well-managed staff, largely out of sight, allowed the owners to indulge a fantasy of carefree Eden.

[75] "My grandfather was the perfect host, always making sure his guests were well provided for and engaged in something they enjoyed." Cynthia Pruyn Green, handwritten notes, August 1992.

The owners' style of life determined the staff organization at a large country house. Unlike Newport, there were no footmen in velvet knee breeches to draw dining chairs at Santanoni, or at any other Great Camp in the Adirondacks. At Kamp Kill Kare, there were not even dining chairs—only benches. That Great Camp required a staff of more than forty to operate, however; Camp Topridge had a staff of about eighty-five.[76]

Santanoni was not so grand a social institution as were some Great Camps. The Pruyns' guest list was usually less than half that of Mrs. Emerson at Sagamore, who enlarged her dining hall to serve forty. If smaller in scale, the inherent logistical problems were the same. Basically a similar range of functionaries provided the same functions, from cooks and chambermaids to gardeners and guides.

Despite its appearance calculated to make the building disappear into the forest, the great log villa, with twenty-four rooms, was larger than the Pruyns' grand city house, which contained twenty-two rooms. Accordingly, a similarly large staff was required, not merely to operate and maintain the villa, but the much larger estate. All told, there were some thirty-five staff bedrooms in the four building complexes at Santanoni Preserve.

We may think it oddly amusing that seekers of the simple life should require a large domestic staff to live in the woods. We may understand why one might want a knowledgeable guide or two when venturing forth into the wild, but a butler? Yes, there was a butler at Santanoni, and probably more maids than required to keep house in the woods. The reason that many purportedly simple country places seem to us over-staffed was not merely that establishments were large, or that labor was cheap, or that employers were indolent. To the contrary, a large staff meant more problems of supervision. Even if not required in the country, some of the townhouse staff required by a more formal regimen in town—key personnel such as the butler—came with the family to the country as a working holiday. More relaxed living in the country usually meant more free time for outdoor recreation, for staff as well as family and guests. The Pruyns provided a recreation pavilion for the staff.[77] Half walls enclosed it, the upper portion screened. ". . .It was big. They sat out there—there was a bunch of them. There was quite a lot of help. . . ."[78] The servants had their own beach at the lakeside service complex, and probably a bathhouse there.

[76] Kaiser, 208.

Butler, maid, and chauffeur at lakeside service complex*

A liberal employment policy also engendered local support for a proprietor, who would be concerned about vandalism, trespass, tax assessment, and volunteer help in emer-

[77] Beatrice Pruyn Thibault recalled the building, part of the service complex behind the kitchen wing of the log villa. Aldrich, 125; also Cynthia Pruyn Green, Aldrich, 112, 125-126.

[78] Cynthia Pruyn Green, Aldrich, 126; beach and bathhouse recalled on 113.

* The butler is caught in dishabille, without his usual jacket and with shirtsleeves rolled up. The maid may have been Sally (see footnote 130).

gencies. Santanoni's first caretaker served as town supervisor, a useful connection.[79]

Families on the Preserve belonged to the Newcomb community. "I can remember Dad taking me by the hand and a lantern in the other and we would walk to the silent movies in the community house which was attached to the Methodist church."[80] Resident families also formed a neighborhood on the estate. "When it was harvest time there would be corn roasts in the field, rides on the sugar-beet wagon."[81]

The Great Camps really depended on local Adirondackers, not only for feasibility of construction and maintenance, but also for regional character. Difference in culture between visitors and locals enhanced the romance of the deep woods. The woodsman who served as prototypical Adirondack guide would not only lead novices, but also—in a driving rain and with perfect good humor—provide for his "sports" a dry shelter and a crackling fire within the half-hour.

Santanoni was year-round home to several families*

Urbanites admired backcountry capability in the wilderness, and enjoyed rustic demeanor. They paid high prices to hear Paul Smith josh them with barbed wit at his fashionable hotel. Such rapport would have been unacceptable at Newport or other more urbane resorts. Nostalgic literature has romanticized the woodsman guide. Not all were so charming; some at Santanoni were in fact "not very nice. . . . Dad [Frederic Pruyn] drank and they hung around him and so forth." Were they really professional guides? "They claimed to be."[82]

Many wealthy camp owners hired a local man who would serve as a guide during the season, and serve as caretaker of the property throughout the year. Raised to survive by subsistence hunting and marginal farming, such local men often became experienced as jacks-of-all-trades, since versatility was required to survive in the remote woods. Elbert Parker served as the first caretaker/guide at Santanoni for at least thirteen and possibly seventeen years.[83]

Before the arrival of the annual spring party, Robert Pruyn would write Parker or his successors to ask if the ice had gone out on Newcomb Lake and, if so, what the water temperature was. In other words, when will the fishing be good? Beyond maintaining the camp's buildings and grounds, the caretaker or superintendent was supposed to know where and when to find fish and game.

The organizational chart of a country house could be complex. Some of the staff came with the family from the city, others were local folk. Some staff was engaged within the house, others without. Generally the household operation was distinct from the rest of the estate function. The lady of the house was more concerned with internal affairs, her husband with external matters.

[79] Elbert Parker served as Supervisor of the Town of Newcomb, while Pruyn successfully petitioned the Town to abandon its rights of way through Santanoni Preserve.

[80] Delilah West Bissell.

[81] Delilah West Bissell.

* From left, the Dunhams–Lester ("Buster") holding Stanley, Madeline and Nellie. From right, the Youngs–"Grandma" Carrie, Carl, and Minnie, and an unknown women behind.

[82] Beatrice Pruyn Thibault, Aldrich, 11-12.

[83] Parker served at least until 1906, according to diary entries. He was Supervisor in 1892. *Essex County Republican*, December 22, 1892.

### Superintendent

A large estate might have a superintendent, who was more an administrator than a caretaker/handyman. A large estate was a business, even if not intended to make a profit, and so was managed as a business. Record keeping was demanded, especially by fastidious owners like Robert Pruyn, who took keen interest in affairs of the estate. Santanoni Preserve, although large, was not so extensive as some vast Adirondack domains, nor was its household run as a veritable private hotel. Robert Pruyn certainly had sufficient interest and ability to manage his own estate. What he lacked was time and presence. When the Farm and Gate Lodge complex greatly expanded the preserve's operations, Pruyn retained a professional estate superintendent who took over the management from Elbert Parker.[84]

Ellis Baker, the "good accountant" from Georgia's Jekyll Island Club, served as the first superintendent from about 1906 to 1915. Charlie Caulfield was the Superintendent from about 1918. He was succeeded by "a man named Hyatt" who was replaced in 1922 by Lester "Buster" Dunham as the "camp boss."[85] Dunham, "who stood 6'-3" or 6'-4" in his stocking feet" was regarded as " a competent guide, a good woodsman, and always ready to tackle any task."[86] Buster, his wife Nellie and children Madeline and Stanley lived at the lakeside caretaker's complex. Buster kept the road open with a snowplow and drove camp children to their Newcomb school in his station wagon.[87] He was dismissed in 1931 when an ailing Robert Pruyn retired and estate operation was reorganized with his bank as trustee.

During their terms, all the superintendents may have lived some of the year in the caretaker's house by the Duck Hole bridge, one-half mile from the main camp. (The Dunhams called it the "way-in house."[88]) Perhaps this lakeside house was more inviting during the summer months, but during the winter the finer Gate Lodge, adjacent to Newcomb hamlet, was more practical as a residence.

After 1931 Arthur ("Art") Tummins, a Newcomb native whom Dunham had hired to work at Santanoni when in his second year of high school, became the lone, full-time staff person at Santanoni until he retired in 1976.[89] After his marriage, he and his family lived in

Art Tummins, 1921

[84] Haynes, "Farm Complex," 74.

[85] Edward Johnson, MD., in his letter to Ethel Bissell, mentioned that Hyatt moved "back to the Boreas, where he had come from."

[86] Haynes, "Farm Complex," 75; Marion Dunham, interview; memo, probably written by Robert Pruyn. Dunham came from Wells, N.Y, Aldrich, 164. He subsequently hired many Santanoni staff from the Wells-Northville area.

[87] Delilah West Bissell.

[88] Caption in Marion Dunham's photo album, recorded by Donald Williams, 1998.

[89] Garrison, "Former Resident Recalls. . . ," interviewing Helen Tummins. Haynes, "Farm Complex", 75, says Tummins retired in 1974.

various places on the estate, at one time in the house near the Gate Lodge, then occupied seasonally by Frederic Pruyn's family. "How I wish this oral history had been done when Art Tummins was alive," commented Frederic's niece, Susan Pruyn King. "He knew every leaf on every tree."[90] Art Tummins worked at Santanoni fifty-one years. He and his wife, Helen, lived on the Preserve for most of their married life.[91]

### Farm Staff

A caretaker/guide, sometimes off in the woods for long days with family and guests, could not attend to day-to-day business of running the estate during the season. Similarly, a skilled superintendent, busy with accounting and management, was not expected to milk cows and tend gardens. Consequently, the expanded farm required additional hands, becoming its own department.

Since Pruyn did not regularly conduct lumbering at Santanoni Preserve, the more continuous business of the estate was agricultural. Although any one of the farm operations was relatively small scale, its operations were diverse enough that the farm required its own manager. Hence on the organizational chart there was a "farm boss" serving under the "camp boss."[92]

Lewis Kinne, remembered as "an imposing man in charge," was farm manager (or "farm boss") from 1910 until farm operations ceased in 1931.[93] The Kinnes came to Santanoni after having worked at the thousand-acre estate and dairy farm of New York Governor Levi P. Morton in Rhinecliff, N.Y.[94] "Boss Kinne" and his wife Minnie Kinne moved into the New Farm House, where they lived for nine years, until moving to the newly built Farm Manager's Cottage.[95]

The chain of command, from Robert Pruyn, through his Superintendent, down to his Farm Manager, continued further to another echelon; a Head Gardener reported to the Farm Manager. The Head Gardener, moreover, supervised an Assistant Gardener and occasional local help. Charles Petoff, a native of Bulgaria who joined the gardening staff in 1915, became head gardener in 1919.[96]

When the Kinne family moved to the Farm Manager's Cottage, Charlie Petoff and his wife Pena ("Nelly") moved into the New Farm House, which then became known as the Gardener's Cottage. Their three children were born in the house.[97] Petoff exercised complete

The Petoffs on the Kinne's porch at the Farm Manager's Cottage, looking toward an icehouse and the Old Farm House.

[90] Thibault interview, July 29, 1992.

[91] Garrison, "Former Resident Recalls...."

[92] George Shaughnessy of Minerva, N.Y., interview, Aldrich, 160.

[93] Mary Petoff Smith, daughter of Head Gardener Charles Petoff. Letter to Robert Engel, September 13, 1992.

[94] Mary Petoff Smith, letter to Robert Engel, September 13, 1992. Also Vice-President under Benjamin Harrison, Morton had *two* Adirondack camps--Eagle Island and Pine Brook on Upper Saranac Lake.

[95] Haynes thinks the Kinnes lived in the New Farm House between 1910 and 1919. "Farm Complex", 75, 149.

[96] Petoff became gardener at Santanoni two years after immigrating to America from Bulgaria, from a climate of similar growing conditions. He learned of the job through Pruyn's Albany tailor, Tancho Vaptsaroff, who had emigrated from the same Bulgarian village. Petoff tilled the Santanoni soil for six years before sending for his wife in 1921. Pena learned English at Santanoni Mary Petoff Smith, letter to Robert Engel, September 13, 1992.

[97] The children were George, Roger, and Marina ("Mary"). A nephew, Lee Markoff, also lived with them. Delilah West Bissell. Petoff had a two-year absence from Santanoni, from 1917-19. Haynes, "Farm Complex," 149.

control over the gardens and orchards. Word was sent to him about what was needed by the Pruyns and employee households, and he alone would pick and deliver the produce. No one else was allowed to browse the garden.

Charles Petoff likewise was relieved of his duties in 1931. At that time Walter West was Assistant Gardener. The West family lived in the old farmhouse ("West Cottage") near the Gate Lodge.[98]

Also reporting to the Farm Manager was the Herdsman, who was responsible for the dairy operations. George Ross, a resident of Newcomb, was clerk at the general store there when engaged as herdsman in 1922.[99] For nine years George lived with his wife Lettie and daughter Rowena in the dark, nineteenth century Old Farm House, renamed the "Herdsman's Cottage" during their tenure. He milked cows by hand twice a day, carrying five-gallon containers by hand to the creamery.[100] In 1931 he too was discharged. He returned to Newcomb and opened a gas station next to his home there.[101]

Caleb Chase had charge of the draft horses during the final years of the farm operation.[102] He and teamster Clifton Parker boarded with the Ross family at the Old Farm House.[103] George Bell was teamster in the 1920s.[104]

The Herdsman's daughter, Rowena, recalled that "my father worked seven days a week for eight years." His "workday started at four a.m. and lasted to six p.m. with an hour or two of free time in the afternoon."[105] George Ross earned a hundred dollars a month, plus "milk, some butter, and on occasion we were given a smoked ham."[106]

Rowena tells of a solitary childhood on the farm. From age eight to sixteen she was the only child around. "I hated it with a passion."[107] After school she would get her roller skates, walk a shoveled path to the barn and, warmed by the animals, skate for hours around and around the smooth concrete floor. As she passed each cow, Rowena would gently touch their rumps and say, "Hi Blanche, hi Castlepolly, hi Fern. . . ."

## Other Estate Staff

Of some staff families who lived or worked on the Preserve, no record has been found. Of others we know little, such as "Vern" and Bertha Pelcher from Wells in Hamilton County and their daughters Jeannette and Marion.[108] Vern was described both as "handyman" and "chauffeur and mechanic."[109] A man named Wilcox managed a "department" that saved practically $1600 in 1911-12, according to the superintendent's annual report.[110]

In addition to resident families, individual "boarders" also lived on the estate. The superintendent and farm manager were responsible for hiring and boarding seasonal laborers. For example, at one point Vern Pelcher boarded with the Dunhams. "The men were so funny, every morning at breakfast, telling jokes," recalls Buster Dunham's daughter, whose mother cooked for the employee boarders.[111]

The work of boarders included cutting firewood for the homes on the farm, and in the

98 Walter and Myrtle West had four children: Delilah, Henry, Everett and Warren. Delilah West Bissell.

99 Dillon and Shaughnessy were proprietors of the store. David Garrison. "A Working Dairy. . . ," 8A.

100 David Garrison. "A Working Dairy. . . ."

101 David Garrison. "A Working Dairy . . . ."

102 Caleb Chase may be the noted Adirondack guide-boat builder.

103 Delilah West Bissell, "My Memories of Pruyn's Preserve."

104 Dan Havron of Paradox, N.Y. to J. W. Aldrich, Aldrich, 159.

105 Garrison says it was a few hours off in the afternoon. "A Working Dairy. . . ."

106 Garrison, "A Working Dairy . . . ," 8A.

107 Rowena Ross Putnam, interview by Robert Engel, tape recording, Newcomb, New York, July 1991.

108 David Garrison. "A Working Dairy . . . ." Delilah West Bissell spelled the daughter's name "Jannette". Vern Pelcher (1875-1963), Bertha Pelcher (1875-1973). Marion became Mrs. William Bacon. Pelcher information from Beverly Williams of Johnstown, via postcard from Don Williams to Howard Kirschenbaum, January 7, 1999.

109 Handyman mentioned in Aldrich, 183. Chauffeur and mechanic mentioned by Marion Dunham, conversations with Donald Williams (1990s), related to Howard Kirschenbaum, December 31, 1998.

110 Reported in Haynes, "Farm Complex", 43.

111 Madeline Dunham Covert, Aldrich 176-177; Pelcher boarding at Dunhams, Aldrich, 183.

Ice Harvest

winter they cut ice" for the estate icehouses.[112] "Although ice had not been harvested for some time, in 1953 one icehouse at the main camp had "ice to a depth of three or four feet still . . . insulated in sawdust below grade."[113]

Arthur Bailey (or "Braley") of Newcomb seasonally tapped about nine hundred maple trees in the sugar bush, and operated the sugar house in the spring. Workers wearing snowshoes carried sap in five-gallon buckets on wooden shoulder yolks from the sugarbush to the laundry building at the service complex, which for a time doubled in season as the sugarhouse, although a sugarhouse also existed along the road to Moose Pond.[114] The Pruyns preferred old-fashioned iron evaporators to stainless steel or tin for the dark color it gave the syrup.[115]

Representative of the many local men who worked at Santanoni Preserve, and of the diverse sorts of tasks they performed, was George Shaughnessy of Minerva. When Pruyn sold some timber from the estate, George cut lumber there for International Paper, during the winter of 1923–24. He stayed on as a seasonal laborer to split firewood, shovel snow from the main camp and boathouse roofs, and harvest ice from Newcomb Lake. Snow was allowed to accumulate on the main camp roof all winter, but with the spring rains the snow became heavier, so the superintendent would get "a gang together to deal with that."[116] The snow would drift so deep around the buildings that Shaughnessy and other workers had to "mow back" the piles to allow more roof snow to accumulate.[117] For four weeks in 1930, Shaughnessy and his brother-in-law, Warren Williams, "brushed out" the entire forty-mile boundary of the

---

[112] Rowena Putnam, quoted by David Garrison. "A Working Dairy . . . ."

[113] J. Winthrop Aldrich, Memorandum to File, May 7, 1996, recording oral commentary of Merle D. Melvin, who thought ice had not been harvested since the 1930s. Susan Pruyn King, remembering as late as 1951, said her brother "Lance and I always assumed it was still being harvested." Manuscript note to authors, January 1999.

[114] Haynes, "Farm Complex", 76; also George Shaughnessy, Aldrich, 160. Madeline Dunham Covert recalled the laundry building used to boil sap, since the Pruyns were absent during the sugaring season. Interview with Rob Engel, Aldrich, 180. Susan Pruyn King recalled the main sugarhouse "down Baldwin Mt. side." Manuscript note to authors. Fisher and Bryant's "Topographic Map of Santanoni Preserve," 1910, shows a "Sugar Camp," not on the road to Moose Pond, but north of the entrance road, on the road toward Baldwin Mountain, shown on the map inside the front cover.

[115] Madeline Dunham Covert, Aldrich, 180.

[116] Aldrich, 36.

[117] George Shaughnessy, interview by J. Winthrop Aldrich, tape recording, Minerva, New York, July 1992, Aldrich, 160.

preserve and posted it with painted metal signs.[118] The job took thirty days.

Newcomb had no veterinarians, so Ed Johnson, the local doctor, also served in that role. Decades later, Johnson recalled: "With the help of Lewis Kinne, who knew how things should go, I and my wife Lillian, who gave the anesthetic, did many procedures that turned out very well. We were both so young and it was a lark to have a part in things."[119] Johnson, who served the town from 1922 to 1952, experienced the Santanoni farm fully staffed in its heyday. "Buster Dunham," he recalled, "was the new caretaker at Newcomb Lake [living at the lakeside service complex]. Next to his headquarters was Arthur Oliver, who scaled [measured] the pulp [softwood timber] for Mr. Pruyn. At the farm was Lewis Kinne in charge, Charlie Petoff as gardener. A relative of Petoff named Lee [Markoff] was the chicken man. George Ross was in charge of the Guernsey cattle. Caleb Chase was in charge of the horses. The pigs were Berkshires, and the sheep were of an excellent breed." Kinne, Johnson recalled, was "a most able man and his dairy was spotless. He made the butter and supervised the smoking of the hams, and everything that was to go to Albany with Art."[120] Art Tummins drove a Larrabee truck once a week to the Pruyn home in Albany "with chickens, eggs, vegetables, fruit, and syrup—and maple sugar," as well as dairy products, smoked bacon, ham, spring water and probably fire wood.[121]

## Domestic Staff

Typically, a large country house would have a head housekeeper, who would report to the lady of the house. The housekeeper would manage others, usually local women, who helped to maintain the interiors. Camp Santanoni was not so hotel-like an operation as to require a very large domestic staff. Nevertheless, merely washing the hundreds of little panes in its many windows became a formidable task, requiring much help, as did the continual sweeping of leaves and needles from its five-thousand square feet of verandahs.

Carrying Sap, March 1905

Rather than bringing one's housekeeper from the city, it seemed more satisfactory to have a woman in the neighborhood serve as camp housekeeper, since she could take charge of making the buildings ready before the family arrived, and cleaning up after their departure. She would supervise others, like Minnie Dunham, caretaker Buster's sister, who boarded at the estate as a seasonal laundress. Minnie's co-workers, Effie Hall and Alice Parker, preferred to commute from the village

[118] George Shaughnessy, Aldrich, 160. The perimeter may be closer to thirty miles.

[119] Dr. Edward Johnson.

[120] Dr. Edward Johnson.

[121] Beatrice Pruyn Thibault, Aldrich, 70.

each day rather than sleep in the "men's camp."[122]

Laundry at a country house was a major project, given the number of guests and a standard of housekeeping that required constant replenishment of linens. Soiled linens and clothing were carried from the villa and staff quarters to the laundry building at the lakeside caretaking complex. It was equipped "with tubs, and stove to heat both the wash water and the old-fashioned flatirons—required in the early years for the ladies' voluminous garments."[123] In the 1920s Nellie Schuyler from Northville spent the main season in residence at Santanoni as laundress. When the Pruyns and their guests were in camp, her sister Fannie Nelson, also from Northville, would assist.[124]

Other domestic help was engaged locally from Newcomb or from other communities as far away as Northville and Wells, in the southern Adirondacks. "Grandma" Carrie Young and her daughter-in-law Minnie worked as cooks or kitchen helpers in the late twenties.[125] Delilah West Bissell remembered four other "girls" who worked at Santanoni: Grace Laurence from Pleasant Valley, Mary Brown from Long Lake, Aunt Jessie Johnson and Threasa Heavron [*sic*] from Newcomb.

If a butler came with the family to the country house, as at Camp Santanoni, his role varied. In the woods, butlers were not required to greet or impress callers. Butlers were not always keen about housekeeping, however, so their area of responsibility generally was restricted to the serving pantry, the china closet, the silver vault, and the wine cellar, as well as attending to errands. Like the guides outdoors, on call all day to provide personal services as needed, a butler sometimes might serve as steward, in charge of acquiring kitchen provisions; but rarely did he invade the province of the chef, who naturally planned the menu and monitored kitchen stores. The dining room, not the kitchen, was the butler's domain. "When my brothers got bored [at long meals], they would surreptitiously pour the water from their goblets into the centerpiece, just to keep the butler busy refilling them."[126] Sis Pruyn Thibault fondly remembered one butler, Hansen, whitewashing her sneakers after a muddy hike to Moose Pond. Cynthia Pruyn Green called Hansen "the perfect butler, polite, efficient." Austin, however—Anna's last butler—attempted to steal family jewelry and was prosecuted.[127]

Often a butler served as the owner's valet at a time when upper-class men as well as women dressed more elaborately. The men might be assisted by a male attendant in

Chauffeur and Butler

[122] Engel, Tummins interview, July 1991. The "men's camp" at the lakeside service complex would be either the Chauffeur's/Stable-men's House or the dormitory wing of the wagon barn/stable.

[123] Cynthia Pruyn Green, Aldrich, 99.

[124] As recalled by Fannie's daughter Josephine Schuyler, who would visit her mother at camp. Josephine Schuyler to Donald Williams (conversations in 1990s), related to Howard Kirschenbaum, December 31, 1998.

[125] They, along with Carl Young (Minnie's husband) and the Dunhams, are identified in a photograph from Marion Dunham's album. Marion (Stanley Dunham's wife, who would have heard it from her husband), told Donald Williams they were "cooks".

[126] Beatrice Pruyn Thibault., referring to Albany luncheons, Aldrich, 97-98.

[127] Green interview, September 23, 1992. Beatrice Pruyn Thibault, Aldrich, 50.

planning, arranging, and maintaining their wardrobe. Sometimes the chauffeur might double as valet, since a driver rarely would be occupied with his vehicle at an hour when the gentleman was dressing. Bud White was chauffeur during the 1920s.[128] Ed Guy of Albany was another Pruyn chauffeur.[129]

The lady of the house generally had the counterpart of her husband's valet, the lady's maid. This most intimate attendant was concerned largely with the mistress's wardrobe. In country house society, where there were few duties for family or guests to perform, changing clothes several times a day often became a painstaking ritual. Women's clothes were extremely elaborate, requiring much coordination of hats, gloves, and parasols, as well as labor-intensive maintenance of starched garments and delicate lace.

Robert and Anna Pruyn came to camp each year with four members of their Albany house staff. The butler, chef, and Suzy, Mrs. Pruyn's unmarried maid, slept on the third floor of the kitchen block.[130] The chauffeur stayed at the service complex, where the garage was located.

In later years, a tutor was retained for the grandchildren while at camp. One young man became very close to the family. When he went on to become a physician, "the boys had a female 'nurse' who didn't last long! The next year a young, beautiful, dark-haired, brown-eyed Mademoiselle was hired. The boys thought she would be 'easy meat' like the other long-suffering ladies, so when told, 'Let's go for a walk,' they promptly climbed a tree in protest as in the past. What they didn't know was that Ma'am had been skiing in the Alps and was in top form, so without a moment's hesitation she was up the tree after them and hauled them all down! After that the boys had a wonderful summer keeping up with her. . . . She was a close friend until her death."[131]

Vern Pelcher, "handyman . . . , chauffeur, and mechanic."

## Relationships

There is little evidence to reveal the relationship of Robert and Anna Pruyn to their staff at Santanoni Preserve. Were employees considered part of the Pruyns' extended family, paid well, and kept on for years, even though the farm clearly was not justified economically? Or were workers exploited for years without holidays or vacations at the relatively low prevailing wages? Testimony is limited.

The assistant gardener's daughter recalled how, "One day R. C. came to the house where we lived and asked Mom if there was anything that would make life easier for her. She said, 'Yes, running water.' He had a hand pump installed in the kitchen and there was a valve that sent it upstairs to a very large tank so we had a bathroom after that. He was very old at the time and walked with a cane."[132] Was "R. C." a considerate employer—or one who took years to give his resident staff running water?

[128] Dan Havron of Paradox, N.Y., to J. Winthrop Aldrich, Aldrich, 159.

[129] Notes, Aldrich, 183.

[130] By another account, an unmarried maid who came with the Pruyns from Albany was named "Sally" and was "very, very good" at her job. Notes, Aldrich, 183. A photograph and caption in Marion Dunham's album also identified a maid named Sally and chauffeur named Ed, presumably Ed Guy referred to earlier. (Donald Williams to Howard Kirschenbaum.)

[131] Beatrice Pruyn Thibault, letter to J. Winthrop Aldrich, August 1, 1992.

[132] Delilah West Bissell.

Charlie Petoff and Lewis Kinne bringing home the venison, inspected by Minnie Kinnie

Marion Dunham still has the pocket watch that Robert Pruyn gave her father-in-law, superintendent Buster Dunham. Apparently upon getting a new watch, Pruyn gave his superintendent the older timepiece, which opened to reveal a portrait of the banker inside. Marion recalled that Buster always prized this gift which was passed on to his son Stanley and then to her, Stanley's widow.[133]

Many of the Preserve's major employees, like caretaker Parker, superintendent Dunham, Farm Boss Kinne, gardener Petoff, and caretaker Tummins, remained at Santanoni for a decade or longer. Although lonely Rowena Ross, the Herdsman's daughter, "hated it with a passion," others left with regret. Santanoni Preserve was home to many who lived there. Delilah West Bissell recalled the day in 1931 when her family moved back to Newcomb village. "It was a sad day when we had to leave that place. Our dog, two cats, a cow and calf were missing . . . next morning, to be found back at the place on Pruyn's. I guess they liked living there also."

[133] Marion Dunham, conversations with Donald Williams (1990s), related to Howard Kirschenbaum, December 31, 1998.

Drawing by Edward Lansing Pruyn

Robert C. Pruyn and his children at Santanoni

Edward Lansing Pruyn ("Ned) is at left; Ruth appears to the right of her father, followed by Robert D. and Frederic ("Fritz") Pruyn. The photograph may have been taken by Anna W. Pruyn—one of the many images she recorded for her many albums. Recalled as the unofficial camp photographer who was camera-shy herself, Anna does not appear in many photographs.

Robert and Anna Pruyn at Santanoni

# 8. The Pruyns in Later Years

"What happened was inevitable."

*Edward Johnson*

Robert and Anna Pruyn ceased the family's long participation in the Dutch Reformed Church. They joined the Episcopal Church, where Robert Pruyn became influential, serving as a member of the board that established the Episcopal hymnal.[1] Change of allegiance was symptomatic, not only of the Pruyns' wish (as suggested by Santanoni's imposing entry gate) to be identified with the Anglo-American establishment, but also of declining Dutch hegemony in Albany at the beginning of the twentieth century.

As a long-established family, the Pruyns were not social climbers. Their circle was largely comprised of old family friends, with whom they associated throughout their long lives. Among their associates were not only relatively obscure Albany businessmen, but also nationally prominent figures such as President Roosevelt and his family.

The Pruyns wintered at the Jekyll Island Club off the Georgia coast among an elite group of bankers and industrialists. In 1899, they acquired an apartment in the club's ex-

[1] Cynthia Pruyn Green recalled that Robert C. Pruyn "was the first one in the family to move from Dutch Reformed to Episcopal." Aldrich, 120. Susan Pruyn King recalled the hymnal involvement. Manuscript note to authors.

clusive Sans Souci annex of six apartments. They purchased theirs in 1899 from Equitable insurance executive Henry B. Hyde; their next door neighbor was financier J. Pierpont Morgan.[2] Robert C. Pruyn was a club member from 1897 to 1931 and was chairman of the committee on golf and sports from 1901 to 1914. At age seventy-five, Pruyn still could "savagely beat" the younger set at golf. "Think of it—*Pruyn*!" lamented the vanquished.[3]

Robert Pruyn also was active in civic and community organizations. He served in the New York State Legislature and on the Board of Regents, which oversees education in New York State.[4] He was a park commissioner of Albany for several years, a vestryman for St. Peter's Church, and a board member of the Albany Boys' Club. He was a founder of the Albany Rural Cemetery and founding member of the Fort Orange Club, and belonged to the University Club and the Albany Country Club.[5] In New York City, Pruyn maintained memberships in the exclusive Century, University, and Metropolitan Clubs. True to his aristocratic roots, Robert Pruyn was also one of the Sons of the American Revolution and member of the Holland Society of New York.[6]

## The Younger Generations

Perhaps the most successful—or at least the most versatile—of the children was the eldest, **Edward Lansing Pruyn** (1874–1950). "Ned" went to a private school in New England but was in Germany for the last year of high school.[7] He attended Harvard from 1894–1898. Later Ned wrote:

Edward Lansing Pruyn ("Ned"), self-portrait

> Most of the years since leaving college have been spent in the study of painting. At this writing I can often distinguish good painting from bad by observing it through a pair of ordinary eyeglasses, and in another twenty-five years hope to put several things on canvas myself which will have no tendency to cause violence.
>
> I have had some experience in surveying and big game hunting. Have also played a lot of golf, about which I possibly know more than any other subject
>
> I notice that . . . I am recorded as a "landscape architect," which I never was and I promise I never will be. I have never altered the landscape except, perhaps, by making a few miles of roads and a few putting greens.[8]

[2] The Equitable Life Assurance Society was investigated by Judge Louis Brandeis and subsequently by the Pujo Congressional Committee. Morgan was a major stockholder.

[3] William Barton McCash and June Hall McCash, *The Jekyll Island Club: Southern Haven for America's Millionaires* (Athens: University of Georgia Press, 1989), 169.

[4] The Legislature made Pruyn a member in 1901; he served two years. Obituary, *New York Times*, October 30, 1934. He served as a regent at the same time, 1901 and 1903.

[5] Susan Pruyn King mentioned the Rural Cemetery role, manuscript note to authors. Other facts in paragraph from "Rutgers College Degree for Robert C. Pruyn," undated (ca. 1929) clipping from unknown newspaper. Pruyn Papers, Albany Institute of History and Art.

[6] Clipping, Albany Institute of History and Art.

[7] Cynthia Pruyn Green recalled that her father attended St. Paul's School, at Concord, New Hampshire. Aldrich, 130.

[8] "Edward Lansing Pruyn," autobiographical article, clipping from a Harvard alumni publication, *Class of 1898– Report IV*, n.d., 430. He left Harvard before graduating to study painting. Susan Pruyn King, electronic communication, January 2000.

Edward Lansing Pruyn, 1912

When nineteen years old, Ned may have assisted in rebuilding sections of the entry road to Camp Santanoni and in the late nineties designed or supervised a second stage of road rebuilding. This experience apparently led to other construction projects.[9] After four years at Harvard, Ned took additional geology and engineering courses at Cornell.[10] The family retains surveying instruments he used to lay out golf courses that he first designed in clay models.[11] Ned designed and first used at Santanoni the road guardrail that later was adapted for many public parkways where a natural character was desired.[12] For a short time, Ned was test manager for the family-held Heldeberg Cement Company.[13] In 1904, after he had contracted diphtheria and unexpectedly recovered, his relieved father offered Ned a guaranteed income of $25,000 a year to study painting with William Merritt Chase, and then to pursue a painting career, an offer he accepted.[14] Chase painted a fine portrait of Robert C. Pruyn. Ned was displeased that his mentor had painted this over another portrait, and three times had to paint out feathers that kept reappearing.[15] Another mentor, prominent Albany artist Walter Launt Palmer who painted with Ned at Santanoni, has been mentioned.

In later years, Ned gave his "business" as "painter." He painted watercolor landscape scenes and did etchings capably, but his art never gained a market. He invented a device to analyze the distinctive proportions of the human face.[16] Ned married Anna Vernon Olyphant, in New York City. They had one daughter, Cynthia Pruyn, who married Douglas Green.[17] After Anna Olyphant Pruyn's death, Ned married Gladys Erickson, known as "Erick";[18] They had two children, Edward and Susan.[19] Susan and her husband, Thomas

[9] Ned supervised construction of part of Route 28N near Newcomb. Aldrich, 94.

[10] Cynthia Pruyn Green regarded her father as a civil engineer. "He got that at Cornell." Aldrich, 93.

[11] Aldrich, 94.

[12] Daughter Cynthia described it as "a log rail running about a foot above the ground (sometimes there were three rails). It was used for a lot of New York's parkways; whoever was in charge of design first came out to Santanoni to inspect them here. You still occasionally see these naturalistic, almost rustic guardrails in use along parkways." Cynthia Pruyn Green. Aldrich, 95. She was not referring to Robert Moses and the Taconic Parkway, for "it was before Robert Moses' day, I guarantee. My father was a little miffed that he never got any credit for it at all." She thought the design was first used for a public highway on the Bronx River Parkway. Historic photographs (e.g., page 42) show a guardrail of the type described along the Santanoni drive.

[13] Cynthia Pruyn Green. Aldrich, 111. R.C. Pruyn's younger brother, Charles Lansing Pruyn, was president of the company. Aldrich, 130.

[14] Daughter Cynthia Pruyn Green recalled that her father studied at the École des Beaux Arts, presumably in Paris, but was uncertain, supposing he worked with Chase wherever he was teaching. Aldrich, 94. Chase, never taught in Paris but had a school of his own in New York, and then taught there at the Art Students' League.

[15] Aldrich, 111-112.

[16] Cynthia Pruyn Green. Aldrich, 94.

[17] Douglas and Cynthia Green had two children. Daughter Sydney Green married Wesley Miller; they had no children. Daughter Cynthia Green married James Sheldon; they have one son, Christopher.

[18] Ned, a widower since 1935, met Susan's mother Gladys Erickson in 1939 when she came to Santanoni as the nurse of Pruyn's ailing lawyer, Jim Cooper.

[19] Edward Lansing Pruyn, Jr. ("Lance" or "Lans") married Betsy B. Smith; they had no children. Susan Yates Pruyn married Thomas I. King. They adopted a daughter, Kirsten. Susan, the youngest of Robert and Anna's grandchildren, was only ten when Santanoni was sold, but she has strong memories of those years.

I. King, live year-round at Long Lake, near Santanoni.[20]

Ned was an avid hunter, spending time in winter at Santanoni occasionally or with his parents at Jekyll Island, where he perfected his golf game.[21] Unlike his brothers, Ned never had a drinking problem.[22]

Edward ("Lance") Pruyn, etching by his father

**Ruth Williams Pruyn Goodrich** (1877–1955), Robert and Anna's second child, is credited with keeping many of the family memorabilia together. Ruth married Ned's Harvard classmate David Marvin Goodrich, Chairman of the B. F. Goodrich Company and son of its founder. Before divorcing, the Goodrichs had one daughter, Anne Marvin "Nancy" Goodrich.[23] Nancy hated her mother and eventually was disowned by her. By all accounts, Ruth was a difficult person. Sis Thibault recalls her aunt Ruth as "a witch. Even her Dad couldn't stand her."[24] While Cynthia acknowledged that her Aunt Ruth had a "rough edge," she recalled that when she was a teenager and her mother died, Ruth showed a special interest in her niece. Ruth traveled with her, then bequeathed her property not only to her two surviving brothers but to Cynthia as well.[25]

**Robert Dunbar Pruyn** (1879–1955), the third of Robert and Anna's children, is least remembered in connection with Santanoni. "I spent a year with a manufacturing company in Albany," he wrote in 1912. "After I was married in 1903, I moved to New York. Since then I have been with two different banking houses. I have found married life a marked success."[26] Bob married Betty Metcalf in New York. They resided with their two children, Robert Lansing and Ruth, in Glen Cove and Syosset on Long Island, and "owned a large farm in Connecticut." They had a place at Islesboro, Maine, a horse farm on the island of Dark Harbor in Penobscot Bay, so were not often at Santanoni.[27]

Bob was less effusive than Ned, whose daughter Cynthia recalled her Uncle Bob, like his father, as "the country-gentleman type, always very poised." Robert, as befitting a proper Wall Street banker, in 1912 belonged to the Harvard Club, The Knickerbocker Club, and the Racquet & Tennis Club in New York City, and the Piping Rock Club on Long Island.

20 The Kings previously resided at Saratoga Springs, New York.

21 Cynthia Pruyn Green. Aldrich, 132.

22 Cynthia Pruyn Green. Aldrich, 140.

23 Anne Goodrich married F. C. Sanford Waters. They adopted five children: Elizabeth, David, Peter, Tom, and John.

24 Beatrice Pruyn Thibault, Aldrich, 6.

25 Beatrice Pruyn Thibault, interview by Robert Engel, tape recording, Santanoni Preserve, July 29, 1992; Cynthia Pruyn Green, Aldrich, 142.

26 Robert attended Harvard 1898-1902. "Robert Dunbar Pruyn," autobiographical article, clipping from a Harvard alumni publication, n.d., 538.

27 *Harvard Class of 1927: Fiftieth Anniversary Report*, 575—576. Delilah West Bissell is quoted: "My Memories of Pruyn's Preserve at Newcomb." Also, Beatrice Pruyn Thibault, Aldrich, 73, and J. Winthrop Aldrich, manuscript note to authors.

Bob and Betty's daughter, Ruth Pruyn, namesake of her aunt, was socially prominent. Ruth first married Ogden Phipps and then Marshall Field III.[28] Ruth Pruyn Field became nationally known as a philanthropist in New York, Chicago, and Connecticut. She died in early 1994, shortly before a scheduled interview about her family and Santanoni. Her Long Island, home, the magnificent Caumsett estate at Lloyd Neck, is now a state park.

Ruth's brother, Robert Lansing Pruyn (Lanny) had his Uncle Ned's versatility. Lanny worked a year in the family bank, then became an aviator, then a stockbroker, then a columnist for the San Francisco edition of the *Wall Street Journal*. Returning to flying, he became an airline pilot, then an account executive in aviation insurance. Lanny married Wilhelmina Duff Balken.[29] Robert Lansing Pruyn died in 1964 at Greenwich, Connecticut.

**Frederic Stanley Pruyn** (1881–1938), Robert and Anna's youngest son, was especially identified with Santanoni, a place he dearly loved. Frederic (known in the family as "Fritz"), married Beatrice Morgan of New York City, daughter of William Fellowes Morgan, whose extended family favored the Thousand Islands. The marriage began a complicated intertwining of families and resorts.[30]

Frederic Pruyn

Frederic and Beatrice had four children: Frederic Pruyn, Jr. ("Fritzi"), Fellowes Morgan Pruyn ("Morgie"), Milton Lee Pruyn

[28] Children of Ruth and Ogden Phipps were Henry Ogden Phipps and Robert Lansing Phipps. Henry married Diana, Countess Sternberg. Their daughter, Alexandra, married Count Seilern und Aspang; they have three children. Robert Lansing Phipps married twice, with no children by either marriage. His second wife is Lee McGrath Phipps.

Children of Ruth and Marshall Field were Phyllis Field and Fiona Field. Phyllis had no children with her first husband, Hernando Samper. With her second husband, Robert Edgar Atheling Drummond, she had three children: Maldwin, Fiona, and Bettina Drummond. There were no children from her third marriage to Count Louis de Flers. Fiona Field married David Rust; they had one daughter, Marina Rust. Her third husband is Jean Kay. They have one daughter, Jeanne Kay.

[29] Robert and Wilhelmina Pruyn had two daughters, Ruth and Alison Pruyn. Ruth married Donald Clark; Alison married Thomas Schneider.

[30] William Fellowes Morgan bought Papoose Island, near Clayton, N.Y., in 1886. The family enjoyed it for three generations. Sis brother Lee Pruyn owned it. Sis Pruyn Thibault. Aldrich, 56. The Pruyns, Morgans, and Goodrichs were part of a coterie of patrician families that summered around the head of Grindstone Island. Prominent guests at Camp Santanoni, the Robert Low Bacons of Westbury, N.Y. and Washington, D.C., also had a summer home on Grindstone Island.

("Lee"), and their sister Beatrice Pruyn Longton Thibault ("Sis").

Frederic, who attended Harvard like his brothers, had a varied career. He was a mining engineer in Mexico, then turned his technical interests to mechanical engineering. He may have been first to propose moving the engine to the rear of buses, and he designed and tested gears for trucks and Otis elevators. Frederic played polo and was versatile as an athlete. He and Beatrice imported Irish Wolfhounds.[31] Frederic claimed to have discovered and promoted not only a prizefighter, but also the famous singer and motion picture actor, Nelson Eddy. Fritz "was a very brilliant man but lost it to booze," regretted his daughter, Sis Pruyn Thibault.[32] Her mother, Beatrice Morgan Pruyn, when their children had grown, divorced Frederic and married David Goodrich, the divorced husband of Frederic's sister, Ruth.[33] The Gate Lodge became a refuge for Fritz in his last years. He died there in 1938 of alcoholism and pneumonia.[34]

In contrast, son Fellowes Morgan Pruyn, ("Morgie") was "the only one in the family who continued with anything," according to his sister, Sis. Morgie became a prominent physician and instructor in medicine at Columbia University. Morgie inherited some of his grandfather's estate-making instinct: "Out of hours I struggle with a seventeen-acre landscape which, after nine years, has almost exhausted me and a good many formidable mechanical aides."[35] He married Agnes Keane; they had no children.

Morgie's brother, Milton Lee Pruyn, attended Harvard for three years, was a professional charter pilot after World War II, then became a real-estate broker.[36] Lee married Antoinette Deltschaft at St. Petersburg, Florida. They had no children together. Lee flew a Grumman Widgeon, which he landed on Newcomb Lake.[37] After retirement, Lee and his wife resided in Palm Beach, Florida.

The eldest son of Frederic and Beatrice, Frederic Pruyn, Jr., was known as "Fritzi," and, after his father died, likewise as "Fritz." He and his wife Helene Wittenberg Scranton had no children.

The youngest child, and only daughter of Frederic and Beatrice, was Beatrice Pruyn, known as "Sis." She married Carl Longton and they had five children.[38] Sis subsequently married John C. Thibault of Clayton, N.Y., where the Thibaults resided. They had no children together, but John Thibault adopted Sis's three youngest.

"R. C. Pruyn was a strange man about his children," observed granddaughter Sis. "He took Frank McCabe into the bank as he might have done for a son, but he did not do so for his sons. Did he expect them to make it on their own? The lives of none of his four children were particularly successful, happy or fulfilled."[39]

That was a subjective judgment by one who was close—possibly too close—to her family. Sis' question, "Did he expect them to make it on their own?" may strike home. Contrary to her implication that R.C. Pruyn should have patronized his offspring, often children indulged by advantaged parents are neither especially successful nor particularly satisfied in life. To the contrary, Robert Pruyn's attitude might be regarded as enlightened "tough love"—determination not to spoil his children. If so, he succeeded only to varying degrees. Not a son, but a grandson was said to be "the only one in the family who continued with anything."

---

31 Beatrice Pruyn Thibault. Aldrich, 155; Otis elevator, Susan Pruyn King, manuscript note to authors.

32 Beatrice Pruyn Thibault. Aldrich, 16.

33 Beatrice Pruyn Thibault, conversations and letter to Paul Malo.

34 Edward Johnson, MD, letter to Ethel Bissell, 1982

35 The estate was at Mt. Kisco, N.Y. "Fellowes Morgan Pruyn," autobiographical article, *Harvard Class of 1931: 25th Anniversary Report*, 791-792.

36 Lee attended Harvard 1931-1933. "Milton Lee Pruyn," *Harvard Class of 1936: 25th Anniversary Report*, 1094.

37 Dan Havron of Paradox, N.Y., and Sis Pruyn Thibault, Aldrich, 159.

38 The children were Anne Louise ("Nancy"), Patricia ("Patsy"), Barbara ("Bobbi"), Susan, and Frederic Henry.

39 Thibault interview, August 1992.

Beatrice Pruyn Thibault ("Sis") at left, Susan Pruyn King (with portrait of their grandfather) and Denise Clark, Sis's granddaughter, at Santanoni, July 1992.

Ned and Fritz served on the board of directors of the National Commercial Bank, but none of the children were encouraged to make banking a career, according to Ned's daughter Cynthia, although her uncle Robert gravitated to Wall Street.

Again, the truth about the father-son relationships is probably more complex than Cynthia's memory suggests. R.C. *did* steer two Adirondack road-building contracts in Ned's direction and would likely have supported his son in similar business ventures if Ned had been so inclined. With his engineering background and his father's business connections, Ned might have done well as a contractor in the lucrative road building field. Similarly, Robert Pruyn *did* place Ned and Fritz on the National Commercial Board. Whether it was the father's lack of encouragement, or the sons' lack of interest or talent, or their health problems, including alcoholism, that accounted for their not following in their father's financial footsteps may never been known.

Whereas their patrician grandparents, Robert and Anna, had preferred country-house life in the isolation of the wilderness, the tastes of Frederic's boys revealed the changing culture of the generations: "Fritzi and Morgan [stayed] in the [Gate] Lodge; they wanted to be out there so that they could go to Tupper and Long Lake to party all the time."[40] An even closer party spot was the Newcomb House, across Route 28N from the Santanoni entrance, where the proprietor "used sardine cans for ashtrays and Morgie and Fritz bartended while Mike [the proprietor] ended up under the table. Once Morgie and Aggie (his wife) were dancing there and one of the men pinched Aggie's behind. Another man reprimanded him, saying, 'you don't do that to a Pruyn!'"[41] But why not? By that time, the respectful comment had become anachronistic. The young Pruyns more rightly were known, not for their grandparents, but for their own behavior.

Even though the children and grandchildren of Robert C. Pruyn may have achieved less than their father and grandfather, the Pruyn family retained its prestige. For almost a century the Pruyns appeared in the *New York Times*, into the fourth generation.[42]

## Santanoni after Robert C. Pruyn

As much as Robert Pruyn loved Santanoni Preserve, from time to time he contemplated selling it. In 1915, he compiled attributes of the preserve in the style of a realtor's description. In 1925 he again described the preserve, probably for a prospective purchaser.[43] A few years later, when he allowed Guy Lee to photograph Santanoni and write a magazine article about it, perhaps Pruyn again had an eye to selling the property.

---

[40] Susan Pruyn King. Aldrich, 12; also Aldrich, 76.

[41] Aldrich, 12.

[42] The *Times* carried obituaries of Robert H. Pruyn (1882), of his son Robert C. Pruyn (1934) and wife Anna W. Pruyn (1939), of their four children, Edward Lansing Pruyn (1950), Ruth Pruyn (1955), Robert D. Pruyn (1955), and Frederic Pruyn (1938), as well as of their grandson, Edward Lansing Pruyn (1950) and granddaughter Ruth Pruyn Phipps Field (1994). Some of these Pruyns appeared in other *New York Times* articles than obituaries, as did some husbands, wives, and Beatrice Morgan Pruyn ("Sis") in 1936. Her brother, Dr. Fellowes Morgan Pruyn ("Morgie") was cited in the *Biography Index*, v. 16 (New York: H. W. Wilson Co., 1990).

[43] Haynes, *Farm Complex*, 44, 51.

The stock market crash of 1929 signaled the end of an initial thirty-seven-year chapter of Santanoni Preserve history. Ironically, the splendid article by Guy Lee, conveying the glory of Santanoni in its full splendor, appeared in *The Sportsman* "the very month that the Market crashed!"[44] "It is estimated that annually $60,000 was spent in upkeep of the estate and a small army of men worked thereon."[45] Although the deflation of investments and subsequent long depression greatly depleted the Pruyn fortune, economic conditions were but one factor in motivating change at Santanoni. More immediate was the physical decline of Robert Pruyn. Then eighty-two years old, he was afflicted with what was then called "dementia", but probably would be diagnosed as Alzheimer's Disease today. In 1931, he retired from the bank. About that time Anna Pruyn and the bank petitioned the court to authorize a custodianship for Pruyn's assets. Three years after retiring, Robert C. Pruyn died.[46]

Perhaps when he last had drawn up his will, Pruyn felt that not all of his children shared his emotional commitment to Santanoni, while separately, few might be financially able to maintain the Preserve. Whether by his own devise or through the custodianship, Pruyn's entire estate was placed in charge of the National Commercial Bank and Trust Co.[47] Establishing a trust would assure that the family seat would remain intact, at least for the rest of Anna's life. Family use of Santanoni actually lasted longer.

Departure: Anna and Robert

For the next three decades, his first- and second-generation descendants received annual income from the trust. To avoid family altercations regarding Santanoni, Pruyn's children were required to apply to the bank for permission whenever they wished to use the property.

The trustees managed Santanoni on a tight budget. "Certainly Mr. Pruyn's mental deterioration and his failure to set up an endowment for [Santanoni's] maintenance resulted in [the] decision to eliminate everyone except Arthur Tummins, who was to act as caretaker of everything."[48] Many workers who had lived at Santanoni Preserve the year around were forced to find not only new employment but also new homes. Tummins alone had been retained as caretaker reportedly because he was the only unmarried worker and would therefore be less expensive to support.[49]

As the new caretaker, Tummins took over the former Petoff residence, the New Farm House next to the Creamery. Initially he kept the farm going, dutifully delivering produce to

[44] J. Winthrop Aldrich, "Memorandum," August 18, 1992, referring to the Guy Lee article, October 1929.

[45] A. B. Recknagel, "History of Robert C. Pruyn Tract, Essex Co., N.Y.," October 1937. The estimate may have been inflated, unless incorporating some costs not included in bank records, which show 1907 expenses totaling $32,180.58. Annual costs in subsequent years through 1916 varied between twelve and twenty-two thousand dollars. National Commercial Bank records.

[46] Robert C. Pruyn died on October 29, 1934, survived by his wife and their four children. Maintenance of his family burial plot at the Albany Rural Cemetery is charged to a trust fund at Key Bank in perpetuity. J. Winthrop Aldrich, manuscript note to authors.

[47] Pruyn's protégé Frank McCabe became the responsible bank official. Edward Johnson, MD; Aldrich, 164.

[48] Edward Johnson.

[49] Helen Tummins interview, July 1991.

Anna's Albany home.[50] A 1931 livestock inventory listed six horses, eight cows, two bulls, eight-hundred to a thousand chickens, and twenty-five pigs.[51] The trustees, however, soon ceased all farm operations, which were not economically viable. By the time the farm was closed, Tummins had married. He and his wife Helen were expecting a child. They moved into the house Walter West's family had recently vacated near the Gate Lodge.

Robert Pruyn's last few years coincided with the Great Depression. During the early 1930s, Santanoni was largely deserted save for the Tummins family. By mid-decade, however, Anna, her children and grandchildren resumed seasonal visits, Anna still assisted by her personal maid. Anna Williams Pruyn died in 1939.

During the late 1930s and 1940s, a whole new generation of Pruyns visited and learned to cherish Santanoni. Frederic's family took over the Gate Lodge and enjoyed half the summer there; the other half was spent at the Thousand Islands with his wife's family, the Morgans. At the "Lodge," as they called it, "there was a sleeping porch where Fritz, Morgie slept w. tutor Leonard Moore."[52] There was a camping area in the field above the Lodge. The nearby boathouse was a launching point for excursions on Harris Lake and adjoining streams.

Edward's family also began visiting on a regular basis, usually occupying the main camp. Although Ned no longer did much painting, he was to be left alone while in his studio, daughter Cynthia recalled.[53] And although he was busy golfing around the world, he would spend a few days most winters at Santanoni.

Despite the family's on-going use of the camp, after Anna Pruyn died the bank began

Santanoni, *adieu*

[50] Tummins interview, July 1991.

[51] Pruyn papers, KeyCorp.

[52] Unsigned, hand-written note in Santanoni photograph album at The Adirondack Museum, 1998.

making plans to sell the preserve. Sis and her brother Morgie sued the trustees, contending that the bank was misinterpreting the intent of the will, which said that the overall estate would be divided into equal parts for each child upon Anna's death. Since Frederic had predeceased his mother, it was possible that his children would be cut out entirely. In light of the lawsuit and the depressed real estate market, the trustees were persuaded to hold and manage the property for an indefinite period.[54] It was also decided that Frederic's share of the estate would be divided equally among his children.

Tenuously, Santanoni Preserve remained in the Pruyn family intact for fourteen years after Anna's death. Records for the 1940s contain spirited entries reminiscent of those a generation earlier: "The men took the kids hunting one evening and startled a buck. The kids heard it but didn't see it! Have new entree for Fritz and his gourmets: 'Bearburgers.'"[55] Fritz (Frederic, Jr.), a devoted hunter and angler, was the grandchild who used Santanoni the most. A 1947 entry reads, "Lee Wulff [a friend of Fritz and a world-renowned sportsman] flew in with Piper Cub on floats . . . Wulff and F.P. hunted Santanoni Brook . . . chipmunks sounded like elephants . . . Wulff got 10 pt. buck . . . flew out with buck on floats of Cub."[56]

A return visit to Santanoni by Cynthia, Sis and Susan in 1992, more than forty years after their last stay there, evoked a long stream of memories for all three.[57] One of their common recollections, though experienced twenty years apart, is of making "moss gardens" on kitchen platters. "We had almost the same childhood here, a generation apart," Sis exclaimed to Susan. By Susan's time, however, servants at Santanoni were a thing of the past. Her mother did most of the cooking and the servants' quarters were used for guests. Because Ned's second family was younger than the others, they used the camp regularly during the late 1940s.

Life at Santanoni became more casual, by inclination as well as by necessity, for the camp no longer could be staffed in the grand manner. The place was more literally a "camp" for the grandchildren of Robert and Anna, whose families in effect camped out in the redundant buildings. Tailored jackets and elaborate gowns disappeared at the dinner table. "When the family had fish they wouldn't eat at the table; they'd start eating right on the kitchen counters!"[58] At breakfast, guava jelly, a Santanoni staple, was flipped from knives across the table.[59]

Like their parents before them, most of the grandchildren became outdoor enthusiasts. Susan, Sis and Cynthia acquired their grandmother's fondness for the woods. A fall hunting party was an annual event.

The main camp and Gate Lodge were maintained on a minimal basis. The trust would authorize repairs for Art Tummins to accomplish with budgetary rather than aesthetic interests foremost. A 1946 handwritten note indicates that the farm and service complexes were in poor condition. Each year family members received statements of the estate's income and disbursements. These indicate that Santanoni was being run at the lowest possible expense—for example, $15,109 in 1949, which included $7,858 in property taxes.[60] The camp was in a holding pattern that could not continue, the bank maintained.

Yet, ironically, Santanoni supported itself in the last dozen years that it was held in trust. The Preserve had not been lumbered since the 1920s, when International Paper Co. harvested

[53] Green interview, September 1992.

[54] Thibault interview, July 1992.

[55] "Santanoni: Record of Fish," entry for November 19, 1946.

[56] "Santanoni: Record of Fish," entry for November 1, 1947.

[57] Susan Pruyn King stayed at Santanoni once more in 1971, but no longer as an owner.

[58] Madeline Dunham Covert. Aldrich, 170.

[59] Cynthia Pruyn Green. Aldrich, 121.

[60] Pruyn papers, KeyCorp. In 1949 town tax was $3,751.55 and school tax was 4,107.17. By another account, taxes were $7,220 annually, apparently reduced later to $3,500. Both examples from "Santanoni Preserve, Newcomb, Essex County, New York." Typescript, n.d., Records of National Commercial Bank.

Cocktail hour, probably late 1940s, with Robert and Anna's grandsons Morgie and Fritz at right.

softwoods. That meant a current crop of hardwood could be cut, and that a new crop of softwoods was coming along. In 1940, the bank commissioned a survey of marketable timber on the estate. The report, by A. B. Recknagel, estimated 6,150 acres of hardwood and several acres of young trees which would provide "the nucleus of a second cut of hardwoods in the future."[61]

The bank contracted a harvest of timber, providing substantial income for several years.[62] The bank cautioned the Pruyns, however, that once these contracts were fulfilled, the property could expect no other source of income for at least two decades while a new timber crop grew. Another assessment contradicted this conclusion, estimating that "there are approximately 3 to 4 million board feet of hardwood left and it is believed that another softwood operation can be performed in another 5 to 10 years."[63] With wise investment of the timber sale proceeds of the 1920s and 1940s and with good forest management, the Preserve might very well have supported itself from silvaculture.

In 1949, the trust hired a mineral consultant to test for ore deposits on the Santanoni Preserve. The idea was overdue. Only six miles east of the camp lies what was once considered the richest iron ore deposit on earth.

---

[61] Survey appended to legal contract between the National Commercial Bank and Trust Company and the Oval Wood Dish Corporation, July 15, 1941. Department of Manuscripts & University Archives, Cornell University, Ithaca, New York.

[62] The bank contracted with the Oval Wood Dish Co. of Tupper Lake to remove a minimum of 5-million board feet per year at a price of $6.50 per thousand feet the first year (or at least $32,500 in income to the estate) and $7.50 per thousand feet in each of the following six years (or $37,500 annual income). Between 1944 and 1949, approximately ten million board feet of hardwood were removed. Pruyn papers, KeyCorp. In 1945, the bank contracted with the Veneer Wood Products Co. to remove softwood trees at a price of $9 per thousand board feet. In March 1947, Trust Officer Charles A. Ten Eyck wrote to Milton "Lee" Pruyn that Veneer Wood Co. had removed 1.7-million board feet and planned to remove three million feet per year for an additional four years. Beatrice Pruyn Thibault papers, Clayton, New York.

[63] "Santanoni Preserve," n.d., typescript in National Commercial Bank records.

Ned Pruyn was convinced, according to daughter Cynthia, that Moose Mountain on the preserve also contained significant amounts of iron ore. He and others had discovered while hunting that compasses were utterly useless in that vicinity. They had assumed it was because of the existence of ferrous metals.[64] But after five days of testing, the consultant concluded, "No mineral concentrations of economic value were anywhere noted. . . ."[65]

The trustees argued that selling the property appeared to be the only way to keep it from draining the trust, a conclusion that Robert and Anna's survivors appeared to share reluctantly.[66] A letter that Fritz Pruyn wrote his brother Lee in October 1948 explained what was being considered. Fritz reported that the trustees proposed selling the property to the State and believed they would get ten dollars per acre ($129,000), one-quarter of which would be divided among the heirs and the rest of which would remain in trust:

> I have for years been dreading the time when the problem of the disposition of Santanoni would inevitably require a decision . . . I believe it must have been an awareness of the social responsibilities of the hypothecation [sic] of such a large chunk of the public domain which led Grandfather to label it a 'preserve for the propagation, etc.' With whatever powers are within our grasp, I think that we should examine the terms of sale . . . to see that it will not be in jeopardy from any responsibilities we may or may not feel either for Grandfather's memory or for the interests of the public, we would thus satisfy our sentimental attachment to the future welfare of the land.[67]

The State did not buy the land, however, then or shortly thereafter when offered again.[68] In 1949 the bank hired a New York City real estate clearinghouse with national distribution, *Previews*, to market the property. The firm recommended targeting institutional investors—religious orders, corporations, or charitable organizations. It produced a two-page brochure with fifteen photographs, describing Santanoni as "ideal for a game preserve, . . . resort, club or colony." The initial asking price was $275,000 if the preserve was sold in four parcels, $195,000 if sold intact. As months passed with no significant interest, the price dropped steadily, but still there were no takers. To defray continuing expenses, the bank contracted with another lumbering firm, to remove what wood they could find.[69] Finally, in July 1953, an auction was held at the Gate Lodge. Under the terms, the preserve would be sold in four parcels, unless a bid on the whole exceeded the sum offered for the four.

At this point, a few of the Pruyn grandchildren decided to bid jointly for one of the four parcels, since as Sis Thibault explained, "None of us individually could afford the upkeep and the property taxes."[70] They expected the cost to be affordable, between $20,000 and $30,000. However, the winning bid—only $79,100 for all 12,900 acres and the structures—came from two brothers, Crandall and Myron Melvin of Syracuse, New York, a banker and lawyer, respectively.

Furnishings were not included in the sale price, and the Melvins indicated they didn't want them. Lee Pruyn wrote to ask the bank

---

[64] Green interview, September 1992. Ned's experience was corroborated by a group of hunters in 1988. David Garrison, "You Can Get There Only By Horseback," *Snow Times*, January 20, 1988, 11A.

[65] Ronald B. Peterson, "Report on a Mineral and Magnetic Reconnaissance of the Santanoni Preserve," undated. Collection Beatrice Pruyn Thibault, Clayton, New York.

[66] A number of bids for repair work were solicited between 1946-48, apparently to ready the camp for sale. Haynes, "Farm Complex," 59. It is not clear which, if any, of these bids, including reroofing the main camp, were accepted or completed.

[67] Frederic Pruyn, letter to Milton Lee Pruyn, October 7, 1951, collection of Beatrice Pruyn Thibault, Clayton, New York.

[68] Again in 1950 the National Commercial Bank and Trust Company, acting for the Estate of Robert C. Pruyn, offered the entire property to the State for $145,000. With no funds available, no action was taken, according to William Rudge and Charles Vandrei, in a chronology that accompanied a presentation to Santanoni Historic Area Citizens Advisory Committee, May 2, 1995.

[69] Bureau Brothers was the lumbering firm. Bank records in the early 1950s show that this group removed 1.6 million board feet plus 131 cords of pulp, paying the trust $36,303.

[70] Thibault interview, July 1992.

Fall hunting, late 1940s. Art Tummins at front left, next to Lee Pruyn. Fritz Pruyn puffs a cigarette in right front center. The party's guides are standing: Lee Hall is at left of back row next to Lewis Parker, Vivian LeCasse (son of Noah) at right.

to sell them off. "There were some back-breaker beds, as I remember."[71] Some of the furniture was not sold, however, and remained with the camp.

Many Adirondack camps and estates have changed ownership frequently. The truly large estates of old established families like the Brandreths, Litchfields, Rockefellers, Whitneys, and Pruyns have been more stable—a few still remain in possession of the original owners. Santanoni Preserve would have three owners in its history. The 1953 sale brought to an end sixty-one years of Pruyn family stewardship, with title for the last nineteen years held by the Robert C. Pruyn Trust. Now the Melvins would preserve Santanoni for two more decades.

[71] Milton Lee Pruyn, letter to Charles Ten Eyck, National Commercial Bank and Trust Company, August 6, 1953. Collection of Beatrice Pruyn Thibault, Clayton, New York.

Drawing by Edward Lansing Pruyn

Abandoned creamery, late 1940s

The Gate Lodge, summer residence of Crandall Melvin, from the Harris Lake boathouse

# 9. The Melvin Years

> The Melvins did not demolish a single building. . . . In 1972 the buildings were generally in better physical shape than they had been in 1953.
>
> *Merle D. Melvin*

For about two decades Santanoni Preserve was the property of the Melvins, a family as prominent in Syracuse as the Pruyns were in Albany. Some similarities notwithstanding, the Melvins were unlike the Pruyns. The Pruyns were Yorkers; the Melvins, Yankees.

Located to the southwest of the Adirondacks, Syracuse is culturally different from Albany, to the southeast. Central New York was settled much later than the Hudson Valley, by different people. Yankees migrated from New England as the nineteenth century began. Syracuse, in the center of New York State, was a Yankee community, largely built of detached frame houses, in contrast to Albany's more urban tradition of masonry row houses. Yankees brought the white meeting house and village green. They carried westward Yankee egalitarianism and individualism, a Yankee work ethic, and the Yankee shrewdness that was disdained by elite Yorkers.[1]

After the initial Yankee influx, post-Civil War industrial development attracted other ethnic groups. More than Albany, Syracuse became a typical American, middle-sized, middle-class city. Larger than the state capital,

[1] Dixon Ryan Fox developed these contrasting characteristics in his *Yankees and Yorkers* (New York: University Press, 1940).

it is more functionally diverse, not being dominated by a single industry or institution such as state government. National corporations and an emigrant elite skimmed much of its wealth. Over the years, patricians declined in importance relative to the city's blue-collar residents, now become largely middle-class. Syracuse has been characterized by more social mobility than Albany. The Melvins were community leaders, but they represented a very different sort of elite, in a different kind of community.

Compared to the Pruyns, the Melvins were not so eminent an Old Family, for Syracuse was not so old a city as Albany. Robert Pruyn's father had been internationally prominent as a diplomat, politician and lawyer, but the father of the Melvin brothers was a farmer—a Yankee trader who amassed land and, in his ripe old age, drove around northern Onondaga County attending to his "extensive real estate interests."[2]

Myron and his brother Crandall were born in a rural village near Syracuse, about a decade after the birth of Robert and Anna Pruyn's youngest child. Both brothers attended public schools. They extended their high school program, attending Central High School in Syracuse in order to prepare for the university.[3] Keenly interested in history, Crandall majored in Classics at Syracuse University, where he was president of the senior class of 1911 and won a prize for his essay, "New York's Share in the American Revolution." Both brothers continued postgraduate studies at the Syracuse University College of Law and formed their own law practice in 1921. The partnership of Melvin and Melvin became one of the most important law practices in Central New York, at one time comprised of twenty-five attorneys and twenty-five secretaries, who occupied the entire seventh floor of the Merchants' Bank Building. The practice continues to this day.[4]

Myron Melvin, the senior partner in the firm, retained the practical Yankee's Calvinist work ethic.[5] He reported for work at six in the morning and rarely left his desk before five in the afternoon. Unlike the conservative Pruyns, Myron was "prominently identified with legal advance" and was regarded as a "leader of progressive thought and action."[6] More fully occupied by his practice, Myron was not so extensively involved as Crandall was in community affairs, but was generous in his contributions to Syracuse University. He was "one of Central New York's best known lawyer-businessmen," who was "considered a multi-millionaire by associates." Myron Melvin died at age eighty-one in 1966.[7]

Younger brother Crandall also was "prominently identified with legal advance." He taught at the Syracuse University College of Law and served on its Board of Visitors, but gravitated from law to banking. Crandall Melvin became President and then Chairman of the Merchants' National Bank and Trust Company of Syracuse.[8] He might have become acquainted with Robert Pruyn through their mutual banking interests, but Pruyn retired the year after Melvin entered banking. Like Pruyn, the Melvins served as directors of

---

[2] Born at Clay, N.Y. in 1859, Asel Melvin married May Belle Soule. Asel was not merely a farmer but had graduated from the New York State Normal School at Oswego, now SUNY Oswego. He taught school before buying a dairy farm in the Town of Salina in 1902, and served as Justice of the Peace. "Asel L. Melvin." Obituary, Syracuse *Post-Standard*, November 6, 1950. Franklin H. Chase gives the parents' names as "Asel J. and May B. Melvin" in *Syracuse and Its Environs: A History* (New York: Lewis Historical Publishing Co., 1924), v. III, 180.

[3] Syracuse *Herald-Journal*, May 4, 1966 (also source of previous information in this paragraph).

[4] The firm relocated elsewhere in Syracuse.

[5] *Herald-Journal*, May 4, 1966.

[6] Franklin H. Chase, 180.

[7] *Herald-Journal*, May 4, 1966 (also preceding quotation).

[8] Crandall Melvin had served eight years as director when he became bank president in 1938. Thomas W. Higgens. "Crandall Melvin, President, 1938-1967," in Crandall Melvin, Sr. *History of the Merchants' Bank and Trust Company of Syracuse, New York: One Hundred and Eighteen Years*, Chapter x. Also: Syracuse *Herald-Journal*, May 4, 1966, and April 21, 1960. The Merchants' Bank was located on Warren Street, then expanded by a new building next door, at the corner of Warren and East Fayette Streets. Merchants' was later absorbed by the Marine Midland Bank which in turn was absorbed the Hong Kong Shanghai Banking Corporation (HSBC).

other corporations and were members of many organizations.

As both were successful bankers, it is not surprising that Robert Pruyn and Crandall Melvin both were Republican in their politics. Otherwise, however, the Pruyns and Melvins were of different American subcultures. Whereas the Pruyns, like most elite Yorkers, became Episcopalian, the Melvins remained Methodist, reflecting their Yankee roots.[9] Crandall Melvin, the brother more involved in community affairs, was keenly interested in social programs like the Boy Scouts and the Salvation Army, to which organizations he made substantial bequests. Crandall's strong sense of communal responsibility was characteristically Yankee.

The Melvins' Yankee sense of egalitarianism, so different from the Pruyns' Yorker sense of *noblesse*, was very evident. Crandall became famous as a landmark, stationed regularly at his desk in the window of his bank, on a main intersection of downtown Syracuse.[10] Crandall, who lived the rest of his life on the working farm that had been his boyhood home, became known as the "Barnyard Banker."[11] He was "the first banker in America to take the bank to the farmer."[12] The Merchants' Bank arranged auctions of livestock and real estate; it conducted sales for a commission and extended credit to purchasers. Crandall's populist sense served him well as a progressive banker, for despite the Great Depression (or to some degree by taking advantage of it) he expanded his banking operations, most remarkably by introducing installment loans for consumers.[13] In his novel consumer orientation, Melvin was regarded as a banking pioneer for innovating relatively easy monthly payments that served merchants as well as consumers during the long Depression.

Merchant's Bank, Syracuse, New York, c. 1965

It is difficult to imagine Robert Pruyn, with manicured beard and high, starched collar, sitting in the front window of his bank, promoting installment loans to hard-pressed consumers—let alone conducting cattle sales at hinterland farms, or posing with a live cow and a beauty queen at the opening of a branch office.[14] It is difficult to imagine the Albany patrician as a member of the Lions' Club and the American Legion, like Crandall Melvin.[15] It is hard to imagine Robert Pruyn enlisting in the U.S. Army as a Private during a war, as did

9 New England settlers brought Congregationalism to Upstate New York, but many subsequently formed Methodist congregations.

10 "He established a precedent by placing his desk out in the open at the entrance in order to be accessible to customers at all times." Thomas W. Higgens. Paul Malo recalls as a youngster passing on the street, seeing the familiar visage of Mr. Melvin regularly.

11 The Merchants' Bank's "Department of Agriculture" was a "pioneer venture in New York State." Crandall Melvin continued his interest in agriculture throughout his life. Higgens, 89, 90.

12 Thomas W. Higgens, 90, 91.

13 *Post-Standard*, April 22, 1980.

14 The illustration, reproduced on the following page, appeared in Crandall Melvin, Sr. *History of the Merchants' Bank and Trust Company of Syracuse, New York: One Hundred and Eighteen Years*, 94.

15 Franklin H. Chase, 181.

Crandall Melvin, the "Barnyard Banker," admiring a prize Jersey at one of his innovative drive-in banks

Crandall Melvin, and certainly Robert Pruyn would seem incongruous directing W. P. A. projects for the unemployed during a Depression, like Crandall Melvin.[16]

Crandall Melvin was identified with "every major banking innovation for nearly 30 years."[17] He devised what was probably the first automobile drive-up window in central New York.[18] He removed the wire cages in his banking room and installed the first, custom-made teller machines in Syracuse, thereby greatly increasing transaction efficiency. He initiated microfilming of checks, sometimes lost or damaged in transit. When Melvin came to the bank, it employed only two women, an imbalance he improved. The Merchants' was the first bank in Syracuse with women on its board of directors.

Crandall Melvin became the first president from Syracuse of the New York State Bankers' Association since 1894 and he served as president of the Merchants' Bank longer than any predecessor. During Melvin's tenure, the number of employees increased tenfold, from forty-one to more than four hundred. The downtown bank was supplemented with thirteen branch offices. In 1961, the Merchants' Bank built a multi-story main office building.[19] Following his presidency, Crandall Melvin served as Chairman of the Board until he retired in 1967. He died thirteen years later at age ninety-one.[20]

The Melvin brothers never gravitated to more fashionable suburbs of Syracuse, but remained loyal to their boyhood home, in the less affluent Town of Salina, where both continued to reside relatively unpretentiously on Buckley Road for the rest of their lives.[21] Both brothers were said to have acquired large real estate holdings in the northern suburbs, which became the primary area of metropolitan growth in the late twentieth century.[22]

Crandall's early interest in history became "a lifetime hobby." The President of Le Moyne College at Syracuse recalled that Crandall Melvin had suggested naming the institution to honor an early Jesuit missionary.[23] Melvin served as President of the Onondaga Historical Association, to which he made a substantial bequest. Like his brother Myron, Crandall Melvin served as President of the Onondaga County Bar Association. He served thirty-six years as a trustee of Syracuse University, where he established and endowed a Syracuse University Law Chair.[24]

Crandall Melvin was eulogized as ". . . a man who made history, wrote history, and lived history." His service to the community was recalled as "a pioneering banker [who] when the Great Depression threatened to overwhelm the community . . . provided the leadership which inspired his competitors to overcome financial handicaps which would have ruined men of lesser vision and courage."[25] He also ". . . brought the county out of the depths by helping to organize WPA make-work projects." He was remembered for his "humility and his humanity."[26]

Chancellor Melvin Eggers of Syracuse University regarded Crandall Melvin as ". . . a tough-minded idealist. . . . He talked as a sage and a saint, but he walked with the common people." Even more generous was the judgment of a Syracuse newspaper: "No individ-

[16] Crandall Melvin served in the Field Artillery, being promoted to Second Lieutenant when he became an instructor at an Artillery school. Franklin H. Chase, 181.

[17] Thomas W. Higgens, 98.

[18] Higgens says first in America (p. 96), but architectural historian Richard Longstreth has identified earlier examples in Indianapolis (1930), outside Los Angeles (1937), and elsewhere by 1941. Letter to Steven Engelhart, December 27, 1998.

[19] Sergeant, Webster, Crenshaw and Folley were architects of the structure, at the northwest corner of Warren and East Fayette Streets in Syracuse.

[20] Crandall Melvin died on April 20, 1980. *Herald-Journal*, April 21, 1980.

[21] Crandall resided with his family at 6834 Buckley Road. *Herald-Journal*, April 21, 1980.

[22] *Herald-Journal*, May 4, 1966; *Post-Standard* April 22, 1980.

[23] Rev. William J. O'Halloran, at a memorial service for Melvin. Ramona B. Bowden. "Service Cites Melvin as 'Giant of a Man.'" *Post-Standard*, May 2, 1980.

[24] Ramona B. Bowden.

[25] *Post-Standard*, April 22, 1980. Also following quotation.

[26] Thomas H. Dyer, past President of the Onondaga Bar Association, quoted by Romona B. Bowden.

ual who lived in Central New York during the twentieth century can be credited with more solid accomplishment than Crandall Melvin."[27]

## The Melvins at Santanoni

Although identified as the summer residence of Crandall and Myron Melvin, the Santanoni Preserve actually was acquired jointly by four of the next generation: Myron, Jr., Merle and May Melvin, three children of Myron and Mabel (Warner) Melvin, and by Crandall Melvin, Jr., son of Crandall and Eliza Ann (Hunter) Melvin.[28] Readers familiar with generational transfer of property will recognize the two lawyers' reason for having the property in their children's names.[29] Nevertheless, Crandall Melvin, Sr., was particularly concerned with the maintenance of the property.[30] His family usually occupied the Gate Lodge, while his brother Myron's larger family occupied the main camp.[31]

Whereas the Pruyn diary entry for July 27, 1896 had recorded: "Six trout . . . Mrs. Pruyn at Inlet. Clear after rain," in the same volume, on the same day of the year, sixty years later, the Melvins wrote: "Cleared out shoreline for storage of lumber. Put on roof of blacksmith shop . . . painted the door of barn."[32] The pattern is consistent throughout the diary notations. The Pruyns and their guests are pictured at play. The Melvins seemed never to stop working. "Crandall Melvin, Sr., enjoyed supervising repairs to the property. . . . Uncle Crandall spent more money than might have seemed warranted in repairing unused buildings, but it was a hobby of his."[33]

Brothers Merle and Myron Melvin Jr. at Santanoni, 1953

When the Melvins acquired Santanoni in the early 1950s, deferred maintenance evidenced two decades of absentee management by remote bankers. Merle Melvin proudly claimed that the condition of most of the Camp Santanoni buildings improved during the twenty years that his family owned them. "The Melvins did not demolish a single building, with the possible exception of the sugar house west of the junction with the Moose Pond Road."[34] Although they retained

27 *Post-Standard*, April 22, 1980.

28 Deed, September 15, 1953. Liber 309, pages 264-276, recorded September 18, 1953. When the property later was sold, the three children of Myron Melvin divided half the proceeds, while the one child of Crandall Melvin received the other half. Franklin H. Chase in 1924 mentioned two children of Myron and Mabel Melvin: Myron S., Jr., born 1920, and Evelyn Barbara, born in 1923. Their mother Mabel was daughter of John J. and Frederica (Kline) Warner of East Syracuse. Eliza Ann Hunter was daughter of John F. and Eltha (Reed) Hunter of Syracuse. Chase, 180, 181.

29 When the two brothers died, the substantial property was not in their estates, so heirs were relieved of tax and title transfer problems.

30 Merle Melvin to J. Winthrop Aldrich, "Memorandum to File" May 7, 1996, recording oral commentary of Merle D. Melvin, 2.

31 Interview with Crandall Melvin, Jr., July 1992. Aldrich, 157. Helen Tummins, who lived on the estate throughout the Melvin years, recalled that "the Melvins were not frequent visitors." Quoted by Dave Garrison, *Post-Star*, December 1, 1987.

32 "Santanoni: Record of Fish and of Some Other Things." 1893-1971. The American Museum of Fly Fishing.

33 The estates of the senior Melvins were reimbursed a total of $280,000 for cost of maintenance and improvement born by the brothers during their life use. The balance of the million-dollar proceeds was divided among their children, as mentioned in a following footnote. Merle Melvin, May 1996 interview.

34 Merle D. Melvin, Esq., interview by J. Winthrop Aldrich, handwritten notes, Syracuse, January 1994; quote from Merle Melvin, May 1996 interview.

Art Tummins as caretaker throughout their entire period of ownership, they performed many tasks with their own labor.

The Melvins repaired houses at the lakeside caretaking complex, and had new roofs put on the farmhouses, silo and Gate Lodge, but the Syracuse contractor would not undertake the elaborate main camp roof.[35] In 1967–68 the original cedar shingle roof of the villa was "probably entirely removed. [The Melvins] could not justify the expense of replacing . . . the same material, to . . . continuing regret [of Merle Melvin]." Rolled asphalt roofing was used.[36]

The Melvins replaced wood stoves with propane stoves. They replaced the Kohler generator with another that did not require cranking, but started automatically on demand. Crandall Melvin, Jr., removed the exterior stairs at the back of the kitchen block "out of fear that his son, an only child, would tumble down them. This was probably a mistake." (Years earlier the Pruyns had replaced the wooden steps in front of the main hall with masonry, after an abandoned cigarette had ignited them and fire threatened the entire villa.[37])

The Melvins had the steel bridge reinforced so logging trucks could safely cross it.[38] They also demolished part of the curving stone wall that had led vehicles under the stone entry arch, thereby creating a more easily negotiated by-pass. As the logging operation manager explained, "You would have done it too if you knew what those French-Canadian log truck drivers were like."[39]

During the Melvin tenure, the farm was inoperative and many of its buildings deteriorated. Nevertheless, between the extensive roofing work and other repairs, the Melvins' legacy at Santanoni is the very existence of its buildings. Had the State of New York, instead of the Melvins, purchased Santanoni from the Pruyn trust, the buildings would have been in jeopardy, as subsequently became evident.

Although the Pruyn trust had assumed that there would be no more marketable timber on the property, the Melvins contracted to cut whatever hardwood remained. As taxes continued to increase, the Melvins also contracted to begin harvesting softwood for pulp.[40] This constituted the fourth serious phase in eighty years of logging at Santanoni. Throughout the 1950s and 1960s, the wood taken out of Santanoni paid the estate's approximate $35,000 annual cost.[41] By another account, "we were able to give the Melvins close to a million dollars from the proceeds of sound timber management" during the late 1950s, and 1960s.[42] This suggests that the Pruyn trust either received poor advice regarding future prospects of lumbering, or was predisposed to terminate its involvement with Santanoni Preserve.

In the long run, however, the prospect of self-sufficiency continued to be bleak, as renewal of the timber resources could not be

---

[35] Stanley Green of Syracuse was the roofer. Merle Melvin, May 1996 interview.

[36] Merle Melvin, May 1996 interview. Melvin could not recall the name of the Plattsburgh firm that installed the roll roofing. Curiously, it was not installed in conventional horizontal manner, but applied vertically. This secured the interiors, for the most part, for about three decades, until architectural grade asphalt shingles were applied from 1995-98.

[37] Merle Melvin, May 1996 interview is source for paragraph. Art Tummins told Melvin about the steps.

[38] Crandall Melvin, Jr. Aldrich, 157.

[39] J. Winthrop Aldrich reported, "When I asked retired manager of the Northern Lumber Company why he removed the wall and rerouted the road, he said. 'Nobody would have wanted to have them drive through that arched gateway.' He said those guys would be going lickity split down the hill with a full load of logs. They wouldn't have cared if they hooked the truck on the side of the building and taken half of it back to Canada with them." Aldrich, 39-40, 157 Susan Pruyn King, however, remembers the section of wall removed when the Pruyns still owned Santanoni, presumably to facilitate *their* lumbering operations. (King to Howard Kirschenbaum).

[40] Hardwoods were harvested by Northern Lumber Company, softwoods by Finch, Pruyn and Co.

[41] Crandall Melvin, Jr. Aldrich, 157.

[42] Duane Irwin of Poland, N.Y., retired Manager of the Northern Lumber Company, telephone conversation with J. Winthrop Aldrich, August 1992. Aldrich, 39-40, 157. Merle Melvin denied Irwin's assertions regarding their profit from the property. Merle recalled modest profit in only three of their twenty-year ownership. Merle Melvin, May 1996 interview, 2, 3.

anticipated for a long duration, during which annual carrying costs and intensive work by the owners would continue.[43]

As the senior Melvin brothers aged, and after Myron died in 1966, their children assumed increasing responsibility for Santanoni. As noted earlier, title already was held by the four—Crandall Melvin, Jr., of Liverpool, N.Y., and Myron's three children: Merle D. Melvin of Syracuse, Myron Melvin, Jr. of Rochester; and May Melvin (Mrs. William) Legg of Liverpool.[44]

Several times the Melvin families explored selling much of Santanoni Preserve to New York State.[45] The first occasion was in 1957. By 1958 an agreement had been reached for the sale of the entire preserve, less fifty acres around the Gate Lodge buildings, which the Melvins would retain. The transaction, however, did not go forward.[46] In 1968, shortly after Myron Melvin, Sr. died, at the time of the main camp's major roof replacement, the Melvins renewed their offer to sell the preserve to the state, less the fifty acres, for $1.5-million. Property values had substantially increased in the decade since prior negotiations and the State still was not prepared to purchase Santanoni.

The impasse was bridged by intervention of a third party. Ironically, the Pruyn family accomplished the breakthrough. The heirs learned the property was for sale from the realtor, probably at the Melvin's suggestion.[47] Edward Pruyn's daughter Susan Pruyn King, her husband Thomas King II, and her brother Lance tried to interest other members of the family in re-purchasing Santanoni themselves. The others were not sufficiently interested, however, and the Kings and Lance could not afford to purchase and maintain the property alone. Late in 1970 the Kings read about The Nature Conservancy in a *Wall St. Journal* article.[48] The Nature Conservancy is a national, non-profit organization, devoted to conserving biological diversity through land protection. It occurred to the Kings that The Nature Conservancy might play a role in preserving the camp as they knew it, while protecting the Preserve from future development. The Kings introduced The Nature Conservancy to the Melvins and Santanoni. Conservancy vice-president Patrick Noonan visited the property

---

[43] During the sixty years the Santanoni Preserve was owned by the Pruyn family, it earned more than a million dollars from timber sales. It might seem that the income could have been placed in a trust fund to acquire interest sufficient to operate the estate indefinitely. However, given the timing of the timber sales and lower interest rates in the first half of the twentieth century, income would not have been sufficient to cover annual costs of fifteen to more than thirty thousand dollars over the sixty years of Pruyn ownership. The Melvins likewise learned that despite lumber sales, operation of the Santanoni Preserve was a money-losing proposition.

[44] These were their addresses on the 1953 Santanoni deed. Crandall Melvin, Jr., born at Liverpool in 1928, grew up at the family farm on Buckley Road. He attended the Liverpool public schools, Culver Military Academy, and Middlebury College (a traditional school of Yankees), and also attended the University of Oslo, Norway. Crandall Melvin, Jr., finally attended Syracuse University, which awarded him baccalaureate and Law degrees. Practicing as an attorney, Crandall Melvin, Jr., like his father has been very active in community affairs. Crandall Melvin III is the only child of Crandall Melvin, Jr. Merle D. Melvin is an attorney with the Melvin and Melvin law firm. He had one son, John D. Melvin, living near Patterson, N.J. Myron Melvin, Jr., later was reported to be a pharmacist living near Baldwinsville, N.Y. and at Geneva, N.Y. Arthur Davis and Connie Schreiber. "B'ville boy hunted: Hundred searching Adirondacks." Syracuse *Herald-Journal*, July 12, 1971, 1; August 1, 1971. May Melvin's husband William Legg in 1971 was secondary education science supervisor in the Liverpool Central School District. The Leggs lived in Liverpool, before moving to Baldwinsville. Davies and Schreiber articles, July 12, 1971, 1; August 11, 1971, 8. The four children of William and May (Melvin) Legg were, by age: Paul, Douglas, Marjorie (Margie) and Linda. Margie was three-years old and Linda was seventeen-months old in August, 1971. Arthur Davis. "Doug's birthday; is he alive?" Syracuse *Herald-Journal*, August 11, 1971, 1.

[45] The following chronology was reported by William Rudge and Charles Vandrei to the Santanoni Citizens Advisory Committee on May 2, 1995.

[46] The Melvins asked $312,000 (about $24/acre) but the State appraised the property at only $177,550 (about $14/acre). Agreement was reached at $19/acre but the legislature failed to provide acquisition funds.

[47] These events were related by Susan Pruyn King in conversations with Howard Kirschenbaum, 1991-92 and electronic communications to Howard Kirschenbaum, May 5 and 6, 1999.

[48] Ray Bender, "State Takes Santanoni Preserve Gift," *Press Republican* (Plattsburgh, NY), February 19, 1972. The article incorrectly said Susan's father and mother, who were deceased, had read about the Nature Conservancy.

in the spring and negotiated with Merle Melvin, obtaining an option to purchase Santanoni Preserve for $1.5 million.[49] Again, the turn of events would prove to be ironic; the Kings' introduction of The Nature Conservancy led to threatened demolition for all of Santanoni's historic buildings.

Whether the Nature Conservancy could have raised an amount that the State of New York had regarded as excessive is not certain. The question is moot, however. The Conservancy had barely begun to explore avenues for raising this substantial sum when a tragedy occurred at Newcomb Lake which led irrevocably to the state's acquisition of the Santanoni Preserve.

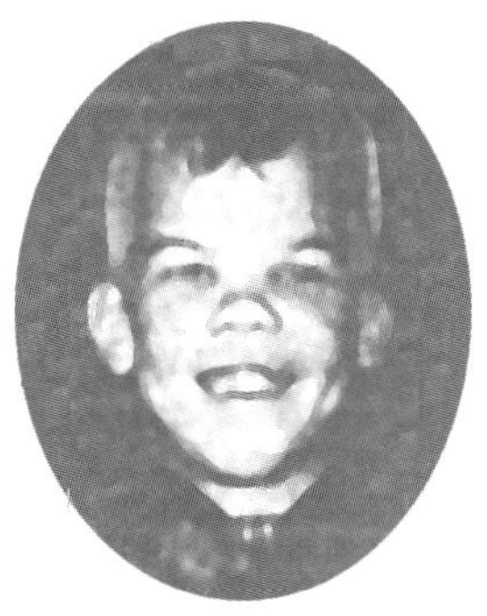

## The Search for Douglas Legg

On Saturday afternoon, July 10, 1971, eight-year-old Douglas Legg was playing with his twelve-year-old brother, Paul, on the entry road, not far from the main lodge.[50] Doug was a stocky boy with exceptionally blond hair. He and his brother were grandsons of Myron Melvin, Sr., then deceased. They were at Santanoni with their parents, May Melvin Legg and William Legg, and their two younger sisters.

According to the headlined story in Monday newspapers, Doug's Uncle Myron told the State Police that he took the youngster on a hike in the afternoon. About three-thirty they encountered rampant poison ivy along an overgrown logging road. Because Douglas was wearing only short pants, his uncle told him to return to the camp. Douglas appeared to walk back to the main lodge. But he did not.

As reported later, when Myron returned to the camp shortly after five-thirty, Doug's absence was discovered. The family immediately called the local fire emergency number to report Doug missing. About nine-twenty p.m. the State Police at Malone were notified.

When Newcomb highway worker Daniel Tefoe heard the news, he dumped a load of stone from his truck and returned immediately to carry volunteers for a search. About thirty people quickly came in from Newcomb village to join the State Police in the search. The boy's father, William Legg, and others worked through the night. The temperature dropped to nearly forty degrees, and Doug was wearing only short blue pants, a white striped shirt, and black sneakers. He had no matches with him.

Day Two: On Sunday about a hundred people continued the hunt. Three State Troopers inspected all buildings and covered about ten miles of logging roads. The search continued through a second night, using lights and bullhorns, while the Troopers searched Newcomb Lake by canoe. "People are religious here," commented a Newcomb man, "and a lot of prayers are being said for the young lad."

Monday, Day Three: State Police estimated that two- to three-hundred volunteers would be given search assignments, beginning eight a.m. at the Town Hall. The New York State Police brought bloodhounds. Three helicopters arrived, one from the State Police, another from the Conservation Department, and the third from the U.S. Air Force. Sixty volunteers

---

[49] Noonan to Howard Kirschenbaum, September 29, 1999. Rudge/Vandrei chronology, fn. 46.

[50] The original version of this section comprised twenty pages of text, including 173 footnotes. To better balance the book as a whole, we have shortened the narration and eliminated the footnotes for this section, most of which referenced stories in the Syracuse *Herald-Journal* from July 12 to August 10, 1971. For the even more detailed version of events, complete with footnotes, readers are referred to the research edition available on disk from Adirondack Architectural Heritage.

came from the Plattsburgh Air Force Base, joined by volunteer firemen from throughout Essex County. Three volunteers dragged the Upper Duck Hole, notoriously dangerous because of its soft bottom. The shallower Lower Duck Hole was scanned visually.

The bloodhounds tracked a scent. "They keep on running towards this one point," state trooper Henry Witt reported. "We've searched the mountain thoroughly but haven't found anything." The dogs lost the scent about a mile and a half from the main lodge. The trooper commented that the hills were "thick, hard going. You'd have to walk pretty close to the boy to see him if he's lying down. We keep hoping he's all right and he'll be able to make it to an open spot."

After Doug had been missing about forty-eight hours, Crandall Melvin, Sr., whose family was in the Gate Lodge, spoke bravely: "They'll find him," he predicted, because Douglas "can't be far away," and he was a "sturdy" boy who was "accustomed to being outdoors." That night the temperature dropped to the freezing mark.

Day Four: On Tuesday morning, Crandall Melvin, Jr., held a press conference for news people, barred from entering the Preserve. The information center was not at Santanoni, however, but the search headquarters at the Newcomb Town Hall, where volunteers cheered the news of new tracks, relayed by police radio. The number of searchers now was about three hundred, including about a hundred and fifty men and women from the Plattsburgh Air Force Base. Four schoolteacher colleagues of Doug's father arrived from Liverpool to help, some of whom left their summer jobs. Twelve deputy sheriffs from Onondaga County volunteered to work without pay, and were released from their duties to do so. About eighty-five faculty, staff and students of the State College of Forestry continued or joined the search, now covering a five-square-mile area.

The fresh tracks, believed to be those of a child, were found near Santanoni Creek, which entered Newcomb Lake on the north shore, the opposite side from where Douglas supposedly had been with his uncle. Lt. R. W. Jones, New York State Police search coordinator, observed that Doug would have had to return past the main camp and continue about a mile beyond the bathing beach to reach the creek.

A State Police bloodhound picked up the scent, following a track due north, up Santanoni Creek, veering northwest toward Ward Pond. The dogs lost the scent at another, more swampy pond, impounded by a beaver dam. The dam was broken and the pond drained, with no result. Two helicopters hovered over as about twenty-five volunteers immediately hunted the rugged, densely-wooded terrain between the creek and larger Ward Pond, about a mile west of the creek, while two other volunteers dragged the pond.

Jim Evans and Brian Howell, adult members of the Adirondack Council of Boy Scouts' search-and-rescue team, with two of their scouts, were conducting an independent search day and night, "using a different approach," searching the Newcomb Farm Road, between the Duck Hole and Beaver Flow.

Newcomb resident Earl Miner reported fresh tracks in the Howard Hill area, north of Beaver Flow, but no sign of the boy there. He observed that there was fresh water and plenty of ripe blueberries to provide emergency food.

The search was difficult, even for seasoned Adirondackers. A volunteer from a local lumbering company, working five additional hours a day on the search, commented that "I've never found it as tiring as yesterday." The hardest part, he observed, was trying to see into the dense woods. Thick brush, soggy bogs and humid swamps were infested with mosquitoes, black flies, horse flies, and deer flies.

Because there had been no rain in two weeks, Forest Ranger Bruce Coon expressed

**Searchers keep in sight of each other as they form their line in a relatively clear area and move into deeper brush.**

Syracuse *Herald-Journal*, July 18, 1971

concern for forest fire with so much intense activity in the woods. Heavy rains dispelled that concern by Tuesday afternoon—a worse turn of events, for they probably washed away scents detectable by search dogs. Strong winds during the storm stopped helicopter operations, and dense fog set in after the four o'clock downpour, further hampering operations. Nearly an inch and a half of rain fell overnight, flooding boggy areas. Temperatures fell to the mid-forties, as about thirty volunteers stayed in the woods overnight, patrolling logging roads in the Ward Pond area. The Melvin families remained at the Preserve, hunting day and night for Douglas.

Wednesday, Day Five: Bo, the State bloodhound, left with Trooper Robert Wotowich two hours before the regular party. Under skies still cloudy, most of the searchers were assigned in one large group back to the Ward Pond area, where dogs had led searchers the preceding day. Tacticians suspected that Doug may have intended to go to Moose

Pond. The family had camped at the lean-to there. Ward Pond is on a straight-line route toward Moose Pond from the point on Santanoni Brook where the track went westward. Later in the day, Woody, another bloodhound, arrived from Buffalo with his owner, policeman John Schultz. Plattsburgh Air Force personnel numbering about one hundred twenty, many here for the fourth day, brought three all-terrain vehicles to be used in lowlands flooded by recent rain. Because the ground was soft, several people fell into sinkholes. There were many cuts and bruises but no serious injuries.

About forty teenage members of the Civil Air Patrol, trained in rescue operations, arrived from points around the state. Participants in an "Adirondack beautification project" joined the search. Volunteers reporting at the Town Hall, now numbering more than three hundred, were used for many tasks, including cooking. Large numbers of participants had to be fed and housed; the Newcomb Fire Department auxiliary prepared food and located lodging for volunteers.

Hundreds of searchers closed in on Ward Pond, but the bloodhounds failed to pick up another scent. Douglas would have had to move about in order for the dogs to find a new scent after the rain. A Trooper commented optimistically, "If the kid is out there, the dog will find him. He just doesn't give up. It's a feeling I have. The dog picked up a scent yesterday and seemed to be on the right track. I think [the kid] may be in the area." State Police and Conservation Department helicopters buzzed the terrain while crews shouted through bullhorns, urging the boy to find a stream or open area. But what if Douglas were injured, and could not move? Air Force representatives requested a plane to photograph the area with infra-red film which detects heat from people and animals after they remain in one spot for some time, as when sleeping.

In the fifth day State Police inspector Donald Ambler took command of the search. He stated, "As far as the pattern indicates, he's heading in a northward direction—that's the assumption that we're going to go on." Probably he meant "northwest," the direction of Moose Pond from the main camp on Newcomb Lake.

Exciting news again was relayed back to the headquarters: Woody, the Buffalo bloodhound, found sneaker tracks and waste, believed to be only one day old, near Ward Pond.

Thursday, Day Six: "Search for Doug intensifies," read the headline of the Syracuse newspaper. The frantic Melvin family issued a plea for more volunteers. The Liverpool School District, near Syracuse, where Doug's father was employed, offered use of its school buses to transport volunteers to Newcomb, advising recruits to bring their own sleeping gear. Essex County Sheriff Kenneth Goodspeed directed recruiting at the Town Hall, where he coordinated all agencies participating in the campaign. A caravan of trucks carried volunteers from the Town Hall into the Preserve each morning. The Sheriff observed that the search had brought more people to Newcomb than in any other time in its history.

Early in the morning an airborne photographer, Jim Evans, took about seventy photographs with infrared film, which would indicate a twenty-foot "glow" where a person had slept the night. Because animals more commonly moved at night, they would not regularly be a factor.

Woody the bloodhound had followed the new scent for about two hours, but heavy rain again washed it away, and the several bloodhounds began anew Thursday morning. About eighty searchers from the State College of Forestry were sent out first, because they were regarded as well trained and better disciplined than most volunteers. They headed for dense thickets that others might avoid.

**The main lodge of the Melvin estate is on-scene search headquarters. The Leggs and Melvins live in the building at the far right when in residence there.**

Syracuse *Herald-Journal*, July 18, 1971

During the afternoon, two more bloodhounds arrived from the Oneida State Police headquarters to join the intensive search now focused southeast of Ward Pond, between it and Newcomb Lake. Five horses came from Syracuse, and five more from Tioga County to facilitate movement through the Preserve. Three Red Cross trucks arrived to assist with food service and first aid.

The rumor that a boy's sneaker had been found was dispelled as false. Nevertheless, State Police Captain R.W. DePuy said he thought that Doug's chances were "still good at this point. We think he's still alive, but we think he's down."

The theory that Doug had intended to reach the camp at Moose Pond initially did not get much support from his family. For an eight-year-old, the boy was not inexperienced—he had climbed the state's highest peak, Mt. Marcy, the previous summer with his parents. But this was just his third trip to Santanoni. He had been only six-years old when he last visited the Preserve. Doug, who was only in the third grade, "didn't know the area at all."

The President of the Newcomb Volunteer Fire Department, Alan Van Auken, spoke for all the searchers: "I'd go home and see my eight-year-old youngster and it would make me want to get out and find this missing boy."

Inspector Ambler broke significant news on this sixth day: Doug's uncle, Myron Melvin, Jr., had changed his report of what had happened on the past Saturday afternoon, when Doug was last seen. Inspector Ambler reported to the press that Douglas did not leave the camp with his uncle, as Myron Melvin previously had stated. Doug "had wanted to go along with his uncle, but the uncle told him to go back to the camp" because he lacked "proper clothing." The main lodge was "a very short distance," no more than fifty or sixty yards away from where Doug was with his older brother, Paul, and a cousin. Myron and Doug had never encountered poison ivy on a logging trail, as earlier stated.

When questioned by reporters about the change of stories, the inspector merely reiterated, curtly, "No, he [Douglas] did not accompany him [Myron Melvin]." At another point, Inspector Ambler stated, "The boy wanted to go along, but the uncle said no, he wanted to go alone." Myron Melvin then departed by himself, apparently leaving Doug with his companions.

The reporters did not speculate about the implications of the new story, or about the reason for its original inaccuracy. Since Douglas had not, as originally reported, started off with his uncle, why did he leave his brother and cousin to go off into the woods alone? No testimony of Doug's companions was reported.

According to a second-hand version related to one of the authors shortly after the event, Douglas was supposed to go on a planned hike, but when the appointed time came he had neglected to change into long trousers. Because he was wearing shorts, he was criticized impatiently for not being dressed as a proper woodsman. Told to go back on the double and put on trousers, Doug instead stormed off into the forest.

Such speculation about motives may be idle, but one may reasonably ask why the boy went off alone, presumably deep into the woods, and why the first report of his departure was reported inaccurately. Because the family was so distraught, these questions may not have been asked at the time—and still may be insensitive to raise, over a quarter century later.

Friday, Day Seven: "Throngs join hunt for boy," read the headline. "Hundreds of Central New Yorkers arrived here today by car, bus, and truck to join in the seven-day-old search for eight-year-old Douglas Legg. . .. Search coordinators have issued a plea for food and other supplies." Doug's grandmother, Mabel Melvin, widow of Myron Melvin, Sr., gave a check for a thousand dollars to the firemen's auxiliary to help provide food and supplies.

Searchers worked in groups of ten to fifteen, accompanied by a leader. State Police said they had plenty of volunteers but lacked "persons familiar with the Adirondack woods to act as search party leaders." About thirty members of the Onondaga Federation of Sportsmen's Club Rescue Team, experienced woodsmen and Adirondack hunters with group-leader potential, were especially welcomed to the search. The volunteers now included a prominent bank chairman, employees of another bank, and two legislators.

Members of the 389th Army Group, Third Battalion, Syracuse, had come last night with another truck to transport volunteers into the main camp assembly area. Eight truckloads of searchers arrived at the log villa early in the morning, prepared to hike northeast to a new search area. Sheriff Goodspeed addressed the searchers before they set out. Some experienced woodsmen had complained that volunteers were avoiding dense growth, and not maintaining line formation to assure uniform coverage. Searchers were instructed to string toilet paper or twine as they moved through the woods, to mark areas covered. The Sheriff stressed the need to look in heavy brush areas, because a lost person may seek shelter and warmth in such places.

Six Liverpool Central School District buses brought about a hundred and fifty new volunteers while another thirty-five or forty arrived on an East Syracuse-Minoa bus. Members of the Newcomb Volunteer Fire Department auxiliary reported that they had exhausted their funds for food and were seeking donations of food and other supplies.

Onondaga County Sheriff's Sergeant David Stevenson commented, "These people have busted themselves and have done everything for this search." He urged all coming up to bring supplies. Food and other supplies

**Searchers wait to board trucks in front of Newcomb Town Hall. Trucks take volunteers to drop off points in wooded areas.**

Syracuse *Herald-Journal*, July 17, 1971

were dropped to searching parties from helicopters.

Corporal, another State Police bloodhound, joined Bo and Woody in their work. Infrared photographs taken the day before showed two "hot spots," but one was judged to be caused by a sleeping bear, the other unexplained. More pictures were taken from a helicopter. Another helicopter inspected a nearby mountain that Doug had wanted to climb.

A State Police officer observed that it was "possible" the boy could be deliberately hiding, or have deliberately run away, but there was "no indication" of this. "I'm convinced there's a very good chance of finding the boy alive," State Police Lieutenant DePuy told reporters. More ominously, another official observed, "Nearly all possible sites where the boy could be have been covered." Still, troopers would "stay as long as it takes to find the boy."

Inspector Ambler, in charge of the investigation, discounted speculation about foul play or kidnapping. He amplified the new version of Saturday's events, reporting that Myron returned from his solo hike about an hour and a half later, to learn that his nephew was not at the villa. Doug's parents had supposed that he had gone with his uncle, Inspector Ambler stated. The inspector did not explain why Doug's parents had reason to suppose that their son was with Myron, if indeed—as was now reported—the boy had spontaneously asked when his uncle passed if he could tag along. The parents would not have known this. William and May Legg more reasonably would have supposed Doug was with Myron if they had previously planned for their son to go on a hike with his uncle.

Tired searchers said the woods were the "thickest and most isolated of any they have ever been in." A week in the woods, under crisis conditions, had been wearing. Some volunteers, kept on stand-by at the Town Hall, griped about poor organization. Police explained the reason: shortage of qualified group leaders. State Police search coordinator Jones observed that he was "satisfied with the operation" considering that "we have so many volunteers. . . . We are going to have some breakdowns at various points, but overall it's looking pretty well."

Saturday, Day Eight: Twenty-nine members of the Mountain Rescue Association flew into Syracuse airport from California, bound for Newcomb. The Melvins paid the airline fares, estimated at about nine thousand dollars. Highly trained in search and rescue missions, the "Sierra-Madre group" had worked in eleven western states, but never before in New York.

About a hundred volunteers of the U.S. Marine Corps Reserve Training Center, 8th Tank Battalion, Mattydale (near Syracuse), arrived Saturday. Twelve mounted horsemen rode in from Lake George. Volunteers now numbered between five and seven hundred. Search expanded eastward to Guideboard Hill, about three miles from the main camp. The Old Newcomb Farm road led from the Upper Duck Hole to this point on the Hudson, at Tahawus.

A third command post, in addition to those at the Town Hall and "Melvin lodge" (main lodge), was established about a mile and a half northeast of Beaver Pond, manned by six forest rangers and three foresters. Their mission was to "mark off trees," presumably as guide posts.

More of Doug's clothes arrived from his home near Syracuse, in order to give the bloodhounds fresh scent. Some police officers complained that searchers' sneakers were leaving prints that were being confused with Doug's.

Searchers headed out for the afternoon in pouring rain and high winds. Among the volunteer searchers was Mayor Oliver Masters of Liverpool, New York, a friend of the family, who reported that they were taking the crisis "well," remaining confident that Doug was "okay and will be found."

Sunday, Day Nine: With "tears in his eyes" Sheriff Goodspeed told of a Liverpool woman "who donated $100, . . . money saved by her family for a vacation."

Eight of the newly-arrived Californians spent Saturday night in the woods, joined by several other volunteers as a ban on night searching was lifted. Late that night searchers discovered a sneaker and hand print about eight miles northeast of the villa. A small child apparently left the prints near Ward Pond Road, an old logging trail three and a half miles north of Guideboard Hill. Because of darkness, further identification had been delayed, so the area became the focus of the next day's main campaign. Because heavy rain would have washed old prints away, searchers were optimistic about the new lead, although woodsmen cautioned that bear tracks often were mistaken for human prints.

On Sunday the Californians broke into four groups, to work their way back from Beaver Pond to the main camp, then head north again. After conferring with the Melvins, the Californians' leader, Doug Temlin, reported an important new fact: Doug's seven-year-old cousin John had seen Doug after Melvin had left him. John was at the bathing beach and he called to Doug, who was passing nearby on the lakeside trail, to come down and join him. Doug ignored his cousin and kept walking. The interviewer derived the impression from the family that Doug had seemed determined to take the forbidden hike, on his own. "The boy's parents think one possibility is that the boy headed out into the woods on a hike anyway." Doug's parents said that their son had shown no personality problems and had not often required punishment, but was characteristically determined and intelligent, liking to do things by himself.

Infrared aerial photographs failed to picture any "hot spots." Further photography would be delayed because the Californians were in the area to be photographed. A Navy helicopter equipped with special heat and sound-detecting equipment arrived. The number of forest rangers doubled, providing leadership for more search parties.

The search peaked this weekend, with seven-hundred to a thousand volunteers at work, representing some seventy-five organizations. The Californians found searching the northeastern forest different from working in the western mountains, because "heavy undergrowth . . . limits vision to less than six feet in spots." Syracusan Nikki Kanaley observed that due to the "very rough" terrain, some youngsters were finding that the search was no "picnic or an Easter egg hunt."

Six divers from the Onondaga County Sheriff and Brewerton Fire Departments' rescue teams continued searching Newcomb Lake. Town of Newcomb highway superintendent, Jim Stringer, was allowing his nine employees to work at the Preserve while he coordinated transportation and supplies. A franchise food chain, Carrols Development Corporation, sent up a truckload of food and drink from Glens Falls, promising to continue to supply provisions. Another truck from Liverpool brought fifteen-hundred sandwiches sent by the Northeast Convention of Rangers, plus another thousand sandwiches made by others. On the truck were two-thousand canned meals, plus five-hundred spaghetti dinners, eighty cases of soda from Canada Dry Bottlers, five-hundred dollars worth of food and paper supplies from Tom Crosby's Super Duper market in Liverpool, including milk, ham, and bread. The Liverpool shipment included money collected by the United Methodist Church of Liverpool. A woman in Fayetteville, N.Y. set up a fund to buy provisions with collection points at branches of the Merchants' Bank.

***Searchers eat a hot dinner***

Syracuse *Herald-Journal*, July 24, 1971

Some volunteers commuted daily from distant homes and motels to the isolated village proudly proclaimed as the "Heart of the Adirondacks." Newcomb, a hamlet of several hundred people, a school, a general store, a volunteer fire department, and three bars, was unprepared to absorb crowds of visitors. Many volunteers slept on the floor of the school gym, others out of doors in tents, cars, and under the stars. Harland and Mary Stubing, both employed with three children at home, opened their home to volunteers, as did other Newcomb families. Mary stayed up late to serve snacks when searchers returned, and got up early to make breakfast for them.

Volunteers were finding the hunt "exhausting, sometimes disorganized, so far in vain, and touched with a sense of mystery that Douglas could vanish without a trace." An Environmental Conservation officer commented, "Essentially . . . something is very funny. I've been looking for people up here for more than ten years and there's always a sign—something—a lost sneaker maybe—or a torn tee shirt. Here there's none. After all this time with all these people looking, there should be something."

Searchers endured not only fatigue, but skin abrasion from working in heavy brush. Many were sinking up to their hips in bogs. Workers were "showing signs of physical and mental strain." Gary Carter, a Newcomb search-party leader who had been in the woods daily since the Saturday that Doug disappeared, reported that the previous day he had stretched string about twenty-two miles, "and this was an easy day." A burly, bearded volunteer from Schenectady, removing his orange hard hat, said that he had gotten '"two hours of sleep each night. . . . I went to call my wife on the phone last night and for a while I couldn't think of my name. That's how mentally tired I am." Instead of slowing down, however, "if anything, we are putting on more miles each day," said Mark Fisher who worked with one of the dog teams. Sheriff Goodspeed, laid up with a swollen leg, observed, "I have never seen anything so beautiful as these people who are helping with the search. Nobody says he's tired. They tell me each night they'll be there the next day to search." The Sheriff, however, noted the shortening of fuses. He, too, was tempted to over-react to annoyances. "I have to catch and remind myself that everybody is tired."

Maggie McMahon, a mother of four, left home at six-thirty every morning for the Town Hall, not leaving until about nine p.m., "if she is fortunate." She lost sixteen pounds during the first two weeks. Ella La Fountain, head of the Fire Department Ladies Auxiliary, said, "I'm tired, but it is the kind of tiredness you can put up with because it's for a good cause." The women of the Ladies Auxiliary complained of sore feet, but not of housework undone. Some could serve because others cared for their younger children. Sally Rockwood said they forgot about time. "We are always thinking of right now, of what has to be done immediately." Mrs. John Duncan added, "We keep thinking of the boy, thinking that he will be found any hour."

Doug's family—his brother Paul and two younger sisters with their parents, grandfather, aunts, uncles, and cousins—remained at Santanoni, waiting for each bit of news. William Legg sent word to the many hundreds of searchers that he wanted to "thank people from the bottom of our hearts for their contributions." Learning that the Newcomb Volunteer Fire Department was exhausting its funds, he said he would seek to help them. The Town of Newcomb likewise was running up large bills for provisions. When money was needed for food and drinks, Town Supervisor Lilbern Yandon charged it off to the town so that they wouldn't have to wait for contributions."

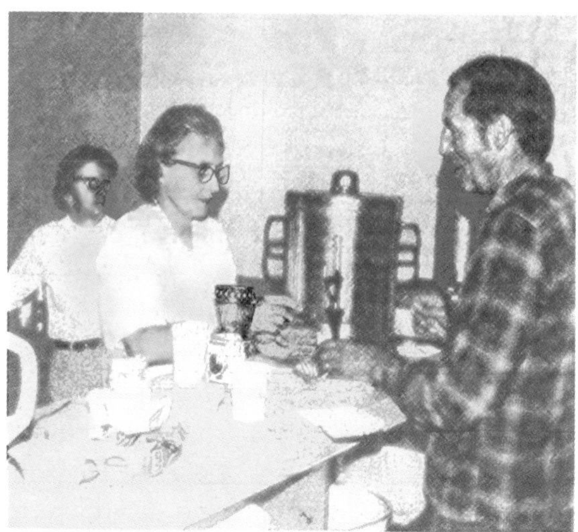

Mrs. Lilbern Yandon, center, serves her ever-moving husband, the town supervisor, a cup of coffee, while Doris Porter, waits to relieve her.

Syracuse *Herald-Journal*, July 25, 1971

Monday, Day Ten: "New scent may lead to Doug." The page-one story reported that a new track had led bloodhounds fifteen miles from the camp, into Franklin County. The dog teams were at Shattuck Clearing, at the juncture of the Cold River and Moose Creek, on the other side of Moose Mountain, northwest of Santanoni Preserve. A system of waterways, lowlands and the old Cold River Tote Road might have provided a fairly accessible route there. One team was air dropped south of Shattuck Clearing; another worked north of the clearing.

WET NIGHT

70s Tomorrow

Full Report and Map on Page 9

SYRACUSE TEMPERATURES

| | | | | | |
|---|---|---|---|---|---|
| 1 a.m. | 55 | 5 a.m. | 53 | 10 a.m. | 68 |
| 2 a.m. | 53 | 6 a.m. | 52 | 11 a.m. | 67 |
| 3 a.m. | 53 | 7 a.m. | 55 | 12 noon | 66 |
| 4 a.m. | 53 | 8 a.m. | 59 | 1 p.m. | 64 |
| 12 mid | 56 | 9 a.m. | 63 | 2 p.m. | 62 |

★ Associated Press

HERA

★ United Press International

SYRACUSE, N. Y., MONDAY, JULY 19, 1971

VOL

An airman from Plattsburgh leads Woody the bloodhound along Santanoni Creek in search for Douglas Legg.

# New scent may lead to Doug

**By ARTHUR DAVIS AND BOB BROWN**

NEWCOMB — A scent trail which could have been left by Douglas Legg led a dog-search team today towards a point at least 15 miles from Newcomb into Franklin County as the search for the missing boy moved into its 10th day.

John H. Terry to ask his help in securing the services of one of the jets.

Doug's father today issued a prepared statement thanking the hundreds of people who have joined the search for the missing boy.

"Our son has been provided with the best possible chance for survival through your efforts. Regardless of the outcome, we will always be mindful of your great expression of concern," he said.

"In our time of need, hundreds of people, volunteers and specialists, have contributed their valuable time and energy in a massive attempt to find our son.

"The persistent attempts of the searchers and prayers of

(Concluded on Page 9)

Griffis Air Force Base at Rome, N.Y. announced orders had come from Washington to send a C-131 Convair to take thermo-radiation photographs of the entire search area. Doug's father, William Legg, had contacted Representative John H. Terry, asking for help.

Then: "In a clarification of conflicting stories, Legg and officials today issued what they say is the explanation of Doug's disappearance."

> Doug went with his uncle down the main road to the lodge [i.e., the entry drive] to a logging road, approximately 200 yards from the main compound.
>
> As they started up the logging road, Melvin told Doug to go back to the house. He escorted the lad to the main road.
>
> Doug walked back to the house and onto a ridge-beach area, where he was seen by his older brother Paul and a cousin John.
>
> They were approximately 200 yards away on the beach, but called to him to come down to the beach. The time was set somewhere between 3 and 4 p.m., July 10, authorities said.
>
> It was not until approximately 6 p.m., when Melvin returned from his hike, that the boy's parents became concerned for his safety. After searching for Doug for another hour, William Legg went into the village at 7:30 p.m. and organized a search party.

The fourth version fused the first three. If Myron had come upon the boys playing together fifty or sixty yards from the villa, as previously stated, apparently Doug tagged along as his uncle walked another few hundred feet down the drive, then accompanied him onto a logging road, where they might have encountered the poison ivy—although the reason for sending Doug back was not mentioned in these later accounts.

The reconciliation of the previous reports did not address the question of whether the hike with his uncle was planned, or whether Doug merely saw his uncle passing and tried to go with him, possibly tagging along uninvited. Either way, Doug might have reacted in anger—to being reprimanded for not being prepared for a planned walk, or being told he was not properly dressed to go on an unplanned one.

Doug's parents apparently expected him to return with Myron, whose arrival without their son caused the first alarm. But why did the Leggs in the interval suppose the boy was with his uncle? Possibly the other two boys may have returned to the villa en route to the beach, perhaps to get swim suits, and at that time might have mentioned to Doug's parents that he had gone off with his uncle.

If this reconciliation of "conflicting stories" finally seemed satisfactory, it left unexplained the reason why Inspector Ambler had taken so long to put the simple pieces together, and why three incomplete and conflicting versions had been given out during the first nine days, versions that never entirely meshed with the final account.

In tandem with this official report, Doug's father issued a prepared statement, addressed to all who had participated in the search:

> Our son has been provided with the best possible chance for survival through your efforts. Regardless of the outcome, we will always be mindful of your great expression of concern. In our time of need, hundreds of people, volunteers and specialists, have contributed their valuable time and energy in a massive attempt to find our son. The persistent attempts of the searchers and prayers of many for Doug's safe return have continually revitalized our strained morale. As the search extends into the tenth day, our family is gravely concerned over the outcome, but we must continue to hope as you do who have looked for Doug every day since Saturday, July 10.

William Legg then mentioned the many groups that had participated in the search. He concluded:

> Finally we especially wish to thank from the bottom of our hearts our relatives, friends, and again the people of Newcomb who have shared this terrible burden with us. We pray to God with all of you, that he will be found alive.

Crandall Melvin Jr., center, with sunglasses and light coat, an uncle of the missing boy, talks to one of search leaders.

Syracuse *Herald-Journal*, July 18, 1971

The formal statements from the police and family suggested some measure of closure, but of course there could be none. Nevertheless, the campaign was winding down. Only about a hundred volunteers remained on Monday, about ten percent of those who had been working over the weekend. There was no shortage of food now, although snacks and cigarettes remained in short supply.

The many others who remained at Santanoni would not give up. "Most of the experienced searchers believe that Douglas is still alive."

The search continued for twenty-three more days. Over the next week a large number of government employees and volunteers continued combing the woods for Douglas Legg. Managers of three franchise restaurants were serving almost four-hundred breakfasts daily. On the twelfth day, about two-hundred-and-fifty of the searchers formed a human chain, walking virtually hand-in-hand close to where Doug was last seen. On Sunday, the sixteenth day, about two-hundred and seventy-five people participated in the search.

Inadvertently, helicopter searcher "Ace Howland" found another missing party—twenty-one Boy Scouts lost in the woods south of Kamp Kill Kare in the Raquette Lake area. But the other Santanoni searchers, exploring one lead and one theory after another, continued to come up empty-handed. The Air Force plane arrived with its sophisticated thermal radiation detection devices and a complete lab on board, with no result. The Sierra-Madre search and rescue team experienced continuing frustration. Unaccustomed to the dense forest of the Northeast, one of them observed that "in California you can look around and find a peak to check your position. Here we've been climbing trees and getting on top of hills and still can't find a peak to go by because the woods are so thick."

In spite of the hardships the search area widened steadily. Teams explored the woods in all directions: north to John Brown's Farm in Lake Placid, west into the adjoining Huntington Wildlife Forest, east to the Hudson River, and south toward Newcomb. Mt. Marcy, Baldwin and other peaks were climbed, some more than once. By day fifteen, eighty square miles had been covered.

When the intensive effort continued to be futile, speculation increased about what had happened to the lost boy. On the twelfth day, as a rumor continued that Doug had been kidnapped, the Sheriff asserted, "We've discounted the possibility of kidnap entirely." The next day, the president of the Newcomb Volunteer Fire Department said, "it is possible he got in with a group of campers who haven't heard any news recently and don't know he's missing." Two days later others speculated that Doug might have joined and be traveling with another party. The next day, after speaking with the family, a searcher revealed that Doug probably had a "definite objective" when he left. Earlier in the day of his departure he had wanted to climb nearby Baldwin Mountain, the searcher said, but his parents had told him it was too late to start. Everyone had his or her theory.

On Monday, the seventeenth day, after most of the weekend volunteers had returned home, the search officially ended. It was announced that "Civilian volunteers who have been searching this area for missing Douglas Legg since July 10 were scheduled to end their efforts as of 6 p.m. today. State Police ordered all volunteers out of the woods."

Although the volunteers left, employees of governmental agencies and armed forces continued searching. The campaign was a joint operation of the State Police, Essex County Sheriff's Department, and New York State Department of Environmental Conservation. By mutual agreement, none of the organizations would withdraw from the search without approval of the others. These lead agencies, together with Green Berets from Fort Devans, Massachusetts, Army Reservists from nearby Fort Drum, other military units and experienced search and rescue teams continued to comb the forest. But throughout the third week of the search their numbers diminished. There were ninety on day seventeen, seventy-five on day nineteen, thirty-five on day twenty-one.

By now well over a hundred square miles had been thoroughly searched. The Sheriff reported, "Every lake in the area has had divers in it twice, and has been dragged." A ranger explained that more than five-hundred miles of string had been strung through the woods. He recalled that about twenty-five hundred volunteers had participated in the search. One of the Newcomb women of the Auxiliary said that she and her friends had made about thirty-five thousand sandwiches.

On Sunday, August 1, when hope of finding Doug was all but extinguished, the expected announcement finally came. "The twenty-three day search for Douglas Legg will end tonight, state police, the Conservation Department, and the Essex County Sheriff's Department jointly announced." A core crew representing the three government agencies would remain one more week at the town hall to receive and check any new leads, maintaining radio communications between participating agencies.

An editorial in a Syracuse newspaper observed, "Nothing is more heartbreaking than to know that a life might have been saved if you were only more skilled in the requirements for such a rescue. . . . Some who participated in the hunt . . . have asked us to support the organization of a skilled, volunteer force always on standby for lost persons."[51]

Still the search went on. The family and many Newcomb neighbors, state employees and assorted volunteers refused to quit. Daily reports from Newcomb continued to appear in the Syracuse newspapers, although no longer as front-page news. One local man who worked nearby at Tahawus returned to his job after volunteering for three weeks. His boss told him, "I think they need you back at Newcomb Lake." As late as the twenty-seventh day, a four-man-four-dog search and rescue team arrived from Seattle.

The next day a nurse from Connecticut advised Newcomb Justice of the Peace Gary Carter that her extra-sensory-perception indicated that Doug had been at Panther Gorge, and that searchers should have "turned left where you took the right turn." The Justice knew that the party had indeed turned right at that point, and that the woman described areas he had known well since childhood so accurately that "it made my hair stand on end." Since her theories "are as good as anything else at this point," she was invited to Newcomb, but failed to find any trace of Doug.

"Doug's birthday; is he alive?" The final newspaper report continued: "Today is Douglas Legg's ninth birthday." May Melvin Legg told the reporter, "We haven't given up hope of finding him and we won't give up hope. . . . It would be wonderful" if he were to be found on his birthday. Both parents believed that "Dougie" had found his way out of the woods and was still alive somewhere. They had talked about climbing nearby Baldwin Mountain, and the family had planned the hike for the day following Doug's disappearance. The Leggs now "felt strongly" that Doug had found the Northville-Placid trail, perhaps following it far out of the area.

[51] Search-and-rescue units within the Department of Environmental Conservation, utilizing local volunteers, were in fact organized as a result of the search for Douglas Legg.

On day thirty-four there was no news from Newcomb. This was to be a story with no end. Douglas Legg was never found.

We may never know what became of Douglas Legg. In the end, the explanation could be simple. Long-time Santanoni caretaker Art Tummins was convinced that Douglas got caught in the quicksand-like muck of the Duck Hole where his body would never surface and be found.[52] Another searcher who reports having worked with the bloodhounds in the early days of the search gave a far more exotic explanation, over a quarter century after the boy's disappearance. He reported that Myron Melvin had confronted a group of "hippies" on the Preserve the day before Doug's disappearance, but they did not leave until the next day. Moreover, the spot where the bloodhounds kept losing the scent was near the Moose Pond road where the hippies were camping. The Melvins, he says, believe that Doug, willingly or not, left Santanoni with this group and is alive today, living in Boston. He says he himself saw a poster in the "Cheers" bar in Boston, in 1996, saying, "Douglas Legg, we still love you. Please come home."[53]

A monument recalls another disaster at nearby Calamity Pond.[54] Similarly, some sort of commemorative plaque might be erected at Santanoni to recall the Newcomb tragedy

[52] Tummins' theory was explained by Sis Pruyn Thibault who recalled, "You didn't want to go in the Duck Hole because it's almost like quicksand way down in the lower end of Upper Duck Hole and you were afraid you'd sink." Aldrich, 26. Susan Pruyn King recalled, "Here at the Main Camp I was given free rein—I could go anywhere by myself except past the bridge into the Duck Hole. As far as I know, nobody could ever go there alone. . . . I don't know if it's quicksand or not, but the muck or silt is so deep you can take a paddle and push it down and you'll never hit bottom." Aldrich, 124.

[53] William MacDonald, a long-time resident of Upper Saranac Lake and Florida, to Howard Kirschenbaum, August 1998. The accuracy of this report cannot be ascertained. It is offered to illustrate how the search for Douglas Legg has entered the annals of Adirondack legend.

[54] Donaldson relates the accidental shooting of David Henderson in *A History of the Adirondacks*, v.1, 143-5.

and the heroic community response. But Santanoni itself is a monument that recalls Douglas Legg, wherever he may be.

The search for Douglas Legg was the most dramatic, most memorable episode in the history of Santanoni Preserve, and the most tragic. But what meaning does the disappearance of an eight-year-old boy have? There may be little significance, in the literal sense, in a senseless tragedy. Why is the lengthy story worth telling, worth remembering?

The search for Douglas Legg was one of the largest community efforts in the history of the Adirondacks.[55] The tragedy brought out the best in family, neighbors, colleagues, and total strangers. It rallied well over a thousand, possibly over two thousand, volunteers. The campaign to find Doug surely was significant—truly heroic. Its lesson is not so much about personal loss, but about community action, for it demonstrates how a crisis creates a community, bonding total strangers in an urgent collective cause. For that alone it is a story worth telling, worth remembering.

The search for Douglas Legg also deepened the historical association of the people of Newcomb with Santanoni Preserve. For generations Newcomb residents had lived and worked at Santanoni. Family histories and Santanoni history were intertwined. The Legg search further merged local history with Santanoni's story. Public response to the family crisis, with so many outsiders passing through the stone entrance arch, marked the end of Santanoni Preserve as a family enclave. The search strengthened the community's identity with the place—a bond that eventually would help save Camp Santanoni from destruction.

## Sale to State

There is another way that the tragedy of Douglas Legg is historically significant—it precipitated the sale of Santanoni Preserve to the State of New York. The Melvin families had no desire to return to Santanoni, nor inclination to prolong the uncertain situation with The Nature Conservancy. They invited the Conservancy's Patrick Noonan, along with Thomas and Susan Pruyn King, to visit Santanoni in the early fall of 1971 to try to reach an understanding.[56] The Melvins volunteered to reduce the price from $1.5-million to one million dollars. Although still far more than the $79,100 paid when acquired, almost twenty years later the property recently had been appraised at $1.75-million. Clearly, the Melvin

[55] Alan Darling. "Santanoni," *Adirondack Life*, September-October, 1981. The Douglas Legg search possibly was equaled subsequently by the massive and sustained search for Sara Anne Wood, victim of serial kidnapper-killer Lewis Lent, who reportedly buried twelve-year-old Sara off the Sagamore Road, near Raquette Lake.

[56] Memorandum from Susan Pruyn King, "To Whom It May Concern," April 16, 1991; the visit was "September or early October . . . when Tom and I brought Pat Noonan and his wife Nancy to stay in the gate House and explore Santanoni." Susan Pruyn King, letter to Howard Kirschenbaum, January 15, 1999.

offer was generous, entailing considerable sacrifice.

The timing was propitious. By late 1971 prospects of public acquisition of Santanoni Preserve had begun to appear less remote. The Temporary Study Commission on the Future of the Adirondacks recently had published its landmark report.[57] Because allocation of State funds to acquire large parcels of land required a deliberative process, the State was disadvantaged when desirable Adirondack land came on the market. Private developers might move more quickly to buy land. The Commission recommended that a not-for-profit organization, which could act more expeditiously than the State, work in concert with the State to purchase private land for addition to the State Forest Preserve.

Out of this recommendation came the Adirondack Conservancy Committee, a committee of the Eastern New York chapter of the national Nature Conservancy. The Adirondack Conservancy Committee eventually became The Adirondack Conservancy, a separate regional chapter of The Nature Conservancy.[58] Santanoni Preserve became its first major project. The fledgling organization was not, however, endowed with ample funds. A million dollars was an enormous sum to be raised.[59]

It was the federal government that soon provided the solution. The Bureau of Outdoor Recreation had a grant program that allowed it to contribute fifty per cent of the cost of acquiring land for public outdoor recreation. Using the $1.75-million appraised value, the U.S. government could contribute $875,000 toward the purchase. The Melvins contributed $750,000 in value as a tax-deductible contribution by lowering the price to one million dollars. On this basis, the Adirondack Conservancy Committee needed to raise an additional $125,000 to complete the transaction.[60]

Susan Pruyn King remembers how she and her husband "worked hand in hand with the Nature Conservancy and the Adirondack Conservancy [Committee] to raise the money to acquire Santanoni and then turn it over to the State of New York. We, carrying our 1892-1903 photographs, went to fund-raisers in New York City, Rensselaerville and Elizabethtown."[61] In spite of everybody's efforts, only fifty-thousand dollars could be raised. If another seventy-five-thousand was not obtained, Santanoni might soon be for sale on the open market. Given Santanoni's ample lake frontages, prospects of real estate development alarmed wilderness advocates.

An anonymous donor contributed the amount, $75,000, required to complete the transaction.[62] Although his wish to remain anonymous was characteristic, it is now appropriate to honor him for his generosity. The donor was the late Harold Hochschild, the well-known businessman, philanthropist and Adirondack historian, who had created and endowed the Adirondack Museum in Blue Mountain Lake. He was also Governor Rockefeller's appointed chairman of the Temporary Study Commission on the Future of the Adirondacks, which had recommended a renewed program of state land acquisition and the creation of the Adirondack Conservancy

[57] Temporary Study Commission on the Future of the Adirondacks, *The Future of the Adirondack Park: Volumes I and II.* (Blue Mt. Lake, N.Y.: The Adirondack Museum, 1972). Volume I contains 181 recommendations on the future of the Adirondack Park. Some of the major recommendations–including the creation of the Adirondack Park State Land Master Plan, the Adirondack Park Land Use and Development Plan, and the Adirondack Park Agency to oversee both plans–were established by law in 1972 and 1973.

[58] The Adirondack Conservancy Committee was comprised of representatives of various Adirondack conservation and environmental groups, state agencies, and the national organization Trout Unlimited. The Adirondack Conservancy's offices are now in Keene Valley, Essex County, N.Y.

[59] A year later, the voters would approve the 1972 State Environmental Quality Bond Act, which would make millions of dollars available for state land acquisition, but in 1971 a million dollars seemed a most ambitious goal.

[60] "State Acquires Santanoni Preserve," *The Post-Star* (Glens Falls, N.Y.), February 19, 1972; Alan Darling. "Santanoni," *Adirondack Life*, September-October, 1981; Letter from W. G. Ives, Jr., Chief, Preserve Protection and Management, DEC to Joan Parkes, February 28, 1986.

[61] King memorandum, April 16, 1991.

[62] Ives letter to Parkes; Rudge and Vandrei state that the donor contributed the entire $125,000 not provided by federal funds.

Committee. Hochschild never received any public credit during his lifetime for the pivotal role he played in the acquisition of Santanoni Preserve.[63]

The federal matching grant required approval of a regional planning body. Local representatives often have been critical of state land acquisition in the Adirondacks, arguing that the State Constitution's requirement to maintain land as "forever wild" prevents development that might provide jobs and community services. Approval was not a foregone conclusion.

Initially, the Lake George-Lake Champlain Regional Planning Board withheld its approval, because board members were uncertain about which state land classification the Santanoni Preserve would be given and how the land would be used. Although physical development would be precluded, the State allows different uses on its Forest Preserve land, depending on how it is classified.

With an end-of-the-year deadline approaching, a meeting of the planning board was held on December 2 in Lake George to hear the state's plans for Santanoni.[64] Representing the New York State Department of Environmental Conservation, Norman Van Valkenburgh explained that it was the state's management plan to classify some parts of the property "wilderness," some parts "primitive," and some portions around the buildings as a "Special Use" area. In this area, said Van Valkenburgh, "The buildings will be preserved due to their architectural and historic interest." The state would continue to pay taxes on the property, as it does on State Forest Preserve lands.

This information satisfied Lilbern Yandon, supervisor of the Town of Newcomb, who spoke in favor of the Santanoni acquisition, since it would become Forest Preserve and the state would pay taxes on it. Later Yandon explained he supported the acquisition "because before it was private land that only a few could use. I recommended it to the Lake George-Lake Champlain Hunting [*sic*] Board that they approve the federal grant. The Essex County Board of Supervisors agreed with me. It will cost the state nothing but future real estate taxes."[65]

Transfer of Santanoni to the State of New York
Patrick F. Noonan of The Nature Conservancy, left,
and DEC Commissioner Henry Diamond

The closing took place on February 18, 1972.[66] Title passed from the Melvins to the

[63] Hochschild's gift "was revealed publicly in June 1992 at ceremonies at the Adirondack Museum attended by the Governor marking the Centennial of the Adirondack Park which [perhaps not] coincidentally was, to the day, the centennial of Hochschild's birth." J. Winthrop Aldrich, manuscript note to authors.

[64] In addition to chairman Noel Brunell and planning board members and staff, others present included Richard Lawrence, Mary Prime and Witman Daniels of the newly created Adirondack Park Agency, and Wayne Byrne and Winifred LaRose of the Adirondack Conservancy Committee. "A-95 Review, DEC Acquisition of Santanoni Preserve. . .Meeting Held at Lake George Institute, Lake George, NY, 10 A.M. December 2, 1971," Lake Champlain-Lake George Regional Planning Board, 3 pp., n.d.

[65] Ray Bender, "State Takes Santanoni Preserve Gift," *Press-Republican* (Plattsburgh, N.Y.), February 19, 1972.

[66] It was held in the county seat of Elizabethtown, in the historic Augustus N. Hand law office--a tiny, mid-nineteenth century, brick building formally owned by the grandfather of Arthur Savage, who as co-chair of the Adirondack Conservancy Committee hosted the event. Also attending the ceremony were Henry Diamond, Commissioner of Environmental Conservation, Patrick Noonan of The Nature Conservancy, Wayne Byrne, co-chair of the Adirondack Conservancy

Nature Conservancy to the State of New York. Representing the Nature Conservancy, Patrick Noonan presented Henry Diamond, Commissioner of Environmental Conservation, with a check for a million dollars, which Diamond in turn would pass to the Melvins to be divided among the four branches of the family.[67] Acknowledging the contribution of the Melvins, the unnamed Hochschild, and other donors, Diamond encouraged further donations to the State Forest Preserve, saying, "I hope this private generosity will be an example and stimulus to other potential donors." The 12,663-acre acquisition was described as "the largest and most significant addition to the forest preserve of the past decade." Newcomb Lake was described as one of the hundred largest in state, important for containing "genetically undisturbed brook and lake trout."[68]

The property conveyed to the state did not include the furnishings at Camp Santanoni. Much of the original Pruyn contents had been dispersed over the years, but many items were still on site. The Melvins took whatever personal effects had meaning to them. The Conservancy Committee and the state had no particular interest in the remaining furnishings. Because the Pruyn family members indicated an interest in a number of personal items that had sentimental value to them, the Conservancy sold to the Kings for $5,000 most of the camp's contents in appreciation for the role they played in the acquisition process.[69] The Kings, in turn, donated four guide-boats and five chairs to the Adirondack Museum, kept many items for their personal use, and sold or disbursed the rest.[70] When the dust settled, Santanoni was empty, save for a lone Great Blue Heron which stood on the mantelpiece in the living room where, as old photographs show, it had stood since the turn of the century.[71]

Committee, Supervisor Yandon of Newcomb, Thomas and Susan Pruyn King, former Sen. Eustis Paine representing Sen. Ronald Stafford, county officials, and representatives of the Adirondack Park Agency and the DEC. The account of the closing is taken from Bender and February 19, 1972 *Post-Star* articles, cited above, and from Alfonso Narvaez, "13,000-Acre Wilderness Tract in Adirondacks Given to State," *The New York Times*, February 19, 1972.

67 Later, when the federal government contributed its $875,000 to the state, this amount would be reimbursed to The Nature Conservancy. Patrick Noonan went on to a distinguished career in conservation, becoming President of The Nature Conservancy, founder of the American Farm Land Trust, and Chairman of the Conservation Fund.

68 Exact acreage given in letter from state official W. G. Ives, Jr. to Joan Parkes, February 28, 1986. Newspaper reports cited the acreage as 12,500, 13,000 and "almost 13,000," figures that have been used ever since. Another often-cited figure is 12,900 acres, which is based on deed descriptions (see Chapter 3).

69 Susan Pruyn King, manuscript note to authors.

70 Susan Pruyn King still retains many of these furnishings and decorative items. Also File Memo from Craig Gilborn, director of Adirondack Museum, September 24, 1990.

71 After the closing, the Adirondack Conservancy Committee went public with its first broad-scale fundraising campaign in May 1972. Their mailing required two eight-cent stamps for postage. Ironically, both were part of a postal series commemorating historic sites, and large letters across the bottom of each stamp read "Historic Preservation."

Abandoned ice house, 1975

The forest reclaims the farm

# 10. State Stewardship

Santanoni will be preserved!

*Governor Mario Cuomo*

After New York State acquired the Santanoni Preserve, public access by motorized vehicle to Newcomb Lake and the area beyond remained closed. Local folk opposed road closure by the State. "People were eager to have the road into the historic Santanoni Lodge stay open, to support tours or restricted traffic. But under the 'forever wild' policy, conflicting uses in wilderness areas are forbidden; roads and buildings are to be closed and removed. The road was closed, and the lodge began to disintegrate."[1]

The area, however, was not classified as "wilderness," the most restrictive of State land use classifications. In fact the lengthy state land classification process was just beginning. Acquisition had come so swiftly that the State's initial intentions and policies toward the newly acquired Santanoni Preserve were not entirely clear—and they have been debated for a quarter of a century. One document, however, clearly describes the Department of Environmental Conservation's original policy regarding Camp Santanoni—to preserve the major buildings and use them for departmental and public purposes.

This management plan, written in the fall of 1971 before the State acquired the property, stated clearly that "All of Santanoni should not be set out as wilderness."[2] Rather 1,550 acres, including a five-hundred-foot buffer zone on both sides of the road to Newcomb Lake and around the three major building complexes, would be designated a "special purpose area." The plan detailed the uses within this area:

[1] Catherine Henshaw Knott, *Living With the Adirondack Forest: Local Perspectives on Land Use Conflicts* (Ithaca, NY: Cornell University Press, 1998), 221. In actuality the road was not open to the public since 1902.

[2] "Management and Use Plan, Santanoni Preserve," Division of Lands and Forests, New York State Department of Environmental Conservation, October 22, 1971. It designated 3,500 acres as wilderness, 7,500 as "primitive," and the remainder as a "special purpose area," described below.

> The main lodge itself is an imposing structure and, if for nothing else, it should be retained for its historical interest as an example of an early Adirondack lodge of the type built by the wealthy summer residents who sought refuge in the wilds of the North Country. However, it will be used as a training and meeting center for employees of the Department of Environmental Conservation. The historical interest will be of importance to those of the general public who will visit and use the property and this historical aspect will be considered as a supplemental purpose. . . . The boathouse and the studio will be retained in their present condition and will be utilized as storage buildings for materials and supplies necessary to the training and meeting center.

The State's management plan also stated that the three residences at Santanoni's farm complex and all the buildings of the Gate Lodge complex (except the Harris Lake boathouse) would be retained. The rest of the buildings throughout the Preserve would be removed. The Gate Lodge, it said, "being immediately adjacent to the bridge, provides an ideal point for the registration of visitor users and the issuance of permits. . . . This building is winterized and will also serve as the headquarters of the caretaker in residence. The present caretaker's house [where the Tummins family was living in summers] will be used by assistant caretakers as needed in the summer season when visitor use is at its peak."

In recognizing the "historical interest" in the buildings at Camp Santanoni, the State was ahead of its time. Few people then thought in terms of "Great Camps," a term that was not common at the time.[3] Large complexes of rustic buildings were widely regarded as "white elephants," demanding high maintenance and inflated taxes. Within ten years all that would change, and surviving Adirondack Great Camps would become appreciated, coveted, and valued properties. That the State immediately recognized the historical value of Camp Santanoni, years before anyone had actually delved into its rich history or architectural significance, demonstrated a forward looking attitude, which in retrospect provides a foundation for more recent decisions about Santanoni's future.

The late Paul Schaefer, widely regarded as a leading advocate for wilderness preservation, was among the first and most influential Adirondackers to embrace preservation of the region's historical buildings, including Camp Santanoni. Others, however, were wary. Not everyone agreed with the State's appreciation or plans for Camp Santanoni. Some environmentalists argued that State retention of the buildings would violate Article XIV, the "forever wild" provision, of the State Constitution. They expressed concern that any initial use would be a precedent and eventually expand to less permissible uses.[4] In response to such concerns, Commissioner Diamond responded that, while the State would manage the Santanoni Preserve in accordance with the October 1971 management plan, the Preserve would also be managed "subject to the provisions of Article XIV" and in accordance with the Conservation Law; if "deemed necessary to protect and preserve the environment and natural resources of the Santanoni Preserve," the various improvements might be removed or public access, hunting or fishing might be limited.[5]

The Commissioner's letter reflected the State's priorities. The State's major interest in acquiring Santanoni Preserve clearly was the addition of some thirteen-thousand acres to the State Forest Preserve. The buildings that came along with the property, as useful and historic as they might be, were of secondary

[3] As discussed in Chapter 2, Arnold Lehman had titled a research report "Great Camps of the Adirondacks" in 1970. The term and concept became more widely known in 1975 when Camp Sagamore was endangered.

[4] Arthur Savage, letter to James Biggane, DEC, February 10, 1972.

[5] Henry Diamond, letter to Arthur Savage, February 15, 1972. Diamond states, "It is the intention and policy of the Department and the Division that future management and use will follow the specific details of the Management and Use Plan dated October 22, 1971, and amended by letter from J. O. Preston, Director, Division of Lands and Forests, to you under date of January 14, 1972. Inquiries by the authors have failed to produce a copy of the January 14 letter.

concern. If, for some reason, there arose an actual conflict between environmental conservation and historic preservation, the buildings would be removed. But in the interim, the State saw neither a legal conflict nor a problem whereby the buildings endangered the natural resources of the Preserve. Accordingly, the Commissioner was able to state clearly that the buildings at Santanoni Preserve could be used for the purposes stated in the management plan, while still respecting the State Constitution and environmental conservation law.

Plan discussion, 1995[6]

People interpreted the Commissioner's letter in light of their own views on Article XIV. For years some would argue that it was understood from the beginning that the buildings at Santanoni would be removed.[7] Others saw just the opposite. Meanwhile, both inside and outside the Conservation Department, employees and advocates quietly or aggressively lobbied for their particular goals for Santanoni. J. Winthrop Aldrich, who shortly thereafter served as assistant to the Commissioner of Environmental Conservation, recalled that "the State selectively demolished soon after acquiring" some buildings, while nothing was done to move ahead with the plan for using Santanoni for training purposes or public visitation.[8] The caretaker's residence, large barn, and other buildings of the lakeside service complex, together with the sheep, poultry and pig houses and other farm buildings were removed. Visitors did, indeed, hike or ski into Santanoni to view the other structures, now available to the public for the first time in their as much as eighty-year history; but there was clearly no consensus within the department or among the interested public regarding the present or future disposition of Camp Santanoni.

### The Broader Issue

To complicate matters, while officials were attempting to clarify their policy about the status of the Santanoni buildings in the Forest Preserve, the State, in short order, came into possession of two-and-a-half more Great Camps.

In 1973 Marjorie Merriweather Post's lavish Camp Topridge was conveyed as a gift to the People of the State of New York. Topridge was the most extensive camp complex in the Adirondacks. On 207 acres overlooking Upper St. Regis Lake and Upper and Lower Spectacle Ponds, this enormous camp suddenly fell into the lap of the State's Office of General Services—apparently too good a deal to refuse but without a publicly-stated plan for its future use and maintenance. Consequently during the seventies the State barely used it at all, except for occasional occupation by the governor and his family—New York State's version of Camp David, as it were.

In 1975 the State acquired the eleven-building caretaking complex at Camp Sagamore in the Raquette Lake area. It almost acquired all twenty-seven buildings of the camp; but at the eleventh hour, just when Syracuse University was about to convey its 1,526-acre Sagamore Preserve to New York State, historic preservationists realized the danger such a conveyance would mean to this outstanding,

[6] From left: unidentified DEC staff; Andy Blanchette, Santanoni Operations staff (DEC); AARCH summer intern Hal Hutchinson; AARCH president Howard Kirschenbaum.

[7] E.g., George Davis, Adirondack Council, letter to Francis Murray, Jr., Asst. Secretary to the Governor, November 21, 1985; Mike DeNunzio, Adirondack Council, speaking to Citizens Advisory Committee on the Santanoni Preserve, January 24, 1996 and other occasions.

[8] J. Winthrop Aldrich, Memorandum to File, May 7, 1996. The 1971 appraisals documented demolished buildings with color photographs.

rustic complex of buildings. If it were to become part of the State Forest Preserve, Sagamore might be destroyed. In the nick of time, the Preservation League of New York State brokered an arrangement that saved the main buildings at Sagamore. The solution was to have the University convey the main buildings of Sagamore on 7.7 acres to the Preservation League, who would then convey it to a third party subject to strict historic preservation covenants. The remaining 1,517 acres, including all of Sagamore Lake, would be conveyed to the State for the Forest Preserve. The last-minute reprieve spared the major landmark buildings, but the State determined to acquire the eleven buildings of Sagamore's caretaking complex—in effect, condemning them.[9]

Finally, in 1979, the State acquired Nehasane Park as part of a complicated deal brokered by the Adirondack Nature Conservancy.[10] Nehasane was part of the remaining 25,000-acre estate of the William Seward Webb family in the west-central Adirondacks. In acquiring most of that acreage, the State also assumed ownership of Forest Lodge and the dozen or so buildings of the camp complex on the shore of Lake Lila. As the Webb family retained several thousand acres of the estate, with other camps on them, it was understood by the family and the State that Camp Nehasane would be razed and the area around Lake Lila reserved for camping and open space recreation.[11]

By the end of the decade, the State of New York had become the proud and confused owner of Camps Santanoni, Topridge, Nehasane, and part of Sagamore—among the most important architectural complexes in the Adirondacks. It would have been hard enough for the Department of Environmental Conservation to decide whether to follow their initial management plan for Camp Santanoni. Now the use of any one camp would set a precedent that might apply to the several other camps under State ownership. The problem had, indeed, become monumental.

It was also no longer a problem recognized only by State officials and interested Adirondack organizations. With all the publicity surrounding the last-minute salvation of Sagamore—including a front-page article in the *New York Times*—the "Great Camps of the Adirondacks" had come to the public's attention.[12] The weekend that the Preservation League passed title to Sagamore's new owner, the League held a conference there which included a tour of Sagamore and two other outstanding Adirondack rustic properties nearby, Camp Uncas and Kamp Kill Kare. The League's statewide network was soon made aware of the importance and uniqueness of Adirondack rustic architecture, an interest that soon spread to the larger community.

In 1977, the new owner of Sagamore, now called Sagamore Institute, began offering annual tours of the Adirondack Great Camps, including Camps Pine Knot, Uncas and Sagamore, led by architectural historian Paul Malo, president of the Preservation League of New York State. The Preservation League undertook a wider survey of thirty-five Adirondack Great Camps.[13] Craig Gilborn, Director of the Adirondack Museum, wrote *Durant: The Fortunes of a Family and their Woodland Camps*, published in 1979, which was the most extensive study to date of William West Durant and the luxurious camps he pioneered in the Adirondacks. Sagamore's co-director Howard Kirschenbaum began leading several weekend

---

[9] Howard Kirschenbaum, *The Story of Sagamore* (Raquette Lake, N.Y.: Sagamore Institute, 1990).

[10] Edith Pilcher, "Nehasane," *Adirondack Life*, 10:5 (Sept./Oct., 1979), 14-17, 42-48.

[11] Paul Malo recalls that Norman Van Valkenburgh, land acquisition officer for the New York State Department of Environmental Conservation, explained that the Webbs did not want their family home used for other purposes. Preferring to have it removed, they made this a condition of transfer to the State.

[12] Harold Faber, "State Buys Vanderbilts' Adirondack Camp," *New York Times*, October 7, 1975.

[13] Mary Ellen Gadski, "Research Report on the Great Camps of the Adirondacks." Unpublished manuscript. (Albany: Preservation League of New York State, 1978).

and weeklong tours each year of Great Camps all around the Adirondacks.

AARCH president Howard Kirschenbaum talks to a tour group at the Gate Lodge

In 1982, Harvey Kaiser's *Great Camps of the Adirondacks*, a pictorial survey of these great rustic estates, brought the camps to an even wider, popular audience.[14] Soon magazine reporters were flocking to the Adirondacks each summer to write features and travelogues on these intriguing properties hidden away in the Adirondack forest. In the mid-1980s, a revival in rustic furniture and design caught on nationwide and brought even greater attention to and emulation of the "Adirondack style" in architecture and the decorative arts.

Public understanding of the Great Camps was increasing throughout the 1970s and early 1980s, but Camps Santanoni and Nehasane and the caretaking buildings at Sagamore deteriorated year after year in the harsh Adirondack climate. Meanwhile the State tried to figure out what to do with all these historic buildings in the Forest Preserve. Ironically, appreciation of these camps grew with each year of their neglect. At Santanoni, sympathetic State employees, troubled to see the empty buildings declining from lack of maintenance, took it upon themselves to sweep and shovel roofs and provide some minimal maintenance to extend the life of the buildings until a real solution could be found.

Meanwhile, meetings were held and letters written exploring different solutions, but there was no consensus to be found among State officials, historic preservation advocates, and environmental organizations concerned with maintaining the integrity of the Forest Preserve. In 1978, Lieutenant Governor Mary Anne Krupsak convened a conference at Camp Topridge specifically to pursue a solution to the dilemma of "cultural heritage in the wilds."[15]

One outcome of the conference was that Peter Berle, Department of Environmental Conservation Commissioner and strong Forest Preserve advocate, publicly committed DEC to retaining all surviving structures at Santanoni until they were listed or determined ineligible for listing on the National Register. "This was significant for Peter Berle had the credibility with the Forest Preserve constituency to make it stick, and his action energized State Parks [i.e., State Office of Parks, Recreation and Historic Preservation] to advance the National Register work."[16] In 1987, in recognition of their historical and architectural significance, ten of the Adirondack Great Camps, including Santanoni, were listed on the National Register of Historic Places.[17]

Another outcome of the conference was the formation of a number of committees to

[14] See Alan Freeman, "Call of the Wild," *Historic Preservation*, (Nov./Dec. 1994), 34-35, for a similar recounting of the "growing understanding of the importance of the approximately forty so-called great camps."

[15] Rosemary Nichols, editor, "Cultural Heritage in the Wilds: Conference Report," Conference at Camp Topridge, N.Y., May 25 and 26, 1978. Office of Lieutenant Governor, Office of Parks and Recreation, and Department of Environmental Conservation. Report undated.

[16] J. Winthrop Aldrich, manuscript note to authors.

[17] "Great Camps of the Adirondacks Thematic Resources." Unpublished National Register of Historic Places Inventory—Nomination Forms (Camps Pine Knot, Echo, Wild Air, Santanoni, Uncas, Sagamore, Moss Ledge, Eagle Island, Prospect Point, and Topridge). Albany: New York State Office of Parks, Recreation and Historic Preservation, 1986.

pursue different aspects of a solution. In these committees, and in other discussions of the problem of State-owned cultural resources in the Forest Preserve, a number of possible solutions typically surfaced. The most obvious and the simplest was for the state to use these historic structures for "administrative purposes"—a long-standing, legally-tested, permissible use within the Forest Preserve. After all, the State used and maintained buildings in the Forest Preserve all the time—for example: offices, residences, and public facilities at State camp grounds; garages and workshops for preserve maintenance; lean-tos and privies for campers; or even Camp Colby, with its stone mansion formerly owned by theatrical agent William Morris, for a Department of Environmental Conservation Environmental Education Camp near Saranac Lake. Although it did not state it explicitly, the State surely would have justified its 1971 management plan for Santanoni, which described its use as a DEC training facility and historic site, as consistent with accepted administrative uses.

A second solution to the problem of historic preservation in the State Forest Preserve was to amend the State Constitution to allow historic preservation. Since there were four historic properties already in limbo, and the State might acquire more in the future, a "land bank amendment" was typically proposed as the best long-term solution. In this approach, a limited amount of acreage would be designated on which the State could maintain and use historic buildings in the Forest Preserve. Four-hundred acres was a figure frequently mentioned for the bank. For example, fifty acres around and under the three building complexes at Santanoni, one hundred acres around the Topridge buildings, and ten acres around the Sagamore caretaking complex could be designated as historical areas. One hundred and sixty acres would be withdrawn from "the bank" for these three sites, leaving two-hundred and forty acres for future use. Such an approach would be comparable to the land-bank amendment that had been passed in 1957 to allow the State to take up to four-hundred acres from the Forest Preserve for State highway improvements.

For every land bank-proponent, there was another advocate who favored "site-specific" constitutional amendments to Article XIV to save particular properties. They cited over a dozen previous amendments to Article XIV as successful case studies of amending the Constitution for narrow but worthy purposes, such as using Forest Preserve land to widen a state ski slope or to lengthen a town airport runway for safety reasons.

Others felt strongly that any tampering with Article XIV of the State Constitution should be avoided at all costs. They pointed to the same dozen or more amendments as evidence that the situation already was getting out of hand. If people felt that Article XIV could be amended every time a town wanted to expand its recreation field into adjoining Forest Preserve lands or every time the State wanted to do some worthwhile project, Article XIV would soon become meaningless. If you could have a land bank for highway expansion and now historic preservation, soon people would be proposing land banks for forestry uses, recreational complexes, tourist facilities, and who knows what else. To this argument others answered, no, Article XIV had been amended relatively few times in over eighty years, and the voters had always exercised wisdom and discretion, voting down many incompatible amendments over the years, while allowing worthwhile projects to proceed.

Agreement seemed almost hopeless. While environmental groups, historic preservation interests, and local officials faced off on preferred solutions, and often argued within their own ranks, State agencies had their own mixed feelings and turf issues. For complex historical reasons, the State office most involved with historic preservation elsewhere—the Office of Parks, Recreation and Historic Preservation—has not been the lead agency for historic preservation in the Adirondack Park.[18] Rather, the Department of Environmental Conservation was responsible for Camp Santanoni and other historic properties in the Forest Preserve, and that department had little experience or interest in historic preservation. Especially when complexes like Santanoni, Nehasane, and Sagamore were located miles within the Forest Preserve, such historic buildings represented major administrative headaches for an agency involved with land and wildlife conservation.

After two years of committee meetings it was clear that the process was going nowhere. By 1980, however, Sagamore Institute, while sensitive to the larger issues involved, was growing desperate about the deteriorating caretaking buildings located literally a few feet from the main camp at Sagamore. They decided to pursue an independent solution for the Sagamore service complex and proposed a site-specific amendment to the State Constitution that would at least solve the Sagamore problem. The amendment provided for Sagamore Institute to buy approximately two-hundred private acres elsewhere in the Adirondack Park and trade that land to the State for incorporation into the Forest Preserve. In return, the State would transfer about ten acres and the caretaking buildings to Sagamore Institute. The Preservation League of New York State, the Department of Environmental Conservation, and the Adirondack Council (the leading environmental advocacy organization in the Park) all agreed to support this amendment. After two more years of lobbying by Sagamore and especially by the Preservation League of New York State, which played a major leadership role throughout the process, the amendment passed the State legislature in 1982 and again in 1983. Finally, it came before the voters on the November 1983 ballot. Public favor was resounding. The voters approved the land exchange amendment with "the largest majority of any referendum in New York State to date."[19] One of the four Great Camp dilemmas had been solved.

Perhaps the problem of the other camps had been solved as well—during this period other legislation was enacted. In 1982, as the momentum for the Sagamore land exchange amendment grew, some groups were supportive of the Sagamore solution, but were wary that this one constitutional amendment might lead to many similar, future amendments, as the State continued to purchase large parcels of property with historic buildings on them. These groups supported the Sagamore land exchange on condition that all parties seek a more comprehensive solution to the problem of historic buildings in the Forest Preserve.

To meet this objection, the Preservation League convened a committee, chaired by Dorothy Miner, League board member and historic preservation lawyer, to work on a broader solution. This resulted in the so-called "Hinchey Bill," named after the Assembly's Conservation Committee Chairman, Maurice Hinchey. This bill passed the legislature as Chapter 351 of the laws of 1983 and later became Environmental Conservation Law 9–0109. The bill had two major provisions. The first was to establish a mechanism that prevented, or at least strongly discouraged, the State from purchasing any more historic properties for the Forest Preserve. Clearly the best solution to this problem was not to create it in the first place.[20] Second, the bill provided that certain historic properties that the State already owned in the Forest Preserve (the drafters had

[18] Normally the Office of Parks, Recreation and Historic Preservation has no jurisdiction inside the Adirondack Park. Two exceptions are John Brown's Farm and Crown Point Battleground. These State Historic Sites are maintained and operated by OPRHP, although nominally under purview of DEC.

[19] Kirschenbaum, *The Story of Sagamore*, 55-58; "The Plan for the Preservation League of New York State, 2000-2004." Albany, N.Y.: Preservation League of New York State, 1999, 5.

[20] This section of the law subsequently has been implemented inconsistently. It was used effectively to save the historic lighthouse on Valcour Island when the State acquired much of the island for the Forest Preserve. Other times the DEC has acquired older, possibly historic buildings for the Forest Preserve without following the law's procedures for evaluating the historic significance of these properties and finding alternative solutions if possible.

Santanoni foremost in mind) could be maintained and used "for public enjoyment and understanding of the forest preserve or for departmental activities necessary in protecting forest preserve lands in the [Adirondack and Catskill] parks. . . ." The law also required that "such maintenance be in accordance with reasonable regulation of the forest preserve in the Adirondack and Catskill parks consistent with Article XIV of the State Constitution." As Governor Mario Cuomo described the bill when he signed it into law:

> The bill will permit the State to maintain historic structures or improvements located within the Adirondack and Catskill Parks and acquired by the State prior to the bill's effective date. This maintenance is only authorized where the structures or improvements are listed or eligible to be listed on the State Register of Historic Places and where the proposed maintenance will not disturb the existing wild forest character of the surrounding land. These limitations will minimize the impact of the maintenance authorized by this bill on the forest preserve while still protecting the indisputably valuable historic resources now in the State's possession in these areas. While the validity of these maintenance provisions may be questioned under Article XIV of the State Constitution, the provisions are not clearly unconstitutional.[21]

By including the last provision about Article XIV, the drafters demonstrated, as did the Governor in his comments, that they were sensitive to the constitutional problem. However, a more critical analysis of the legislation might characterize the bill as saying, "It's now legal to preserve Camp Santanoni, as long as it doesn't violate the Constitution to do so." And the Governor could be interpreted to have said, "It's possible this law is unconstitutional, but that's not clear, so we're going to approve it." This is precisely how a number of environmental advocates saw the legislation—as an illegal end-run around the State Constitution. They argued that the legislature could not override the Constitution by making the maintenance and use of Santanoni legal, if it was not legal to begin with.[22]

Other knowledgeable attorneys and environmentalists, such as Assemblyman Hinchey's advisor and frequent drafter of environmental legislation Paul Bray, maintained that the reference to the Constitution simply referred to the long tradition of cases and Attorney Generals' rulings which established that certain uses in the Forest Preserve were permissible. He argued that the second part of this legislation did not authorize new, previously unauthorized uses of the Forest Preserve, but merely reiterated and clarified previous rulings about what was permissible. The new legislation, then, was essentially an "administrative solution," said Bray. Thus Santanoni could be maintained and used within the parameters of previous administrative precedents.[23]

There was strong disagreement on this matter, and those who hoped that the Hinchey legislation would provide the solution for Santanoni and other historic properties in the Forest Preserve were disappointed to see no further action. Beyond the *enabling* legislation, political will was required to galvanize action. The political consensus around Santanoni was not yet present.

Meanwhile, the fate of Camp Topridge and Camp Nehasane was resolved. As with Saga-

[21] Mario Cuomo, Memoranda, Chapter 351, "Adirondack and Catskill Parks—Protection of Historic Resources," June 21, 1983.

[22] E.g., Letter from David Gibson, Association for Protection of the Adirondacks to Robert Bendick, DEC, October 23, 1991; Harold Jerry, Public Service Commission to Howard Kirschenbaum, September 25, 1991. Both letters state they would support constitutional amendments to preserve Camp Santanoni.

[23] Letter from Paul Bray to Howard Kirschenbaum, May 6, 1982, with accompanying memorandum, citing particularly Association for the Protection of the Adirondacks v MacDonald, 253 N.Y. 234 (1930). In practical terms, interpretations of constitutionality rest with the Attorney General, until the Court or Legislature determine otherwise. The Attorney General *could* interpret the Constitution to allow retention of historic buildings. It is his call. Other opinions and interpretations are relatively inconsequential, except as *political* issues. Except for blatant violations, every questionable practice is "legal" until it is contested, and confirmed or condemned by the Attorney General, the Court, or the Legislature.

more, few people wished to see Topridge destroyed. Since its acquisition by the State, it had been used first as an executive retreat and more recently as a State training and conference center and for public tours. But Governor Cuomo believed it was too great a drain on the State's budget and determined to divest the State of its interest in the luxury camp. In 1985, while maintaining ownership of the undeveloped portion of the property for the Forest Preserve, the State auctioned off 102 acres and the buildings at Topridge to the highest bidder.[24] Although the Adirondack Council and other environmental groups believed this to be an unconstitutional sale of State Forest Preserve land, they decided not to sue the State, as the actual outcome was probably the best solution that could be achieved.

The problem of Camp Nehasane was then resolved in short order. The State burned down the buildings—the usual fate for structures acquired in the Forest Preserve.

Vestige of a Great Camp, Nehasane; even the chimneys have since been removed

The Richard Hudnut property, Fox Lair, likewise had been torched.[25] Historic preservation groups raised no serious objection to Nehasane's removal; not only was Nehasane regarded as less outstanding architecturally or historically than Sagamore, Topridge and Santanoni, but the Webb family had made demolition of the main lodge at Nehasane a condition of sale.[26] The site of Webb's Forest Lodge and other buildings along the shore of Lake Lila were bulldozed and filled, covering the last remnants of one of the earliest Adirondack Great Camps built on a vast wildlife and timber preserve.

And then there was Santanoni, still sitting empty in the forest, still deteriorating year after year from the harsh Adirondack elements.

Art Tummins retired as caretaker in 1976, and little or no maintenance was done on the buildings.[27] For a brief period, from 1978–79, the State had used the Gate Lodge for "administrative purposes." It provided housing for a short-lived, federally funded program called the Youth Conservation Corps and housed ski troops from the US Army's 10th Mountain Division for security against terrorists during the 1980 Winter Olympics in Lake Placid. For a summer or two, a State employee lived at the main camp, providing a deeper presence for safety and supervision in the Forest Preserve. The Department of Environmental Conservation also experimented with renting rowboats to the public on Newcomb Lake. But throughout the 1980s Santanoni remained mostly vacant, experiencing the DEC's unofficial policy of benign neglect, as solutions for the State-owned camps were debated in Albany, in the Adirondacks, and at meetings and conferences around the State.

The public, however, continued to visit the Santanoni Preserve in gradually increasing numbers. Hikers, skiers, the occasional horseback riders, and a growing number of bicyclists came down the 4.7-mile road from the Gate Lodge parking area to the main camp.

[24] Howard Kirschenbaum, "Camp Topridge for Sale?", *Adirondack Life*, March-April, 1985, 17-19.

[25] Elisabeth Hudnut Clarkson, *An Adirondack Archive: The Trail to Windover* (Utica, N.Y,: North Country Books, 1993).

[26] Van Valkenburgh to Malo, footnote 11.

[27] Art and Helen Tummins had purchased a home in Newcomb two years earlier. Art died in February, 1985. Dave Garrison. "Former resident recalls life in area preserve." Glens Falls *Post-Star*, December 1, 1987.

At Newcomb Lake they enjoyed the forest, lake, and mountain views of the Preserve and marveled at the intriguing, abandoned buildings from a by-gone era.

Two local residents, Tom Dillon and Ken Helms, operated horse-drawn wagons that transported visitors into the Santanoni Preserve. Their volume of customers grew steadily through the eighties as their earlier business in hauling hunters and fishing parties and their gear to campsites in the preserve was augmented by the growing number of day visitors who wanted to view the Great Camp on Newcomb Lake.

In addition to individuals making the trek to Camp Santanoni, more and more organized outings visited the preserve. Sagamore Institute led trips to Santanoni at least once every spring, summer and winter through most of the eighties. The Adirondack Mountain Club also made Santanoni a regular destination for its hiking and cross-country ski trips. The approximate ten-mile round trip ski to Santanoni's main camp became known as one of the most enjoyable and lovely cross-country ski outings in the Adirondacks.

Winter vistors

When the new Adirondack Park Visitor Interpretive Center was located in the Town of Newcomb, it too made Santanoni a regular destination for guided nature and history tours. In fact, for a brief period the Gate Lodge at Camp Santanoni was considered a possible location for the new Visitor Center, to be operated by the Adirondack Park Agency. It was felt that the vast Adirondack Park lacked a coordinated system of interpretation and that an official interpretive center would begin to address this need. A number of locations around the Adirondacks were proposed for this purpose, including Newcomb due to its central location and need for the economic stimulation which a visitor center might foster.[28] Seeing an opportunity for linking the proposed visitor center with Santanoni, Howard Kirschenbaum widely circulated a proposal: the Sagamore Institute and the Adirondack Mountain Club would work together with the State to operate Santanoni's main camp for public recreation and education. The Gate Lodge complex would house the State's interpretive center.[29] The proposal was based on the legal justification of the Hinchey legislation of 1983. After an initial indication of interest, the Adirondack Mountain Club determined not to participate in the plan because of the constitutional problem, among other reasons.[30] The Adirondack Council and Adirondack Park Agency also opposed the idea.[31]

The Governor finally decided to locate the main visitor center at Paul Smiths in Franklin County and to locate a "satellite visitors center" at Newcomb, employing the Santanoni Gate Lodge.[32] The Department of Environmental Conservation lacked enthusiasm for this idea—and for Camp Santanoni in general. Evidence of DEC attitude was an official statement to a representative of the Adirondack Mountain Club in March, 1986: "It is

---

[28] Shawn Tooley, "Remote Newcomb Site Wins Center Sweepstakes," *Adirondack Daily Enterprise*, August 26, 1985.

[29] "A Proposal for Saving and Using Santanoni," Sagamore Institute, undated (August 1985); Howard Kirschenbaum, "To Save Santanoni," *Adirondack Life*, Jan./Feb. 1986, 53-54.

[30] "Camp Santanoni," resolution amended and approved by the ADK executive committee, December 14, 1985.

[31] George Davis, Program Director, Adirondack Council, letter to Henry G. Williams, Commissioner, DEC, September 19, 1985; Robert Glennon, letter to Woody Cole, Chairman, APA, "Re: Santanoni—Kirschenbaum Memo," August 1, 1984 [sic, actually 1985].

[32] "Santanoni Gatehouse Use May Become Test Case," *Adirondac*, Feb./March 1986, 4.

the general feeling within the Department, for a variety of reasons, that the buildings associated with the Santanoni complex should be removed from State lands. The one possible exception is the Gate Lodge at the edge of the property. This is being considered, in cooperation with the Adirondack Park Agency, for possible use as a satellite visitor information center. If a decision is made to maintain this latter structure, appropriate steps will be taken to ensure that it is in compliance with the Constitution, any applicable laws and the Adirondack Park State Land Master Plan."[33]

With such resistance within his own State agencies, and with continuing opposition from the Adirondack Council, Governor Cuomo eventually chose another Newcomb location for the visitor center. A large new facility was constructed on Rich Lake in the Huntington Memorial Forest, on lands leased from the State University College of Environmental Science and Forestry in Syracuse. As the Huntington Forest adjoins the Santanoni Preserve on its western side, the Santanoni farm and main camp became favorite destinations for field trips from the new Visitor Center.

When the latest flurry of activity around Santanoni died down, things returned to business as usual in the Santanoni Preserve. The buildings continued to deteriorate year after year, slowed down only temporarily by the occasional State forest ranger or operations staff who would sweep the pine needles out of the roof valleys, board up a broken window, or discourage vandalism by their presence. In small groups and large, visitors would make their way to Santanoni to hike, ski, hunt or fish, often unaware of the old buildings located throughout the preserve. And so they would cross the iron bridge to marvel at the grand entrance arch, pause at the farm complex and admire the graceful lines of the barn and stone creamery, and above all stand astonished by the log villa overlooking Newcomb Lake. There visitors regularly commented on the haunting, mysterious, almost mystical quality they experienced at the abandoned main camp. A participant on one of Sagamore's organized trips to Santanoni in the late eighties, described what it was like to discover the lakeside camp for the first time:

> Just when I'm beginning to believe that this is a walk to forever, the road begins to go downhill. After a short half-mile we glimpse a lake through the trees, then old buildings half hidden in second growth woods. We have arrived. At first it is almost an anti-climax; these massive, dark, boarded up buildings are it? Was this what I walked so far to see or was the walk the thing? Selfishly I let others unpack . . . right now I must explore.
>
> It doesn't take me long to discover that this place is so right! It justifies its own existence by just being here. Immense roofed porches that wind around and connect separate buildings call me to follow them. . . These building built with massive logs stand in faded glory overlooking Newcomb Lake and the mountains that encircle with wilderness this abandoned habitation. . .
>
> The windows allow me to peer in—to spy on empty rooms with bare floors; stairways that go up only to end in deep shadow; huge granite fireplaces, soot-stained and cold-hearthed for too many years. A stuffed Great Blue Heron, plumage dark with dust and age, stands sentinel on a massive hand-hewn mantle. It watches—for what? If people came back to live here, to care for these crumbling buildings—would its job be done? Has the spirit of the wild heron—elusive, regal—been holding back final ruin until Santanoni is safe again?
>
> Sitting on the porch steps, looking out over the lake through the wild growth of brush and trees that are reclaiming the view, I thought I heard rockers creaking on the porch behind me, the sound of children's bare feet running across the warm boards, the rustle of long skirts brushing the floor. . . . Suddenly it's time to leave. Too soon—not enough time to explore, to dream, to seek answers to half-formed questions.[34]

[33] Norman Van Valkenburgh, Director, Division of Lands and Forests, DEC, letter to David Newhouse, Co-Chairman, Forest Preserve Advisory Committee, March 24, 1986.

[34] Margaret Ackenback-Villanova, typescript, late 1980s, undated.

And so it went. Now approaching two decades of abandonment and neglect, Santanoni's fate remained unresolved. While most of the buildings remained remarkably sound, a testimony to their outstanding construction, serious problems could not be forestalled indefinitely. Many leaks had begun to appear in the main camp's vast roof structure. The boathouse showed gaping holes in its roof, and rafters were starting to give way. Moss was growing on the cedar shingles of the Artist's Studio. Some of the outbuildings of the main camp were collapsing. Daylight showed through many cracks in the barn roof. The rear roof of the Old Farm House had caved in, and the building was open to the weather with serious damage resulting. One of the masonry arches of the Creamery was cracking and separating. The porch and porch roof of the West Cottage by the Gate Lodge was falling in.

Historic preservationists and others who appreciated Santanoni had been saying it for years; now the truth was unmistakable. If something weren't done soon, it would be too late to save Camp Santanoni.

## New Hope: Adirondack Architectural Heritage

In 1990, Howard Kirschenbaum, who had recently retired as executive director of Sagamore Institute, invited a number of leaders in Adirondack and New York State historic preservation to discuss the possibility of forming an Adirondack historic preservation organization. One of the goals of this organization would be to find a solution for preserving Camp Santanoni.

The meeting took place in Alexandria Bay, on May 4, at the annual conference of the Preservation League of New York State.[35] Kirschenbaum shared his perception that, although numerous individuals around the Adirondacks and New York State loved Camp Santanoni and cared deeply about its future, there was no organized constituency to fight in a concerted, ongoing way for Santanoni's preservation. He reminded the group that there had been previous interest in forming a regional historic preservation association.[36] He invited the group to consider forming such an organization now, with its first major project being to advocate for the preservation of Camp Santanoni.

The response was enthusiastic. Adirondack Architectural Heritage ("AARCH" for short) was formed on June 26, as a non-profit, tax-exempt organization, with the following purposes:

> To enhance public understanding and appreciation of the architectural and historical resources of the Adirondack Park.
>
> To facilitate mutual support among organizations and individuals working to protect the architectural and historical resources of the Adirondack Park.
>
> To seek solutions for endangered historical and architectural resources of the Adirondack Park.

AARCH's first officers were Kirschenbaum as President, Mary Hotaling as Secretary, and Craig Gilborn, Director of the Adirondack Museum, as Treasurer. Members of the board's Santanoni Committee were Kirschenbaum, Paul Malo, Newcomb Town Supervisor George Canon, and architect Carl Stearns. AARCH's board represented the leading historic preservation groups and other influential constituencies in the Adirondack Park, giving the new organization immediate legitimacy in addressing park-

[35] In attendance were: Clare Adams and David Gillespie, NYS Office of Parks, Recreation and Historic Preservation; Steven Engelhart, Friends of Keeseville; Anthony N.B. Garvan, Preservation League of NYS; James Hotaling, Adirondack Park Agency; Mary Hotaling, Lake Placid-North Elba Historic Preservation Commission; Bill Johnston, Essex County Planning Office; Paul Malo, architectural historian, past president Preservation League; Sue Rathbun, Pride of Ticonderoga, Anthony Wood, J. M. Kaplan Fund.

[36] Arnold Markowitz had convened a meeting for this purpose at the Preservation League's annual conference at The Sagamore, Bolton Landing, April 25, 1987.

wide issues, among them the future of Camp Santanoni.[37]

AARCH had an invaluable partner in Newcomb Town Supervisor George Canon. Long-time Newcomb resident, 30-year employee of the recently-closed National Lead Company mining operation at Tahawus, recent President of the Newcomb Historical Society, Canon believed that Newcomb's history and future were tied to that of Camp Santanoni. Members of many of the town's families had worked on the preserve over the years, some for several generations. Santanoni was a part of their family history, their cultural heritage. Canon also saw Santanoni as an asset for local economic development. The town's population had decreased from 1,200 to 541.[38] Tourism was now one of the few areas for potential economic growth in Newcomb.

Canon became an important figure on AARCH's board of directors, not only for the leading role he played on the Santanoni issue but also in helping legitimize historic preservation as a positive agenda among local officials and citizens around the Park.

In planning its campaign to "save Santanoni," AARCH made three strategic decisions. First was to take a different tack than had been employed in previous attempts to develop a consensus around Santanoni. These attempts had foundered over the enormous diversity of viewpoints that State agencies, environmentalists, historic preservationists, and local constituencies brought to the table. Not only did these groups often differ with one another; they frequently were divided among themselves. Some environmentalists, for example, supported Santanoni's preservation and some did not. Of those who were supportive, some felt the Hinchey legislation was the logical justification and opposed a constitutional amendment, while others insisted that a constitutional amendment was the only possible solution. For eighteen years since the State's acquisition of Santanoni, the major players in Adirondack policy formation had been unable to agree on a solution. Rather than have everyone sit around the table again only to repeat an exercise in futility, AARCH determined instead to work initially with Santanoni's supporters only. The plan was to develop a coalition of organizations and individuals who were united in their support for preserving Santanoni. By developing a strong foundation of support, by the time potential opponents and skeptics entered the

AARCH Executive Director Steven Engelhart with tour group at the main lodge

[37] Other founding board members were Steve Engelhart, Anthony N.B. Garvan, Robert Hammerslag, Barbara Parnass, Sue Rathbun, Barry Silverstein and Michael Wilson. The new organization spent its first few months getting organized internally and developing future plans, then went public in early 1991 with a successful membership drive funded by the J.M. Kaplan Fund.

[38] Dick Sage, Chairman of the Newcomb Planning Board, quoted by Knott, 220. He mentioned that the last census showed the population declined 20.1 % during the decade 1980-1990.

discussion, there would be enough momentum for preservation already underway that the movement could not be derailed.

AARCH's second strategic decision was to lay out a positive vision for how Santanoni would be used. In past discussions on the subject, there were always three related problems to solve: the legal problem of how to justify any preservation or use of the Santanoni buildings, then the practical problem of what to do with them, and finally the financial problem of who would pay for it all. Prior discussions revealed that some individuals and groups who did not have a particular problem with the legal aspects of the situation still could not get motivated on behalf of Santanoni, because they had no idea who would take responsibility for funding the restoration and operating the property. The State certainly was not interested in doing so. Private entrepreneurs were out of the question. So why go through the time and effort of a constitutional amendment, for example, if in the end, there was no feasible plan for maintaining and using Santanoni?

AARCH and the Town of Newcomb addressed this problem by going on record with a plan for Santanoni's use and a willingness to take responsibility for implementing the plan, if necessary. In a document they quietly circulated among potential supporters, they wrote:

> It may be years before the best utilization and management plan for Camp Santanoni is evolved. The following goals are proposed initially for utilizing the buildings at Camp Santanoni. Any additional uses would be consistent with the values implied below.
>
> 1. Stabilize the buildings to prevent further deterioration.
>
> 2. Gradually restore these buildings, in a manner consistent with the Secretary of Interior's Standards for Rehabilitating Historic Buildings.
>
> 3. Serve as a destination for educational and recreational outings by the general public and the nearby Adirondack Visitor Center at Rich Lake.
>
> 4. Conduct educational tours of the camp.
>
> 5. Serve lunch, in season, to the hiking, skiing, hunting, fishing and horseback-riding public—thus enhancing Santanoni as an excellent location for day-long outings in the Forest Preserve.
>
> 6. Offer simple, hostel-like accommodations to the public, in season, for approximately 20 people maximum (e.g., bring your own sleeping bag).
>
> 7. Offer educational programs and/or displays to enhance public appreciation and understanding of the surrounding Forest Preserve.
>
> 8. Operate Santanoni in a manner that harmonizes with the surrounding Forest Preserve (e.g., continue non-motorized access).
>
> 9. Operate Santanoni in a manner that models the most enlightened, ecologically-sensitive practices.[39]

Having outlined a vision for Santanoni's operation, the document also addressed the question of who might carry out such an operation. It acknowledged that other non-profit organizations and State agencies were capable of doing so, but stated, "If necessary, the town of Newcomb and Adirondack Architectural Heritage have agreed to assume joint responsibility for operating Camp Santanoni in the manner outlined above, or to find another appropriate non-profit organization to do so."

As a final strategic decision, AARCH's board of directors concluded that a constitutional amendment was the best, long-term solution for Santanoni—preferably a land bank amendment, which would also provide a solution for other State-owned historic properties in the Forest Preserve.

Having formulated a strategy, by fall of 1990 AARCH and the Town of Newcomb were ready to launch their campaign. It began with the AARCH board passing a formal resolution, which became the model for other organizations.

> WHEREAS, Camp Santanoni, in the Town of Newcomb, Essex County, is an important historical, cultural and architectural resource for all the people of New York State; and

---

[39] "Using Camp Santanoni," Adirondack Architectural Heritage proposal, 2 pp., n.d.

WHEREAS, Camp Santanoni has played an important role in the family histories of many residents of the Town of Newcomb and Essex County; and

WHEREAS, Camp Santanoni has great recreational value for hikers, skiers, hunters, fishermen, horseback riders, photographers and other recreationists; and

WHEREAS, Camp Santanoni offers great educational opportunities for school groups, environmental education and the general public interested in history, architecture and nature; and

WHEREAS, Camp Santanoni is well situated to enhance the programming at the nearby New York State Visitors' Interpretive Center at Rich Lake; and

WHEREAS, Camp Santanoni has great potential to contribute significant economic benefits to the local and regional community; and

WHEREAS, Camp Santanoni can be preserved and utilized in a manner that harmonizes with the surrounding New York State Forest Preserve,

THEREFORE, BE IT RESOLVED, that Adirondack Architectural Heritage endorses all efforts to preserve and utilize Camp Santanoni for public recreation and educational purposes; and

BE IT FURTHER RESOLVED, that Adirondack Architectural Heritage would support amending Article XIV of the State Constitution, if necessary, to accomplish this purpose.[40]

The Town of Newcomb passed the same resolution simultaneously.[41] Under Canon's leadership, the Essex County Board of Supervisors followed suit.[42] Naturally, the Preservation League of New York State lent its support, although having borne the brunt of work on the Sagamore land exchange amendment of 1983, and having initiated the Hinchey legislation, it clearly favored the latter solution over a constitutional amendment for Santanoni.[43]

Throughout the fall, Kirschenbaum and Canon made numerous calls and visits to State legislators, the governor's office, State agencies, and the leaders and boards of various Adirondack organizations. The effort yielded further resolutions and letters of support. In December, the executive committee of the Adirondack North Country Association (ANCA), the leading economic development group for the park, approved a letter of support for efforts to save Camp Santanoni.[44] The same month, Julia Stokes, New York State's Deputy Commissioner for Historic Preservation wrote that she was convinced Santanoni "should be saved and used."[45] By January, Ronald Stafford, the North Country's Republican State senator and the second most powerful member of that body, had given his initial support, as had Anthony Casale, the area's Republican State assemblyman, and Betsy Boyd, the State Department of Economic Development's regional tourism director.[46]

Meanwhile, AARCH had been working on getting Democratic support for Santanoni in Albany. Newcomb was located in solid Republican territory, where local government officials and State legislators typically opposed State land use regulation and supported initiatives that promised economic development. But the Democrats controlled the Governor's Office and the State Assembly, and they supported most environmental legislation and protections. They would be much more careful about supporting any measure that might threaten or be perceived to threaten the integrity of the State Forest Preserve. On the other hand, the Democratic leadership in Albany was not doctrinaire, and many of them with strong environ-

[40] "Board Resolution on Camp Santanoni," Adirondack Architectural Heritage, September 11, 1990.

[41] Town resolution, untitled, signed by George H. Canon, September 10, 1990.

[42] "Resolution Supporting the Use of Camp Santanoni in the Town of Newcomb for Public Recreation and Education," Board of Supervisors of Essex County, October 1, 1990.

[43] "The Preservation League, along with the newly formed Adirondack Architectural Heritage and the Town of Newcomb, are committed to saving the Great Camp and are confident a solution can be found that will satisfy all concerned." *Newsletter*, Preservation League of New York State, Fall 1990, 3.

[44] Thomas Tobin, executive director, ANCA, letter to Howard Kirschenbaum, December 19, 1990.

[45] Julia Stokes, letter to Howard Kirschenbaum, December 12, 1990; second letter to the same effect on February 12, 1991.

[46] Sen. Stafford, his influential assistant Peter Repas, and Assemblyman Casale offered their support verbally to George Canon and Howard Kirschenbaum in meetings in their offices on January 14, 1991; formal letters of support came later in the year; Betsy Boyd, letter to Howard Kirschenbaum January 23, 1991.

mental records believed it was possible to balance environmental protection with historic preservation in the Adirondacks. Kirschenbaum contacted two of them with whom he had worked closely on the Sagamore land exchange amendment a decade earlier.

One was Assemblyman Maurice Hinchey, powerful chairman of the Assembly's Environmental Conservation Committee. He was very receptive to another campaign to save an important Adirondack landmark. After viewing a slide presentation on Santanoni in his office, Hinchey scheduled a January ski trip to visit the camp personally, but hurt his back at the last minute and had to postpone the visit. Still he offered his tentative support until he could see Santanoni for himself. Ironically, while his advisor Paul Bray considered the "Hinchey Bill" of 1983 to be the logical legal basis for preserving Santanoni—after all, the legislation was written with Santanoni in mind—Hinchey himself was quite open to the constitutional amendment approach which AARCH advocated.[47]

Governor Cuomo's assistant, Joseph Martens, was the second important Democrat to meet Kirschenbaum and Canon in Albany. Martens oversaw Adirondack matters and other environmental issues. Martens was supportive of Santanoni's preservation and, in turn, arranged a meeting for AARCH board members with Robert Bendick, the new State Deputy Commissioner for Natural Resources at the Department of Environmental Conservation. Following that meeting, Bendick skied in to Santanoni to see the area and buildings for himself and from then on was a steady supporter for preservation, while still remaining responsive to the concerns voiced by the environmental community. Bendick's support represented a major change in departmental policy toward Santanoni.

That winter and spring of 1991, additional supporters joined the informal coalition. Canon secured the official endorsement of the Intercounty Legislative Committee of the Adirondacks, the organization representing county legislators throughout the park.[48] The full board of the Adirondack North Country Association passed a resolution of support, which it immediately forwarded to the governor, legislative leaders and others.[49] DEC's Robert Bendick answered ANCA by stating that the department's internal policy group had determined that "the existing buildings should be stabilized and retained. DEC has no intention of demolishing Santanoni." Rather, "the Department is in the process of exploring strategies for selective restoration and interpretation of the buildings" which should be preserved as "an important resource which remains to enhance our understanding of the history of the North Country."[50]

As summer approached, AARCH finally began contacting the environmental organizations. When Senator Stafford made public his support for Santanoni in July, it became clear that a formidable coalition had been formed for Santanoni's preservation. On the state level there were endorsements from the governor's office, the leadership of both chambers of the State legislature, the Department of Environmental Conservation, and the State Office of Parks, Recreation and Historic Preservation. Local government officials throughout the Park supported Santanoni's preservation, as did the Adirondacks' leading economic development organization, as well as the Preservation League of New York State, and the Park's historic preservation community, led by Adirondack Architectural Heritage.

[47] Paul Bray, letter to Howard Kirschenbaum, March 11, 1991. Hinchey is currently U.S. Congressman from the Catskill region.

[48] "Resolution Supporting the Use of Camp Santanoni in the Town of Newcomb for Public Recreation and Education," April 25, 1991.

[49] "Resolution to Support the Use of Camp Santanoni for Public Recreation and Education," passed June 13, 1991; "Memorandum," June 21, 1991.

[50] Robert Bendick, letter to Daniel Palm, executive director, ANCA, June 5, 1991.

Robert Engel (in shorts) with tour group

Not every organization and State official agreed on the legal solution; clearly there were still differences in approach, with some parties favoring the Hinchey legislation and administrative solutions, while others advocated a constitutional amendment. Nevertheless, there now appeared to be enough momentum and enough agreement about solutions that, after twenty years of indecision, Adirondack organizations and officials appeared to be heading toward a final resolution for Camp Santanoni.

Knowing that coalitions can easily fall apart, however, Adirondack Architectural Heritage decided to keep the momentum building. With a grant from the Open Space Institute, for the summer of 1991 the organization hired a graduate student intern, Robert Engel, who would become co-author of this book. Engel was to camp in the Santanoni Preserve near Newcomb Lake, to greet visitors at the main camp, to inform them of Santanoni's history and significance, and to develop further public support for its preservation. AARCH was prepared to do this on its own, with Engel moving camp every few days if needed, if a long-term camping permit was not obtained. This proved unnecessary. DEC officials recognized that AARCH's intern would also be performing a public service by keeping an eye on the buildings and educating the visiting public, so they gave AARCH a long-term permit for a campsite on Newcomb Lake. They also allowed AARCH's intern to station himself on the main camp porch, act as an interpreter, and survey public opinion about Santanoni.

Having accompanied hundreds of people to Santanoni over the years, AARCH board members were convinced that the large majority of visitors supported Santanoni's preservation, restoration, and modest use. AARCH developed a short questionnaire asking visitors two simple questions:[51]

> How has the presence of the buildings at Camp Santanoni affected your excursion into the Santanoni Preserve today?
>
> ___ The buildings enhance the experience.
>
> ___ The buildings detract from the experience.
>
> ___ The buildings make no difference.
>
> Ideally, what would you like to see happen with the buildings at Camp Santanoni?
>
> ___ Tear them down or allow them to rot. Let the area return to wilderness.[52]

---

[51] A third question asked visitors how often they had visited Santanoni. 514 (69%) said they were visiting for the first time; 156 (21) had visited 2-4 times, and 76 (10%) had come five or more times. Responses were comparable for first time and multiple visitors.

[52] Later in the summer this item was changed to "Remove them and let the area return to wilderness."

___ Preserve them just as they are now.

___ Restore them and use them for historic tours and public education and recreation, on a modest scale.

A total of 746 respondents, about half of all visitors, completed the survey.[53] The results were overwhelmingly in favor of Santanoni's preservation—far more positive than AARCH had expected. Ninety-eight per cent of the visitors said the buildings enhanced their experience in the preserve![54] As to the future of the buildings, eighty-three per cent voted to restore them and use them for historic tours and public education and recreation on a modest scale. Fifteen percent said preserve them just as they are now. Only two percent advocated removing them and letting the area return to wilderness.

A space on the survey for additional comments produced scores of statements expressing visitors' strong emotional reactions to the architecture and setting. The words gave additional meaning to the survey's statistical results.

> Given the proliferation of shoddy building methods, log construction on the scale of Santanoni ought to be preserved so that future generations can have the opportunity to see what people were capable of doing.
>
> Buildings are unique. Where else on the planet does architecture like this exist?
>
> My three children were completely awestruck when they saw it. I would like to believe that it can be preserved for many future "young eyes" to see.
>
> Places like this are rare and should be treated as such. Once demolished there can be no replacement. As a tribute to both 19th century architecture and NY State history, Santanoni must be preserved.[55]

Log detail at the main camp

AARCH wasted no time in publiciczing the results of its survey. To all those who argued that the Santanoni buildings take away from the wilderness experience and are inconsistent with the Forest Preserve, AARCH answered, "Say's who?" The people who sit in their offices and write passionate prose about wilderness values, or the masses of people from all walks of life who actually hike and bike and ski into the Forest Preserve and experience it for themselves? As AARCH wrote in a cover letter disseminating the survey results, "Certainly this strong indication of public support does not resolve the thorny legal issues involved, nor does it address the financial realities of preserving Santanoni. But it does indicate a goal shared equally by lovers of history, architecture and wilderness and by Adirondack residents, other New Yorkers and out-of-state visitors alike, for all were well-represented among the respondents. It is our hope that

---

[53] The survey was available to all visitors who arrived at the main camp between June 29 and September 2, 1991. Engel estimated that about one in two visitors completed the survey. Most indicated their name and address on their survey forms, although this information was optional.

[54] 1.4% said the buildings made no difference, and .6% said they detracted from the experience. The surveys are on file for inspection in the offices of Adirondack Architectural Heritage.

[55] Comments of Susanne Bloes, Sherburne, NY: Gerard Dunphy, Ithaca, NY; a Mr. or Ms. Livingston, Duanesburg, NY; and Mark Brozozowski, Philadelphia, Pennsylvania.

this almost universally shared goal—preserving Camp Santanoni and using it as a public educational and recreational resource—will guide our ongoing deliberations."[56]

Throughout the summer, board members of Adirondack organizations and State officials hiked in or rode the wagons to see Camp Santanoni for themselves. Clearly the momentum for a decision was building and they needed to formulate, or in some cases rethink, their organizational positions. In August, Robert Bendick called together in Newcomb representatives of the major State agencies (Environmental Conservation, Historic Preservation, and Adirondack Park Agency), historic preservation groups (Preservation League of NYS, Adirondack Museum and Adirondack Architectural Heritage) and the Town of Newcomb for a meeting on the future of Santanoni. There he outlined a compromise solution for Camp Santanoni. The buildings would be preserved but not actively used. They would be, in effect, an educational exhibit whose interpretation would enrich the public's understanding of Adirondack history and architecture. While the legal rationale for preservation was not fully determined, it was felt that legal justification existed for administrative purposes or as authorized by the 1983 Hinchey legislation. Could we all live with this compromise?

It was about as much preservation and use as some could accept and less than others had been working for. Some said, yes, they could support this solution. Others, like AARCH and Newcomb, said possibly. There was more thinking to be done by some and more discussions as staff went back to their boards or agencies to clarify their official positions. Yet there was a sense in the meeting that, although some were not prepared to reach an agreement that day, a consensus was, in fact, emerging. As one state official summarized the meeting, "It was an impressive gathering of organizations and agencies, all with the common goal for the preservation of this significant resource. The meeting was productive and the agreements reached are terrific."[57]

After the summer the activity continued. Assemblyman Hinchey, his assistant Diana Swain and advisor Paul Bray hiked into Santanoni with Kirschenbaum, and they all rode out in the wagon together with Supervisor Canon. Hinchey was so impressed by what he saw that he called DEC to urge them to undertake emergency stabilization measures on behalf of some of the most endangered buildings, and he promised to call the governor immediately to urge his support for Santanoni's preservation. It was probably no coincidence that a week later, on October 10, 1991, Governor Mario Cuomo announced publicly that Santanoni would be preserved.[58]

High-level decisions like this are influenced by many sources. While legislators and lobbyists were weighing in with the governor, so was his secretary, part-time Newcomb resident Pam Broughton. When Governor Cuomo emerged from his press conference in Lake Placid after announcing Santanoni's preservation, a reporter asked him if he had visited Santanoni. The governor answered, "I have not, but my secretary lives there. After fifteen years as my secretary, when she read last week that we were doing Santanoni, she said, 'you've finally done something right.'"[59]

---

[56] Howard Kirschenbaum, AARCH President, cover letter, September 15, 1991.

[57] Julia Stokes, Deputy Commissioner for Historic Preservation, NYS Parks, Recreation and Historic Preservation, letter to J. Winthrop Aldrich, Assistant to the Commissioner, DEC, August 27, 1991. The Adirondack Park Agency then was less than enthusiastic about employing "an historic preservation land use category in the State Land Use Plan and applying it to a portion of Santanoni Preserve. . . . Bendick felt that we could not ask the APA to reclassify any Wilderness, so we were limited to Wild Forest. This is a problem for repair of the stone bridges, the re-establishment of the [Newcomb Lake] overlook view, and of Delia Lake spring water works." J. Winthrop Aldrich, manuscript note to authors.

[58] Address at Lake Placid, New York, October 10, 1991.

[59] Governor Cuomo's response was captured on tape. "Adirondack Great Camps: Part II: The Saranacs, St. Regis and Santanoni." New York: Media-M-Productions. Videotape, in press.

Environmental organizations quickly responded. The Association for the Protection of the Adirondacks went on record in favor of the compromise solution—for limited use—provided that this be authorized by a constitutional amendment.[60] The Adirondack Mountain Club wrote the DEC Commissioner and APA director a four-page letter:

> ". . . to inform you that ADK's Board of governors voted on November 2nd to support the preservation of Camp Santanoni as a permanent exhibit of a unique and extraordinary Adirondack style of architecture and as a facility to promote public enjoyment and understanding of the Forest Preserve.
>
> After considerable legal research, we believe that the Department of Environmental Conservation's plan for limited rehabilitation and interpretation of the buildings at Camp Santanoni is expressly permitted by ECL 9–0109. We do not believe a Constitutional Amendment is either necessary or desirable. Our research revealed no judicial decision precluding the maintenance of buildings on Forest Preserve."[61]

Several more pages of careful legal argument followed. The Residents Committee to Protect the Adirondacks issued its own statement endorsing Santanoni's preservation.[62]

Following the Hinchey visit in October, the Department also got to work stabilizing portions of those buildings most in danger of collapse, such as the Boat House and sections of the main lodge. By the year's end, the Governor could announce:

> We have acted to preserve Camp Santanoni from the ravages of the winter, in cooperation with the Town and the historic preservation community. It is our hope that the deterioration of these =landmark buildings can be halted and proposals to use the site for cultural education will advance in 1992–the centennial year of both Santanoni and the Adirondack Park.[63]

[60] David Gibson, executive director, letter to Robert Bendick, October 23, 1991.

[61] Neil Woodworth, Counsel and Conservation Chairman for letter to Thomas Jorling and Robert Glennon, November 12, 1991.

[62] *Adirondack Voices*, Fall 1991, 3.

[63] Press release from Executive Chamber, December 30, 1991.

## Planning for the Next Hundred Years

The following spring DEC's Robert Bendick called together in Albany the leaders of the historic preservation and environmental community most involved in the Adirondacks to hammer out a final compromise solution on Santanoni. Now that the governor had committed the state to preserve Camp Santanoni, Bendick made it clear that the department was proceeding to implement this policy. He hoped everyone around the table could be comfortable with the concept of preserving Santanoni as a passive exhibit, which would not be used to provide public accommodations or food service but would be restored to a point and be interpreted to the public. When asked about the legal justification for this approach, he indicated the department attorneys felt that Santanoni could be preserved and used for administrative purposes or in accordance with the Hinchey legislation or both. He was not there to argue the fine legal points but to see if we all could live with this solution.

Apparently almost everybody could, notwithstanding some disclaimers about needing to consider the matter further, discuss it with their boards, or wait to see how the plan actually would be implemented as further details were decided. The meeting ended with a plan to proceed on several fronts. The department would draft the "unit management plan," which would describe in detail how the Santanoni Preserve would be used and managed. This would take about a year to complete and would then go to the public hearing stage. Meanwhile, the Preservation League of New York State, with AARCH's assistance, would work on a historic structures report that would guide future stabilization work on the buildings. AARCH and the Town of Newcomb would continue to provide interpretation at Santanoni and make plans for actual stabilization work to begin.

Preservation League of New York State presents check for farm historic structures report*

Immediately after the meeting a state-issued press release announced the agreed arrangement:

> Following legal and planning measures now to be implemented by the State, the camp buildings will be preserved through the joint efforts of the Department of Environmental Conservation, the Town of Newcomb, the Preservation League of New York State, Adirondack Architectural Heritage and other government and private organizations. . . . This action is in accordance with Governor Cuomo's pledge last fall in Lake Placid to devise a plan for Santanoni that balances the need to protect the integrity of the forest preserve while recognizing the importance of maintaining important historic sites.[64]

In the release, Commissioner of Environmental Conservation Thomas Jorling said:

> It is appropriate in this centennial year of the Adirondack Park that this classic example of rustic camp architecture be preserved as an historic landmark for future generations. We will draft a management plan that both respects the character of the surrounding forest lands and provides the public with a better understanding of the rich cultural heritage and wilderness values of the region. We appreciate the efforts of

* Report author, consultant Wesley Haynes, left; Town of Newcomb Supervisor George Canon; AARCH President Howard Kirschenbaum receiving check; AARCH Executive Director Steven Engelhart; Tania Werbizky presenting check from Preservation League; Barbara Sweet, Town of Newcomb Councilwoman and Adirondack Park Agency Commissioner; J. Winthrop Aldrich, Deputy Commissioner for Historic Preservation, New York State OPRHP; Richard Cipperly, New York State DEC.

64 Department of Environmental Conservation press release, March 23, 1992.

> the town and the historic preservation community to work in partnership with us on this important effort.

This plan set the pattern for the rest of the decade. While the state presumably was working on its unit management plan, the other parties slowly but surely moved forward with their parts of the bargain.[65] The Preservation League and AARCH, with financial support from the Open Space Institute and the J.M. Kaplan Fund, began work on a series of historic structures reports. These projects analyzed the existing condition of the buildings and the work necessary to stabilize them, as well as documenting the history of many of the structures. Preservation consultant Wesley Haynes of Argyle, New York, took the lead on most of this seminal work, which provided invaluable information to guide future interpretation and preservation of Santanoni. His work was helped immeasurably by the original research conducted by Robert Engel for his master's thesis and by DEC's J. Winthrop Aldrich, who in 1994 became Deputy Commissioner for Historic Preservation at State Parks, Recreation and Historic Preservation.

Each summer, with funding from the Town of Newcomb, AARCH hired and supervised one or more interns to greet the public, interpret Santanoni's history and significance to visitors, and continue to build public support for the camp's preservation. The intern also performed a valuable service in watching over the buildings, as Robert Engel discovered the first summer. He interrupted a group of campers who had made a cooking fire on the main lodge porch, with only a sheet of aluminum foil between the fire and the wooden decking! The charred wood was visible for years until the porch was rebuilt.

Each year, AARCH's working relationship with the state matured. The first year, officials merely tolerated intern Robert Engel's presence; he could not officially guide visitors through the camp. The second year, intern James Mudd again camped near the main camp and was given a key to open and close the front door to the lodge each day. Although he could not officially guide people around, this was the first time that the public was able, legally, to view the interior of Santanoni's main lodge. The third year, interpreters Mark Montaine and Richard Sweet were allowed to guide visitors inside the main building. The fourth year, DEC permitted intern Carolyn Cipperly to live in the Artist's Studio—essentially camping in the building without utilities.

Through the summer of 1993 neither had stabilization work begun, nor had writing of the unit management plan commenced. AARCH became concerned that the Santanoni effort might be losing momentum. So it asked the department for permission to organize a late-autumn work project to replace the deteriorated cedar shingle roof of the Artist's Studio—a difficult offer to refuse. The Town of Newcomb purchased all the materials and paid the contractor. The Preservation League developed the work plan which was supervised by Tupper Lake contractor Randy Burgoyne and Kirschenbaum, who coordinated the volunteer effort. The project took place over four days in October and November.[66] Ironically, on October 28, while the volunteer crew was working on the roof, they could look across Newcomb Lake and see about thirty U.S. Air Force and State Police raking the largest island for Douglas Legg's remains, unsuccessfully following up on the latest lead in the unsolved mystery.

[65] The following chronology is documented in successive issues of Adirondack Architectural Heritage's *Newsletter*, from 1992 through 1999.

[66] The crew included AARCH volunteers Irv Francis, Joe and Nancy Pfeiffer, board member and architect Carl Stearns who had worked on the preservation plan, Don and Beverly Williams, Melissa Brewer, Dan Edelstein, George Petkov, Danny Otts and Warren Lipa; Newcomb Supervisor George Canon and Historical Society Director Virginia Hall; and DEC's Andy Blanchette, Richard Cipperly and Phil Johnstone. A work crew from the state prison "shock program" at Moriah cleaned up the debris. At least eighty percent of the roof was completed that fall. Burgoyne and Otts returned the following spring to complete the work.

AARCH and Newcomb regarded the studio roof restoration as a turning point for Santanoni. Not only had significant, visible work begun; the state's own employees had officially participated in the restoration. The Town of Newcomb had spent a substantial amount on materials. AARCH publicized the accomplishment. There could be no turning back now.

However, by the spring of 1994 the state had taken no further action—neither authorizing further work, committing funds of its own, nor beginning the unit management plan. Again, AARCH was placed in the role of advocate, urging the state to fulfill its commitments. In a three-page letter to the deputy commissioner, AARCH's president wrote,

> But in spite of all the good intentions, the fact is that Santanoni is in worse shape now than it was three years ago—seriously worse shape. The boathouse caved in. The department placed an enormous, intrusive metal gas tank right in the middle of the Gate Lodge complex. The main lodge, the barn and other buildings are deteriorating rapidly. While the bureaucracy grinds on, Santanoni is falling down![67]

Expressing the hope that it would not be necessary to mobilize the coalition again to encourage the state to take action, AARCH suggested three practical steps that could be done immediately:

> 1. Give AARCH and the Town of Newcomb permission to begin to stabilize the main lodge roof.
>
> 2. Authorize DEC operational staff, working with Newcomb and AARCH volunteers, to begin to stabilize the barn roof.
>
> 3. Give the Unit Management Plan for Santanoni the highest priority.

The state's response was positive. Richard Cipperly, Assistant Regional Forester for the area was given additional authority for the Santanoni project and continued to work closely with AARCH and Newcomb, as did Chuck Vandrei, DEC's new historic preservation officer, doing all they could to move the project forward. AARCH's new executive director, Steven Engelhart, took on an increasing portion of the responsibility of coordinating with the DEC, as the state invested significant staff time in replacing most of the cedar shingle roof of the main barn, using materials provided by the Town of Newcomb. AARCH and Newcomb began work on the main lodge roof, getting about ten percent of it completed that year—another important, symbolic beginning.

DEC Preservation Officer Chuck Vandrei and Howie Kirschenbaum on main camp roof.

The unit management plan, however, remained in limbo, preventing any serious long-term planning or fund raising for the project. Many other unit management plans around the Adirondacks were years behind schedule. The state did not appear to be consciously avoiding work on the plan, but rather to be distracted by competing priorities. One of these was the gubernatorial election of 1994.

When Republican George Pataki became governor, replacing Democrat Mario Cuomo, some Adirondack watchers were anxious about the new administration's environmental and historic preservation policies. Governor Pataki, however, protected more land in the Adirondacks, through purchase and conservation easements, than any recent governor. His administration also became a strong supporter of Camp Santanoni's preservation. The new

[67] Howard Kirschenbaum, letter to Robert Bendick, May 25, 1994. The state eventually fenced the gas tank and now plans to move it to a less conspicuous location. Also in the Gate House complex, DEC replaced the old barn that had burned, which their operations crew used for vehicle storage and maintenance activities, with a new garage of appropriate design located mostly out of sight beyond the visitor parking area.

Commissioner of Environmental Conservation, John Cahill, hiked into Santanoni Preserve and camped on Newcomb Lake with his family several times. The previous administration had been supportive; nevertheless each of its actions involving Santanoni had been taken with extreme caution. With the new administration, preservation and interpretation activities were authorized more confidently.

In March of 1995, the new DEC leadership assembled a Santanoni Historic Area Citizens' Advisory Committee. This group helped to plan the future of Camp Santanoni by providing input for the writing of the unit management plan, then two years behind schedule. Beginning that May, the committee met about a dozen times over the next eighteen months to deliberate on many aspects of Santanoni's future.[68] With the same players from state agencies, environmental groups, historic preservation organizations and local government, one had a recurring sense of *deja vu*. Issues about appropriate use of the Forest Preserve that had been raised throughout the past twenty years were raised once again and debated once more. Under the leadership of now Supervising Forester Cipperly, however, the committee's work moved forward, with many areas of apparent consensus achieved.

According to the evolving plan, following the precedent of two other historic areas in the Adirondack Park—John Brown's Farm and the battlefield at Crown Point—a Historic Area would be created within the Santanoni Preserve. This area would include the three building complexes at Santanoni and the road connecting them, with a minimal amount of acreage around the Gate Lodge and Main Camp complexes, and a somewhat larger area around the Farm that included some of the original fields. Just how many acres would be included and just how much trimming of foliage would be permitted in order to restore some of farm's landscaping was not determined.

The Historic Area would still be part of the Forest Preserve and no public motorized vehicles would be permitted. Access to the farm and main camp would still be by foot, ski, horse, bicycle, or horse-drawn wagon. The buildings would be stabilized and restored to a degree, but the extent of restoration was not determined. The buildings would not be used for public accommodations or the serving of food. The buildings would, in effect, be exhibits that would be interpreted to the public. Not only would the interpretation focus on the historical and architectural interest of the Great Camp, the interpretation would help visitors appreciate the relationship of Santanoni and other Adirondack camps in the growing conservation movement in the Adirondacks and the nation. Exhibits and guided tours would both be appropriate forms of interpretation, but the specifics were left to future planning. Some furnishings and artifacts might be part of the interpretation, if security concerns were addressed. Nature interpretation would best be left to the nearby Adirondack Park Visitor Center.

Many other issues were discussed, from whether both horse-drawn sleighs and cross-country skiers could use the road in winter (probably not; the horses ruin the ski trail), to whether bicycle rentals at the Gate Lodge would be appropriate (probably not; best that commercial activity be handled in Newcomb wherever possible). On the other hand, the Gate Lodge would make a logical visitors' center for Santanoni—for interpretation, safety orientation, and the sale of some items to raise funds for Santanoni's preservation. A "Friends organization," such as those that exist for many state historic sites, would be an appropriate way to gain public support for Santanoni's preservation and interpretation.

While most organizations represented seemed more or less comfortable with most of the features of the evolving plan, there was by no means complete agreement. At the final

[68] Minutes were kept for meetings from May 2, 1995 through October 10, 1996.

committee meeting in the fall of 1996, the Adirondack Council's representative made it clear they "never agreed to go along with the majority decision" and "reserved the right to disagree or sue." Some members voiced disappointment that after all the time and effort put into the planning process, there was still not a consensus on some important issues.[69] The department promised to synthesize the group's decisions and discussions, make some judgment calls of its own, and produce the long-awaited unit management plan within about six months. At that time the committee would meet again to review the draft, the department would make any further revisions, and the draft plan would go to public hearing.

## New Developments

It would be three more years before the unit management plan was completed. Aside from the usual problems, one reason for the delay was the controversial issue of motorized access for handicapped individuals in the State Forest Preserve. In the late 90's, Santanoni Preserve, with its passable roads to Newcomb Lake and Moose Pond, became a focal point for this controversy. There apparently was some concern that whatever the Santanoni Unit Management Plan said about handicapped access could be a precedent for the entire Adirondack Park; therefore the plan was held up while the larger issue was deliberated.

Finally released in October of 1999, the Camp Santanoni Historic Area Unit Management Plan held few surprises.[70] For the most part it reflected the ideas and plans that had been discussed during the Citizens Advisory Committee deliberations: reclassifying a clearly defined "historic area" around the buildings and road; allowing a clearly defined level of restoration and interpretive activities within that envelope; and maintaining the wild forest character of the area. In presenting the legal justification for preserving Santanoni, Commissioner Cahill stated that, based on "legislative history and judicial interpretation, . . . the stabilization, rehabilitation and maintenance of the Camp Santanoni buildings and their curtilage, and their use for purposes of historical and cultural interpretation, are compatible with the purposes of Article XIV and the reasonable regulation of the Forest Preserve."[71]

At this writing, Adirondack organizations and interest groups are framing their responses to the document. When public hearings are held, no doubt some constituencies will argue that the State was too timid in its proposed Historic Area boundaries and plans for restoration, interpretation, and use. Others will say such plans go too far. The State's decision to allow disabled persons motorized access between the Gate Lodge and Newcomb Lake will be controversial. There may be further argument over the legal justification for preserving Camp Santanoni, even by Santanoni's supporters.

Meanwhile, in the years of awaiting the unit management plan, tangible progress at Santanoni has continued. The interpretation of Santanoni has become more extensive. In 1996, AARCH and Newcomb hired *two* interns to spend the summer at Santanoni.[72] One lived in the Artist's Studio, as had become the pattern, and conducted oral interpretation at the main camp. The other lived at the Gate Lodge, and for the first time in its existence, the Gate Lodge was open to the public. Each year since then, a little more work has been done at the Gate Lodge, to restore the interior and begin creating a Santanoni Preserve visitors' center there.

Each year the stabilization of some of the buildings has continued, guided by profes-

[69] Minutes of the October 10, 1996 meeting.

[70] "Camp Santanoni Historic Area and Related Areas of the Vanderwhacker Mountain Wild Forest Draft Unit Management Plan" (Albany: New York State Department of Environmental Conservation, October, 1999).

[71] Camp Santanoni Unit Management Plan, 2. "Curtilage" means the enclosed land surrounding the buildings.

[72] Hal Hutchinson was the intern in 1995; Mark Brebach and Kirsten Merriman in 1996; Taya Dixon, Eric Meulemans and Zeph Parmenter in 1997; Joanna Doherty and Kurt Leasure in 1998; Amanda Mason and Renee Norris in 1999.

Log craftsman Michael Frenette

sionally developed plans reviewed and approved by the State Office of Historic Preservation.[73] The state completed most of the barn roof restoration in 1995. The Town of Newcomb and AARCH have kept working on the main lodge roof, each year advancing the project until 20%, 50%, 80% and, by 1999, virtually all of the extensive surface has been re-shingled. In 1998–99, funded by the town, log building specialist Mike Frenette spent most of the summers at Santanoni restoring major sections of the main lodge porch and porch roof support beams.

[73] "Camp Santanoni Main Camp Complex Documentation, Stabilization and Maintenance Plan," prepared by The Preservation League of New York State (Albany), Crawford and Stearns Architects (Syracuse), Ryan-Biggs Associates (Troy), and Wesley Haynes Historic Preservation (Argyle), 1993. Haynes' "Farm Complex""and "Gate Lodge Complex" reports also contain detailed stabilization recommendations. Prepared separately, over many years, these reports should be combined, updated, and extended to produce a more detailed plan for Santanoni's stabilization and long-term restoration.

In 1999, the state began an extensive exterior and structural restoration of the Old Farm House, with a grant from the state Environmental Protection Fund. It was an eleventh-hour save for this building, the oldest at Santanoni, which had been open to the weather and was deteriorating rapidly.

Although significant work has taken place on some buildings, other important structures have continued to deteriorate. The Boat House roof has collapsed and the building requires reconstruction. The Farm Manager's Cottage and West Cottage are slowly declining. A new bridge, reasonably compatible, has recently replaced the 1890's iron bridge to the Gate Lodge, but some of the historic character of the preserve's entry has been lost.

When considering the camp as a whole, it has been difficult in some years to tell whether the stabilization was outpacing the deteriora-

Old Farm House restoration begins, 1999

tion, or vice versa. Now, as the century turns, it seems clear that the tide has changed and preservation momentum is gaining ground.

Two other developments have been initiated recently. In 1998, building on a seven-year track record of increasingly close cooperation, the Department of Environmental Conservation asked Adirondack Architectural Heritage to form a Friends of Santanoni group to assist and support the department in its efforts to preserve Camp Santanoni and interpret it to the public. Many state-owned historic sites around New York have such support groups, which are typically independent non-profit organizations that can operate more flexibly and creatively than the state in raising funds and recruiting volunteers in support of a historic site. Thus, Friends of Camp Santanoni was formed, to be:

> . . . a partnership of non-profit organizations, the Town of Newcomb, the NYS Department of Environmental Conservation, other state agencies and the thousands of people who love this special place and believe in its preservation and use for public education, recreation and inspiration. The purpose of the Friends is to provide support for the ongoing preservation, interpretation and use of Camp Santanoni through fundraising, staffing, volunteer work, promotion, educational programming and interpretation. . ..The Friends of Camp Santanoni is managed by Adirondack Architectural Heritage, the non-profit, historic preservation organization for the Adirondack Park. [74]

With a distinguished Advisory Board and growing membership, Friends of Camp Santanoni is mustering public support, both financial and political, for Santanoni's preservation.[75]

Finally, after years of planning between the State Office of Historic Preservation, the Department of Environmental Conservation, and the National Park Service, Santanoni —already listed on the National Register of Historic Places— Historic Places--was classified as a National Historic Landmark. This is the premier distinction for the nation's most important historical and architectural sites.[76]

Friends of Camp Santanoni and National Landmark status should do much to advance the cause of Santanoni's preservation. Meanwhile, on the ground at Santanoni, as the twentieth century ends, visitors to the preserve see vibrant activity in all three camp complexes.

New signs direct the public to the Visitors' Center in the Gate Lodge, staffed daily, where

---

[74] "Friends of Camp Santanoni: Supporting New York State's Adirondack Great Camp," Friends of Sananoni brochure, 1998.

[75] Friends of Santanoni's first Advisory Board represented the broad coalition that ultimately was responsible for preserving the historic site: Stuart Buchanan, Region 5 Director, NYS Department of Environmental Conservation; Sandra Bureau, Director, Adirondack Park Interpretative Centers; George Canon, Supervisor, Town of Newcomb; Susan Dineen, Adirondack Museum; Virginia Hall, President, Newcomb Historical Society; William Johnston, Essex County Planner; Susan Pruyn King, Long Lake; Howard Kirschenbaum, Adirondack Architectural Heritage; Reid Larson, Essex County Historian; Hon. Elizabeth Little, New York State Assembly; Hon. Ronald Stafford, New York State Senate; and Darlene McCloud, President Preservation League of New York State.

[76] Camp Santanoni was approved for National Landmark status at a National Park Service meeting on April 14, 2000. The nomination forms were prepared by Wesley Haynes.

Volunteers work on porch floor restoration

they view an attractive new exhibit on Santanoni's history, funded by AARCH and executed by students at the Cooperstown Graduate Program.[77] Rooms are being painted. Friends of Camp Santanoni brochures and other literature are available. Items may be purchased to raise funds for restoration.

Farther into the preserve, an interpretive sign announces arrival at "Santanoni Farm." Lawns around the Creamery and two main farmhouses have been cleared of brush and mowed, creating for the first time in years a sense of care and occupation. A large area around the Old Farm House is ribboned off as a work area. Scaffolding around the building, piles of new lumber, and visible work in progress on large portions of the building signal the state's serious intention to preserve Santanoni. Visitors can walk through the barn and Creamery and gain some sense of the extensive farm operation that existed here.

At Newcomb Lake, on approach to the main lodge, visitors may be struck by the new roof shingles that cover the expansive structure. Walking under the porte cochere onto the main camp porch they see work in progress on the front facade—log bracing, jacks, come-alongs and cables, large areas of new log floor joists carefully fitted together and awaiting decking, other areas of new porch flooring recently laid. On some days visitors may see volunteers working with Mike Frenette, learning the techniques of log construction while restoring the great log villa.

To avoid the porch work areas, visitors are routed through the cabins, for the first time fully available for public viewing. The summer interpreter provides guided tours of the

[77] The history and museum studies program at Cooperstown is conducted by the State University of New York College at Oneonta.

main camp and displays a growing collection of historic photographs and other interpretive materials. Once the unit management plan is approved, there will be impetus for the preparation of a comprehensive interpretive plan worthy of a National Landmark property.

Over the past quarter century, then, Camp Santanoni has gone from a completely intact Adirondack Great Camp to an abandoned derelict in danger of removal to a distinguished historic site starting on the long road to restoration. In the past decade, it has gone from a relatively unknown property hidden deep in the forest to one of the best-documented of the historic Adirondack camps.

In the past few years, its owner, the State of New York, has gone from resisting its preservation to actively and proudly promoting and supporting it as one of the state's valued historic places. And in the past two years, the unofficial coalition of organizations and individuals that successfully campaigned for Santanoni's preservation has come together as the Friends of Camp Santanoni to help it achieve its long-term potential. Just what that potential is remains to be determined. The official plan for its future is about to be debated. Yet Santanoni's future *is* being created with each new step in its restoration, interpretation, and national recognition.

A midsummer night's idyll

# Departure

She was told it would never last—but it has.

*Cynthia Pruyn Green*

Santanoni Preserve is a property of New York State; as such, it belongs to the people of the State. In a larger sense, as recognized by its national historic designation, Santanoni belongs to all Americans.

Several decades after facilitating Santanoni's transfer from the Melvins via The Nature Conservancy to public ownership, Patrick Noonan reflected, "When I think back on the many conservation projects I've been involved with, probably thousands, this one stands at the forefront."[1]

Santanoni Preserve is not merely a superlative natural resource, but an equally important cultural resource. A bequest to future generations, this historic site is not preserved as a memorial to the families that built and occupied its structures, however; for with passing years the Pruyns and Melvins, like most of us, will become increasingly less relevant to those yet to come. The owners of Great Camps were only visitors to their occasional retreats, but even those who called these places their real homes, like Art and Helen Tummins, who lived most of their married life on the Preserve, will recede into distant history. Santanoni is preserved as a historic landmark because it represents more broadly the early occupants' times, talents, tastes, their way of life—in a word, their "culture." Beyond merely representing a period, moreover, Santanoni conveys attitudes and values that are timeless.

What does Camp Santanoni tell us—what does it mean? The place was not primarily a hunting lodge. Except for the ritual fall parties, most of the Pruyns were not avid hunters. Santanoni Preserve contained an ambitious agricultural establishment. Its farm—the only publicly-owned, largely intact, gentleman's farm planned by the leading agricultural expert and farm designer of the period—is an important historical site in its own right. Yet, given its setting in the Adirondack wilds, it operated not as a practical farm, but more as romantic fantasy. As such, the wilderness farm might be dismissed as personal folly, but it represents a deeper human value.

Robert Pruyn represented a motivation, as Anthony N. B. Garvan observed, that was stimulated by challenge, the prize being more coveted because of the difficulty. In this sense, Santanoni Preserve may have been a trophy, but it was not ostentatious evidence to the public of Robert Pruyn's accomplishment. Rather, like many Great Camps of the Adirondacks, the trophy was hidden in thousands of acres of wilderness. The achievement was personal. Rather than a contest between human competitors, it was a confrontation between man and the environment. Although his farm was "impractical for farming purposes," it was undertaken, as Robert Pruyn said, as a "patient contest with nature."[2] That phrase might convey an essential motivation for the Great Camp—to confront nature once regarded as hostile and evolve a way to live harmoniously with it, savoring and even revering the wilderness.

The game required rules. Rules are necessary if there is to be a challenge—even if the rules are arbitrary and apparently contradictory. Robert Pruyn wore high, starched collars at camp, but his metal bed had a Spartan horsehair mattress. Patrician conser-

[1] Patrick Noonan to Howard Kirschenbaum, September 29, 1999. Noonan's distinguished career in conservation was summarized in Chapter 9, footnote 67.

[2] Haynes, "Farm Complex," 18. Otto Jantz, Appraiser, 1935 inventory. Haynes, "Farm Complex," 56.

vatism eschewed modern shortcuts and labor-saving equipment. Just as the Pruyns never had any motor boats on the lakes, so Robert Pruyn "never allowed mechanization here. Everything had to be done the old-fashioned way. They had sugar bushes around the property and the sap buckets had to be carried to the sugarhouse by the young men using shoulder yokes, sometimes two or three miles."[3] Anna Pruyn "knitted her own wool."[4] Although Robert Pruyn was a multi-millionaire, he had no telephone at Santanoni.[5] There was no electricity at his country home during his lifetime. Even after his children installed a generator, "there were just a few lights, and when you wanted to go from cabin to cabin at night, you had a candle with a chimney and you would light your candle and go to bed."[6] Ice was cut from the lake years after his death, although electrical refrigeration was available. The same ascetic impulse in quest of authenticity has characterized the wilderness conservation movement, likewise patrician in origin. "Roughing it" is intentionally impractical; the camper's intention is aesthetic. Beatrice Morgan Pruyn was a leading advocate of the amendment to the New York State Constitution that banned billboards in the Adirondacks.[7] The current prohibition, not only of motor boats, but of motor vehicles at Santanoni Preserve is consistent with the Pruyn aesthetic.

Santanoni Preserve, an early forest reservation, was perhaps the first of the self-sufficient Great Camps. When built the great log villa was "the largest and finest in the entire forest."[8] Yet it is not only for its grandeur that Santanoni's main lodge is valued, nor even for the quality of its native craftsmanship alone, but as a work of art.

Although Japan provided an essential influence for the great log villa at Santanoni Preserve, the Adirondack log country house was really an invention for which there was little or no historic precedent. The Santanoni villa is devoid of period style. For this reason, time has proven it to be relatively timeless. It strikes us, even today, more than a century later, as astonishingly fresh, because it seems so *natural*, so imbued with what the Japanese call *shibui*. Transcending period style, Santanoni remains relevant and speaks to us; its message appeals instinctively to throngs of visitors. What is that appeal? It is evocation of nature as timeless. The observer, ". . . in repose, able for the moment to cast a philosophical eye on his world, [finds] something to be loved and cherished, because it gives definition and meaning to his life."[9]

Whereas the prototypical Great Camp of the Adirondacks, William West Durant's Camp Pine Knot, had been a relatively naïve adaptation of the lumber camp—a casual accretion of small cabins—the great log villa at Santanoni Preserve, 265 feet wide, is neither a vernacular building, nor is it provincial architecture. As synthesis of local vernacular and elite Japanese cultures, the Pruyn country house attained creative distinction and a quality of universality. The great log villa was the first work of significant architecture in the Adirondack Mountain region, the first local building that, more than being merely

3 George Shaughnessy of Minerva to J. Winthrop Aldrich, 36. A tractor was acquired "probably in the '30s" after Robert C. Pruyn's tenure. It appeared in the 1953 inventory. Aldrich, 74.

4 Hallie Bond. "Notes Taken During a Trip Into Santanoni on July 29, 1986 . . . . " Typescript, 1988, NYSDEC. Sis Pruyn Thibault recalled that ". . . we had sweaters from sheep wool. We did the knitting, but I don't know who spun the yarn." Sis remembered her grandmother only in Anna's later years.

5 Cynthia Pruyn Green. Aldrich, 115.

6 Cynthia Pruyn Green. Aldrich, 117.

7 Sis Pruyn Thibault recalled that, "It took her years to get it on the floor. She was President of the Women's Republican Club in Albany and was friends with several Senators and she still had a tough time, but finally got it passed." Aldrich, 56. Mrs. Frederic Pruyn, who became Mrs. David Goodrich, was prominent in the women's garden club movement. Aldrich, 56.

8 NYS Forest Commission, *Annual Report*, 1: 178.

9 Aldo Leopold, *Sand County Almanac* (New York: Oxford, 1949), 265.

"artistic," became architecture as art. Robertson's great log villa is the major architectural achievement of a region widely known for its distinctive regional style.

The main camp at Santanoni Preserve may have no great interior space so imposing as that of Camp Topridge; neither is its log construction so remarkably monumental nor inventive as that of Camp Uncas. More than other important regional buildings, however, Robertson's villa is distinguished by integral unity, enhanced by metaphorical significance. As a whole, this Great Camp has more architectural substance than any other.

Santanoni's centerpiece villa, amplified by its satellite clusters of ancillary buildings, is "significant," in the literal sense of that term as a "sign," or symbol to convey meaning. The Great Camp of the Adirondacks embodies not merely an aesthetic but an ethical ideal. "This Arcadian view advocated a simple, humble life for man with the aim of restoring him to a peaceful coexistence with other organisms."[10] The Great Camp represents a utopian attempt to find a way of living intimately with nature.

If the simple life required thirty-five bedrooms for staff, no matter—after all, Eden had provided amply for the the needs of the first couple to dwell in harmony with their environment. Compared to the Pruyn's great masonry residence in town, their forest villa was rustic, and its way of life seemed refreshingly idyllic.

Santanoni Preserve represents not only a socially conservative aesthetic, but an emerging wilderness ethic. Pioneer wilderness advocate Aldo Leopold observed that "conservation is a state of harmony between men and land."[11] Pioneer modern architect Walter Gropius predicted that "the Japanese approach of persuading and stimulating nature will have a greater future value than the predominant Western method of 'conquering' and 'exploiting' her."[12]

Old-growth pine on a Newcomb Lake island

Santanoni Preserve, more than a complex of buildings, is a wilderness reservation, envisioned as an unspoiled world in microcosm. It may be regarded as romantic, nostalgic, privileged, and escapist, hence irrelevant to critical issues of the real world from which it insulates itself.[13] Santanoni is, however, poetic, and it is beautiful. It is, as Walter Gropius said of Katsura and the artful Japanese house, "the lofty abode of man in equilibrium, in serenity."[14]

[10] Donald Worster, *Nature's Economy: A History of Ecological Ideas* (New York: Cambridge, 1985), 2.

[11] Leopold, 243.

[12] Gropius, in Ishimoto, 67.

[13] As Tange observes, Japanese *haiku* poetry, so highly regarded as a rarefied "intensely personal" art form, into which the Japanese "poured all their feelings and aspirations . . . did not aim at confronting reality. On the contrary, it [was] an attempt to escape from the world." Tange, in Ishimoto, 35.

[14] Gropius, in Ishimoto, 8.

Santanoni Preserve represented ideals of Robert Clarence Pruyn, but no less those of Anna Williams Pruyn, who first proposed an estate in the Adirondacks. It was she who wanted architecture appropriate to the mountain wilderness that she had grown to love as a child. It was she who wanted a rustic summer home, not a conventional country house.

Anna loved Santanoni Preserve to the end of her long life. Her cabin nearest the boathouse, where she stayed alone after Robert's death, contained a scriptural motto, "This, too, shall pass." Anna "was told [Santanoni] would never last," recalled her granddaughter Cynthia, "but it has."[15]

Santanoni may continue to last, so long as visitors recognize and appreciate its unique integration of East and West, of civilized culture and natural wilderness. As Robert C. Pruyn observed, "There is independence, delight, and peace in the isolation." As he, his wife Anna, and their architect intended, a recollection of the Japanese temple, realized in the building style of the Adirondacks, has given us unique architecture and a shrine to nature.

We depart, meeting others who arrive, seeking those rare qualities—others who will begin new chapters in the continuing history of the Santanoni Preserve.

Arrival

[15] Cynthia Pruyn Green, Aldrich, 121.

# The Illustrations 

The older photographs of Santanoni may be attributed in large part to Anna Pruyn. As mentioned previously, granddaughters recalled her as camera-shy but an avid photographer. Her son Edward Lansing Pruyn also photographed some of the illustrations, perhaps for his future reference as a painter. An artist's eye for composition is often evident. Ned may have inherited this visual sensitivity from his mother, who was an intent observer of nature.

The Pruyn albums at the Adirondack Museum provide the largest source of Santanoni photographs, barely tapped for this book. Prior to placement in the Museum, many of the Pruyn photographs were copied by Carl Stearns for the AARCH archive, from which some have been reproduced here. Members of the family hold additional historic images. Susan Pruyn King has lent the Edward Lansing Pruyn self-portrait together with some of his other drawings, etchings, photographs, and other memorabilia reproduced here. The late Beatrice Pruyn Thibault ("Sis") likewise shared her own photograph albums and negatives. Donald Williams donated copies of photographs of Santanoni staff families from his private collection. Charles Vandrei has shared reproductions from DEC files.

The Adirondack Museum has provided photographs reproduced on the following pages: front cover, 5, 22, 25, 27, 36, 38, 42, 74, 79, 81, 94, 99, 101, 102, 103 (barns), 104, 106, 112, 119, 120, 121, 123, 125, 135, 141, and back cover (all except upper left).

The rare photograph of Zempukuji Temple by the pioneer photographer of Japan, Felix Beato, is reproduced by permission of Princeton University Press. The aerial view of Katsura Imperial Villa appears with permission of Yale University Press.

Carl Stearns provided the main camp roof plan that opens Chapter 4. The main camp floor plan in Chapter 5 was adapted from a drawing by Vicki Howard.

Mike Minnetta obtained the photographic portrait of Robert Robertson in Chapter 4, courtesy of Shelburne Farms, Shelburne, Vermont. Biltmore Estate in Asheville, North Carolina contributed the photograph of Edward Burnett and associates in Chapter 6. The photographs of Crandall Melvin and the Merchants' Bank are from Thomas Higgins' *History of the Merchants' Bank and Trust Company,* cited in the bibliography.

Joanna Donk, Harvey Kaiser, James Swedberg, and Bill McDowell granted permission for use of their photographs as the frontispiece and on pages 50, 76, and 181, respectively.

We are grateful to Austin O'Brien, Margaret Prime, Eileen Freer, and John Stoller, who each contributed one or more modern illustrations. AARCH executive director Steven Engelhart is photographer of other recent views, as are co-authors Robert Engel and Howard Kirschenbaum. Co-author Paul Malo drew the aerial reconstruction of the main camp, and prepared the map and site plans, which are composites, derived from various base maps prepared by Wesley Haynes, the Department of Environmental Conservation and others.

Permission is required to reproduce illustrations from this book in any media. Permission may be obtained from holders of the original material, or otherwise from Adirondack Architectural Heritage.

Virtually all of the photographs have been digitally enhanced to varying degrees to improve printed reproduction. Old images required correction of exposure and sharpness, while most modern slides required adjustment when converted for black-and-white presentation. Occasionally images have been cropped or straightened. Photographers who are displeased may blame the picture editor, Paul Malo, who has done the digital enhancement.

The *Ho-o-den*

Chicago, 1893

# Bibliography

The Albany Institute of History and Art holds the Robert C. Pruyn papers, and the Key Trust Company (successor to the National Commercial Bank), Albany, holds papers of the Robert C. Pruyn Estate. Rutgers University has papers of the Orientalist, William Elliot Griffis, with whom Robert Pruyn corresponded.

The Adirondack Museum Library, Blue Mountain Lake, New York, has several volumes of camp memorabilia, including daybooks ("Santanoni: Record of Fish and Some Other Things," 1893–1931), journals and scrapbooks, gifts of Susan Pruyn King. The Santanoni guest book in three volumes is on long-term loan to the Adirondack Museum from the late Cynthia Pruyn Green. Other photographs, albums and mementos are retained by family. An extended daybook (1893–1971) was given to the American Museum of Fly Fishing, Manchester, Vermont by the Melvin family.

The New York State Department of Environmental Conservation retains a large Santanoni archive, including much material collected by J. Winthrop Aldrich. Wesley Haynes' "Farm Complex" report (see entry) provides a more complete bibliography of the DEC collection. Adirondack Architectural Heritage (AARCH) also has a substantial Santanoni archive, containing copies of most of the DEC materials, as well as other letters, documents and photographs collected by the authors and by AARCH.

Numerous additional references are provided in footnotes throughout the text.


Adirondack Architectural Heritage. *Newsletter.* Issues from 1992 through 1999. Keeseville, N.Y.

*Adirondack News.* Newcomb, N.Y.: Adirondack News Company, Washington Chase, ed., v. 1, 1893.

Aldrich, John Winthrop. Memorandum to File, May 7, 1996. Recording oral commentary of Merle Melvin.

______*Santanoni Preserve: Source Book #1.* Albany: New York State Department of Environmental Conservation. 1992–93. Typescript transcribing oral interviews.

*American Legislative Leaders, 1850–1910.* Charles F. Ritter and Jon L. Wakelyn, eds. New York: Greenwood, 1989. "Robert Hewson Pruyn."

*Appleton's Cyclopaedia of American Biography.* Six volumes. James Grant Wilson and John Fiske, eds. New York: D. Appleton & Co., 1888–1889. Reprint. Detroit: Gale Research, 1968, "Robert Hewson Pruyn," "Robert Henderson Robertson."

Ballagh, Margaret Tate Kinnear. *Glimpses of Old Japan, 1861–1866.* Tokyo: Methodist Publishing House, 1908.

Barnard, Ed and Betty. "The Family of Johannes Pruyn (1614–)." Typescript, 1994, Onondaga County Public Library.

Bedford, Steven M. "Country and City: Some Formal Comparisons." The Country House Tradition in America." *The Long Island Country House, 1870–1939.* Southampton, N.Y.: Parrish Art Museum, 1988.

Bennett, Allison P. *The People's Choice: A History of Albany County in Art and Architecture.* Albany: Albany County Historical Association, 1984.

*Biographical Annals of the Civil Government of the United States, During Its First Century, from Original and Official Sources.* Charles Lanman, ed. Washington. DC: James Anglilm, 1896. Reprint. Detroit: Gale Research, 1976. "Robert Hewson Pruyn."

*Biography Index: A Cumulative Index to Biographical Material in Books and Magazines.* August, 1949–August 1952. New York: H. W. Wilson Co, 1953. "Crandall Melvin," "Robert Hewson Pruyn," "Edward Lansing Pruyn," "Fellowes Morgan Pruyn."

Bissell, Delilah West. "My Memories of Pruyn's Preserve at Santanoni." Unpublished manuscript, Town of Newcomb Archives, Office of the Supervisor, Newcomb, N.Y., June 12, 1991.

Bond, Hallie. "Notes Taken During a Trip Into Santanoni on July 29, 1986." Typescript, NYSDEC, 1988. Recording commentary of Helen Tummins.

Bowden, Ramona B. "Service Cites Melvin as 'Giant of a Man.'" Syracuse *Post-Standard*, May 2, 1980.

Burr, David H. *An Atlas of the State of New York: Containing a Map of the State and of the Several Counties*. Ithaca, N.Y.: Stone and Clark, 1829, 1839, and subsequent editions.

______"Map of the County of Essex" [New York]. Ithaca, N.Y.: Stone and Clark, Republishers, 1840.

______"Map of the State of New York," 1841.

Chase, Franklin H. *Syracuse and Its Environs: A History*. New York: Lewis Historical Publishing Co., 1924.

Commission on the Adirondacks in the Twenty-First Century. *The Adirondack Park in the Twenty-First Century*. Albany: State of New York, 1990.

Coughlin, Claire and Hope Irvin Marston. *Santanoni Sunrise*. A Christian romance novel set at Santanoni. Uhrichsville, Ohio: Heartsong Presents, 1994.

Darling, Alan. "Santanoni," *Adirondack Life*, September-October, 1981.

*Dictionary of American Biography*. New York: Scribner, 1928–1936. "Robert Hewson Pruyn."

*Dictionary of American Diplomatic History*. First and second editions. John E. Findling, ed. New York: Greenwood, 1980, 1989. "Robert Hewson Pruyn."

Dillon, Tom. Interview by Robert Engel, handwritten notes. Santanoni Preserve, August 1991.

Division of Lands and Forests, New York State Department of Environmental Conservation. "Management and Use Plan, Santanoni Preserve." October 22, 1971.

______*Camp Santanoni Historic Area and related areas of the Vanderwhacker Mountain Wild Forest Draft Unit Management Plan*. Albany: Department of Environmental Conservation, October 1999.

Dixon, Taya. "Edward Burnett: An Agricultural Designer on Gentlemen's Estates." Unpublished master's thesis, University of Pennsylvania, 1998.

Donaldson, Alfred L., *A History of the Adirondacks*. New York: Century, 1921, 2 v; reprinted, Fleischmanns, N. Y.: Purple Mountain, 1996; Harrison, N.Y.: Harbor Hill Books, 1977.

*The Dream City: A Portfolio of Photographic Views of the World's Columbian Exposition with an Introduction by Prof. Halsey C. Ives*. St. Louis: N.D. Thompson, 1893.

Dunham, Marion. Interview by Robert Engel, tape recording. Santanoni Preserve, August 17, 1992.

Engel, Robert. "A History of Camp Santanoni, The Adirondack Retreat of Robert C. Pruyn." Unpublished master's thesis, Cooperstown Graduate Program, 1996.

Engel, Robert and Howard Kirschenbaum. "A Great Camp Memoir." *Adirondack Life*, May-June 1993: 46–49.

Engel, Robert, Howard Kirschenbaum, and Paul Malo. *Santanoni: From Japanese Temple to Life at an Adirondack Great Camp: Early Draft With Additional Research Material*. On disk. Keeseville, N.Y.: Adirondack Architectural Heritage, 1998.

Engel, Robert and Judith Watson. "TR's Midnight Dash: From Mt. Marcy to Washington." *New York State Conservationist*, v. 54, no. 2, October 1999: 20–21.

Essex County Land Grantee Books #103, 104, 106, 107, 108, 111, 113, 114, 115, 116, 127. Office of the County Clerk, Essex County, N.Y.

Fennessey, Lana. *The History of Newcomb, Essex County, New York*. Elizabethtown, N.Y.: Denton Publications, 1977.

Fisher and Bryant. Map of Santanoni Preserve, 1910. Reproduction of original map in files of Department of Environmental Conservation.

Fox, Dixon Ryan. *Yankees and Yorkers*. New York, University Press; 1940.

Freeman, Castle. "Shelburne Farms." *Country Journal*, v. 10, no. 6, June, 1983.

Gadski [Domblewski], Mary Ellen. "Research Report on the Great Camps of the Adirondacks." Unpublished report. Albany: Preservation League of New York State, June 1978.

Garrison, David. "Former Resident Recalls Life in Area Preserve." *Glens Falls Post Star,* December 1, 1987.

______"A Working Dairy in the Middle of the Mountains." *Snow Times,* February 3, 1988.

Gilborn, Craig. *Durant: The Fortunes and Woodland Camps of a Family in the Adirondacks.* Blue Mountain Lake, N.Y.: The Adirondack Museum, 1981.

Graham, Frank, Jr. *The Adirondack Park: A Political History.* Syracuse, N.Y.: Syracuse University Press, 1978.

Green, Cynthia Pruyn. Handwritten notes, August 1992.

______Interview by J. Winthrop Aldrich, handwritten notes. Walpole, Mass., February 26, 1993.

______Interview by Robert Engel, tape recording. Santanoni Preserve, July 29, 1992.

______Interview by Robert Engel, tape recording. Santanoni Preserve, September 23, 1992.

______Letter to J. Winthrop Aldrich, c. to Robert Engel, August 1992.

Griffis, William Elliot *Japanese Fairy Tales.* New York: T.Y. Crowell Co., 1908.

Hamlin, Huybertie Pruyn. *An Albany Girlhood.* Edited by Alice P. Kenny. Albany, N.Y.: Washington Park Press, 1990.

______Collected papers. McKinney Library, Albany Institute of History and Art, Albany, N.Y.

______"Four Spring Parties to Santanoni," Collected Papers, Locator #AF121.

Harada, Jiro. *The Lesson of Japanese Architecture.* London, The Studio; New York: Studio Publications, 1936.

Havron, Don. Interview by J. Winthrop Aldrich, tape recording. Paradox Lake, N.Y., June 1992.

Haynes, Wesley. "Farm Complex, Santanoni Preserve, Newcomb, New York: Historic Structure Report." Prepared for Adirondack Architectural Heritage, 1996.

______"Gate Lodge Complex, Santanoni Preserve, Newcomb, New York: Historic Structure Report." Prepared for Adirondack Architectural Heritage, 1998.

Higgens, Thomas W. "Crandall Melvin, President, 1938–1967," in Crandall Melvin, Sr. *History of the Merchants' Bank and Trust Company of Syracuse, New York: One Hundred and Eighteen Years,* Chapter 10. Syracuse: Syracuse University, 1969.

*Historic Preservation in the Adirondack Park.* Colloquium Proceedings, December 4, 1982. The Adirondack Research Center, Union College, Schenectady, N.Y.

Hochschild, Harold. *The MacIntyre Mine: From Failure to Fortune.* Blue Mountain Lake, N.Y.: The Adirondack Museum, 1962.

Hotaling, Mary B. "Robert H. Robertson, Architect of Santanoni." *Adirondack Architectural Heritage Newsletter,* v. 5, no. 1, June 1996: 1, 3–4.

Ishimoto, Yasuhiro, editor, photographer, and co-author. *Katsura: Tradition and Creation in Japanese Architecture.* New Haven: Yale University Press, 1960. Contains articles by Walter Gropius and Kenzo Tange.

Ito, Teiji. *The Japanese Garden: An Approach to Nature.* New Haven: Yale University Press, 1972.

Jantz, Otto. Inventory and Appraisal, November 1934, from Surrogate's Court, Albany County, order Assessing Transfer tax upon the Estate of Robert C. Pruyn, March 27, 1935.

Johnson, Dr. Edward. Letter to Ethel Bissell, Town of Newcomb, Office of the Supervisor. Undated, circa 1982.

Johnson, Eugene J. *Style Follows Function: Architecture of Marcus T. Reynolds.* Albany: Washington Park/Mount Ida Presses, 1993.

Kaiser, Harvey H. *Great Camps of the Adirondacks.* Boston: David R. Godine, 1982.

Kennedy, William. *O Albany! An Urban Tapestry.* New York: Viking, 1983.

Kenny, Alice P. *The Gansevoorts of Albany: Dutch Patricians in the Upper Hudson Valley.* Syracuse, N.Y.: Syracuse University, 1969.

King, Susan Pruyn. Interview by Robert Engel, tape recording. Santanoni Preserve, July 29, 1992.

______Letter To Whom It May Concern, April 16, 1991.

Kirschenbaum, Howard. *The Story of Sagamore.* Raquette Lake, N.Y.: Sagamore Institute, 1990.

______"To Save Santanoni." *Adirondack Life,* January-February 1986: 53–54.

______"Thirty-Four or More?" *Adirondack Life,* May-June 1985: 9–12.

Lancaster, Clay. *The Japanese Influence in America.* New York: Rawls, 1963; New York: Abbeville Press, 1983.

Landau, Sarah Bradford. *Edward T. and William A. Potter: American Victorian Architects.* New York: Garland, 1979.

Lee, Edwin B. "Robert H. Pruyn in Japan, 1862–1865." *New York History*, April 1985: 123–139.

Lee, Guy H. "Estates of American Sportsmen: Santanoni, the Adirondack Camp of Robert C. Pruyn, Esq. of Albany, New York." *The Sportsman*, v. 6, no. 4 , October 1929: 71 ff.

Lee, Sherman E. *A History of Far Eastern Art.* New York: Abrams, n.d.

Lehman, Arnold. "Great Camps of the Adirondacks." Blue Mountain Lake, N.Y.: The Adirondack Museum, 1978.

Longstreth, Richard. "Historical Bibliography of the Built Environment in the Adirondack Region of New York State." Society of Architectural Historians website, 1996, revised 1999, www.SAH.org/bibs/adrbib.html.

Malo, Paul. "Adirondack Architecture and the Culture of Exurbia." *Forever Wild: The Adirondack Experience.* Katonah. N.Y.: Katonah Museum of Art, 1991.

______"A Home to Call Our Own: Getting to the Heart of Native Architecture." *Adirondack Life*, v. 28, no. 7, November-December, 1997: 56–79.

______"Nippon in the North Country: Japanese Inspiration in Form and Philosophy." *Adirondack Life*, v. 29, no. 7, Collectors' Issue 1998-99: 50–55.

Manuscript Notes to Authors. Extensive commentary by J. Winthrop Aldrich, Susan Pruyn King, and other readers. Notes on manuscript draft, December 1998-January 1999.

Masten, Arthur H. *The Story of Adirondac.* Syracuse, N.Y.: Syracuse University Press, 1968.

Masters, Raymond D. *A Social History of the Huntington Wildlife Forest (Which Includes Rich Lake and the Pendelton Settlement).* Utica, N.Y.: North Country, 1993.

McCash, William Barton and June Hall McCash. *The Jekyll Island Club: Southern Haven for America's Millionaires.* Athens, Ga. and London: The University of Georgia Press, 1989.

McMartin, Barbara. *The Adirondack Park: A Wildlands Quilt.* Syracuse: Syracuse University Press, 1999.

______ *To the Lake of the Skies: The Benedicts in the Adirondacks.* Canada Lake, N.Y.: Lake View Press, 1996.

Melvin, Crandall, Jr. Interview by J. Winthrop Aldrich, tape recording. Syracuse, N.Y., July 1992.

Melvin, Crandall, Sr. *History of the Merchants' National Bank and Trust Company of Syracuse, New York: One Hundred and Eighteen Years.* Syracuse: Syracuse University, 1969.

Melvin, Merle. Correspondence with J. Winthrop Aldrich and oral commentary transcribed in Aldrich, 1996.

Morse, Edward S. *Japanese Homes and Their Surroundings.* Boston: Ticknor, 1886.

Murphy, Eloise Cronin. *Theodore Roosevelt's Night Ride to the Presidency.* Blue Mountain Lake, N.Y.: The Adirondack Museum, 1977.

"National Commercial Bank and Trust Company of Albany, N.Y.: Improvements and Additions with a Brief History [The]." Albany, N.Y., 1922.

*National Cyclopaedia of American Biography [The],* Volumes 6, 13, 26. New York: James T. White & Co., 1937. Entries for: Pruyn, Robert C.; Pruyn, John V. L.; Pruyn, Robert H.; Pruyn, Charles L.; Robertson, Robert H.; Williams, Chauncey P.

"Newcomb, New York in the Adirondacks," real estate sales brochure No. 43030, 2/50, New York: Previews, February, 1950. Description and photographs of Santanoni.

*New York Genealogical and Biographical Record,* July 1884. "Robert H. Pruyn".

New York State Forest Commission. "Private Preserves in the Adirondack Forests," [Eighth] *Annual Report of the New York State Forest Commission for the Year 1893.* Albany: James B. Lyon, State Printer, 1894, 1: 178–179.

*New York Times.* Indexed articles other than obituaries: Beatrice Morgan Pruyn, Edward L. Pruyn, Frederic Pruyn, Mrs. Frederic Pruyn, John V. L. Pruyn, Robert C. Pruyn, Robert D. Pruyn, Robert L. Pruyn, Robert H. Pruyn, Ruth Pruyn.

______Obituaries: Anna W. Pruyn, Edward Lansing Pruyn, Frederic Pruyn, Robert C. Pruyn, Robert D. Pruyn, Robert H. Pruyn, Robert H. Robertson, Robert H. Robertson, Jr.

Notehelfer, F. G., ed. *Japan Through American Eyes: The Journal of Francis Hall, Kanagawa and Yokohama, 1859–1866*. Princeton: Princeton University Press, 1992.

Nouët, Noël. *The Shogun's City: A History of Tokyo*. Sandgate, England: Paul Norbury, 1990.

Ooka, Minoru. *Temples of Nara and Their Art*. New York: Weatherhill/Heibonsha, 1973.

"Portraits of the Presidents of National Commercial Bank & Trust Co." Albany: The Bank, 1970. McKinney Library, Albany Institute of History and Art, Albany, N.Y.

Preservation League of New York State, et al. "Camp Santanoni Main Camp Complex: Documentation, Stabilization and Maintenance Plan, Draft Report." August 23, 1993.

Pruyn, Frederic. Letter to Milton Lee Pruyn, October 7, 1951. Collection of Beatrice Pruyn Thibault, Clayton, N.Y.

Pruyn, John V. L., Jr. "Pruyn Family, American Branch." *New York Genealogical and Biographical Record*, v. 15, July 1884: 97–98. Cited by Edwin B. Lee, fn. 3, 124.

Pruyn, Milton Lee. Letter to Charles Ten Eyck, National Commercial Bank & Trust Co., August 6, 1953. Collection of Beatrice Pruyn Thibault, Clayton, N.Y.

Pruyn Papers. Albany Institute of History and Art, McKinney Library, Albany, N.Y. Collection of letters, newspaper articles, personal notes and ephemera of Robert Hewson Pruyn and Robert Clarence Pruyn.

Pruyn, Robert C. Business correspondence 1898-1902. Collection of Susan Pruyn King, Long Lake, N.Y.

______Collection of papers. KeyCorp Trust archives. Albany, N.Y. Miscellaneous papers and correspondence relating to Pruyn's Santanoni Preserve.

[Pruyn, R. C.] "Santanoni Preserve, Adirondack Mountains." Typescript. May, 1915.

Putnam, Rowena Ross. Interview by Robert Engel, tape recording. Newcomb, N.Y., July 1991.

Rathbone, Cornelia Kane. "A Dethroned Ideal." *Godey's Magazine*. September 1893.

Recknagel, A. B. "History of the Robert C. Pruyn Tract, Essex Co., N.Y." Typescript, October 26, 1939.

______"Report on Timber Estimate and Growth Study on the R. C. Pruyn Estate, Newcomb, Essex Co., N.Y." Typescript, September 1, 1940.

"Register of Pedigree." Bound volume of handwritten genealogy of the ancestry of Robert C. Pruyn and Anna Williams Pruyn. Collection of Cynthia Pruyn Green, Walpole, Mass.

"Robert C. Pruyn, 87, Financier, is Dead." Obituary, *New York Times*, October 30, 1934, 19.

"Robertson, Robert H." *Who's Who in America*, 1920–21.

"Roosevelt in the Adirondacks." *The Essex County Republican*, v. 59, no. 39, May 25, 1899.

Roosevelt, Theodore. Letter to Robert C. Pruyn, May 27, 1899. Theodore Roosevelt Papers, Library of Congress, V8-P399, Washington, DC.

Rudge, William and Charles Vandrei. "Santanoni Chronology." Typescript, NYSDEC. Presented to Santanoni Historic Area Citizens Advisory Committee, May 2, 1995.

Rudofsky, Bernard. *The Kimono Mind: An Informal Guide to Japan and the Japanese*. Garden City, NY: Doubleday, 1965.

Santanoni "Bits of Fact and Fiction by All: 1893–1915." The Adirondack Museum Library, Blue Mountain Lake, N.Y. Poems, letters and comments by visitors.

"Santanoni Guest Book." 1893–1937, vols. I–III. Collection of Cynthia Pruyn Green. Signatures, comments, photographs and illustrations by guests to Camp Santanoni.

"Santanoni Photograph Albums." 7 vols., 1892–1931. The Adirondack Museum Library, Blue Mountain Lake, N.Y. The seven albums plus separately mounted and loose photographs contain more than one thousand images.

"Santanoni Preserve," n.d., typescript in National Commercial Bank records.

"Santanoni Preserve/Adirondack Mountains," typescript, c. 1925, at New York State Department of Environmental Conservation.

"Santanoni Preserve, Newcomb, Essex County, New York." Typescript, n.d., Records of National Commercial Bank.

"Santanoni: Record of Fish and Some Other Things" [Diary] 1893–1931. The Adirondack Museum

Library, Blue Mountain Lake, N.Y. Daily entries of camp activity, mostly fishing.

"Santanoni: Record of Fish and of Some Other Things." 1893–1971. The American Museum of Fly Fishing, Manchester, Vt. Daily entries of camp activity, mostly fishing.

[Santanoni Scrapbooks.] 1893–1931. The Adirondack Museum Library, Blue Mountain Lake, N.Y. Poems, letters, photographs, illustrations by family and guests.

Schuyler, Montgomery. "The Work of R. H. Robertson." *Architectural Record*, v. 6, October, 1896: 184–219.

Shaughnessy, George. Interview by J. Winthrop Aldrich, tape recording. Minerva, N.Y., July 1992.

Smith, Bradley. *Japan: A History in Art*. New York: Gemini, 1964.

Smith, H. Perry. *History of Essex County, New York*. Syracuse: D. Mason, 1885.

Smith, Mary Petoff. Letter to Robert Engel. September 13, 1992.

Smith, Raymond W., and Richard C. Youngken. *National Register of Historic Places Inventory-Nomination Form, Camp Santanoni (Component 4)*, 1987.

______*National Register of Historic Places Inventory-Nomination Form. Great Camps of the Adirondacks Thematic Resources*, 1987.

Suzuki, Kakichi. *Early Buddhist Architecture in Japan* . Tokyo: Kodansha, 1980.

*Syracuse Herald Journal*. Douglas Legg stories, July 12 to August 10, 1971. Melvin obituaries, May 4, 1966, April 21, 1980.

Terrie, Philip G. *Contested Terrain*. Syracuse, N.Y.: Adirondack Museum/Syracuse University Press, 1997.

Thibault, Beatrice Pruyn. Interview by Robert Engel, tape recording. Santanoni Preserve, July 29, 1992.

______Interview by Robert Engel, tape recording. Clayton, N.Y., August 17, 1992.

______Letter to J. Winthrop Aldrich. August 1992.

Thornton, Tamara P. *The Meaning of Country Life among the Boston Elite*. New Haven, Conn.: Yale University Press, 1989.

Treat, Payson J. *Japan and the United States, 1853–1921*. Boston: Houghton Mifflin, 1921.

Tummins, Helen. Interview by Robert Engel, handwritten notes. Newcomb, N.Y., July 1991.

*The Twentieth Century Biographical Dictionary of Notable Americans*. Rossiter Johnson, ed. Boston: The Biographical Society, 1904. Reprint, Detroit: Gale Research, 1968. "Robert Hewson Pruyn."

VanValkenburgh, Norman J. *The Adirondack Forest Preserve: A Chronology*. Ann Arbor, Mich.: University Microfilms International; Blue Mt. Lake, N.Y.: Adirondack Museum, 1979.

Waite, Diana S., ed. *Albany Architecture: Guide to the City*. Albany: Mount Ida Press, 1993.

Wallace, E. R. *Descriptive Guide to the Adirondacks (Land of the Thousand Lakes.)* New York: American News Co., 1876.

______ *Descriptive Guide to the Adirondacks (Land of a Thousand Lakes.)* Syracuse: 1895.

*Who's Who in America*, 38th edition, 1974–1975. Wilmette, Ill.: Marquis Who's Who, 1974. "Crandall Melvin, Jr."

*Who's Who in American Law*. Second edition. Wilmette, Ill.: Marquis Who's Who, 1979. "Crandall Melvin."

*Who Was Who in America*, Historical Volume, 1607–1897. Revised Edition. Chicago: Marquis Who's Who, 1967. "Robert Hewson Pruyn."

*Who Was Who in America* Volume 4, 1961–1968. Chicago: Marquis Who's Who, 1960. "Crandall Melvin."

*Who Was Who in America* Volume 8, 1982–1985, Chicago: Marquis Who's Who, 1985. "Robert Henderson Robertson."

Wight, J. B. "Japanese Architecture at Chicago." *The Inland Architect and News Record*, v. 20, no. 5, December 1892.

Wilson, Richard Guy. "Picturesque Ambiguities: The Country House Tradition in America." *The Long Island Country House, 1870–1939*. Southampton, N.Y.: Parrish Art Museum, 1988.

______"Delano and Aldrich." In Robert B. MacKay et al, eds. *Long Island Country Houses and Their Architects, 1860–1940*. New York: W.W. Norton, 1996.

Withey; Henry F. and Elsie Rathburn Withey. *Biographical Dictionary of American Architects*. Los Angeles: New Age, 1956. "Robertston, Robert H."

#  Index 

Page numbers in italics indicate illustrations

High Fields, pencil drawing on paper by Edward Lansing Pruyn

Drawing by Edward Lansing Pruyn

........................................

*Format for this book was arranged in Microsoft Word. Regular text was set in Times and display fonts in Palatino electronic fonts. Paul Malo prepared the manuscript and cover/dust jacket for reproduction and enhanced most of the illustrations with Adobe Photoshop.*

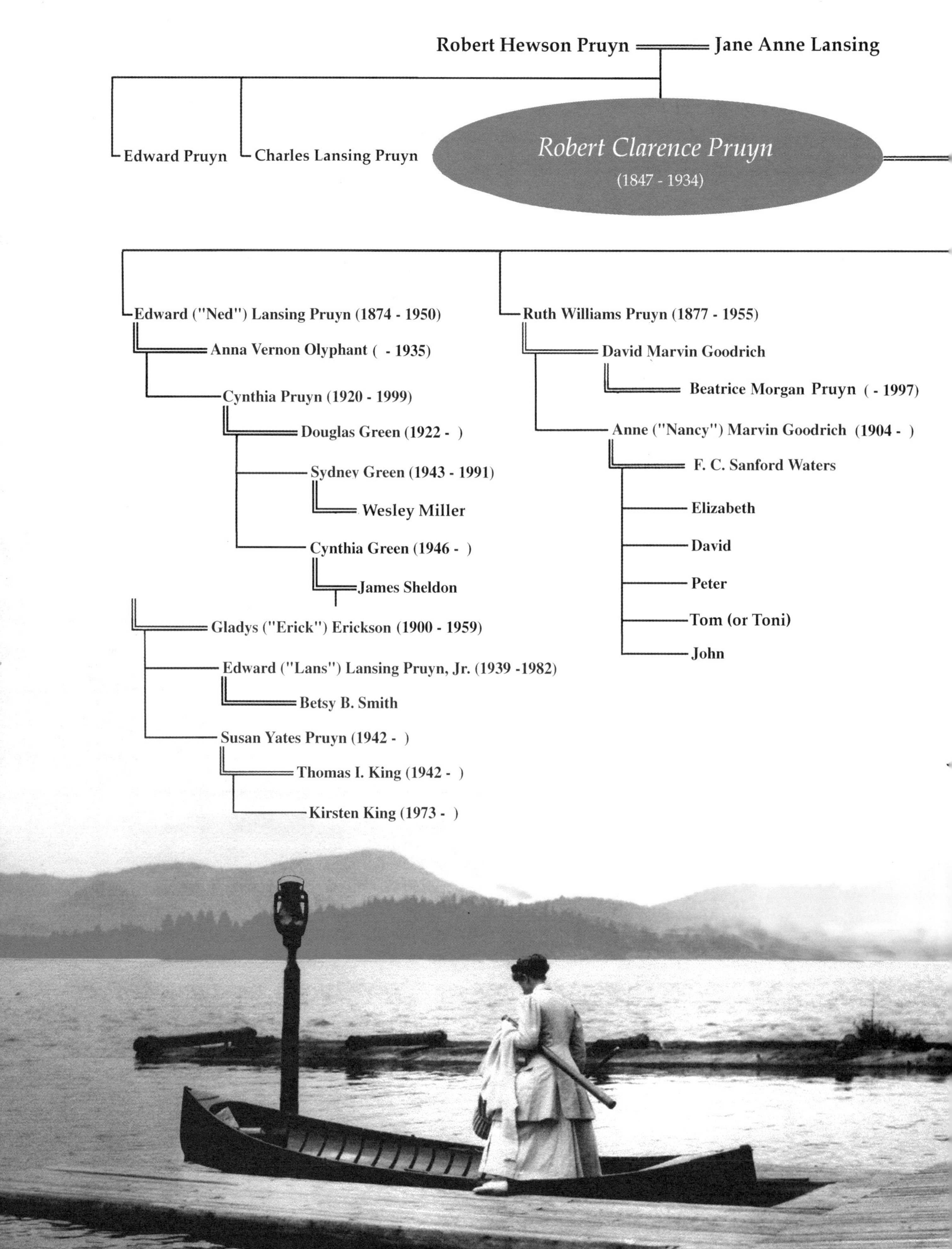
Robert Hewson Pruyn
Jane Anne Lansing
Edward Pruyn
Charles Lansing Pruyn
Robert Clarence Pruyn
(1847 - 1934)
Edward ("Ned") Lansing Pruyn (1874 - 1950)
Anna Vernon Olyphant ( - 1935)
Cynthia Pruyn (1920 - 1999)
Douglas Green (1922 - )
Sydney Green (1943 - 1991)
Wesley Miller
Cynthia Green (1946 - )
James Sheldon
Gladys ("Erick") Erickson (1900 - 1959)
Edward ("Lans") Lansing Pruyn, Jr. (1939 -1982)
Betsy B. Smith
Susan Yates Pruyn (1942 - )
Thomas I. King (1942 - )
Kirsten King (1973 - )
Ruth Williams Pruyn (1877 - 1955)
David Marvin Goodrich
Beatrice Morgan Pruyn ( - 1997)
Anne ("Nancy") Marvin Goodrich (1904 - )
F. C. Sanford Waters
Elizabeth
David
Peter
Tom (or Toni)
John